# Anorexia Nervosa

## A MULTIDIMENSIONAL PERSPECTIVE

# *Anorexia Nervosa*

## A MULTIDIMENSIONAL PERSPECTIVE

Paul E. Garfinkel, M.D., F.R.C.P. (C)

Psychiatrist-in-Chief,
Toronto General Hospital;
Professor of Psychiatry,
University of Toronto;
Graduate Faculty,
Institute of Medical Sciences

and

David M. Garner, Ph.D.

Director of Research,
Department of Psychiatry,
Toronto General Hospital;
Associate Professor of Psychiatry,
University of Toronto

BRUNNER/MAZEL, *Publishers* • NEW YORK
BOOK CENTER • MONTREAL

SECOND PRINTING

**Library of Congress Cataloging in Publication Data**

Garfinkel, Paul E., 1946-
  Anorexia nervosa.

  Includes bibliographies and index.
  1. Anorexia nervosa.  I.  Garner, David M., 1947-  .
II.  Title.  [DNLM:  1.  Anorexia nervosa. WM175 G231a]
RC552.A5G37                 616.85'2                 82-1337
ISBN 0-87630-297-5                                    AACR2

Copyright © 1982 by Paul E. Garfinkel
and David M. Garner

Published by
BRUNNER/MAZEL, INC.
19 Union Square
New York, New York 10003

Distributed in Canada by
BOOK CENTER
1140 Beaulac Street
Montreal Quebec H4R 1R8

MANUFACTURED IN THE UNITED STATES OF AMERICA

For Dorothy and our children, Jonathan, Stephen and Joshua

and

For Maureen, Wiley and Lorraine

# FOREWORD

Many psychiatric disorders are multidetermined, but probably none more so than anorexia nervosa. As a clinical entity it is the final common pathway of forces as diverse as fashion, social expectation, familial tension, and delusional belief.

Once the drive towards being thin is established, the condition acquires autonomous characteristics. These too are products of numerous factors: starvation, which generates its own obsessions and characteristic physiological responses; endocrinological pathology; the difficult pattern of control-seeking; and the highly resistant disorders of self-perception.

In spite of claims made from time to time, treatment of anorexia nervosa cannot be defined by a simple formula. It demands attention to the highly individual pathology of the patients, and any Procrustean recipe will inevitably be misapplied to a large group of patients falling outside its scope.

In this book, Garfinkel and Garner demonstrate the complex interaction of cause, disease pattern and treatment modality. Recognizing the complexity of the syndrome, they do not provide simple or predictable solutions in their scholarly survey of this tragic, frustrating disorder. They do, however, outline treatment strategies which are effective and give hope to the treating physician, the patient and the family.

*Vivian Rakoff, M.A., M.B.B.S., F.R.C.P.(C)*

# CONTENTS

# *PREFACE*

As its title implies, this book presents a model for understanding and treating anorexia nervosa as a multidimensional disorder. The intended audience is both the academic who is interested in a synthesis of the scientific literature related to anorexia nervosa and the health practitioner who is primarily concerned with understanding and treating individuals with the disorder. The book begins by describing clinical features and addressing historical diagnostic controversies which have yet to be resolved. The physical and psychological mechanisms which may predispose, precipitate, and perpetuate the disorder are described, and we acknowledge the influence of Professor H. Weiner's thinking applied to other psychosomatic illnesses in the development of our multidimensional perspective of anorexia nervosa. We have attempted to describe in detail the parameters of both inpatient and outpatient treatment of the disorder as well as complications that have been common in our patients.

Because of the sex distribution of the disorder, we have adopted the convention of using feminine pronouns or referring to individuals with the disorder as female (we recognize that the illness is by no means confined to women). Also, our sample size varies throughout the text since we have different amounts of information available depending on measures employed or data base available at the time of writing a particular section. We recognize that there is some overlap and perhaps repetition in different sections, but it has been our intention that the various chapters stand independently as potential sources of reference.

We have grown through the experience of writing this text. In many ways the experience can be compared to the therapeutic process embarked upon by so many of our patients. It began with some apprehension and a vague appreciation of the magnitude of the prospective task. It has involved a meaningful collaboration filled with hard work, insight, frustration, gratification and, finally, the crystalization of an understanding of issues which have personal meaning. Probably the closest analogy is the recognition that when the process is finished it has only just begun. Writing this volume has set the occasion for new challenges and it has provided a foundation from which to further our understanding.

## ACKNOWLEDGMENTS

Many individuals have contributed in a professional and personal way to the production of this book and it would be impossible to recognize all of them adequately here. However, we are particularly indebted to Professor Vivian Rakoff, Chairman of the Department of Psychiatry, University of Toronto and Director of the Clarke Institute of Psychiatry, who has been most helpful in his encouragement as well as his review of the manuscript. We wish to thank Dean Frederick Lowy of the Faculty of Medicine, University of Toronto for his original suggestion to put our ideas into book form. Drs. Joel Sadavoy, Padraig Darby, and Frances Frankenburg were generous with helpful comments in different sections. Drs. Harvey Stancer and Harvey Moldofsky have provided an important role in contributing to our understanding of the illness. Dr. Gregory Brown, Chairman of the Department of Neurosciences, McMaster University, has been an extremely valued collaborator in aiding our understanding of the hypothalamic-pituitary relationships in the disorder.

We are grateful to Marion Olmsted and Cathy Spegg for statistical advice. Stacey Douglas and Brenda Berck were helpful in proofreading the manuscript. Finally, we appreciate the painstaking typing and technical help from Judy Noble, Noreen Resnick, Rita McConnell, Bernadette Montsegue, Dilly Ratansi, and Martha O'Shaughnessy.

We are also appreciative of the outstanding nursing and other professional staff of the Psychosomatic Medicine Unit for their care and sensitivity in the treatment of the patients at the Clarke Institute of Psychiatry. We are grateful for the generous support of the Ontario Mental Health Foundation, Medical Research Council (Canada) and the National Institute of Mental Health. Finally, we would like to acknowledge the cooperation and many ideas that have come directly from our patients and to express our appreciation to them for their generous participation in the many investigations reported in this volume.

Paul E. Garfinkel, M.D.
David M. Garner, Ph.D

# Anorexia Nervosa

A MULTIDIMENSIONAL PERSPECTIVE

CHAPTER 1

# The Clinical Picture

# of Anorexia Nervosa

While once considered to be a rare disorder, recent studies have confirmed the clinical impression that anorexia nervosa is a relatively common
problem of adolescence (Crisp, Palmer and Kalucy, 1976). Anorexia nervosa is a syndrome characterized by the relentless pursuit of a thin body size
(Bruch, 1970). It is associated with an exaggerated dread of weight gain and
fat, often in spite of emaciation, and to the detriment of other physical and
psychological aspects of the individual's life. The person with anorexia nervosa begins dieting in an attempt to lose weight. Over time, achievement of
ever decreasing weights becomes a sign of mastery, control, and virtue.
Anorexia nervosa is often considered to be a disorder of eating. In the most
precise sense this is incorrect. It is a disorder in which the drive for a thinner
shape is secondary to concerns about control and/or fears about consequences of achieving a mature shape. The pursuit of thinness becomes
necessary for the individual to feel a sense of mastery or control over her
body.

In this chapter the signs and symptoms of anorexia nervosa will be
reviewed and in the following one the historical development of the concept
and the criteria usually required for the diagnosis will be outlined; there will
be some overlap between the two chapters. While the cardinal feature of the
disorder is the overriding pursuit of thinness, other signs and symptoms are
frequently present and have been assigned varying degrees of importance
depending on the author. We will describe these features, under the following headings: 1) the drive for thinness; 2) psychopathological features;
3) the effects of starvation; and 4) physiological complications. The complications will be fully discussed in Chapter 11.

This description is largely for convenience and there is some overlap between symptoms; for example, some psychopathological features are those of starvation. However, whenever possible an attempt will be made to distinguish those features specifically related to starvation from those which appear to be independent of it. As Kubie (1971) has said, all illnesses are "processes"; in any illness there "is an important distinction between the initial process which is the core of the illness and the sick life which gradually results and which may persist long after the sickness, as an active process of pathology, is over. The sick life of a quadriplegic will last for many years after the active infection with the virus of poliomyelitis has disappeared" (p.303).

The interactive relationships developed between an individual's inner and outer worlds, her symptoms, and later by her battle against her symptoms are important in considering a person with anorexia nervosa. Some of the symptoms present in anorexia nervosa generate other symptoms and distortions in the patient's life and in the lives of those close to her. The secondary elaboration of symptoms can become of great clinical importance particularly when considering a patient who has had anorexia nervosa for several years. For example, laxative abuse to reduce weight may produce electrolyte disturbances which are then responsible for weakness or convulsions. Or an anorexic may withdraw socially; the withdrawal is, in part, due to starvation and, in part, to feelings of lowered self-worth, but it results in other symptoms such as loneliness, isolation, and poor social skills. The secondary elaboration of symptoms in anorexia nervosa is a major factor in the perpetuation of the disorder and the chronicity which all too frequently develops.

## THE DRIVE FOR THINNESS

The central feature of anorexia nervosa is the individual's marked pursuit of thinness with the associated conviction that her body is too large. Although this may seem to begin with dieting like that of many North American and European adolescents, it evolves from roots which antedate the diet. Often the patient has been slightly overweight and may begin to diet in response to comments about her size from family members, peers, or a boyfriend. A particular part of her body (e.g., her stomach, thighs, or buttocks) may feel too large. The initial intent is to "lose a few pounds."

At first she will cut out sweets, desserts and high-calorie snacks; this behavior is rewarded by family and friends, particularly in our health and nutrition-conscious society where this may be a sign of being "more in control." However, when her weight goal has been attained, she still feels somewhat overweight and then gradually decides to further restrict her intake of foods. Usually this takes place over several months and goes unnoticed by those around her. By the time others do notice it, she is stubbornly refusing to eat normal amounts of food. Usually the intake is limited to about 600-800 calories per day (Brooks, Braithwaite and Barbato, 1978; Marshall, 1978; Russell, 1970). There is some variability in what these young women eat, but in general, they will select high protein, low carbohydrate foods that are presumed to be low in calories. Many patients will develop extreme rigidity in their eating habits in an effort to control their weight.

While anorexia nervosa patients have an overriding drive to be thin, they do not offer any explanation; they merely say they will feel better the thinner they are. The drive for thinness is ego-syntonic, and is not viewed as something they would like to see changed. They don't perceive themselves as abnormal (Theander, 1970). Consequently, they do not wish help to reverse their weight loss. If they want help it is only for some sequelae of the illness. This severe denial of illness is an important feature early in the disorder. Lasègue (1873) described it well:

> . . . an inexhaustible optimism, against which supplications and menaces alike are of no avail: "I do not suffer and must then be well . . .". So often have I heard this phrase repeated by patients, that now it has come to represent for me a symptom — almost a sign . . . the whole disease is summed up in this intellectual perversion (p. 151).

More recently Mayer (1963) has suggested that the clinical picture of anorexia nervosa centers around a triad of denials — denial of hunger, of thinness, and of fatigue.

Central to the concept of the distorted drive for thinness in anorexia nervosa is a disturbance in body image. This has been clearly described by Bruch (1962) and will be covered in detail in Chapter 6. In spite of the severe and progressive weight loss, many anorexics are unaware of their emaciated state. They may deny several aspects of the disorder but especially the fact that their changed bodies are not healthy or beautiful. Lasègue (1873) wrote:

> The patient, when told that she cannot live upon an amount of food that would not support a young infant, replies that it furnishes sufficient nourishment for her, *adding that she is neither changed nor thinner* (p.150).

The disturbance of body image is an overvalued idea and is of near or actual delusional proportions. In a general sense it can take several forms: Most commonly, patients either deny the extent of the weight loss or they feel that, while they have lost weight generally, a particular body part remains far too large. Strong feelings of self-loathing are the usual emotional component to the body image. Some patients may fleetingly display an emotional reaction of pleasure in their bodies but this is related only to thinness and avoidance of fat.

Crisp (1967) has described anorexia nervosa as a "weight phobia"; over time food may also become a phobic object but only secondarily to the weight fears. Many foods are never allowed. In particular, high carbohydrate foods become feared and must never be eaten. As time passes, the fear that these foods will produce undue weight gain increases. Later, the diet is increasingly rigidly restricted: cottage cheese, salads, fruits, and vegetables. Some patients will eat exactly the same foods every day for months. Lasègue described this in 1873: ". . . one alimentary substance being replaced by another for which an exclusive predilection may be manifested for weeks together" (p. 148). Exceeding the daily "allotment" of any food will induce intense guilt and a desire to cut back food intake even further on the next day.

Because of social pressures to eat, most patients indulge in deceptive behaviors in attempts to hide the extreme dieting from others. Food that is served at home is fed to the dog, flushed down the toilet, or thrown into the garbage. Often parents are told, "I'm not hungry, I ate at a friend's house." Many anorexics will induce vomiting after meals, and some begin to misuse laxatives as a device to prevent weight gain, while pleasing others by eating. The deceptive behaviors aimed at hiding the degree of dieting may antagonize parents, siblings, and medical staff who are not familiar with the psychology of the illness. They result in intense and characteristic struggles for control. The behavior is not due to malice, but to the extreme fear of weight gain.

A large subgroup of anorexics alternate between not eating and bulimia (gorging). The distinction between these and diet-restricting anorexics is more fully developed in Chapter 3. It has been long recognized that bulimia occurs in some anorexic patients. Gull (1874) wrote: "Occasionally for a day or two the appetite was voracious" (p.133). The bulimic patients are usually more distressed by their behavior and feel alternately an intense sense of self-control while dieting and a total lack of control and self-loathing when bulimic. When busy they usually restrict food intake, but during solitary leisure time they will overeat to the point of exhaustion. During the bulimic episode foods that are "forbidden" by the self-prescribed diet are ravenously consumed: rich cakes, desserts, and ice cream. These are foods which are forbidden in the self-imposed diet, but they are not disliked. Some patients will eat whatever is available at the time, e.g., a jar of honey, or pastries that are still frozen. Enormous quantities of food may be eaten during these periods — dozens of doughnuts may be consumed at one sitting.

Following the binge some patients will restrict their food intake for several days, while others will begin to vomit or misuse laxatives for the purposes of preventing weight increases. The bulimia-vomiting cycle may last for many hours and an individual may vomit several times over the course of one evening. A considerable amount of money may be required to buy these foods and some patients begin to steal to support this behavior. The bulimic patients have many characteristics which differentiate them from restricting anorexics. In our view they represent a distinct subtype of the anorexia nervosa syndrome (Garfinkel, Moldofsky and Garner, 1980).

Vomiting usually, but not always, occurs in the bulimic group. It may begin spontaneously after overeating or the patient may have read or heard about it as a means of weight control. A variety of methods are used — sticking a finger or toothbrush down the throat is most frequent but it is not uncommon for patients to develop the ability to vomit spontaneously and some rely on emetics. Russell (1979) has described patients who developed calluses over the dorsum of the hand as a result of the repeated friction of skin against incisors. The patient's feelings associated with the vomiting are generally mixed: At first, there is great relief at having found a way to be able to eat and still maintain a low weight. One of our patients said, "I thought I had the problem licked; I couldn't understand why everyone didn't eat and then vomit."

After beginning to vomit the patient may increase the frequency of bulimic episodes. But there is also a sense of shame in having to rely on vomiting. Over time, what started out as a means to control weight becomes something that must be done or extreme guilt is felt — the patient then becomes "a slave" to the vomiting. When this happens and the person has been vomiting two, three or more times daily for many months, she will rarely be able to stop it on her own and needs a controlled hospital environment.

While the term "anorexia" implies a loss of appetite, this does not usually occur until very late in the starvation process (Ceaser, 1979; Garfinkel, 1974; Pardee, 1941; Theander, 1970). Hunger may be absent if the patient fasts totally and ketosis develops (Dally, 1969). Most patients report normal awareness of hunger but express terror at giving in to the impulse to eat. Because of the intense hunger, some patients are driven to misuse appetite suppressants such as amphetamines or other "diet pills," or drink large quantities of fluid. Others reinterpret resisting their hungry state as a sign of their self-discipline.

By contrast, satiety perception is extremely distorted. Patients report severe bloating, nausea, and distension after eating even small amounts of food, and they do not feel rested or satisfied after eating as most people do. Instead, there is usually a marked sense of guilt for having "given in." It is not yet certain how much, if any, of this satiety disturbance is related to altered gastrointestinal function subsequent to starvation. Constipation is a regular feature due to the restricted food intake and starvation state. This in turn leads to further symptoms of bloating and reduced dietary intake. Some patients begin to treat themselves with laxatives or enemas. From this point others develop the idea of using laxatives to prevent the absorption of foods and further weight gain.

The lack of recognition of inner states goes beyond the awareness of body size but extends, according to Bruch (1973), to a variety of inner feelings, including fatigue. Instead of being exhausted while starving, these young women enjoy boundless energy until late in the illness. Gull (1874), wrote, "It hardly seemed possible that a body so wasted could undergo the exercise which seemed so agreeable" (p. 133); and Lasègue (1873) noted: "So far from muscular power being diminished, this abstinence tends to increase the aptitude for movement" (p. 148). The exercise is, in part, directed to burning up calories and losing further weight. As with the dieting, however, with time the exercise eventually becomes an issue of self-discipline; anorexics cannot allow themselves to miss even one day of the exact amount of self-prescribed activity. Blinder, Freeman and Stunkard (1970) have used pedometers to demonstrate the marked increase in these patients' activity levels, even when in hospital. Crisp (1967) has suggested that the patient's level of physical activity returns to normal after adequate nutrition is restored, thereby implying that hyperactivity is a result of the starvation. This increased activity is not, however, seen in people seriously starving from other causes (Keys et al., 1950), may often antedate significant weight loss (Bruch, 1973), and may remain after restoration of normal weight (Kron et al., 1978).

Amenorrhea is a constant feature in female patients with anorexia nervosa if only because many investigators require its presence for a formal diagnosis of the condition (Russell, 1970; Garrow et al., 1975). The amenorrhea indicates the complexity of many of the anorexic's symptoms: It appears largely, but not entirely, to be the product of weight loss and starvation. It has been repeatedly observed that for many women (70%), amenorrhea develops shortly after the onset of the weight loss (Fries, 1977). However, in a significant proportion (estimates vary between 7-24%) amenorrhea actually appears to precede the weight loss (Fries, 1977). At present, it is not known whether the patients' emotional distress or other independent hypothalamic dysfunction triggers the amenorrhea. However, for most patients amenorrhea is related to weight loss. This is discussed in detail in Chapter 4.

## PSYCHOPATHOLOGICAL FEATURES

The psychopathology of anorexia nervosa is closely intertwined with both the drive for thinness and the manifestations of starvation. The drive for thinness is related to the anorexic's intense fears of obesity and of being out of control. While our culture as a whole is preoccupied with a desire for thinness, the anorexic lets this dominate her life. She becomes terrified of any real or imagined manifestations of fat on her body, even in places where fat is stored normally. Any slight weight increase is perceived as a threat which must be halted promptly. This fear of obesity and weight gain is coupled with an intense food preoccupation common to all starving people. The result is the opposite of what the anorexic wishes: While avoiding foods and eating to reduce her size, she becomes increasingly preoccupied with thoughts of foods and food-related activities. The starvation-induced food preoccupation magnifies the anorexic's fears of not being able to control her appetite and forces her to increase her dieting behavior.

There is a desperate avoidance of normal body proportions. Often, the individual sets a weight limit for herself to allow "a margin of safety." One of our patients described it: "I have to allow myself a few pounds' room in case I have an emergency binge." This weight limit is below the weight necessary for normal hormonal production or biological maturation. The weight limit is generally determined quite arbitrarily but is then followed religiously. In addition to the stated upper weight limit, many patients rely on the way certain clothes feel. Charcot noted this many years ago when he observed a young girl with a ribbon tightly bound around her waist. She explained to him that the ribbon was a measure which the waist was not to exceed (quoted in Janet, 1929, p.233). If a particular pair of jeans begins to feel too tight, the anorexic feels she is approaching her upper weight limit. While this type of behavior is common in normal weight-conscious individuals, what differs is the unrealistic and often dangerous highest allowable upper limit. Russell, Campbell and Slade (1975) have shown that the cognitive process of "what the scales say" is the most important regulating feature of this. They altered the scales to record lower than actual weights and found anorexic patients would then readily gain weight. Obviously this is not recommended as a therapeutic technique, because deception does not help these patients in the long term, but it does indicate the extent of the cognitive controls on their upper weight limits.

The rigidly held weight limit exemplifies the dichotomous thinking of the anorexic (Garner and Bemis, 1982). She feels that, "If I am not 85 lbs, then I might as well be 200 lbs." That is, exceeding her weight limit by even one pound is equal, in her mind, with being totally out of control. In their thinking, anorexics are unable to recognize "in-betweens"; everything in their world is either black or white — there are no grays. A preoccupation with good and evil pervades all their activities (Meyer and Weinroth, 1957). This occurs in all areas requiring self-control — in eating versus not eating, exercising versus not exercising, studying versus recreation. It may also be evident in attitudes to sexuality (abstinence versus promiscuity) and even self-worth (all good versus all bad). It may also extend to the therapeutic setting; the therapist is either idealized or villified. One important aspect of psychotherapy is for the patient to learn for herself appropriate "in-betweens" in each of these areas.

As with other starving people, the anorexic gradually narrows her interests. Many entirely restrict their activities to exercise, schoolwork, and dieting, while all other activities fall by the wayside. They have often been model children premorbidly (Bruch, 1973), involved in a variety of usual activities. With the onset of the illness they restrict their interests but continue to study and prepare homework endlessly; their high grades in school are usually the result of overachieving. Significantly, most girls lose interest in their friends early in the dieting. Bruch (1973) has suggested that this is a most important early signal of the problem; that is, dieting which was begun to enable the person to feel better about herself and to be more involved with others does not lead to improved relationships but to withdrawal and isolation. By the time the weight loss has progressed to the point of medical intervention, the anorexic may be totally isolated. This isolation results in loneliness and a sense of social inadequacy. These, in turn, accentuate the worries about self-control and further the preoccupation with weight loss as time passes.

The moods of anorexic patients are quite variable. Initially, there is a denial of all problems including mood changes; anorexics display a stubborn defiance about most matters, with a marked lack of concern for personal problems. Lasègue observed this in 1873: "Not only does she not sigh for recovery, but she is not ill-pleased with her condition" (p.151). This denial is another of the major symptoms of anorexia nervosa unrelated to starvation and again demonstrates that anorexia nervosa is not merely excessive dieting. The denial conceals the feelings of helplessness these patients later describe when they have improved. Depression and lability of mood are common when the disorder becomes chronic and relate to both the starvation process and the adjustment to such a serious illness.

Patients with anorexia nervosa lose all interest in sex and avoid encounters with the opposite sex. When sexual experiences do occur, they are usually not enjoyed. In part, this is related to starvation (Keys et al., 1950), but it also may continue after weight restoration. Anorexics experience little pleasure from their bodies. Bruch (1973) has described this as part of the defect in recognizing and acting spontaneously on a variety of internal processes. Crisp (1970) has postulated that the central psychopathology underlying the "weight phobia" relates to a basic avoidance of psychosexual maturity — that is, problems which to the girl are vague and intangible become displaced onto her body and concretized: "What is wrong with me is my body size." These problems often relate to learning to regulate their inner and outer worlds and become evident in a variety of situations — for example, separations, deaths, or sexual events. According to Crisp, although the specific symptoms are largely focused on eating and weight, the underlying problem is a profound resistance to sexual and psychological maturity. But while fearful of aspects of adulthood, these girls also long to be adults. As Selvini Palazzoli (1974) has observed, it is an oversimplification to insist that the anorexic merely wants to revert to childhood. Rather, she wishes to become an autonomous adult in a distorted sense — by rejecting those aspects of the feminine body which, to her, signify potential problems.

While the disorder itself may partially represent a fear of psychosexual maturity, its predisposition appears rooted in basic ego-deficits. In particular, Bruch (1973) has linked anorexia nervosa to an overwhelming sense of ineffectiveness. That is, the individual's intense efforts to control her weight reflect basic deficits in mastery over eating, sexual and aggressive drives and impulses. Bruch has hypothesized two disturbances to be closely related to this sense of ineffectiveness, namely disturbances in one's body image and the misperception of affective and visceral sensations.

Closely related to the sense of ineffectiveness and lack of basic self-control is a sense of personal mistrust. In contrast to the paranoid patient who generally trusts himself but not others, the anorexic not only mistrusts herself but she fears her own impulses. Selvini Palazzoli (1974) has described this as both "interoceptual mistrust" (p. 92) and "intrapsychic paranoia" (p. 94). The anorexic patient does not trust her body; rather she is afraid of it. The lack of internal trust seen in these patients may be rooted in their misperception of internal states and thus may be linked to Bruch's (1973) hypothesized genesis of the disorder. Alternatively, it may derive from the chronic internal battle to control weight. Regardless of whether this lack of internal trust is pathogenic or a complication of the disorder, recognition and treatment of it is fundamental to the patient's recovery.

A further aspect of the psychology of anorexia nervosa relates to the regulation of self-esteem. The feeling of self-worth in anorexic patients is closely bound to external standards for appearance and performance. High achievement expectations are less the product of internal drives than of the desire to please others. The confused search for a personal identity is expressed through mimicry of cultural role models. Thus, self-esteem may be directly bound to a "look" or an "image" reflecting aesthetic and performance ideals. In this regard, recent cultural trends may have had an influence on the increased frequency of anorexia nervosa in Western societies (Garner and Garfinkel, 1978, 1980). Pressures on women to be thin and to achieve, and also conflicting role expectations which force women to be paradoxically competitive, yet passive, may partially explain why anorexia nervosa has increased so dramatically. Patients with anorexia nervosa respond to these pressures by equating weight control with self-control and this in turn is equated with beauty and "success."

Anorexia nervosa can be considered a "psychosomatic" disorder for several reasons. On the one hand, anorexic patients represent the extreme of the split between mind and body — that is, the patient has decided that her mind must subdue her body. This is not a suicide wish — the starvation is a statement about autonomy, not an attempt at self-destruction. Psychoanalytic writers have conceptualized this mind/body split to be related to an incorporation of the maternal object from which the girl wants to separate (Selvini Palazzoli, 1974). Anorexics have a sense of anhedonia with a desire to remove the physical and live only through their mental beings. This sense of severe physical anhedonia has been empirically demonstrated to be closely related to the patient's disturbed body image (Garfinkel, 1981). Anorexia nervosa can be considered a psychosomatic entity at another level; most patients present with starvation which in itself produces psychological symptoms. These are discussed more fully in the following section. Psychological distress can therefore produce physical changes which will then introduce further psychological symptoms. These symptoms will then tend to perpetuate the disorder and it is partly for this reason that weight restoration is an important, non-negotiable aspect of the early management.

## THE EFFECTS OF STARVATION

Many of the symptoms regularly ascribed to the anorexia nervosa syndrome are a direct result of starvation and occur in starving people, whatever its cause (Casper and Davis, 1977). This is particularly noticeable for the food-related features. Anyone who has worked closely with anorexics will have recognized their paradoxical food refusal while being preoccupied with eating. They have collected and assiduously read nutritional books, have attended gourmet cooking classes, and are often avid cooks. Many enjoy feeding others while forbidding themselves food. It is not uncommon for them to enter food-related professions (e.g., dietitian, cook, or waitress). Often they will display unusual eating behaviors at meals. Many treat eating with various rituals and great secrecy, something that must be done only in total privacy. Some refuse to eat if anyone else is present. Others can eat only in darkness or only when standing. Often they spend increasingly lengthy periods of time at a meal, at times barely completing lunch before supper. At the dinner table, non-diet-related food habits may become very obvious — putting ketchup on salads and mixing a variety of spices on all foods. These features together are often described as part of the "anorexic behavior" but in actual fact many have been clearly described in the Minnesota studies (Keys et al., 1950) of semi-starvation.

During World War II, 36 psychologically normal conscientious objectors were placed on semi-starvation diets for six months to learn more about the psychobiological effects of starvation. This study is of particular relevance in evaluating the symptoms of anorexia nervosa, since, unlike natural starvation due to famine or war, these volunteers were starving but were surrounded by food and people who were eating well. These volunteer males displayed many so-called "anorexic" features: intense preoccupation with food, "food fads," mixing unusual food combinations, and "dawdling" over meals.

Toward the end of the starvation, men would spend two hours over a meal which previously they would have consumed in minutes. They spent hours planning how they would handle their day's food quota (Keys et al., 1950). Food became the dominant topic of conversation. Nineteen of the men began reading cookbooks and collecting recipes. Some planned to become cooks after the study was completed. Unusual mixing of food combinations was regular. There was a sharp rise in coffee and tea consumption; many men drank over 15 cups of coffee a day. Subjects attempted to keep their stomachs full by drinking large quantities of other liquids (water, soup) as well. Gum-chewing, smoking, and nail-biting increased dramatically. These features are usual in anorexic patients.

The bulimia which occurs in many anorexic subjects was also described in four subjects in the Minnesota studies (Schiele and Brozek, 1948), and as in anorexia nervosa, this was followed by remorse. As in bulimic anorexics, a few of the starved volunteers began to steal small items that they could otherwise afford. Some men had vivid food-related dreams. In earlier studies of starvation (Benedict et al., 1919; Sorokin, 1942), food dreams and dreams of breaking dietary restrictions were common, as were occasional food dreams of an aggressive or cannibalistic nature (Schiele and Brozek, 1948) not unlike those recently purported to be of particular significance for anorexia nervosa (Levitan, 1979).

It has been repeatedly observed that patients with anorexia nervosa frequently manifest obessional behaviors (Dally, 1969; Solyom et al., in press.). At times it has even been suggested that anorexia nervosa is basically a compulsion neurosis (Palmer and Jones, 1939; Solyom et al., in press). However, obsessive thinking about foods and compulsive behaviors as well as heightened obsessionality may occur in starving people in general. For example, indecisiveness was frequently observed in Keys et al.'s (1950) starved men. "Excessive" gum-chewing (up to 40-60 packages per day) was described in some of the starved volunteers in the Minnesota studies (Schiele and Brozek, 1948); this was initially begun "to alleviate hunger and nervous tension but was continued compulsively in spite of the fact that it failed to give the desired result (p.48) and resulted in severe pain.

Another starving "normal" subject became obsessed with the idea of rummaging through garbage. "Hoarding" and acquisitiveness are common in both anorexia nervosa and other starvation states; in the Minnesota studies food-related hoarding (hot plates, cookbooks, coffee pots) was common as was hoarding of non-food-related items (old books, secondhand clothes). Hoarding of food has also been demonstrated in rats when their body weight was reduced by fasting (Fantino and Cabanac, 1980).

The obsessional characteristics of the anorexic are clearly not entirely starvation-related, however. They don't disappear but may improve following weight restoration. While this compulsive behavior in anorexics may serve the purpose of increasing a sense of self-control, other starvation effects work directly against this. For example, a reduced ability to concentrate was reported by 66% of the Minnesota subjects and self-discipline, alertness, and ambition were also reduced (Keys et al., p. 821). Problems with concentration and alertness are frequently reported by anorexics as distressing and these increase their worries about self-control; but rather than deal with the cause of these symptoms — starvation — anorexics further starve to feel more in control. This clearly serves to increase the cognitive symptoms.

These starvation studies also documented an exaggeration of subjects' previous personality traits. Many subjects became increasingly indecisive. A narrowing of interests, social withdrawal, and irritability were common responses. Subjects generally became inhibited. These are also seen as a major part of the symptom complex in anorexia nervosa. On the MMPI the Minnesota subjects displayed an elevation of the depression, hypochondriasis, and hysteria scales in comparison with prestarvation baseline scores

(Keys et al., p. 865). Lability of mood was common and one subject was admitted to hospital with a brief hypomanic state.

While these men were initially well, psychologically, several had to stop the experiment because of their personality changes and for many of the others recovery did not occur immediately on refeeding; Schiele and Brozek (1948) observed that often more than the 12 weeks of rehabilitation were necessary to observe complete recovery. In fact, the initial refeeding period was often quite stressful. For example, extreme hunger was often reported after eating a large meal. When, as is common, this occurs in anorexic patients, it is associated with a terror of losing control. This is why the period of refeeding in anorexia nervosa is so significant. The patient may initially experience great discomfort; however, weight restoration is absolutely necessary. It must be stressed that there is great individual variability in the presence and severity of these starvation symptoms. This variability depends on the individual's premorbid personality, the rapidity and degree of starvation, sleep loss and the damaging effects of the social isolation (Bruch, 1979).

Sleep disturbance is a regular complication of the starvation process. Crisp (1970, 1980) observed that insomnia, especially early morning awakening, was a feature in most patients with anorexia nervosa and that the sleep disturbance was not a result of mood changes. Later, Crisp, Stonehill and Fenton (1971) and Crisp and Stonehill (1971) confirmed these earlier observations using sleep self-reports, EEG recordings, measurements of body weight, and psychoneurotic status before and after weight restoration. Crisp and Stonehill (1971) found that weight loss, and less and more fragmented sleep, as well as early waking, were unrelated to mood state or psychiatric morbidity in a large group of psychiatric outpatients. They proposed that nutritional change is associated with changes in sleep patterns independent of mood state. More recently, this same group compared the sleep EEG of ten anorexics before and after weight restoration with the sleep of matched controls. They found that undernourished low body weight anorexics had less sleep and more restlessness, but during refeeding and weight gain their slow wave sleep increased and returned to normal levels. At that point, their increased duration of sleep was associated with increased REM. They speculated that the increase in slow wave sleep might reflect previously hypothesized bodily synthetic processes and the "rekindling of the pubertal process."

Loss of sexual interest was marked in the volunteers of the Minnesota experiment. Subjects were struck by this: "I have no more sexual feeling than a sick oyster" (Keys et al., 1950, p. 839). Not only did interest in the opposite sex and dating decline; masturbation, sexual fantasies, and dreams ceased or were greatly reduced. Anorexic patients also lose sexual interests and avoid contact with the opposite sex. Like the amenorrhea, this is presumably complexly determined. In part it represents a complication of the starvation but it frequently persists, at least in part, after weight restoration. In this sense it is also tied to the individual's fears of being unable to control or discipline herself, particularly in areas in which bodily feelings are concerned.

## THE SIGNS OF ANOREXIA NERVOSA

Allbutt (1910) vividly described a patient:

A young woman thus afflicted, her clothes scarcely hanging together on her anatomy, her pulse slow and slack, her temperature two degrees below the normal mean, her bowels closed, her hair like that of a corpse dry and lustreless, her face and limbs ashy and cold, her hollow eyes the only vivid thing about her . . . This wane creature whose daily food might lie on a crown piece, will be busy yet on what funds God only knows (p. 398).

Many of the signs of anorexia nervosa are the direct products of starvation. The patient appears emaciated, in extreme cases "like a skeleton only clad with skin" (Morton, 1694). The characteristic female curves disappear. The degree of weight loss is extemely variable but can be greater than 50% of the person's premorbid weight. Our patients' average weight on first presentation is 65% of the Canadian average for their age and height. Only 4% have lost less than 25% of their premorbid weight (Garfinkel, Moldofsky and Garner, 1980). Using water dilution techniques (Ljunggren, Ikkos and Luft, 1961) it has been found that the lost tissue is mostly composed of solid matter, with water accounting for only 32% of the total. The amount of body fat is greatly reduced, for example to 8% of body weight in one study (Fohlin, 1977).

In addition to the emaciated appearance, the anorexic usually has a dry cracking skin and may have lost some hair from her scalp. Pubic and axillary hair is generally unchanged (Beck and Brochner-Mortensen, 1954). The nails become brittle. Lanugo hair, a fine downy growth, over the cheeks, neck, forearms and thighs is common. The patient's hands and feet are usually cold and blue. Cyanosis may extend to the nose and ears. Carotene pigmentation may be present on the palms and soles; this may be due to frequent ingestion of high carotene-containing foods (Russell, 1970) or to an acquired defect in carotene metabolism. There may be a perioral dermatitis from repeated exposure to vomitus. Bradycardia and hypoten-sion may be marked and bruises from subsequent falls may be evident. The patient's temperature may be low. Patients with repeated vomiting of long duration display a variety of dental problems, including dissolution of enamel and caries (Hurst, Lacey and Crisp, 1977). Peripheral edema is com-mon especially when a severely malnourished patient is rapidly refed. Some patients may also develop edema after being bulimic on high carbohydrate foods or ingesting large amounts of coffee or salt. This is not an indication for using diuretics. Dehydration may occur from fluid restriction combined with repeated vomiting and diuretic or laxative misuse.

Anorexics display a preservation of their secondary sexual characteristics, except for some reduction in breast tissue (Beck and Brochner-Mortensen, 1954). This differs from patients with primary pituitary illness. Other changes due to hypothalamic dysfunction, including the amenorrhea, are described in Chapter 4.

## PRESENTATION, DIFFERENTIAL DIAGNOSIS, AND INVESTIGATIONS

Because of the multiple symptoms of the illness and because of its many complications (see Chapter 11), patients with anorexia nervosa present in a variety of ways. Most commonly, the weight loss, which does not concern the individual herself, becomes noticeable to a family member, teacher, or friend and the girl is then brought to the family doctor. The common reasons for the consultation are the severe weight loss, postprandial bloating, amenorrhea, or family disputes around eating. With the increased attention recently given to the disorder, parents or school nurses may have identified the illness before the girl is seen by the physician.

At times the patient herself may request medical help — not for the weight problem, but for some sequelae of the disorder which she finds unpleasant. For example, the individual may wish treatment for her severe constipation, sleep disturbance, or impaired concentration. Occasionally, the patient may be concerned about her unhappiness, labile mood, or severely restricted interpersonal relationships. Some complain of "bloating" and request diuretics; others may actually first present in order to obtain "diet" pills and specific weight-reducing diets. Some patients, particularly those with bulimia, become dependent on alcohol or sedative drugs and may present with this feature. Some present primarily with gastrointestinal symptoms — constipation, abdominal pains, and bouts of watery diarrhea if laxatives are being misused. At times this may lead to laparotomy. Anorexic women may first consult physicians because of amenorrhea or infertility and some present to sexual dysfunction clinics with vaginismus and frigidity. Others are not seen medically until they have regained weight on their own and have maintained this weight through vomiting or laxative misuse. They may present with the complications of these behaviors — weakness, hypokalemia, tetany, or convulsions.

A number of other illnesses must be differentiated from anorexia nervosa. These are chronic wasting diseases such as tumors or tuberculosis, hypothalamic diseases, regional enteritis, and several primary endocrine disturbances: anterior pituitary insufficiency, Addison's disease, hyperthyroidism, and diabetes mellitus. Several functional disorders may also be confused with anorexia nervosa. These are: primary depressive illness, schizophrenia, hysteria, and obsessive-compulsive neurosis; they are described in further detail in the following chapter.

The primary somatic causes of weight loss are generally readily distinguished from anorexia nervosa on the basis of a thorough history and physical examination. Of importance in the history is the patient's desire for the weight loss, her conviction that her emaciated body is not too thin, and her deliberate dieting. Often there will also be evidence of disposing of food, self-induced vomiting, laxative misuse, and the marked drive for activity with excess energy. If such a clear history is available one can be reasonably certain of the diagnosis.

While the symptoms of weight loss and amenorrhea are common in hypothalamic tumors, it is rare to have a tumor present with the actual symptoms of anorexia nervosa (see Chapter 4). An EEG, skull x-ray, and at times a CAT scan will be required to clarify the picture. The latter is indicated if the clinical picture does not resemble "typical" anorexia nervosa, if neurological signs are present, or if the illness begins to take an unexpected course. In anterior pituitary insufficiency there is a reduced BMR and amenorrhea, but these constitute the major resemblance to anorexia nervosa. There is rarely serious weight loss in Simmonds' disease and there is also loss of secondary sexual characteristics. On laboratory testing, the presence of low growth hormone (growth hormone is often elevated in starving anorexics), hypothyroidism or other, end organ hypofunction is clearly discernible.

In hyperthyroidism, significant weight loss may occur but the remainder of the clinical picture is of a hypermetabolic state (elevated pulse, respiration and blood pressure, sweaty warm extremities, etc). This is generally quite different from most presentations of an anorexic; however, bulimic patients may display some of these features — a hot flushed appearance, tachycardia, and restlessness after periods of prolonged overeating (Crisp, 1977). Their thyroid function tests will definitely not be in the hyperthyroid range. Occasionally a physician who measures serum thyroxine and finds it low in anorexic patients will consider the individual hypothyroid and treat her with thyroxine. While it is true that anorexic patients may display a thyroid conservation response to starvation (see Chapter 4), this is not a true hypothyroid state. Thyroxine has no place in the management of anorexia nervosa.

Diabetes mellitus may be suspected on the basis of weight loss in association with ingestion of large volumes of fluid and polyuria; however, in anorexia nervosa these are due to attempts to control hunger with low calorie fluids, rather than thirst.

Addisonian patients may most closely resemble anorexics in that they display weight loss, vomiting, reduced food intake, hypotension, and occasionally hypoglycemia. Skin pigmentation may occur in Addisonian patients but has, on occasion, been observed in anorexics as well (Dally, 1969). However, the weight loss of adrenal insufficiency is due to anorexia, not an aversion to weight gain. They are inactive and have markedly reduced energy, at times being bedridden. On laboratory testing, the elevated potassium and reduced sodium are different from the potassium depletion that is common in anorexia nervosa. If uncertainty exists, provocative and suppressive tests of adrenal-cortical function will confirm the diagnosis.

Some patients, with specific localized symptoms may require detailed investigation. For example, with a presentation of weight loss in conjunction with postprandial pain, bloating, and constipation, gastrointestinal radiography is indicated. These additional studies may be required in specific instances. In general, however, with a detailed collateral history from someone who knows the patient well and physical examination it is uncommon to require extensive laboratory testing to confirm the diagnosis. On the other hand, it is often necessary to have the anorexic patient undergo specific tests in order to determine the extent of the sequelae. In this regard patients with vomiting or laxative abuse or fairly marked starvation require regular monitoring of their hematologic indices, electrolytes, and hepatic, cardiac and renal function. The specific sequelae to anorexia nervosa are more fully described in Chapter 11.

## REFERENCES

Allbutt, T.C.: Neuroses of the stomach and of other parts of the abdomen. In: T.C. Allbutt and H.D. Rolleston (Eds.), *System of Medicine*. London: The Macmillan Company, 1910.
Beck, J.C. and Brochner-Mortensen, K.: Observations on the prognosis in anorexia nervosa. *Acta Med. Scand.,* 149:409-430, 1954.
Benedict, F.G., Miles, W.R., Roth, P. and Smith, H.M.: Human vitality and efficiency under prolonged restricted diet. Carnegie Institute, Washington. Publication No. 280, 1919.
Brooks, M.H., Braithwaite, S.S. and Barbato, A.L.: Anorexia nervosa. *Compr. Ther.,* 4:44-50, 1978.

Blinder, B.J., Freeman, D.M.A., and Stunkard, A.J.: Behavior therapy of anorexia nervosa: Effectiveness of activity as a reinforcer of weight gain. *Am. J. Psychiatry,* 126:1093-1098, 1970.

Bruch, H.: Perceptual and conceptual disturbances in anorexia nervosa. *Psychosom. Med.,* 24:187-194, 1962.

Bruch, H.: Instinct and interpersonal experience. *Compr. Psychiatry,* 11:495-506, 1970.

Bruch, H.: *Eating Disorders.* New York: Basic Books, 1973.

Bruch, H.: Anorexia nervosa. In: J.J. Wurtman and R.J. Wurtman (Eds.), *Nutrition and the Brain.* New York: Raven Press, 1979.

Casper, R.C. and Davis, J.M.: On the course of anorexia nervosa. *Am. J. Psychiatry,* 134:974-978, 1977.

Ceaser, M.: Hunger in primary anorexia nervosa. *Am. J. Psychiatry,* 136:979-980, 1979.

Crisp, A.H.: The possible significance of some behavioural correlates of weight and carbohydrate intake. *J. Psychosom. Res.,* 11:117-131, 1967.

Crisp, A.H.: Premorbid factors in adult disorders of weight, with particular reference to primary anorexia nervosa (weight phobia). *J. Psychosom. Res.,* 14:1-22, 1970.

Crisp, A.H.:Sleep, activity, nutrition and mood. *Br. J. Psychiat.,* 137:1-7, 1980.

Crisp, A.H. and Stonehill, E.: Aspects of the relationship between psychiatric status, sleep, nocturnal motility and nutrition. *J. Psychosom. Res.,* 15:501-509, 1971.

Crisp, A.H., Stonehill, E. and Fenton, G.W.: The relationship between sleep, nutrition and mood: A study of patients with anorexia nervosa. *Postgrad. Med. J.,* 47:207-213, 1971.

Crisp, A.H., Palmer, R.L. and Kalucy, R.S.: How common is anorexia nervosa? A prevalence study. *Br. J. Psychiatry,* 128:549-554, 1976.

Dally, P.: *Anorexia Nervosa.* New York: Grune and Stratton, 1969.

Fantino, M. and Cabanac, M.: Body weight regulation with a proportional hoarding response in the rat. *Physiol. Behav.,* 24:939-942, 1980.

Fohlin, L.: Body composition, cardiovascular and renal function in adolescent patients with anorexia nervosa. *Acta. Paediatr. Scand.,* (Suppl) 268:1-20, 1977.

Fries, H.: Studies on secondary amenorrhea, anorectic behavior, and body image perception: Importance for the early recognition of anorexia nervosa. In: R. Vigersky (Ed.), *Anorexia Nervosa.* New York: Raven Press, 1977.

Garfinkel, P.E.: Perception of hunger and satiety in anorexia nervosa. *Psychol. Med.,* 4:309-315, 1974.

Garfinkel, P.E.: Some recent observations on the pathogenesis of eating disorders. *Can. J. Psychiatry,* 26:218-223, 1981.

Garfinkel, P.E., Moldofsky, H. and Garner, D.M.: The heterogeneity of anorexia nervosa: Bulimia as a distinct subgroup. *Arch. Gen. Psychiatry,* 37:1036-1040, 1980.

Garner, D.M. and Bemis, K.M.: A cognitive-behavioral approach to anorexia nervosa. *Cog. Ther. Res.,* 6:1-27, 1982.

Garner, D.M. and Garfinkel, P.E.: Sociocultural factors in anorexia nervosa. *Lancet,* 2:674, 1978.

Garner, D.M. and Garfinkel, P.E.: Socio-cultural factors in the development of anorexia nervosa. *Psychol. Med.,* 10:647-656, 1980.

Garrow, J.S., Crisp, A.H., Jordon, H.A., Meyer, J.E., Russell, G.F.M., Silverstone, T., Stunkard, A.J. and Van Itallie, T.B.: Pathology of eating, group report. In: T. Silverstone (Ed.), *Dahlem Konferenzen, Life Sciences Research Report 2.* Berlin, 1975.

Gull, W.W. Anorexia nervosa. *Trans. Clin. Soc.* (London), 7:22-28, 1874. Reprinted in: R.M. Kaufman and M. Heiman (Eds.), *Evolution of Psychosomatic Concepts. Anorexia Nervosa: A Paradigm.* New York: International Universities Press, 1964.

Hurst, P.S., Lacey, J.H. and Crisp, A.H.: Teeth, vomiting and diet: A study of the dental characteristics of seventeen anorexia nervosa patients. *Postgrad. Med. J.,* 53:298-305, 1977.

Janet, P.: *The Major Symptoms of Hysteria.* New York: Macmillan, 1929, p.233.

Keys, A., Brozek, J., Henschel, A., Mickelsen, O. and Taylor, H.L.: *The Biology of Human Starvation, Vol. 1.* Minneapolis: University of Minnesota Press, 1950.

Kron, L., Katz, J.L., Gorzynski, G. and Weiner, H.: Hyperactivity in anorexia nervosa: A fundamental clinical feature. *Compr. Psychiatry,* 19:433-440, 1978.
Kubie, L.S.: Multiple fallacies in the concept of schizophrenia. *J. Nerv. Ment. Dis.,* 153:331-342, 1971.
Lasègue, C.: De l'anorexie hystérique. *Arch. Gen. de. Med.* 385, 1873. Reprinted in: R.M. Kaufman and M. Heiman (Eds.), *Evolution of Psychosomatic Concepts. Anorexia Nervosa: A Paradigm.* New York: International Universities Press, 1964.
Levitan, H.: Implications of certain dreams reported by patients with anorexia nervosa syndrome. Post-graduate Board, Royal Victoria Hospital and McGill University, Montreal, April, 1979.
Ljunggren, H., Ikkos, D. and Luft, R.: Basal metabolism in women with obesity and anorexia nervosa. *Br. J. Nutr.,* 15:21-34, 1961.
Marshall, M.H.: Anorexia nervosa: Dietary treatment and re-establishment by body weight in 20 cases studied on a metabolic unit. *J. Hum. Nutr.,* 32:349-357, 1978.
Mayer, J.: Anorexia nervosa. *Postgrad. Med.,* 34:529-534, 1963.
Meyer, B.C. and Weinroth, L.A.: Observations on psychological aspects of anorexia nervosa. *Psychosom. Med.,* 19:389-398, 1957.
Morton, R.: *Phthisiologica: Or a Treatise of Consumptions.* London: S. Smith and B. Walford, 1694.
Palmer, H.D. and Jones, M.S.: Anorexia nervosa as a manifestation of compulsion neurosis: A study of psychogenic factors. *Arch. Neurol. Psychiat.,* 41:856-860, 1939.
Pardee, I.: Cachexia (anorexia) nervosa. *Med. Clin. North Am.,* 25:755-773, 1941.
Russell, G.F.M.: Anorexia nervosa: Its identity as an illness and its treatment. In J.H. Price (Ed.), *Modern Trends in Psychological Medicine, 2.* London: Butterworths, 1970.
Russell, G.F.M.: Bulimia nervosa: An ominous variant of anorexia nervosa. *Psychol. Med.,* 9:429-448, 1979.
Russell, G.F.M., Campbell, P.G. and Slade, P.D.: Experimental studies on the nature of the psychological disorder in anorexia nervosa. *Psychoneuroendoctrinology,* 1:45-56, 1975.
Schiele, B.C. and Brozek, J.: "Experimental neurosis" resulting from semistarvation in man. *Psychosom. Med.,* 10:31-50, 1948.
Selvini Palazzoli, M.P.: *Self-starvation.* London: Chaucer Publishing Co., 1974.
Solyom, L., Miles, J.E. and O'Kane, J.: Comparative study of anorexia nervosa. *Can. J. Psychiatry* (in press).
Sorokin, P.A.: *Man and Society in Calamity.* New York: Dutton, 1942.
Theander, S.: Anorexia nervosa: A psychiatric investigation of 94 female patients. *Acta. Psychiatr. Scand.* [Suppl.], 214:1-194, 1970.

# CHAPTER 2

# Anorexia Nervosa:

# The Concept and Diagnosis

## ANOREXIA NERVOSA AS A DISTINCT DISORDER VERSUS ITS RELATIONSHIP TO OTHER ILLNESSES

There has been considerable controversy over the years about whether anorexia nervosa exists as a discrete disorder or whether it represents a variant of other illnesses. Gull (1874) considered anorexia nervosa to be a distinct disorder. Similarly, Gilles de la Tourette (1895) and Déjérine and Gauckler (1911) differentiated it from loss of appetite in psychosis and depression. However, Dubois (1913) challenged this distinction with his description of an adolescent girl with anorexia nervosa and early signs of schizophrenia. Simmonds' (1914) subsequent description of a patient with anterior pituitary damage and weight loss resulted in a long period of diagnostic confusion between anorexia nervosa and primary endocrine illness; this is described more fully in Chapter 4.

There have been many psychiatrists who have considered anorexia nervosa to be a variant of some other psychiatric illness, such as schizophrenia, affective disorder, obsessional neurosis, or hysteria. Of these, the most frequent has been that anorexia nervosa is an expression or form of affective illness, since depression is a common feature. According to Thoma (1967) and Dally (1969) this was Kraepelin's position. The German psychoanalyst Wulff (1932) and later Meyer and Weinroth (1957) compared the fluctuations of some patients between bulimia and depression, and fasting and elation, to the mood swings of manic-depressives. Zutt (1948) reported on six patients with anorexia nervosa, of whom four experienced depressed mood; he thought the illness was related to manic-depressive psychosis.

It is easy to see why blurring between the syndromes may occur, since many symptoms are common to the two disorders. Kay (1953), for example, noted "depressive mood" in 50% of his anorexic patients and Rollins and Piazza (1978) reported depressive symptoms in 74% of their sample. Carlson and Cantwell (1980) found that, while anorexic adolescents frequently described such depressive symptoms as dysphoric mood, low self-esteem, hopelessness, and suicidal ideation (in 16-67% of patients), their scores on a global rating for depression were significantly less than adolescents with a primary affective disorder. The vegetative features of depression, insomnia, fragmented sleep, weight loss, constipation, reduced libido, and amenorrhea are all part of the anorexic's symptomatology. In addition, cognitive features of depression such as indecisiveness, poor concentration, loss of interests, and social withdrawal also occur. Moreover, the fall in self-esteem which is central to depressive psychopathology also occurs in anorexia nervosa, but in the latter becomes tied to body weight or appearance.

In addition to the shared symptoms of the two disorders, the recent work of Cantwell et al. (1977) has documented both the prevalence of depression in anorexic subjects over time and also the frequent occurrence of affective illness in the mothers of anorexics. These investigators followed 26 patients for an average of five years after treatment. About two-thirds of the patients could be given a psychiatric diagnosis other than anorexia nervosa at the time of follow-up and one half of these met criteria for affective disorder. Moreover, two fathers, 15 mothers and six siblings were diagnosed as suffering from an affective disorder. Kalucy, Crisp and Harding (1977) also reported that 14% of the fathers of their patients, but none of the mothers, suffered from manic-depressive illness. They concluded that this relationship may be associated with concern about controls and marital disharmony in such families rather than pointing to a primary connection between affective disorder and anorexia nervosa. Dally (1977) has stated that about three-quarters of the mothers of his younger (< 15) patients have been depressed. Winokur, March and Mendels (1980) recently compared the relatives of anorexic patients with controls. Twenty-two percent of the former but only 10% of the latter had evidence of primary affective disorder. On the other hand, Theander (1970) observed a morbid risk for depression of only 2.6% in the parents of his anorexic patients. We, also, did not find a high frequency of affective disorder in the parents from our series (Garfinkel, Moldofsky and Garner, 1980), but the diagnoses were made on historical information rather than direct interviews with relatives.

While the findings of depression on follow-up and depression in the relatives are noteworthy, it is important to distinguish between the symptoms of dysphoric mood which is common in chronic illness and a primary depressive syndrome. In addition, if depression is diagnosed by signs and symptoms on a structured interview or rating scale, anorexics may frequently be so classified simply by virtue of symptoms, some of which are induced by starvation. Finally, it may not be surprising to find depression in members of these families given other observations of their style of interaction (Minuchin, Rosman and Baker, 1978). Crisp, Harding and McGuinness (1974) noted that as anorexics improve, their parents frequently manifest depressive and anxious symptoms. Depressive symptoms and even suicide attempts are not uncommon in anorexia nervosa. And it has been suggested that the use of tricyclic antidepressants to treat both depression and anorexia nervosa further links these illnesses (Needleman and Waber, 1976). However, there is no controlled double-blind investigation delineating the efficacy of these medications in anorexia nervosa and even if there were, it would be fallacious to conclude common mechanisms for the disorders based on similar drug responses. While there are clinical features common to both anorexia nervosa and affective disorder, and while depression is a common symptom in chronic forms of anorexia nervosa, the fundamental drive for thinness which dominates the anorexic's clinical picture warrants a separate classification of the illness. At the same time, the reported increase in relatives with primary affective disorder may represent a predisposition to the illness either via genetic or psychological mechanisms.

Other writers have suggested a connection between schizophrenia and anorexia nervosa. Grace Nicolle (1939) held this point of view in a paper entitled, *Prepsychotic Anorexia,* which also implicated a primary endocrine disorder in the pathogenesis. Binswanger (1944) described *The Case of Ellen West,* who clearly had anorexia nervosa and whom both he and Bleuler diagnosed as a simple schizophrenic. Some features of schizophrenia may be observed in anorexia nervosa. In particular, anorexics often show social withdrawal, negativism, and indecisiveness, which superficially resemble a volition defect. The distorted self-perceptions of the body of the anorexic may resemble psychotic perceptions of schizophrenics, but in the former relate only to her body and not to others. Rarely anorexic patients may describe their sense of helplessness as a feeling of being controlled externally; while this has some semblance to "made feelings," care should be taken not to confuse this with a delusion that conforms to a "first rank" symptom. Bleulerian thought process and affective disturbances and Schneiderian first rank symptoms are absent in anorexia nervosa. In addition, there is no increased risk for schizophrenia in the families of anorexics (Theander, 1970). Schizophrenic patients may occasionally lose weight;

however, this is generally due to a delusion about food or catatonic symptoms and not to a preoccupation with body size.

While a clear differentiation can readily be made between schizophrenia and anorexia nervosa, there are some patients who present with anorexia nervosa and later develop overt psychoses (Kay and Leigh, 1954; Meyer, 1961). There are several possibilities to account for these: transient schizophrenic-like states can occur in severely starved patients (Keys et al., 1950; Dally, 1969) or in individuals with borderline personality organizations (Gunderson and Singer, 1975). But these should be differentiated from the eventual development of schizophrenia, which is uncommon in anorexia nervosa. For example, Dally (1969) reported one of 140 anorexics to be schizophrenic on follow-up and Theander (1970) found one of 94 patients to be borderline psychotic. These figures are not out of keeping with the 1% lifetime risk for schizophrenia in the population as a whole (Babigan, 1975).

Many anorexic symptoms are of an obsessive nature — the relentless pursuit of thinness, calorie counting, repeated checking of weight, meticulous habits, and indecisiveness all resemble obsessive symptoms. Palmer and Jones (1939) concluded that anorexia nervosa was basically a compulsion neurosis and Du Bois (1949) called this disorder "compulsion neurosis with cachexia." Smart, Beumont and George (1976) confirmed the highly obsessional nature of a group of anorexic subjects using psychometric tests. This was recently confirmed by Solyom, Miles and O'Kane (in press). Using the Leighton Obsessional Inventory, anorexics were found not to differ in degree of obsessional features from severe obsessive-compulsive neurotics if the main obsession of the neurotics were eliminated from the analysis. Symptom severity did not differ between the groups. They concluded that about one-half of their anorexic patients suffered from an obsessive neurosis.

Although some obsessionality is present in anorexic subjects when they are ill, this may be a product, in part, of severe starvation, as shown in the Minnesota experiments (Keys et al., 1950). Moreover, since these studies by Smart et al. and Solyom et al. were based on relatively small numbers of chronically ill subjects and since obsessionality has been thought to be a poor prognostic feature (see Chapter 12), they may suffer from sampling bias. Large numbers of patients without this degree of obsessionality who may recover more quickly may be excluded from the sample. Obsessive-compulsive character traits are frequently present in anorexics, but they do not signify an obsessive-compulsive neurosis; these traits occur in a wide variety of other disorders. For example, obsessive-compulsive behaviors are also common in schizophrenia (Lewis, 1936). In obsessive-compulsive neurotics these symptoms are ego-alien; while the anorexic is preoccupied with weight, body shape, and food, only the latter is ego-alien. Indeed, it is one of the major tasks of therapy to have the patient consider her drive for thinness to be ego-alien.

Lasègue (1873) had observed hysterical symptoms in his anorexic patients. He termed the disorder "anorexie hystérique" and, like his contemporaries, viewed hysteria as a predominantly hereditary disturbance of the central nervous system. Gilles de la Tourette (1895) also considered primary anorexia nervosa to be a manifestation of hysteria which had to be differentiated from "anorexia gastrique"; this was due to gastrointestinal symptoms resulting in the refusal of food. Shortly after this, Janet (1919) observed that not all anorexic patients had hysteria but that they constituted a significant subgroup, a position later supported by Dally (1969).

Periodically the link between hysteria and anorexia nervosa has been revived; for example, Hobhouse (1938) felt that anorexia nervosa was a form of conversion hysteria. While the definition of hysteria has now been replaced by such terms as hysterical personality disorder, somatization disorder (Briquet's syndrome) and conversion disorder, anorexia nervosa does not fit neatly into any of these categories. Some, but not all, anorexic patients display hysterical personality types (Beumont, George and Smart, 1976; Dally, 1969).

Occasionally people with somatization disorder may present with vomiting and weight loss, but they are readily differentiated from the true anorexia nervosa patient. In contrast to the anorexic, the person with somatization disorder presents with a long history of being sickly, having had numerous operations and suffering from multiple complaints. They may also manifest conversion or dissociative symptoms and generally they use their symptoms to draw attention to themselves while anorexics in contrast try to avoid notice. Conversion disorders may resemble anorexia nervosa in that they are both physical disorders representing underlying psychological disturbance. In both conditions there may be significant elements of secondary gain; that is, the symptoms gain benefits for the patients they would not ordinarily receive. An essential difference between the two entities is that in conversion disorders the individual does not experience the sense of controlling or withdrawal of the symptoms; rather they develop suddenly after particular environmental circumstances and often have symbolic value and represent an underlying conflict. Anorexia nervosa, on the other hand, is characterized by the individual's willful and deliberate determination to lose weight. Garfinkel, Kaplan, Garner, and Darby (1982) have recently demonstrated marked clinical and psychometric differences between anorexics and a group of women with conversion disorders who presented with vomiting and weight loss. In none of the hysterical disorders is the preoccupation primarily with body shape as it is in anorexia nervosa.

In addition to physicians who have thought anorexia nervosa to be a subtype of depression, schizophrenia, obsessive illness, or hysteria, a second viewpoint regards anorexia nervosa as a nonspecific symptom of a group of disorders linked only by the fact that significant weight loss occurs as a result of emotional problems. Bliss and Branch (1960) presented such an opinion based upon their finding that the literature was confusing with regard to distinguishing anorexia nervosa from other forms of malnutrition. This was due not only to inaccurate reports, but also to the fact that some of the features attributed to anorexia nervosa were (as we have previously noted) signs of starvation; they develop in starving people, regardless of the underlying cause. As a result of this definition, anorexia nervosa was considered to be an umbrella diagnosis encompassing weight loss due to schizophrenia, depression, or other emotional causes. Therefore, they did not view anorexia nervosa as a distinct clinical entity but on the contrary claimed "anorexia nervosa is a symptom found at times in almost all psychiatric categories." This viewpoint has been the subject of criticism from others (Bruch, 1973, 1977; Theander, 1970; Thoma, 1967) since it results in  masking those individuals with the core symptoms of primary anorexia nervosa, and it has the effect of making use of the term meaningless.

In contrast to the preceding points of view, most clinicians would now recognize a core syndrome of primary anorexia nervosa that is distinct from other illness. This is the position historically taken by Gull (1868) and Lasègue (1873) when they originally described the syndrome. Gull was particularly careful to eliminate the possibility of underlying somatic illnesses. Gilles de la Tourette (1895) and Déjérine and Gauckler (1911) had also recommended differentiating a primary form from other psychiatric disturbances. Today, Bruch (1970, 1973), Crisp (1965), Frazier (1965), King (1963), Russell (1970), and Thoma (1963), as well as our group (Garfinkel et al., 1980), have recognized the existence of a definite syndrome of primary anorexia nervosa with characteristic signs and symptoms distinguishable from other causes of weight loss. While some differences may exist regarding exact diagnostic criteria, these investigators are fundamentally in agreement: they conceive of primary anorexia nervosa as defined by a preoccupation with body size and the intense efforts of the individual to reduce her weight at the expense of other areas of her life.

By contrast, in the so-called secondary forms of the disorder, weight loss occurs not because of the pursuit of thinness per se, but is related to disinterest in foods, delusions that the food is poisoned, psychogenic dysphagia, vomiting not related to pursuit of thinness, etc. Bruch (1973) has added another group in addition to this nonspecific group; these are what she describes as "atypical" anorexics — in whom weight loss occurs because of various symbolic misinterpretations of the eating function, rather than because of weight preoccupation. It is our opinion that these patients should not be diagnosed as suffering from anorexia nervosa. It is more useful to describe them according to their primary diagnosis (e.g. schizophrenia, conversion disorder, etc). For this reason the term "secondary anorexia nervosa" will be dropped and will not be discussed further in this book.

## DIAGNOSTIC CRITERIA FOR ANOREXIA NERVOSA

While most clinicians readily recognize patients with anorexia nervosa, there is no unanimity of opinion regarding the clinical features necessary for a diagnosis (see Bhanji [1979] for a discussion of various features considered essential for the diagnosis by a random sample of both psychiatrists and consultant physicians). This is partly because different individuals have focused on different aspects of the illness. Nevertheless, the central feature of the disorder has been repeatedly described in slightly different words. Thus, for Bruch (1970) it is the "self-inflicted starvation and *relentless pursuit of thinness*" (p. 3); for Selvini Palazzoli (1974) it is "not the lack of appetite that holds the key to anorexia nervosa — the true cause is a *deliberate wish to slim*" (p. 24). According to Ziegler and Sours (1968) it is "the *pursuit of thinness as a pleasure in itself* and a frantic concern with establishing control over the body and its functions." Crisp (1977) described anorexia nervosa as a "weight phobia." Central to this is the "preoccupation of the anorectic with maintaining *a low subpubertal body weight and of avoiding any weight gain* . . . Within the potential anorectic there emerges the increasing conviction that her body shape and volume is governing her destiny" (Crisp, 1977, p. 465). This relentless pursuit of a thin body size in spite of emaciation is the central phenomenon that must always be present for a diagnosis of anorexia nervosa.

Beyond the basic drive to be thin, various other diagnostic criteria have been established. For some, such as Theander (1970), the diagnosis hinges only on the totally preoccupying pursuit of thinness; no strictly defined degree of weight loss, age of onset, or biological changes are necessary. All that is required for the diagnosis is that the patient should have changed her attitudes towards food, eating, and body weight and that this should have caused some weight loss. Clearly this approach may cause the excessive application of the anorexic label to relatively benign conditions.

Most investigators, however, have attempted to define more objective criteria for anorexia nervosa, whether they relate to psychopathology or descriptive signs and symptoms. In considering these, one should recognize that the symptomatology in anorexia nervosa consists of a number of factors: 1) the drive for thinness and its related manifestations (e.g., starvation, vomiting, laxative misuse, hiding foods); 2) the effects of starvation; 3) psychopathological features; and 4) complications or sequelae. For Bruch, the diagnosis is based on the drive for thinness in conjunction with three interrelated psychological disorders. These are disturbances in the body image, disturbances in one's internal perceptions, both viscerally and affectively, and an overall sense of personal ineffectiveness or helplessness in one's world (Bruch, 1973). These are important issues and will be further discussed in later sections. However, they are difficult to determine objectively, may not be uniformly present in all patients, and may therefore not be useful for routine clinical diagnosis.

For this reason a number of objective diagnostic criteria have been developed, both clinically and for use in clinical research. If they are to truly differentiate anorexics from others who have lost weight, these criteria must focus more on the core features of anorexia nervosa and less on the starvation effects and sequelae. These diagnostic criteria (e.g., Dally, 1969; Morgan and Russell, 1975) usually require evidence of a psychobiological disturbance in addition to the fear of weight. For example, Russell's (Morgan and Russell, 1975; Russell, 1970) criteria for a diagnosis of anorexia nervosa are: 1) that the patient resorts to a variety of devices aimed at achieving weight loss (starvation, vomiting, laxatives, etc.); 2) that there is evidence of an endocrine disorder, amenorrhea in the female and loss of sexual potency and interest in the male; and 3) that the patient manifests the characteristic psychopathology of a morbid fear of becoming fat. This is often accompanied by a distorted judgment by the patient of her own body size. A specific degree of weight loss is not required.

Dally (1969) has used similar criteria and has quantified the specific features; for example, in addition to refusal to eat, the patient must have lost at least 10% of her previous body weight; amenorrhea must be of at least three months' duration if menses were previously regular; the age of onset should be between 11 and 35 years. And Dally required that there be no evidence of preexisting schizophrenia, severe depression, or organic disease.

Rollins and Piazza (1978) have attempted to integrate both psychopathology and physical changes in their diagnostic criteria. According to this group the essential psychopathology consists of 1) evidence of a weight phobia and/or a distorted body image and 2) a "pervasive sense of inadequacy.'' The physical criteria consist of either a weight loss of 20% or more body weight or weight loss to less than 80% of average for age and height; and amenorrhea is a necessary feature in females.

Recently, the Pathology of Eating Group addressed itself to the definition and classification of eating disorders. In their report (Garrow et al., 1975), they advanced a succinct and useful definition of anorexia nervosa. All three features must be present:

1) Self-inflicted severe loss of weight, using one or more of the following devices: a) avoidance of foods considered to be "fattening" (especially carbohydrate-containing foods); b) self-induced vomiting; c) abuse of purgatives; and d) excessive exercise.
2) A secondary endocrine disorder of the hypothalamic anterior pituitary gonadal axis manifest in the female as amenorrhea and in the male by a diminution of sexual interest and activity.
3) A psychological disorder that has as its central theme a morbid fear of being unable to control eating and hence becoming too fat.

This group did not define a specific degree of weight loss, nor a defined range of ages of onset, nor the absence of preexisting illness.

The slightly older criteria of Feighner et al. (1972) were devised for use in clinical research; that is, they were intended to be rather strict so that investigators from various centers could be reasonably certain of the comparability of patients in different studies. While generally useful for clinical research, they exclude many individuals who have the essential features of the disorder but miss some ancillary symptoms, and several of their criteria are misleading:

1) They require the presence of anorexia — most anorexics do not truly experience loss of appetite until rather late in the illness (Garfinkel, 1974) and, therefore, this is not a useful diagnostic requirement;
2) Age of onset prior to 25 years is unduly restrictive as some patients may develop the illness in their late twenties or thirties (Dally, 1969; Garfinkel et al., 1980) and occasionally even later (Kellett, Trimble and Thorley, 1976; Launer, 1978; Ryle, 1936);
3) According to these criteria, weight loss must exceed 25% of original body weight. If someone were relatively thin at the onset or still growing and lost only 15-20%, it should not negate the diagnosis.

Just how restrictive the Feighner et al. (1972) criteria may be is exemplified by Rollins and Piazza's (1978) report that, of their anorexic patients who were diagnosed clinically, only 23% would meet a rigid interpretation of the Feighner criteria.

We feel that the Pathology of Eating Group's descripton of anorexia nervosa is the most appropriate and clinically applicable. The requirement of an hypothalamic-pituitary axis dysfunction eliminates individuals with so-called "normal" but excessive dieting, while the avoidance of a weight criterion prevents the definition from being arbitrarily restrictive. The recently revised Diagnostic and Statistical Manual of Mental Disorders (1980) has partially taken account of these diagnostic problems and no longer specifies an age of onset or the need for anorexia. While a weight loss of 25% is still required for a diagnosis, this may be modified for younger children. We will further discuss this concept of a specific degree of weight loss later in this chapter when we address the question of whether anorexia nervosa may be viewed as the extreme end of a continuum of behaviors.

The patients described in our clinical investigations throughout this book have met the Pathology of Eating Group's criteria and have generally also met the Feighner et al. (1972) criteria excluding the three points discussed above (Garfinkel et al., 1980). About 9% of our patients did not meet the Feighner criteria because they were either too old (5%) or had lost only 15-25% (4%) of their original weight.

## THE EATING ATTITUDES TEST (EAT):
## AN INDEX OF THE SYMPTOMS OF ANOREXIA NERVOSA

In an effort to quantify the broad range of symptoms of anorexia ner-vosa, we have constructed a 40-item self-report questionnaire, the Eating Attitudes Test (EAT). The construction and validation of the EAT have been described elsewhere (Garner and Garfinkel, 1979). While the EAT measures symptoms commonly found in anorexia nervosa, the diagnosis of anorexia nervosa remains a clinical one, based on the criteria listed above. A high score on the EAT does not invariably reflect anorexia nervosa nor does a low score invariably rule it out (on a self-report questionnaire people may not respond honestly). However, in practice, the EAT has been shown to be quite accurate in predicting group membership. For example, in earlier studies (Garner and Garfinkel, 1979, 1980) we found that a "cut-off" score of 30 maximally differentiated anorexics from normal weight university students. When this score was used, false negatives were mini-mized (6% of patients with anorexia nervosa were excluded) and false positives were relatively infrequent (12% of subjects without anorexia ner-vosa according to strict criteria scored >30 on the EAT). Using a discrimi-nant function analysis procedure, the EAT was 91% accurate in classifying both normal controls and a large group of anorexic patients.

It is important to stress that the EAT was designed to assess the broad range of anorexic symptoms — it does not reflect only symptoms of starvation. In fact, we have found insignificant correlations in a large group of dance students between EAT score and body weight or between EAT score and percentage deviation from premorbid weight. Recently we have conducted an analysis to further determine the psychometric and clinical correlates of the EAT for a large sample of female anorexia nervosa patients (N = 160) and normal comparison subjects (Garner, Olmsted, Bohr, and Garfinkel, submitted for publication). An abbreviated 26-item version of the EAT (EAT-26) is proposed based on a factor analysis of the original scale (EAT-40). The EAT-26 is highly correlated with the EAT-40 (r = .97) and the three factors form subscales which are meaningfully related to bulimia, weight, body-image variables and psychological symptoms. The original EAT-40, as well as the items comprising EAT-26, are in the Appendix.

The EAT appears to have utility as a screening device for assessing the symptoms commonly found in anorexia nervosa. However, those appearing to be anorexic on the EAT should be clinically interviewed, to confirm the diagnosis. The EAT score may also serve as an index of improvement since recovered patients have normal scores (Garner and Garfinkel, 1979).

## ANOREXIA NERVOSA AS A DISCRETE SYNDROME VERSUS A CONTINUUM OF BEHAVIORS

Since the drive for thinness and fear of fat, which are central to anorexic symptomatology, are present to some degree in most young women in Western society, it is reasonable to question whether anorexia nervosa represents the extreme of a continuum of fear of fatness, dieting behaviors, and starvation effects. Alternatively, anorexia nervosa may be a distinct syndrome and not merely dieting that has gradually got out of control. This type of question has been raised for other disorders. For example, hypertension has at times been thought to be the extreme end of a normal distribution of blood pressures and at times to be symptomatic of a group of distinct illnesses. Similar questions arise within the diagnosis of depression — where do normal grieving and unhappiness end and where does the depressive syndrome begin? For years there has also been controversy between the viewpoint that depression itself exists on a continuum (Kendell, 1976) versus the idea of a discrete dichotomy between reactive and endogenous forms of depression (Kiloh and Garside, 1963). More recently the understanding of depression as a "final-common pathway" (Akiskal and McKinney, 1975) in response to a variety of risk factors has gained in popularity. We feel this is also applicable to the understanding of anorexia nervosa.

With regard to anorexia nervosa, previous writers have suggested both its qualitative distinctness and its existence along a continuum. Crisp (1970, 1977) has emphasized the specific and qualitative biological changes which distinguish anorexia nervosa from other forms of excess dieting. He characterized anorexia nervosa by dietary restriction of proportions sufficient to force the individual below the menstrual weight threshold or "critical weight" which purportedly inhibits or reverses the neuroendocrine mechanisms first mobilized at puberty. This causes biological and experiential "regression" to the prepubertal state which Crisp views as a functional avoidance response to the adolescent state for which the anorexic patient and her family are unprepared. For Crisp, the psychobiological regression to a prepubertal state clearly differentiates anorexia nervosa from excessive dieting or weight concerns. A definite degree of weight loss is therefore necessary, that is, one which gets the individual below the "critical weight" for normal menstruation. At the same time, Crisp writes that "anorexia nervosa can blend both quantitatively and qualitatively with the normal" (Crisp, 1980, p. 19).

Bruch (1973) concurs that anorexia nervosa is not merely excess dieting accompanied by starvation symptoms but has important psychological antecedent events. In accordance with this view, she has also recognized a group of "thin-fat people" with the psychological characteristics of anorexics and little weight loss. Rollins and Piazza (1978) have hypothesized that the expression of the syndrome is partly related to severity of psychological factors but also that qualitative differences, possibly in psychophysiology and partly in "fantasies which accompany the body-image distortion" (p. 135), may distinguish the full-blown syndrome. However, as we will discuss in Chapter 4, those physiological neurohumoral changes which have been delineated at present are not known to be predisposing factors, but rather appear to be due to the syndrome.

On the other hand, others, particularly in Europe, have suggested a continuum of dieting behaviors from benign dieting to anorexia nervosa. Berkman (1948), at the Mayo Clinic, first suggested such a continuum

> . . . in which the symptoms are so mild that the individual merely appears thin, to instances in which the symptoms are so severe that the starvation results in emaciation and cachexia. In other words no sharp diagnostic line separates simple malnutrition from anorexia nervosa and the minimal requirements for the making of the diagnosis of the latter are to a certain extent only a matter of personal opinion (p. 237).

Loeb (1964) advanced a similar view. Fries (1977) has emphasized the role of simple dieting in the development of secondary amenorrhea, "anorexic" symptoms and anorexia nervosa. He suggests that "true" anorexia nervosa represents a final stage on a continuum of symptoms. In a comparison of 21 patients with clearly defined anorexia nervosa with 17 women with long-standing amenorrhea and weight loss who did not meet research criteria for anorexia nervosa, Fries was unable to differentiate these groups on self-estimates of body size or anorexic symptoms. J.A.O. Russell (1972) has suggested that a "forme fruste" of anorexia nervosa may be common. However, the statistical procedures used in his study were not explicit nor were the psychological or behavioral measures of anorexia nervosa. Nylander (1971) comprehensively studied Swedish adolescents and reported that the prevalence of serious cases of anorexia nervosa was 0.6% in females but that a further 10% had "mild cases." He suggested that the difference between the mild and serious cases was of degree only. Holmberg and Nylander (1971) found evidence for this view in an investigation of 54 consecutive patients with secondary amenorrhea who presented to a gynecological clinic. Fifty-one of the 54 women reported that they had lost some weight at the time of onset of amenorrhea; the average reported weight loss was about 11 kg and almost one-half of the total group were less than 80% of average weight for their age and height. Seventy-five percent of these women described some symptoms characteristic of anorexia nervosa. Yet only three had been previously diagnosed as having the anorexia nervosa syndrome.

Our study of dancing students (see Chapter 5 for full details of this study) offers some support to the notion of a continuum of at least anorexic symptoms in this population. We found that 38% of dancers studied (versus only 12% of university students) displayed EAT scores in the anorexic range. But only 7% of the dancers had anorexia nervosa according to strict diagnostic criteria on clinical interview. The others with these high scores displayed marked concerns with body shape and weight. Furthermore, psychological symptomatology as measured by the Hopkins Symptom Checklist (Derogatis, Lipman, Rickels, Uhlenhuth and Covi, 1974) was related to elevated EAT scores in this group. Their weight concerns therefore went beyond benign dieting, and were associated with significant psychopathology, but they did not display the fully developed anorexia nervosa syndrome.

We feel that the evidence to date suggests that anorexia nervosa is not only a condition of excessive dieting. The extreme dieting and drive for thinness must interact with other predisposing forces. Denial, body image disturbance, and hyperactivity are some of the clear indicators that anorexia nervosa is not simply excessive dieting. However, starvation effects, which account for some of the dramatic manifestations of anorexia nervosa, do occur on a continuum from mild to severe. Of even greater significance is the fact that many of the psychological predispositions to the disorder also occur to varying degrees in the population as a whole. Examples of these include concerns with control over one's life, identity, autonomy, self-worth, and bodily preoccupations. A drive for thinness, starvation manifestations, and predisposing risk factors may all occur to varying degrees in the general population, and we feel that anorexia nervosa itself may occur along a continuum of severities. Nevertheless, while the disorder represents a continuum which may gradually tend toward normal, there is real merit in distinguishing the full-blown syndrome with changes in the hypothalamic-pituitary axis from very mild forms. The distinction is partly, but not entirely, related to severity both in terms of starvation effects and likely in psychological predisposing and perpetuating factors.

It is important to recognize the existence of young women who have weight concerns that interfere with their psychological well-being but who nevertheless do not have full-blown anorexia nervosa. We speculate that these women may be using weight control to deal with issues similar to those of anorexics — the regulation and expression of self, autonomy, and self-control. We prefer the term "anorexic behavior" (Fries and Nillius, 1973) to describe such people, who appear to correspond to Bruch's (1973) "thin-fat people."

While these individuals with "anorexic behavior' may be preoccupied with body weight like anorexics, they do not develop the full syndrome. This is similar to the situation that may develop with other illnesses. Tuberculosis is due to a definite infectious agent. But not everyone exposed to the pathogen, the tubercle bacillus, will develop symptoms of TB and even in those who do, the manifestations can be extremely variable — ranging from a discrete lesion in the lung or spine to a disseminated form. Similarly, many young women possess predisposing factors and are exposed to pathogenic circumstances related to the development of anorexia nervosa. These will be described in later sections but include concerns with self-worth, control and autonomy, personal mistrust, conceptual/perceptual distortions, and familial relationships.

While these predisposing factors are seen in many, not everyone will develop overt dieting/weight problems and of those who do some will display "anorexic behaviors" while a few will develop the full syndrome, anorexia nervosa. It is not clear at present what protective factors prevent the development of the full syndrome in individuals at risk. Possibly these involve such things as less disturbed interpersonal and familial functioning, social supports, ability to trust in others, a more internalized sense of self-worth, healthy autonomous ego functioning, and a more abstract level of conceptual development. Clearly, however, this is a fruitful area for further study, for if we were able to learn what protective factors prevent the full expression of the syndrome, improvements in treatment would be likely to follow.

REFERENCES

Akiskal, H.S. and McKinney, W.T., Jr.: Overview of recent research in depression. Integration of ten conceptual models into a comprehensive clinical frame. *Arch. Gen. Psychiatry,* 32:285-305, 1975.

Babigan, H.M.: Schizophrenia: Epidemiology, In: A.M. Freedman, H.I. Kaplan, and B.J. Sadock (Eds.), *Comprehensive Textbook of Psychiatry.* Baltimore: Williams and Wilkins, Second Edition, 1975.

Berkman, J.M.: Anorexia nervosa, anterior-pituitary insufficiency, Simmonds' cachexia, and Sheehan's disease: including some observations on disturbances in water metabolism associated with starvation. *Postgrad. Med.,* 3:237-246, 1948.

Beumont, P.J.V., George, G.C.W. and Smart, D.E.: Dieters and 'vomiters and purgers' in anorexia nervosa. *Psychol. Med.,* 6:617-622, 1976.

Bhanji, S.: Anorexia nervosa: Physicians' and psychiatrists' opinions and practice. *J. Psychosom. Res.,* 23:7-11, 1979.

Binswanger, L.: Der Fall Ellen West. Schweiz. *Arch. Neurol. Psychiat.,* 54:69-117, 1944.

Bliss, E.L. and Branch, C.H.H.: *Anorexia Nervosa: Its History, Psychology and Biology.* New York: Paul B. Hoeber Inc., 1960.

Bruch, H.: Instinct and interpersonal experience. *Compr. Psychiatry,* 11:495-506, 1970.

Bruch, H.: *Eating Disorders.* New York, Basic Books, 1973.

Bruch, H.: Psychological antecedents of anorexia nervosa. In: R.Vigersky (Ed.), *Anorexia Nervosa.* New York: Raven Press, 1977.

Cantwell, D.P., Sturzenberger, S., Burroughs, J., Salkin, B. and Green, J.K.: Anorexia nervosa; an affective disorder? *Arch. Gen. Psychiatry,* 34:1087-1093, 1977.

Carlson, G.A. and Cantwell, D.P.: Unmasking masked depression in children and adolescents. *Am. J. Psychiatry,* 37:445-449, 1980.

Crisp, A.H.: Clinical and therapeutic aspects of anorexia nervosa — study of 30 cases. *J. Psychosom. Res.,* 9:67-78, 1965.

Crisp, A.H.: Premorbid factors in adult disorders of weight, with particular reference to primary anorexia nervosa (weight phobia). A literature review. *J. Psychosom. Res.,* 14:1-22, 1970.

Crisp, A.H.: Diagnosis and outcome of anorexia nervosa: The St. George's view. *Proc. Roy. Soc. Med.,* 70:464-470, 1977.

Crisp, A.H.: *Anorexia Nervosa: Let Me Be.* London: Academic Press, 1980.

Crisp, A.H., Harding, B. and McGuinness, E.: Anorexia nervosa. Psychoneurotic characteristics of parents: relationship to prognosis. A quantitative study. *J. Psychosom. Res.,* 18:167-173, 1974.

Dally, P.J.: *Anorexia Nervosa.* New York: Grune and Stratton, 1969.

Dally, P.J.: Anorexia Nervosa: Do we need a scapegoat? *Proc. Roy. Soc. Med.* 70:470-480, 1977.

Déjérine, J. and Gauckler, E.: *Les manifestations fouctionelles des psychonevroses, leur traitement par la psychotherapie.* Paris: Masson, 1911.

Derogatis, L., Lipman, R., Rickels, K., Uhlenhuth, E.G.H. and Covi, L.: The Hopkins Symptom Checklist (HSCL): A self-report symptom inventory. *Behav. Sci.,* 19:1-15, 1974.

*Diagnostic and Statistical Manual of Mental Disorders, Third Edition,* Washington, D.C.: American Psychiatric Association, 1980.

Dubois, R.: De l'anorexie mentale conume prodrome de la demence precoce. *Ann. Med. Psychol.,* 10:431-438, 1913.

Du Bois, F.S.: Compulsion neurosis with cachexia (Anorexia Nervosa). *Am. J. Psychiatry,* 106:107-115, 1949.

Feighner, J.P., Robins, E., Guze, S.B., Woodruff, R.A., Jr., Winokur, G. and Munoz, R.: Diagnostic criteria for use in psychiatric research. *Arch. Gen. Psychiatry,* 26:57-63, 1972.

Frazier, S.H.: Anorexia nervosa. *Dis. Nerv. Syst.,* 26:155-159, 1965.

Fries, H.: Studies on secondary amenorrhea, anorectic behavior, and body image perception: Importance for the early recognition of anorexia nervosa. In: R. Vigersky (Ed.), *Anorexia Nervosa.* New York: Raven Press, 1977.

Fries, H. and Nillius, S.J.: Dieting, anorexia nervosa and amenorrhea after oral contraceptive treatment. *Acta Psychiatr. Scand.,* 49:669-679, 1973.

Garfinkel, P.E.: Perception of hunger and satiety in anorexia nervosa. *Psychol. Med.,* 4:309-315, 1974.

Garfinkel, P.E., Kaplan, A., Garner, D.M., and Darby, P.L.: The differentiation of vomiting and weight loss as a conversion disorder from anorexia nervosa. Presented at the American Psychiatric Association Annual Meeting, Toronto, 1982.

Garfinkel, P.E., Moldofsky, H., and Garner, D.M.: The heterogeneity of anorexia nervosa: Bulimia as a distinct subgroup. *Arch. Gen. Psychiatry,* 37:1036-1040, 1980.

Garner, D.M. and Garfinkel, P.E.: The Eating Attitudes Test: An index of the symptoms of anorexia nervosa. *Psychol. Med.,* 9:273-279, 1979.

Garner, D.M., and Garfinkel, P.E.: Socio-cultural factors in the development of anorexia nervosa. *Psychol. Med.,* 10:647-656, 1980.

Garner, D.M., Olmsted, M.P., Bohr, Y. and Garfinkel, P.E.: The eating attitudes test: Psychometric features and clinical correlates. Submitted for publication.

Garrow, J.S., Crisp, A.H., Jordan, H.A., Meyer, J.E., Russell, G.F.M., Silverstone, T., Stunkard, A.J. and Van Itallie, T.B.: Pathology of eating, group report. In: T. Silverstone (Ed.), *Dahlem Konferenzen, Life Sciences Research Report 2.* Berlin, 1975.

Gilles de la Tourette, G.A.E.B.: *Traite Clinique et Therapeutique de l'Hysteric.* Paris: Plou, Nourit et Co., 1895.

Gull, W.W.: The address in medicine delivered before the annual meeting of the BMA at Oxford. *Lancet,* 2:171, 1868.

Gull, W.W.: Anorexia nervosa. *Trans. Clin. Soc.* (London), 7:22-28, 1874. Reprinted in: R.M. Kaufman and M. Heiman (Eds.), *Evolution of Psychosomatic Concepts. Anorexia Nervosa: A Paradigm.* New York: International Universities Press, 1964.

Gunderson, J. and Singer, M.T.: Defining borderline patients: An overview. *Am. J. Psychiatry,* 132:1-10, 1975.

Hobhouse, N.: Discussion of paper by Grace Nicolle on prepsychotic anorexia. *Proc. Roy. Soc. Med.,* 32:153-162, 1938.

Holmberg, N.G. and Nylander, I.: Weight loss in secondary amenorrhea. A gynaecologic, endocrinologic and psychiatric investigation of 54 consecutive clinic cases. *Acta Obstet. Gynecol. Scand.,* 50:241-246, 1971.

Janet, P.: *Les Obsessions et la Psychasthenie.* Paris: Felix Alcan, 1919.

Kalucy, R.S., Crisp, A.H. and Harding, B.: A study of 56 families with anorexia nervosa: *Br. J. Med. Psychol.,* 50:381-395, 1977.

Kay, D.W.K.: Anorexia nervosa: study in prognosis. *Proc. Roy. Soc. Med.,* 46:669-674, 1953.

Kay, D.W.K. and Leigh, D.: Natural history, treatment and prognosis of anorexia nervosa, based on study of 38 patients. *J. Ment. Sci.,* 100:411-431, 1954.

Kellett, J., Trimble, M. and Thorley, A.: Anorexia nervosa after the menopause. *Br. J. Psychiatry,* 128:555-558, 1976.

Kendell, R.E.: The classification of depressions. *Br. J. Psychiatry,* 129:15-28, 1976.

Keys, A., Brozek, J., Henschel, A., Mickelsen, O. and Taylor, H.L.: *The Biology of Human Starvation,* Minneapolis: University of Minnesota Press, 1950.

Kiloh, L.G. and Garside, R.F.: The independence of neurotic depression and endogenous depression. *Br. J. Psychiatry,* 109:451-463, 1963.

King, A.: Primary and secondary anorexia nervosa syndromes. *Br. J. Psychiatry,* 109:470-479, 1963.

Lasègue, C.: De l'anorexie hystérique. *Arch. Gen. de Med.* (1873) Reprinted in: R.M. Kaufman and M. Heiman (Eds.), *Evolution of Psychosomatic Concepts. Anorexia Nervosa: A Paradigm.* New York: International Universities Press, 1964.

Launer, M.A.: Anorexia nervosa in late life. *Br. J. Med. Psychol.,* 51:375-377, 1978.

Lewis, A.: Problems of obsessional illness. *Proc. Roy. Soc. Med.,* 29:325-336, 1936.

Loeb, L.: The clinical course of anorexia nervosa. *Psychosomatics,* 5:345-347, 1964.

Meyer, B.C. and Weinroth, L.A.: Observations on psychological aspects of anorexia nervosa. *Psychosom. Med.,* 19:389-398, 1957.

Meyer, J.E.: The anorexia nervosa syndrome. Catamnestic research. *Arch. Psychiat. Nervenkr.,* 202:31-59, 1961.

Minuchin, S., Rosman, B.L., and Baker, L.: *Psychosomatic Families: Anorexia Nervosa in Context.* Cambridge, MA: Harvard University Press, 1978.

Morgan, H.G. and Russell, G.F.M.: Value of family background and clinical features as predictors of long-term outcome in anorexia nervosa: four year follow-up study of 41 patients. *Psychol. Med.,* 5:355-371, 1975.

Needleman, H.L. and Waber, D.: Amitriptyline therapy in patients with anorexia nervosa. *Lancet,* 2:580, 1976.

Nicolle, G.: Prepsychotic anorexia. *Proc. Roy. Soc. Med.,* 32:153-162, 1939.

Nylander, I.: The feeling of being fat and dieting in a school population. An epidemiologic interview investigation. *Acta Sociomed. Scand.,*3:17-26, 1971.

Palmer, H.D. and Jones, M.S.: Anorexia nervosa as a manifestation of compulsive neurosis. *Arch. Neurol. Psychiat.,* 41:856-860, 1939.

Rollins, N. and Piazza, E.: Diagnosis of anorexia nervosa. A critical reappraisal. *J. Am. Acad. Child Psychiatry,* 17:126-137, 1978.

Russell, G.F.M.: Anorexia nervosa: Its identity as an illness and its treatment. In: J.H. Price (Ed.), *Modern Trends in Psychological Medicine,* 2. London: Butterworths, 1970.

Russell, J.A.O.: Psychosocial aspects of weight loss and amenorrhea in adolescent girls. In: *International Congress of Psychosomatic Medicine in Obstetrics and Gynecology,* 3. London, 1972.

Ryle, J.A.: Anorexia nervosa. *Lancet,* 2:893-899, 1936.

Selvini Palazzoli, M.P.: *Anorexia Nervosa.* London: Chaucer, 1974.

Simmonds, M.: Ueber embolische Prozesse in des Hypophysis. *Arch. F. Path. Anat.,* 217:226-239, 1914.

Smart, D.E., Beumont, P.J.V. and George, G.C.W.: Some personality characteristics of patients with anorexia nervosa. *Br. J. Psychiatry,* 128:57-60, 1976.

Solyom, L., Miles, J.E. and O'Kane, J.: Comparative study of anorexia nervosa. *Can. J. Psychiatry,* (in press).

Theander, S.: Anorexia nervosa. A psychiatric investigation of 94 female cases. *Acta Psychiat. Scand.* [Suppl], 214:1-94, 1970.

Thoma, H.: *Anorexia Nervosa,* translated by G. Brydone. New York: International Universities Press, 1967.

Winokur, A., March, V. and Mendels, J.: Primary affective disorder in relatives of patients with anorexia nervosa. *Am. J. Psychiatry,* 137:695-698, 1980.

Wulff, M.: Uber einen interessanten oralen Symptomenkomplex und seine Beziehung zur Sucht. *Int. Ztschr. Psychoanal.,* 18:281-302, 1932.

Ziegler, R. and Sours, J.: A naturalistic study of patients with anorexia nervosa admitted to a university medical center. *Comprehens. Psychiat.,* 9:644-651, 1968.

Zutt, J.: Das psychiatrische krankheitsbild der pubertatsmagersucht. *Arch. Psychiat. Nervenkr.,* 180:5-6, 1948.

# APPENDIX
## Eating Attitudes Test

Please place an (X) under the column which applies best to each of the numbered statements. All of the results will be *strictly* confidential. Most of the questions directly relate to food or eating, although other types of questions have been included. Please answer each question carefully. Thank you.

| Always | Very often | Often | Sometimes | Rarely | Never | |
|---|---|---|---|---|---|---|
| ( ) | ( ) | ( ) | ( ) | ( ) | (X)† | 1. Like eating with other people. |
| (X) | ( ) | ( ) | ( ) | ( ) | ( ) | 2. Prepare foods for others but do not eat what I cook. |
| (X) | ( ) | ( ) | ( ) | ( ) | ( ) | 3. Become anxious prior to eating. |
| (X) | ( ) | ( ) | ( ) | ( ) | ( ) | 4. Am terrified about being overweight. |
| (X) | ( ) | ( ) | ( ) | ( ) | ( ) | 5. Avoid eating when I am hungry. |
| (X) | ( ) | ( ) | ( ) | ( ) | ( ) | 6. Find myself preoccupied with food. |
| (X) | ( ) | ( ) | ( ) | ( ) | ( ) | 7. Have gone on eating binges where I feel that I may not be able to stop. |
| (X) | ( ) | ( ) | ( ) | ( ) | ( ) | 8. Cut my food into small pieces. |
| (X) | ( ) | ( ) | ( ) | ( ) | ( ) | 9. Aware of the calorie content of foods that I eat. |
| (X) | ( ) | ( ) | ( ) | ( ) | ( ) | 10. Particularly avoid foods with a high carbohydrate content (e.g. bread, potatoes, rice, etc.). |
| (X) | ( ) | ( ) | ( ) | ( ) | ( ) | 11. Feel bloated after meals. |
| (X) | ( ) | ( ) | ( ) | ( ) | ( ) | 12. Feel that others would prefer if I ate more. |
| (X) | ( ) | ( ) | ( ) | ( ) | ( ) | 13. **Vomit after I have eaten. |
| (X) | ( ) | ( ) | ( ) | ( ) | ( ) | 14. Feel extremely guilty after eating. |
| (X) | ( ) | ( ) | ( ) | ( ) | ( ) | 15. **Am preoccupied with a desire to be thinner. |
| (X) | ( ) | ( ) | ( ) | ( ) | ( ) | 16. Exercise strenuously to burn off calories. |
| (X) | ( ) | ( ) | ( ) | ( ) | ( ) | 17. **Weigh myself several times a day. |
| ( ) | ( ) | ( ) | ( ) | ( ) | (X) | 18. ‡Like my clothes to fit tightly. |
| ( ) | ( ) | ( ) | ( ) | ( ) | (X) | 19. Enjoy eating meat. |
| (X) | ( ) | ( ) | ( ) | ( ) | ( ) | 20. Wake up early in the morning. |
| (X) | ( ) | ( ) | ( ) | ( ) | ( ) | 21. Eat the same foods day after day. |
| (X) | ( ) | ( ) | ( ) | ( ) | ( ) | 22. Think about burning up calories when I exercise. |
| ( ) | ( ) | ( ) | ( ) | ( ) | (X) | 23. Have regular menstrual periods. |
| (X) | ( ) | ( ) | ( ) | ( ) | ( ) | 24. Other people think that I am too thin. |
| (X) | ( ) | ( ) | ( ) | ( ) | ( ) | 25. Am preoccupied with the thought of having fat on my body. |
| (X) | ( ) | ( ) | ( ) | ( ) | ( ) | 26. Take longer than others to eat my meals. |
| ( ) | ( ) | ( ) | ( ) | ( ) | (X) | 27. Enjoy eating at restaurants. |
| (X) | ( ) | ( ) | ( ) | ( ) | ( ) | 28. **Take laxatives. |
| (X) | ( ) | ( ) | ( ) | ( ) | ( ) | 29. Avoid foods with sugar in them. |
| (X) | ( ) | ( ) | ( ) | ( ) | ( ) | 30. Eat diet foods. |
| (X) | ( ) | ( ) | ( ) | ( ) | ( ) | 31. Feel that food controls my life. |
| (X) | ( ) | ( ) | ( ) | ( ) | ( ) | 32. Display self control around food. |
| (X) | ( ) | ( ) | ( ) | ( ) | ( ) | 33. Feel that others pressure me to eat. |
| (X) | ( ) | ( ) | ( ) | ( ) | ( ) | 34. Give too much time and thought to food. |
| (X) | ( ) | ( ) | ( ) | ( ) | ( ) | 35. *Suffer from constipation. |
| (X) | ( ) | ( ) | ( ) | ( ) | ( ) | 36. Feel uncomfortable after eating sweets. |
| (X) | ( ) | ( ) | ( ) | ( ) | ( ) | 37. Engage in dieting behaviour. |
| (X) | ( ) | ( ) | ( ) | ( ) | ( ) | 38. Like my stomach to be empty. |
| ( ) | ( ) | ( ) | ( ) | ( ) | (X) | 39. Enjoy trying new rich foods. |
| (X) | ( ) | ( ) | ( ) | ( ) | ( ) | 40. Have the impulse to vomit after meals. |

† The 'X' represents the most 'symptomatic' response and would receive a score of 3 points.
* $P < 0.05$, *t*-test.      ** $P < 0.01$, *t*-test.      ‡ $P > 0.05$, *t*-test.
For all remaining items, group means differed at the $P < 0.001$ level of confidence with a *t*-test.

*Note.* The analysis reported in the body of the paper is a point biserial correlation coefficient where item score was correlated with group membership to establish the validity of individual items as predictors. The *t*-test results reported above simply demonstrate the magnitude of the differences between mean item scores for the AN and NC cross-validation sample.

Reprinted with permission from Garner and Garfinkel (1979)

# APPENDIX
## EAT-26 Factor Structure

| Item Number | Item Content | Factor Loading |
|---|---|---|
| | Factor 1 (26.4% of variance): Dieting | |
| 37 | Engage in dieting behavior. | .72 |
| 30 | Eat diet foods. | .69 |
| 36 | Feel uncomfortable after eating sweets. | .68 |
| 39 | Enjoy trying new rich foods. | .66 |
| 29 | Avoid foods with sugar in them. | .64 |
| 10 | Particularly avoid foods with high carbohydrate content. | .58 |
| 15 | Am preoccupied with a desire to be thinner. | .51 |
| 38 | Like my stomach to be empty. | .48 |
| 22 | Think about burning up calories when I exercise. | .47 |
| 14 | Feel extremely guilty after eating. | .46 |
| 4 | Am terrified about being overweight. | .45 |
| 25 | Am preoccupied with the thought of having fat on my body. | .45 |
| 9 | Aware of the calorie content of foods that I eat. | .45 |
| | Factor 2 (10.8% of variance): Bulimia and Food Preoccupation | |
| 40 | Have the impulse to vomit after meals. | .78 |
| 13 | Vomit after I have eaten. | .75 |
| 7 | Have gone on eating binges where I feel that I may not be able to stop. | .63 |
| 34 | Give too much time and thought to food. | .60 |
| 6 | Find myself preoccupied with food. | .59 |
| 31 | Feel that food controls my life. | .55 |

| Item Number | Item Content | Factor Loading |
|---|---|---|
| | Factor 3 (5.0% of variance): Oral Control | |
| 8 | Cut my food into small pieces. | .81 |
| 26 | Take longer than others to eat meals. | .69 |
| 24 | Other people think that I am too thin. | .69 |
| 12 | Feel that others would prefer if I ate more. | .62 |
| 33 | Feel that others pressure me to eat. | .62 |
| 5 | Avoid eating when I am hungry. | .52 |
| 32 | Display self-control around food. | .41 |

# CHAPTER 3

# Subtypes of

# Anorexia Nervosa

Attempts at distinguishing subtypes of anorexia nervosa date back at least to Janet (1919), who recognized hysterical and obsessional (psychasthenic) forms. A major difference between these two forms was the preservation or absence of hunger; obsessional patients were thought to maintain hunger but refused to give in to the desire to eat, but the hysterical patient, in addition to losing hunger, often displayed hyperactivity, anesthesia, and had a past history of hysterical behavior.

Janet's classification system was totally ignored until Dally (1969) utilized it in his careful study of a large number of anorexic patients. He defined three groups: an obsessional group, an hysterical group and a group of "mixed etiology." Because individuals were classified not only by whether they were obsessional or hysterical, Dally preferred the terms group O, H, and M. About half of his sample consisted of group O subjects and the other two groups comprised one-quarter each. Group M reflected "secondary" forms of anorexia nervosa. In comparing the first two groups, Dally observed major differences, as did Janet, including the loss of hunger in Group H. The O group also frequently displayed bulimia and vomiting, and had labile moods.

More subtle differences were also described. For example, individuals in Group H did not "mirror gaze" and displayed an "involuntary" increase in activity and energy. Both Janet's and Dally's classification systems relied heavily on the presence or absence of hunger and appetite. However, we have previously observed that most anorexics maintain their feelings of hunger (Garfinkel, 1974); when an individual is ketotic as in severe starvation, hunger will be inhibited, but this depends on the physiology of the

40

starvation process rather than on some inherent difference between individuals. Other differences such as mirror gazing and involuntary hyperactivity are often difficult to elicit accurately. Dally's classification system is therefore quite limited. However, Janet and Dally both noted that certain symptom groups tend to cluster together; for example, Dally observed that vomiting, bulimia, and labile mood often occur together in a given patient. He found that stealing was confined to his group O patients.

More recently, Beumont and his group (Beumont, 1977; Beumont, George and Smart, 1976) pursued an earlier suggestion by Meyer (1961) that clinical differences existed between those anorexia nervosa patients who lost weight by restricting food intake, and those in whom vomiting is a major symptom. All female patients seen over a two-year period, who met rigorous criteria for primary anorexia nervosa, were reviewed. Of the 31 patients studied, 17 were "dieters" (i.e., lost weight solely through caloric restriction) and 14 were "vomiters and purgers" (i.e., lost weight through vomiting, laxative, or diuretic misuse).

A number of clinical differences were observed between the two groups. Specifically, the vomiters and purgers were likely to have been obese premorbidly, to be more sexually active, and to have histrionic personalities. When 22 of these patients were studied by psychometric tests (Beumont, 1977), both groups were observed to be highly obsessional on the Leighton Obsessional Inventory. The "dieters" were characterized by introversion on the Eysenck Personality Inventory. Vomiting, which is a poor prognostic sign in anorexia nervosa (Garfinkel, Moldofsky and Garner, 1977), may be related to the duration of illness. That is, patients may first present with caloric restriction and only as the illness becomes chronic will they vomit or abuse laxatives. While this occasionally occurs, the differentiating features between the groups which Beumont documented with regard to premorbid obesity and sexual activity predate the onset of anorexic symptoms.

The Pathology of Eating Group (Garrow, Crisp, Jordan, Meyer, Russell, Silverstone, Stunkard and Van Itallie, 1975) distinguished one group of chronic anorexia nervosa patients that seemed to display many aspects of addiction; they habitually overate and vomited large quantities of foods, usually in secret. They retained a terror of weight gain and had a need to control their weight, yet they had a psychological craving for food. Metabolic consequences of their vomiting and diarrhea (e.g., fluid and potassium depletion) were thought to further stimulate their ingestive behavior, thereby perpetuating this cycle. Other features of this group included use of drugs known to facilitate weight loss and the use of alcohol for sedative effects. They frequently smoked to excess. No data were provided to support the description of this group or whether the group could be satisfactorily discriminated from anorexic patients who tended to restrict their caloric intake and never engage in bulimia. Similarly, Boskind-Lodahl (1976) described women with bulimia and referred to them as bulimarexic,'' although clinical features to distinguish them from bulimic and restricting anorexic patients were not provided.

Russell (1979) has recently reported on a group of 30 patients with 1) an irresistible urge to overeat; 2) followed by self-induced vomiting or purging; and 3) a morbid fear of becoming fat. He used the term "bulimia nervosa" to describe these individuals; Russell's detailed account stressed the close association between bulimia and vomiting or laxative misuse, and reviewed the possible complications of this disorder. The metabolic and emotional consequences were observed to differ between bulimic and restricting anorexics. In particular, hypokalemia, impaired renal function, convulsions, and depression were common to this bulimic group. While he recognized a core set of features to this disorder, he suggested that it was premature to consider this a distinct syndrome except in its most narrow sense of shared signs and symptoms. He felt, however, that this syndrome did not imply a common etiology; in fact, he stressed that the etiology was largely unknown. Of the 30 patients studied, 24 met his criteria for a past history of anorexia nervosa and six displayed these symptoms without any history of weight loss and therefore could not be classified as having anorexia nervosa. This led him to conclude that bulimia nervosa may be a disturbance with different causes, one of which was anorexia nervosa. At present it is not known how commonly bulimics have had frank episodes of anorexia nervosa, since Russell's patients were probably self-selected to overrepresent anorexics, given his long-standing interest in the illness.

In a large, multihospital collaborative study of anorexia nervosa, 105 patients were divided into two groups according to the presence or absence of bulimia and then compared on a variety of clinical, developmental, and psychosocial parameters (Casper, Eckert, Halmi, Goldberg and Davis, 1980). Forty-seven percent of the sample had periodically been bulimic, 16% on at least a daily basis. The bulimic patients were significantly different: Clinically, they were more likely to vomit than dieting restricters (57% versus 18%), admit to a strong appetite (69% versus 46%), and engage in compulsive stealing (24% versus 4%). Socially, the bulimic patients were said to be more outgoing, more interested in sex and to have had some heterosexual experience. On psychological tests, they displayed higher depression and somatization scores. Bulimic patients also tended to be older; they clustered in the over-18-year-old group, but mean ages at onset did not differ between the groups (Casper et al., 1980; Halmi, Casper,

Eckert, Goldberg and Davis, 1979). With regard to this last point, these investigators suggest that bulimia may therefore be a sign of chronicity or that a "certain degree of . . . maturation is a necessary requirement for bulimia to develop."

In a similar effort to determine whether these anorexic patients who repeatedly overingested foods ("bulimic") were a distinct subgroup within the primary anorexia nervosa syndrome, we reviewed our consultation files on all our anorexic subjects who met the modified Feighner, Robins, Guze, Woodruff, Winokur and Munoz (1972) criteria described in Chapter 2. We were careful to exclude non-anorexic patients with bulimia, as bulimia may exist in obese or other non-anorexic disorders.

From 1970 to 1979, we had consulted on or treated 207 patients who met these criteria. Since 1973, a relatively standard series of questions were asked over the two-to-three hour consultation period. Data from these consultations were coded using a standard format and provided the clinical base of information for each patient. Bulimia was defined as an abnormal increase in one's desire to eat, with episodes of excessive ingestion of large quantities of food which the patient viewed as ego-alien and beyond her control. Bulimic episodes were characterized by the eating of large quantities of food (e.g., two dozen doughnuts, one gallon of ice cream), usually high in carbohydrates. This was usually done secretly when the individual was alone. The duration of the eating was highly variable but could take several hours or more. Crisp (1980) has estimated that the mean daily caloric intake of bulimics is 4,000-5,000 calories per day, but it is not uncommon to see patients whose ingestion during bulimic periods far exceeds this.

We have collated data from 193 of our patients. They were successive consultations who were seen during various phases of their illness and with varying degrees of chronicity (Table 1). Of the total sample, 97 experienced bulimia at the time of initial consultation and 96 did not. In the remaining 14 patients these data were not clear; therefore, they were omitted from the analyses. Of the bulimic patients, 39 experienced episodes of excessive ingestion of food at least on a daily basis; 38, one-to-five times per week and 20, one-to-three times per month. Patients who clearly did not display bulimia and only curtailed dietary intake were placed into the "restricting" group.

The results of our comparison of the two groups on demographic characteristics are displayed in Table 1. Both groups of patients showed similar social characteristics, with the upper and middle social classes being overrepresented in comparison with the general population. This issue will be further discussed in Chapters 5 and 7. There were no significant dif-

## TABLE 1

### Clinical Demographic Features in Two Groups of Anorexia Nervosa Patients

|  | Bulimic (N = 97) | Restricting (N = 96) | Level of Statistical Significance |
|---|---|---|---|
| Age | 22.2 ± 0.5 | 21.2 ± 0.6 | NS |
| Marital Status (%) |  |  |  |
| Single | 76.3 | 86.5 ) |  |
| Married | 22.7 | 11.5 ) | NS |
| Separated | 1.0 | 2.0 ) |  |
| Religion (%) |  |  |  |
| Protestant | 37.4 | 43.0 ) |  |
| Jewish | 17.6 | 20.4 ) | NS |
| Catholic | 23.0 | 15.0 ) |  |
| Other | 21.9 | 21.6 ) |  |
| Duration of Illness (months) | 50.2 ± 4.8 | 40.2 ± 6.3 | NS |
| Social Class | 2.8 ± 0.2 | 2.7 ± 0.2 | NS |
| Sex (F/M) | 94/3 | 91/5 | NS |

ferences between the bulimics and restricters in age of onset or duration of illness, but there was a tendency for bulimics to have been ill longer. Of patients who developed bulimia, the onset of bulimic episodes occurred at varying phases of the disorder. In some patients, it preceded or was coincidental with the weight loss. For those patients, on whom these data were available in an earlier study, we found that bulimia developed $19.2 \pm 8.0$ (m ± SEM) months after the onset of dieting (Garfinkel, Moldofsky and Garner, 1980). Russell's (1979) "bulimia nervosa" patients also developed bulimia relatively early after the onset of the dieting behavior; in 18 out of the 30 patients the overeating commenced within one year of beginning to diet. Similarly, 14 of Dally's (1969) 23 anorexic patients — who were bulimic — developed this within 18 months of beginning to diet.

There were major differences between our bulimic and restricting groups on weight-related clinical features (Table 2). Bulimic patients had a history of weighing more ($p < 0.005$), and in fact over 20% were obese (defined as >115% of average for age and height) premorbidly. By contrast, obesity was rare in the restricters (8%) ($p < 0.02$). Similarly, bulimic patients weighed significantly more at the time of our initial contact ($p < 0.001$), and at their minimum weights ($p < 0.05$). Casper et al. (1980), however, were unable to find premorbid or minimal weight differences in their sample. In

## TABLE 2

### Weight-related Clinical Features in Two Groups of Anorexia Nervosa Patients

|  | Bulimic | Restricting | Level of Statistical Significance |
|---|---|---|---|
| Birth weight (kg) | $7.2 \pm 0.3$ | $7.0 \pm 0.2$ | NS |
| Maximum premorbid |  |  |  |
|   weight (kg) | $61.4 \pm 1.0$ | $56.8 \pm 1.2$ | $p < 0.005$ |
|   % of average | $104.4 \pm 1.7$ | $97.9 \pm 1.8$ | $p < 0.01$ |
| Premorbid obesity | 19/92 (20.6%) | 7/90 (7.7%) | $p < 0.02$ |
| Minimum |  |  |  |
|   weight (kg) | $39.6 \pm 0.7$ | $36.5 \pm 0.8$ | $p < 0.005$ |
|   % of average | $66.8 \pm 1.1$ | $62.7 \pm 1.2$ | $p < 0.02$ |
| Weight at consultation |  |  |  |
|   (kg) | $45.6 \pm 1.0$ | $39.5 \pm 0.8$ | $p < 0.001$ |
|   % of average | $77.2 \pm 1.7$ | $68.0 \pm 1.1$ | $p < 0.001$ |
| Height (cm) | $163.4 \pm 0.6$ | $162.4 \pm 0.8$ | NS |
| Menarche (yrs) | $12.9 \pm 0.2$ | $12.8 \pm 0.2$ | NS |

agreement with our weight data, both Russell (1979) and Beumont (1977) reported higher than expected weights in their bulimic and "vomiter-purger" samples.

The groups studied by us, not surprisingly, showed clear differences in the methods they used to lose and maintain a low weight (Table 3). The restricters relied heavily on avoiding meals whenever possible, and when this was not possible, on selecting low carbohydrate foods. They also hid foods frequently. Vigorous compulsive exercising aimed at burning calories was also common. The bulimic patients did all of this but also frequently vomited and misused laxatives. Vomiting was present in 68.1% of bulimics versus 22.6% of the restricters ($p < 0.001$); laxative misuse, for the deliberate purpose of weight loss, was surprisingly common in both groups but much more so with bulimics (46.7%) than restricters (22.6%) ($p < 0.01$). Diuretic misuse, however, was uncommon in both groups (about 4%). Similarly, both Russell (1979) and Casper et al. (1980) have reported that their bulimic patients relied heavily on devices other than starvation for weight control.

The bulimic group differed from the restricters on a variety of impulsive behaviors: these are indicated in Table 4. Twenty-one percent of the bulimics versus 11% of the restricters had misused street drugs (p = 0.06). Alcohol use ($p < 0.05$) and stealing occurred significantly more frequently in

## TABLE 3

### Eating-related Clinical Features in Two Groups of Anorexia Nervosa Patients

|  | Bulimic | Restricting | Level of Statistical Significance |
|---|---|---|---|
| Eats regular meals (at least once per week) | % | % |  |
| Breakfast | 31.8 | 43.0 | NS |
| Lunch | 35.2 | 37.6 | NS |
| Dinner | 53.4 | 62.4 | NS |
| Snacks | 15.4 | 14.1 | NS |
| Food faddishness | 91.8 | 69.5 | $p < 0.01$ |
| Vomiting | 68.1 | 22.6 | $p < 0.001$ |
| Laxatives | 46.7 | 22.6 | $p < 0.001$ |
| Diuretic use | 4/87 (4.6%) | 3/92 (3.3%) | NS |

## TABLE 4

### Impulse-related Clinical Features in Two Groups of Anorexia Nervosa Patients

|  | Bulimic | Restricting | Level of Statistical Significance |
|---|---|---|---|
|  | % | % |  |
| Street drug use | 21.2 | 10.9 | $p < 0.10$ |
| Alcohol use (weekly or more) | 18.3 | 5.9 | $p < 0.05$ |
| Stealing | 11.7 | 0.0 | — |
| Self-mutilation | 7.4 | 3.3 | NS |
| Suicide attempts | 19.1 | 7.7 | $p < 0.05$ |
| Lability of mood | 35.0 | 16.0 | $p < 0.02$ |

bulimics. While 12% of the bulimics reported stealing (usually food or money), this was never displayed by restricting patients. Suicide attempts ($p < 0.05$) and deliberate acts of self-inflicted injury without suicide intent were more common in the bulimic group, but the latter were not statistically significant. For example, 7% of bulimics and 3% of restricters had previously harmed themselves in this way, usually by cutting. Twenty percent of bulimics and 8% of restricters had made prior suicide attempts.

Lability of mood was more frequent in bulimics as determined in the mental status examination ($p<0.02$). Russell (1979) had previously described subjective depression to be common in his bulimic patients; 11 of his 30 patients had also attempted suicide.

Sexual and social characteristics of the two groups are shown in Table 5. The restricting group were relatively isolated and formed few friendships. Less than one-fifth of these individuals were involved in social relationships and found them satisfying. Bulimics were less commonly isolated and more frequently engaged in transient and nonsatisfying relationships. Patients in the bulimic group were more sexually active and more likely to use oral contraceptives. However, they did not describe their sexual relationships as pleasant. Crisp (1967) had observed previously that this group "rushed into one relationship after another . . . in the mistaken belief that they would then feel secure and wanted" (p. 128). He noted that their sexual relationships were frequently characterized by fellatio and that this was followed by vomiting. Russell (1979) had also noted the increased social and sexual behavior of "bulimia nervosa" patients as had Beumont et al. (1976) and Beumont, Abraham and Simpson (1981) in their studies of anorexics who vomit.

## TABLE 5

### Sexual/Social Behaviors in Two Groups of Anorexia Nervosa Patients

|  | Bulimic | Restricting | Level of Statistical Significance |
|---|---|---|---|
| Social Relationships | % | % |  |
| Isolated | 28.6 | 46.7 | ) |
| Uncommon and not satisfactory | 15.4 | 20.7 | ) |
| Common, intermittent and not satisfactory | 27.5 | 14.1 | ) $p<0.05$ |
| Consistent and satisfactory | 28.5 | 18.5 | ) |
| Sexual Intercourse |  |  |  |
| Never | 36.8 | 65.2 | ) |
| Rare and not satisfying | 36.8 | 26.1 | ) |
| Infrequent | 22.4 | 5.8 | ) $p<0.003$ |
| Frequent and pleasant | 4.0 | 2.9 | ) |
| Oral contraceptives | 44.4 | 25.9 | ) $p<0.01$ |

The family histories of our patients are demonstrated in Table 6. Of importance, both groups show an overrepresentation of anorexia nervosa in siblings (6%) and multiple births (4.2%). In the total sample there were seven cases of twins and one set of triplets. The mothers of bulimic patients were frequently obese (49% versus 32%) in the restricting group. No difference was found in the history of parental mental illness between groups. Using these clinical factors, a discriminant function analysis was previously found to be accurate in predicting group membership in 79.2% of the subjects (Garfinkel et al., 1980); 85.9% of restricters were classified accurately and 72.4% of the bulimics were classified accurately. These data indicate that there were real differences between the groups.

Data such as these that rely on historical information must be treated with some caution. And it must be recognized that patients with anorexia nervosa frequently lie or deny aspects of their illness, which may distort the

## TABLE 6

### Family History in Two Groups of Anorexia Nervosa Patients

| | Bulimic | Restricting | Level of Statistical Significance |
|---|---|---|---|
| Mother's age at patient's birth (yrs.) | 29.2 ± 0.6 | 30.1 ± 0.7 | NS |
| Mother dead (%) | 5.3 | 3.1 | NS |
| Mother's history of obesity (%) | 48.7 | 32.4 | p < 0.05 |
| Mother's history of mental illness (%) | 16.7 | 11.6 | NS |
| Mother working (%) | 44.0 | 39.1 | NS |
| Mother previously married (%) | 7.7 | 7.5 | NS |
| Father's age at patient's birth (yrs.) | 32.5 ± 0.8 | 34.0 ± 0.8 | NS |
| Father dead (%) | 8.4 | 8.3 | NS |
| Father's history of obesity (%) | 20.3 | 15.1 | NS |
| Father previously married (%) | 8.6 | 4.4 | NS |
| Patient's birth order | 2.0 ± 0.1 | 2.3 ± 0.1 | NS |
| Number of siblings | 3.1 ± 0.1 | 3.2 ± 0.1 | NS |
| Multiple birth (%) | 4.1 | 4.2 | NS |
| AN in sibs (%) | 4.2 | 7.3 | NS |
| Obesity in sibs (%) | 15.6 | 12.6 | NS |
| Patient adopted (%) | 2.1 | 6.4 | NS |

findings. Furthermore, these results were obtained at one point in time, i.e., our first consultation, and it is possible that further symptoms appear in any given patient as the illness evolves: A patient who displayed no bulimia or vomiting when first seen may have developed these symptoms later. The fact that we have seen each of these patients ourselves, that we have utilized a standard assessment technique and independent raters to extract the relevant data, and that most patients were seen after they had been ill for several years (on average four years) may help to reduce these deficiencies. A further problem with all studies by people who are particularly "interested" in a disorder it that of the referral or selection bias. Our sample is not necessarily representative since we only investigate subjects referred to us. In large measure our sample is one of rather chronically ill people who have often failed in therapies elsewhere. In this regard, bulimics, and in particular severely ill bulimics, are likely overrepresented. Just how common bulimia is in anorexia nervosa is not known. While studies such as those of Casper et al. (1980), Hsu, Crisp and Harding (1979), and our own report figures of 44-50%, these are highly selected samples. Other investigations have found bulimia to be less frequent: for example, Theander (1970) in 16%; Rollins and Piazza (1978) in 27%. Crisp's (1980) estimate of bulimia occurring at some point in the illness in about 30% of anorexic patients is probably reasonable, if one discounts the selection biases referred to above.

In spite of the limitations of this type of study, significant differences between bulimic and restricting anorexics have been observed. In our patients these included premorbid obesity, weight, food and impulse-related problems during the illness, and maternal obesity associated with the bulimic patients. Taken together, these characteristics suggest a different group of women who are predisposed to develop the bulimic type of anorexia nervosa. These women have frequently been premorbidly obese and their mothers also have been obese, as had been suggested by Garrow et al. (1975). The 49% prevalence for obesity in our bulimic patients' mothers is even more striking when one considers the reduced frequency of obesity in North American women of upper social classes (Stunkard, 1975). The fact that bulimics have frequently been obese and often have a family history of obesity highlights the conflicts these individuals face. As Ellen West described it, "Fate wanted me to be heavy and strong but I want to be thin and delicate" (Binswanger, 1944). Stordy, Marks, Kalucy and Crisp (1977) have recently shown that the thermic response to a carbohydrate meal differs in anorexics who were previously obese; they gain weight more readily. To achieve their desired degree of thinness they must inflict greater dietary restraint upon themselves or resort to vomiting and laxatives, but they never reach as low a weight as other anorexics. Others may use pharmacologic agents such as amphetamines to reduce appetite, or diuretics to reduce bloating. For example, Ellen West misused thyroid pills to the point of developing hyperthyroidism.

Bulimic patients are sexually active but usually feel misused and are unable to enjoy sex. They often report that a feeling of being out of control, sexually, exacerbates the bulimia. As in their eating and other areas of self-control, they do not know "in-betweens" in sexual behavior. Moreover, their moods are labile and they frequently feel out of control. They behave in harmful, impulsive ways: For example, 19% of our bulimic patients had previously attempted suicide and 12% were involved in stealing. Crisp, Hsu and Harding (1980) have reported that stealing occurred in 14 out of 102 anorexic patients seen by them; in 13 of the 14 cases stealing occurred in conjunction with bulimia. Some may become alcoholics (five of our bulimic patients had been members of Alcoholics Anonymous). This abuse of alcohol by bulimic anorexics has also been described elsewhere (Brosin, 1941; Casper et al., 1980).

We found that 7% of our bulimics had previously engaged in self-mutilation. Several authors have also observed the association of self-mutilation, particularly genital self-mutilation, with disturbances in eating (French and Nelson, 1972; Goldney and Simpson, 1975; Rosenthal, Rinzler, Wallsh and Klausner, 1972; Simpson, 1975). For example, in Rosenthal et al.'s series of 24 wrist-cutting patients, 15 described either compulsive overeating, or severe anorexia, or both; 18 of 24 self-mutilators in Simpson's (1975) study experienced such eating problems, versus only two subjects in a control group. Goldney and Simpson (1975) went so far as to link the occurrence of genital self-mutilation, eating disturbance, and hysterical personality under the dubious title of "Caenis Syndrome." There is no clear rationale for separating such a syndrome, but these symptoms are all indicative of the degree of disturbance in psychosexual identity and impulse control experienced by this group of patients. These studies highlight the frequency of disturbances in eating behavior and possibly anorexia nervosa, in groups of self-mutilators.

Selvini Palazzoli (1974) has described differences in psychological characteristics of bulimic versus restricting anorexics. Using the Rorschach test, she observed that her bulimic patients displayed serious disorders in thought and communication not present in restricters. She also felt that families of bulimics, like the patients themselves, were more chaotic, demonstrating "psychotic confusion, violence and a complete breakdown of family communication" (p. 205). These findings, however, were impressionistic and Bruch (1973, p. 268) was unable to confirm such differences using a similar scoring technique. With regard to the families of bulimics,

Crisp, Harding and McGuinness (1974) described excessive obsessionality in the fathers. Their standards for performance and self-control were considered to be an important factor in the disorder. (This will be discussed further in Chapter 7.)

On psychometric tests the bulimic patients display differentiating characteristics. These relate largely to their reduced impulse control, increased extraversion, and mood variability. Casper et al. (1980) administered a variety of psychometric tests to their large sample. These included the MMPI, the Hopkins Symptom Checklist, and the Raskin Mood Scale. Bulimic patients experienced increased anxiety, depression, and guilt and reported more somatic preoccupation. Those patients who were bulimic every day displayed more significant psychopathology as evidenced by elevations on the MMPI subscales for schizophrenia, depression, psychopathic deviance, paranoia, and psychasthenia. Strober (1980) studied a smaller number of young subjects (all less than 17) and found "bingeing-vomiters" had reduced self-control but were more psychologically minded and flexibile on the California Personality Inventory. In this small sample, restricting and bulimic groups were observed to share a variety of psychological features. By contrast, Stonehill and Crisp (1977) and Hsu and Crisp (1980) administered the Crown-Crisp Experiential Index (formerly the Middlesex Hospital Questionnaire) and found that anorexic patients who vomited had significantly more psychopathological symptoms, especially depression. This finding persisted when patients were retested on follow-up.

Beumont's (1977) findings regarding increased extraversion in vomiting patients have already been described. Furthermore, patients with cycles of bulimia and vomiting compared with restricting anorexics are more inaccurate in self-estimates of their body sizes (Button, Fransella and Slade, 1977). They also showed more severe and refractory body image disturbances (Strober, Goldenberg, Green and Saxon, 1979) which may be indicative of the severity of psychopthology.

Not only do bulimics appear to have characteristic clinical features and to be more psychologically disturbed, but of greater importance, bulimia has repeatedly been found to be a poor prognostic sign in anorexia nervosa (Crisp, Kalucy, Lacey and Harding, 1977; Garfinkel et al., 1977; Morgan and Russell, 1975). Bulimic anorexics experience a far more chronic course to their illness than do restricters. Sir Aubrey Lewis has remarked that where knowledge about an illness is limited, a requirement for its identification as a "clinical entity" is that it breeds true (quoted in Russell, 1970). While the overall course of anorexia nervosa is highly influenced by a number of variables which will be later discussed, it appears that the very different responses to treatment of bulimic and restricting anorexics further emphasize the different nature of their disorders. Furthermore, due to their marked electrolyte losses bulimics are at greater risk for metàbolic complications. (This will be discussed in Chapter 11.)

Although there are differences, the two groups share common features. In particular, the vigorous pursuit of a thin body, regardless of weight, is similar in both groups. A bulimic, Ellen West, described typical anorexic concerns: "My thoughts are exclusively concerned with my body, my eating, my laxatives. And to be thin becomes my life's ideal" (quoted in Lifton, 1979, p. 258). Anorexic women, like most women in our culture, have a strong drive to appear thin. However, the bulimic group, partly because of their constitutional or developmental predisposition to obesity and partly because of their personality characteristics and ego-deficits, deal with this drive in an extreme fashion, by alternating bouts of starvation and bulimia. Other factors probably contribute to the presence of bulimia. Crisp (1967) suggests bulimia is related to chronicity and often first occurs when a patient is forced to gain weight rapidly, rather than through a process of gradual desensitization to her body size. He has suggested that the drive to bulimia increases with the duration of carbohydrate restriction. Selvini Palazzoli (1974) agrees with Crisp in suggesting that bulimia may often result from iatrogenic factors; for example, force-feeding in a setting of inadequate psychological support. Crisp also cites two patients treated with leucotomy, who then displayed bulimic episodes (Crisp, 1967) and bulimia has followed therapy with tricyclic antidepressants (Kendler, 1978).

The group of bulimic patients described here bear many similarities to Beumont et al.'s (1976) "vomiters and purgers." However, we believe that dividing the groups on the basis of the presence or absence of bulimia relates more to the core psychological difficulties of these patients: their poor mastery of their eating, sexual, and aggressive drives and impulses. The reliance on vomiting and purgatives is an external manifestation of their lack of self-control. Moreover some patients are bulimic without vomiting; when they were studied as a separate group they closely resembled the other bulimic-vomiting patients. Our bulimic group also show some overlap with Dally's (1969) group O. Again, however, the presence or absence of hunger cannot be utilized as a reliable distinguishing feature as many patients in both groups retain a sense of hunger unless they are in the final stages of starvation (Garfinkel, 1974).

Guiora (1967) has suggested that anorexia nervosa and bulimia are not separate syndromes but the extreme ends of the same disorder. He examined six patients in whom these extremes alternated and used the term "dysorexia" in an attempt to avoid the use of anorexia nervosa. His patients would appear to conform to our bulimic subtype of the anorexic syndrome. Guiora emphasized the possibility that individual patients may alternate between the two extremes. But while he is correct in saying that the bulimic group alternate between starvation and overeating, the majority of anorexic patients never give in to the impulse to overeat.

While our data clearly show that bulimic patients with anorexia nervosa can be differentiated from restricting anorexics, not all people with bulimia have anorexia nervosa. For example, Nogami and Yabana (1977) described three groups of patients with what they termed Kibarashi-gui (binge eating). Only one group had anorexia nervosa. Other groups consisted of patients who were chiefly 1) neurotic and depressed and 2) borderline or schizophrenic. Although vomiting after overeating could be observed among members of all three groups, they felt that habitual voluntary vomiting was only seen among the anorexic group. We, however, have seen self-induced vomiting in patients with somatization disorders and therefore this criterion cannot be used to separate bulimic individuals with anorexia nervosa from others. Nogami and Yabana (1977) reported that the bulimia in the neurotic group was a transient stress-related phenomenon and in the schizophrenic group usually also transient and part of a psychotic clinical picture; only in the anorexic group did the bulimia run a chronic course. We do not agree that the duration of bulimia is a distinguishing feature; however, bulimia can clearly be a manifestation of a variety of illnesses, including many organic brain diseases.

At present the distinction between bulimia with anorexia nervosa versus bulimia in the absence of anorexia nervosa is based purely on clinical descriptive criteria — whether the individual's preoccupation is with body shape or not, the presence of weight loss, and associated psychobiological features as noted in the previous chapter. Palmer (1979) has recently addressed the diagnostic problem by coining the term "dietary chaos syndrome" to describe a group of individuals who may or may not have had a previous diagnosis of anorexia nervosa. According to Palmer (1979), the features of this syndrome include: 1) a grossly disturbed pattern of eating (abstinence, vomiting, bulimia, etc.); 2) a preoccupation with eating and food, and sometimes with weight, which overrides other thoughts (the impulse to eat is experienced as out of control); and 3) body weight may change over a few kilograms in hours or days in response to the balance of intake and output.

Although this syndrome may be associated with anorexia nervosa, this is not always the case. At times it may occur without a history of weight loss and amenorrhea. This description essentially corresponds to that of DSM III's definition of bulimia, with the addition of depressive moods and self-deprecating thoughts following episodes of binge eating (DSM III, 1980).

However, DSM III excludes all anorexic patients within the bulimia diagnosis, as it does when the bulimia is symptomatic of schizophrenia. Both Palmer and the authors of DSM III appear to be responding to a need to describe a group of patients who do not fit previous diagnostic categories. While we agree with the need for such a diagnosis, several important questions remain unanswered. First, we do not know how common such behavior is in a nonclinical population or how commonly bulimia is present independently of anorexia nervosa. Second, how do those bulimic patients without the core features of anorexia nervosa differ psychopathologically from those with anorexia nervosa? Are they merely individuals who never lose much weight and whose major preoccupation has shifted from body size to control of food intake but otherwise resemble anorexics or are they fundamentally different from bulimic anorexics?

**PERSONALITY TYPES IN BULIMIC VERSUS RESTRICTING ANOREXICS**

Personality features may blend with the symptoms caused by the illness, especially when its onset is in early adolescence before full maturation of the personality (Morgan and Russell, 1975). For this reason it is often difficult to make an accurate comment about the individual's personality. As noted previously, when emaciated, many individuals present with obsessional features but these are, at least in part, manifestations of the starvation state. After weight restoration it is common to observe hysterical and schizoid personality characteristics in addition to the obsessional traits. There is therefore no one personality type exclusively seen in anorexia nervosa. However, given the cluster of clinical features coexisting in bulimic patients, it is reasonable to question whether bulimics are not frequently individuals with borderline personality organizations. While this term has slightly different uses according to different authors and while there is considerable overlap with other personality diagnoses (Perry and Klerman, 1978), there has been recent consensus on its core features (Gunderson and Singer, 1975; Gunderson and Kolb, 1978; DSM III, 1980).

Bulimic anorexics often have labile affect, loss of control, and a sense of emptiness described by Gunderson and Singer (1975) as typical of borderlines. It is partly this labile affect and unhappiness which has caused some to suggest that these anorexics suffer from bipolar mood disorders; but their moods are rarely sustained, or are related to their physical anhedonia. They do not feel pleasure from their bodies but rather a sense of intolerance and a need to "control their bodies." Their behavior is characterized by poor impulse control which, as noted earlier, may take many forms beyond the bulimic episodes themselves. They include misuse of drugs and alcohol, stealing, mutilation, and suicide attempts. Their sexual patterns are often impulsive and like a "binge" with frequent periods of abstinence followed by indiscriminate sexual activity and little pleasure. The sexual activities are often attempts at closeness and are not associated with satisfaction but rather a sense of being misused.

Their interpersonal relationships fluctuate between transient, superficial ones and intense dependent ones that lead to further personal devaluation and anger. These individuals may maintain adequate school and work performance. However, this is often a surface adjustment masking a severely disturbed personal identity. This is hidden by superficial identifications with others and their responding to the expectation demands of parents and peers. These bulimic patients also experience brief but repeated depersonalization experiences, as do borderlines. The remaining features of the borderline, their overt psychoses and response to projective psychological tests, have not been directly studied by us. However, based on the other features in common we feel it is justified to conclude that many individuals with the bulimic form of anorexia nervosa have borderline personality organizations.

To say that bulimic anorexic patients may frequently have borderline personalities may not in itself significantly improve our understanding of the pathogenesis of this form of the disorder. However, if one views such borderline patients as frequently having marked problems with emotional separation and autonomy and if the latter are predispositions to anorexia nervosa, it may help explain why this group is vulnerable to the illness. The complex multidetermined nature of anorexia nervosa is also underlined by these observations — not all borderline individuals develop anorexia nervosa when faced with separation or other stress and not all anorexics, or even most, have borderline personalities. In this regard, the borderline personality cannot be considered as either necessary or sufficient for the later development of anorexia nervosa. This view of the development of anorexia nervosa in response to several different predisposing and precipitating factors will be further discussed in Chapter 8.

## REFERENCES

Beumont, P.J.V., George, G.C.W. and Smart, D.E.: "Dieters" and "vomiters and purgers" in anorexia nervosa. *Psychol. Med.,* 6:617-622, 1976.

Beumont, P.J.V.: Further categorization of patients with anorexia nervosa. *Aust. N. Z. J. Psychiatry,* 11:223-226, 1977.

Beumont, P.J.V., Abraham, S.F. and Simpson, K.G.: The psychosexual histories of adolescent girls and young women with anorexia nervosa. *Psychol. Med.,* 11:131-140, 1981.

Binswanger, L.: Der Fall Ellen West, *Schweiz Arch. Neuro. Psychiat.,* 54:69-117, 1944.

56                                                                Anorexia Nervosa

Boskind-Lodahl, M.: Cinderella's step-sisters: A feminist perspective on anorexia nervosa and bulimia. *Signs: J. Wom. in Cult. Soc.,* 2:342-356, 1976.
Brosin, H.W.: Anorexia nervosa; case report. *J. Clin. Endocrinol.,* 1:269-271, 1941.
Bruch, H.: *Eating Disorders.* New York: Basic Books, 1973.
Button, E.J., Fransella, F. and Slade, P.D.: A reappraisal of body perception disturbance in anorexia nervosa. *Psychol. Med.,* 7:235-243, 1977.
Casper, R.C., Eckert, E.D., Halmi, K.A., Goldberg, S.C., and Davis, J.M.: Bulimia. Its incidence and clinical importance in patients with anorexia nervosa. *Arch. Gen. Psychiatry,* 37:1030-1034, 1980.
Crisp, A.H.: The possible significance of some behavioral correlates of weight and carbohydrate intake. *J. Psychosom. Res.,* 11:117-131, 1967.
Crisp, A.H.: *Anorexia Nervosa: Let Me Be.* New York: Grune and Stratton, 1980.
Crisp, A.H., Harding, B. and McGuinness, B.: Anorexia nervosa. Psychoneurotic characteristics of parents. A qualitative study. *J. Psychosom. Res.,* 18:167-173, 1974.
Crisp, A.H., Hsu, L.K.G. and Harding, B.: The starving hoarder and voracious spender: Stealing in anorexia nervosa. *J. Psychosom. Res.,* 24:225-231, 1980.
Crisp, A.H., Kalucy, R.S., Lacey, J.H. and Harding, B.: The long-term prognosis in anorexia nervosa: Some factors predictive of outcome. In: R. Vigersky (Ed.), *Anorexia Nervosa.* New York: Raven Press, 1977, p. 55-65.
Dally, P.: *Anorexia Nervosa.* London: William Heineman Medical Books, 1969.
Diagnostic and Statistical Manual of Mental Disorders, Third Edition. Washington D.C.: American Psychiatric Association, 1980.
Feighner, J.P., Robins, E., Guze, S.B., Woodruff, R.A., Jr., Winokur, G. and Munoz, R.: Diagnostic criteria for use in psychiatric research. *Arch. Gen. Psychiatry,* 26:57-63, 1972.
French, A.P. and Nelson, H.L.: Genital self-mutilation in women. *Arch. Gen. Psychiatry,* 27:618-620, 1972.
Garfinkel, P.E.: Perception of hunger and satiety in anorexia nervosa. *Psychol. Med.,* 4:309-315, 1974.
Garfinkel, P.E., Moldofsky, H. and Garner, D.M.: The outcome of anorexia nervosa: Significance of clinical features, body image and behavior modifications. In: R. Vigersky (Ed.), *Anorexia Nervosa.* New York: Raven Press, 1977, pp. 315-329.
Garfinkel, P.E., Moldofsky, H. and Garner, D.M.: The heterogeneity of anorexia nervosa: Bulimia as a distinct subgroup. *Arch. Gen. Psychiatry,* 37:1036-1040, 1980.
Garrow, J.S., Crisp, A.H., Jordan, H.A., Meyer, J.E., Russell, G.F.M., Silverstone, T., Stunkard, A.J. and Van Itallie, T.B.: Pathology of eating, group report. In: T. Silverstone (Ed.), *Dahlem konferenzen,* Life Sciences Research Report 2. Berlin, 1975.
Goldney, R.D. and Simpson, I.G.: Female genital self-mutilation, dysorexia and the hysterical personality: The Caenis Syndrome. *Can. Psychiatr. Assoc. J.,* 20:435-441, 1975.
Guiora, A.Z.: Dysorexia: A psychopathological study of anorexia nervosa and bulimia. *Am. J. Psychiatry,* 124:391-393, 1967.
Gunderson, J.G. and Kolb, J.: Discriminating features of borderline patients. *Am. J. Psychiatry,* 135:792-796, 1978.
Gunderson, J.G. and Singer M.T.: Defining borderline patients: An overview. *Am. J. Psychiatry,* 132:1-10, 1975.
Halmi, K.A., Casper, R.C., Eckert, E.D., Goldberg, S.C. and Davis, J.M.: Unique features associated with age of onset of anorexia nervosa. *Psychiat. Res.,* 1:209-215, 1979.
Hsu, L.K.G. and Crisp, A.H.: The Crown-Crisp experiential index (CCEI) profile in anorexia nervosa. *Br.J. Psychiat.,* 136:567-573, 1980.
Hsu, L.K.G., Crisp, A.H. and Harding, B.: Outcome of anorexia nervosa. *Lancet,* 1:61-65, 1979.
Janet, P.: *Les Obsessions et la Psychasthenie.* Paris: Felix Alcan, 1919.
Kendler, K.S.: Amitriptyline-induced obesity in anorexia nervosa: A case report. *Am. J. Psychiatry,* 135:1107-1108, 1978.
Lifton, R.J.: *The Broken Connection.* New York: Simon and Schuster, 1979.

Meyer, J.E.: The anorexia nervosa syndrome. Catamnestic research. *Arch. Psychiat. Nervenkr.,* 202:31-59, 1961.

Morgan, H.G. and Russell, G.F.M.: Value of family background and clinical features as predictors of long-term outcome in anorexia nervosa: Four-year follow-up study of 41 patients. *Psychol. Med.,* 5:355-372, 1975.

Nogami, Y. and Yabana, F.: On Kibarashi-gui (binge eating). *Folia Psychiatr. Neurol. Jpn.,* 31:294-295, 1977.

Palmer, R.L.: The dietary chaos syndrome: A useful new term? *Br. J. Med. Psychol.,* 52:187-190, 1979.

Perry, J.C. and Klerman, G.L.: The borderline patient. A comparative analysis of four sets of diagnostic criteria. *Arch. Gen. Psychiatry,* 35:141, 1978.

Raymond, F. and Janet, P.: *Les Obsessions et la Psychasthenie.* Paris: Felix Alcan, 1903.

Rollins, N. and Piazza, E.: Diagnosis of anorexia nervosa. A critical reappraisal. *J. Am. Acad. Child Psychiatry,* 17:126-137, 1978.

Rosenthal, R.J., Rinzler, C., Wallsh, R. and Klausner, E.: Wrist-cutting syndrome: The meaning of a gesture. *Am. J. Psychiatry,* 11:1363-1368, 1972.

Russell, G.F.M.: Anorexia Nervosa: Its identity as an illness and its treatment. In: J.H. Price (Ed.), *Modern Trends in Psychological Medicine, 2.* London: Butterworths, 1970.

Russell, G.F.M.: Bulimia nervosa: An ominous variant of anorexia nervosa. *Psychol. Med.,* 9:429-448, 1979.

Selvini Palazzoli, M.P.: *Self-Starvation.* London: Chaucer Publishing Co., 1974.

Simpson, M.A.: The phenomenology of self-mutilation in a general hospital setting. *Can. Psychiatr. Assoc. J.,* 20:429-434, 1975.

Stonehill, E. and Crisp, A.H.: Psychoneurotic characteristics of patients with anorexia nervosa before and after treatment and at follow-up 4-7 years later. *J. Psychosom. Res.,* 21:189-193, 1977.

Stordy, B.J., Marks, V., Kalucy, R.S. and Crisp, A.H.: Weight gain, thermic effect of glucose and resting metabolic rate during recovery from anorexia nervosa. *Am. J. Clin. Nutr.,* 30:138-146, 1977.

Strober, M.: A cross-sectional and longitudinal (post weight restoration) analysis of personality and symptomelogical features in young, nonchronic anorexia nervosa patients. *J. Psychosom. Res.,* 24:353-359, 1980.

Strober, M., Goldenberg, I., Green, J. and Saxon, J.: Body image disturbance in anorexia nervosa during the acute and recuperative phase. *Psychol. Med.,* 9:695-701, 1979.

Stunkard, A.J.: Presidential address — from explanation to action in psychosomatic medicine: The case of obesity. *Psychosom. Med.,* 37:195-236, 1975.

Theander, S.: Anorexia nervosa. A psychiatric investigation of 94 female cases. *Acta Psychiat. Scand. (Suppl.),* 214:1-194, 1970.

# CHAPTER 4

# *Hypothalamic*

# *Pituitary Function*

## HISTORICAL PERSPECTIVE

From its earliest description, anorexia nervosa was recognized to resemble, but also to be distinct from, entirely somatic disorders. Thus Richard Morton (1694) described two patients whom he differentiated from other tubercular individuals as having nervous consumption. Since then, the history of the concept of anorexia nervosa in relation to primary somatic illness can be divided into three phases. Initially, anorexia nervosa was described as a psychological disturbance in which starvation was considered to be responsible for many of the prominent symptoms. After the description of pituitary insufficiency there followed a period of 25 years of confusion between these disorders. More recently, there has again been a clarification of the differences between primary pituitary illness and the hypothalamic-pituitary manifestations of anorexia nervosa and the associated mechanisms involved in their production.

Gull's 1868 Address in Medicine at Oxford contained a short reference to the disorder which he would later name anorexia nervosa:

> At present our diagnosis is mostly one of inference, from our knowledge of the liability of the several organs to particular lesions; thus we avoid the error of supposing the presence of mesenteric disease in young women emaciated to the last degree through hysteric apepsia, by our knowledge of the latter affliction, and by the absence of tubercular disease elsewhere (Gull, 1868, p. 175).

Gull's method of diagnosing hysteric apepsia (anorexia nervosa) included

58

both relying on its clinical manifestations and the exclusion of somatic causes of weight loss. Six years later Gull began to use the term "anorexia nervosa" and discussed factors he felt were important in the pathogenesis; he thought the "morbid mental state" and a perversion of the "ego" relating to a disturbed nerve force to be significant. At the same time, Lasègue (1873) independently described the disorder. In addition to his detailed clinical descriptions, Lasègue stressed that the patient's active psychological disgust for food leads to the weight loss and he noted familial involvements in the disorder. He described hysterical symptoms in seven of the eight patients on whom he based his reports. He termed the disorder "anorexie hystérique" and, like his contemporaries, viewed hysteria as a predominantly hereditary disturbance of the central nervous system.

During the next few years anorexia nervosa was clearly defined in the literature; for example, Sir Clifford Allbutt (1910) described a "typical" case in his *System of Medicine*. Déjérine and Gauckler (1911) described patients with "mental anorexia," whose origin was presumed to be purely emotional. Also, Stephens (1895) published an autopsy report of an anorexic patient; the brain was described to be "normal throughout." Thus, the initial period of attention to anorexia nervosa was characterized by description of the syndrome, its clinical manifestations, and its distinction from primary somatic illness.

In 1914 the pathologist Morris Simmonds described a patient in whom cachexia was associated with destruction of the adenohypophysis. He amplified these observations in papers between 1916-1918 which described four more cases and the condition began to be called Simmonds' disease. In 1930, Smith found that removing the anterior lobe of the rat's hypophysis without injury to adjoining portions of the brain produced an experimental model of Simmonds' disease. He also showed that the hormonal deficiency could be relieved by implanting the pituitary gland. Throughout the 1920s and 1930s many articles were written on Simmonds' disease, although it seems in retrospect that in a number of instances these were cases of anorexia nervosa (Berkman, 1948, Nemiah, 1950). For example, Sheldon (1939) estimated that "there are over 80 instances of this mis-reporting and approximately half of the published cases of anorexia nervosa are indexed under other names," and he described Kylin's (1935) monograph as "a monograph on Simmonds' disease which will always be one of the more important papers on anorexia nervosa." What occurred in the 1930s was a steady "rediscovery" and ultimately a renaming of the disorder. Falta (1928) described anorexia nervosa as a defect in appetite secondary to abnormal insulin metabolism. Korbsch (1936) felt it was due to a primary atrophy of the gastric mucous membrane. Krause and Muller (1937) described it as severe anterior pituitary weakness. By 1939, Kylin recognized these patients differed from Simmonds' patients and called the illness "wasting of late female puberty, a disease form sui generis." A few years later Escamilla and Lisser (1941) reviewed 595 cases in the literature described to be Simmonds' disease, of which only 101 could truly be so described and who were subsequently pathologically verified.

Not surprisingly, in view of the confusion between anorexia nervosa and Simmonds' disease, a number of hormonal preparations were recommended as treatment for anorexia nervosa. Levi (1922) had considered the condition to be due to hypothyroidism and Josefson (1933) recommended thyroid hormone as particularly helpful. By contrast, Allison and Davies (1931) and Richardson (1939) noted the alarming further weight loss that resulted from thyroid hormone and that others had failed to perceive any benefit from it in anorexic patients, Krause (1937) attributed anorexia nervosa to "shrinkage" of the adrenal cortex, as had Leeds (1928), who assumed it was "pluriglandular" in origin but adrenal insufficiency was thought to play the major role. Reiss (1943) advocated treatment with corticotrophic hormone and even based the efficacy of the treatment on a rising output of ketosteroids after its administration. Furthermore, Von Bergman (1934) and Kylin (1935) recommended treatment of implanting a calf's hypophysis in the omentum. Richardson (1939) found that intramuscular injection of extract of the anterior lobe of the pituitary was ineffective in anorexia nervosa.

The clear distinction between Simmonds' disease and anorexia nervosa was made in a series of papers beginning in the late 1930s. Ryle, Richardson and Sheldon independently published reports reintroducing the work of Gull (Richardson, 1939; Ryle 1939; Sheldon, 1939). Sheldon wrote:

> How is it that so many observers — men like ourselves except that so far as they are concerned Sir William Gull might never have existed — how is it that they universally regard the condition as organic and with almost complete unanimity incriminate the anterior pituitary as the cause of the disease? (p. 739).

In North America, Farquharson and Hyland (1938), Richardson (1939) and McCullagh and Tupper (1940) wrote on the psychogenic nature of anorexia nervosa and its distinction from Simmonds' disease. Escamilla and Lisser (1942) published a comprehensive report of Simmonds' disease, reviewing the literature and including a comparison group of anorexic patients. In 1948, Berkman summarized his extensive experience with anorexia nervosa and pituitary insufficiency at the Mayo Clinic. Sheehan and Summers (1949) provided a detailed review of pituitary insufficiency, based on pathological diagnosis, and differentiated it from other disorders, including anorexia nervosa. These articles significantly clarified the diagnostic confusion that had existed. In fact, Berkman (1948) correctly concluded that the clinical differentiation of anorexia nervosa from pituitary insufficiency was quite easy. Sheehan and Summers (1949) stated there were only two symptoms common to Simmonds' Disease and anorexia nervosa: amenorrhea and a low basal metabolic rate. Anorexia nervosa, unlike pituitary insufficiency, is associated with extreme weight loss; only one quarter of Simmonds' patients show severe weight loss (Sheehan and Summers, 1949). Moreover, in contrast to the lassitude of the patient with Simmonds' disease, the anorexic patient is frequently active both physically and mentally. Differentiating signs included additional hair growth in anorexia nervosa and the loss of pubic and axillary hair in Simmonds' disease. Today, we would add the vigorous pursuit of thinness, denial of illness, disturbances in body image, and intense efforts at weight loss (disposing of food, vomiting, laxatives, etc.) as important differentiating clinical features.

## MENSTRUAL FUNCTION AND FERTILITY

Amenorrhea is a characteristic feature of anorexia nervosa. While this is usually a secondary amenorrhea, depending on the age of onset of the illness, some young women may present with primary amenorrhea. For example, in an earlier study (Garfinkel, Moldofsky and Garner, 1980), 4% of our patients presented with primary amenorrhea. With a slightly younger group (Hurd, Palumbo and Gharib, 1977), 11% of the sample were prepubertal at the onset. Mean menarchal age, however, is not abnormal in anorexic patients (mean of $12.8 \pm 0.2$ years, Garfinkel et al., 1980; Theander, 1970), although Crisp (1970) has suggested that menarche may in fact occur at an unusually young age.

For many patients (70%), loss of menses occurs shortly after the onset of the weight loss (Fries, 1977; Hurd et al., 1977). However, in a significant proportion (estimates vary between 7-24%), amenorrhea appears to precede the weight loss (Fries, 1977). Obviously, these findings are limited by the imprecise retrospective reports. Nevertheless, for some patients, amenorrhea appears to be the first manifestation of the illness. It is not clear whether this is due to the emotional upheaval preceding the dieting behavior (for example, it has been noted that social isolation begins to occur in the year prior to dieting) or because of an independent hypothalamic abnormality. But the marked retrospective bias in reporting onset of dieting behavior and the known effects of emotional disturbance on menstrual function (Drew, 1961; Rakoff, 1962) make it premature to conclude the latter. Earlier studies by Bass (1947) on women in concentration camps demonstrated that for most (60%) with amenorrhea the cessation of menses occurred immediately after internment, before their nutritional status had been seriously impaired.

For most anorexic patients, amenorrhea is related to the degree of weight loss. This is also true for the female population as a whole: Fries and Nillius (1973) have noted a high occurrence of dieting and weight loss in women who presented with "post-pill amenorrhea"; approximately 75% of 75 such subjects were judged to be underweight at the time of onset of amenorrhea; their average weight loss was over 9 kg. Four patients had anorexia nervosa and another six women showed anorexic traits. Similarly, in a random sample of a Swedish population, Pettersson, Fries and Nillius (1973) found that 6% of the females under 25 had secondary amenorrhea for more than three months. In a follow-up investigation, the amenorrheic women in this sample were found to be significantly underweight when compared to controls. Richardson and Pieters (1977) also found adolescent girls in South Africa who had primary amenorrhea weighed less and had significantly less body fat than their menstruating peers. Moreover, Garner and Garfinkel (1980) recently studied female ballet students and found that 28% in a professionally-oriented school were amenorrheic. These women weighed significantly less than their menstruating peers (80.4% versus 84.5% of average). Similarly, Frisch, Wyshak and Vincent (1980) studied 89 young ballet dancers. They observed a significantly delayed onset of menarche in this group in comparison with the general population. Also, 15% of the group reported secondary amenorrhea and 30% had irregular cycles. Only 33% of the dancers reported regular cycles. Significantly, dancers with amenorrhea or irregular cycles weighed less than those with regular menses. Since this group of ballet students began serious studies at an early age (nine years), it was concluded that the low calorie intake and rigorous training accounted for the amenorrhea rather than particular selection factors relating to late maturers choosing ballet.

Weight is not the sole critical factor determining menstruation, however. In a study by Feicht, Johnson, Martin, Sparkes and Wagner (1978) on female athletes, they found 19/54 were amenorrheic but those in the amenorrheic sample did not weigh less than the others. In a separate study of menstrual function in female athletes, Dale, Gerlach and White (1979) found that serious "runners" had more frequent irregular and absent menses than controls. Not only was their body weight less but the runners' body fat was markedly reduced. Amenorrhea may relate more to the percentage of body fat, extent of exercise, or the degree of stress the individual is under than to the actual weight. Therefore, while weight is one important variable in amenorrhea, it is not the only one.

Patients with anorexia nervosa usually, but not always, resume menstruation after their weights are restored. This is true even for patients who have been amenorrheic for many years. For example, Beck and Brochner-Mortensen (1954) estimated that 68%, Theander (1970) 76%, and Dally (1969) 59% of surviving patients resumed normal menses. Kay (1953) reported that 55% of his patients resumed normal regular menses. The others were equally distributed among amenorrheic women and oligomenorrheic ones. Of the group with persisting amenorrhea, all but one patient was chronically ill and underweight. Morgan and Russell (1975) found that exactly 50% of their sample had normal menses on follow-up four to eight years after presentation. Again there was a clear relationship with weight; regular menses with only one exception were confined to those women whose weight had returned to normal. In a later study of similar design, Hsu, Crisp and Harding (1979) followed up 102 patients. Twenty-eight had persistent amenorrhea and 11 of the group were of normal body weight. Garfinkel, Moldofsky and Garner (1977) found that almost 50% of their patients were menstruating regularly two years after treatment. Return of menses is quite common but not invariable when patients regain weight to more than 90% of average for their age and height (Table 1).

These findings are in accord with the concept proposed by Frisch (1977) that the onset and maintenance of regular menstrual function are both dependent upon maintenance of a minimum weight for height. This minimum weight for height is proposed to represent a critical fat storage (Frisch and McArthur, 1974) and implies that a particular body composition of fat/lean or fat/body weight may be an important determinant for reproductive ability in the human female (Frisch, 1977). Frisch and McArthur (1974) estimated that for the onset of menarche, fat must constitute an estimated 17% of body weight and that a body composition of about 23% fat is necessary for the maintenance of regular ovulation. It has been sug-

## TABLE 1

Relationship Between Return of Menses and Weight on Follow-up

| Follow-up | Menses | |
| Weight (% average) | Present | Absent |
| --- | --- | --- |
| 90-125% | 11 | 1 |
| 80-89% | 6 | 8 |
| <80% | 2 | 11 |
| Total | 19 | 20 |

Chi-square = 14.83, df = 2, p <0.001.
Reprinted with permission from Garfinkel et al., 1977.

gested that the reduced metabolic rate associated with reaching this "critical" level of body fat may trigger the onset of menses. This reduction may diminish the steroid feedback sensitivity of the hypothalamus and allow for sufficient rise in estrogen secretion to support menstruation (Richardson and Pieters, 1977).

However, not all studies on anorexia nervosa are in accord with this hypothesis; for example, Katz, Boyar, Roffwarg, Hellman and Weiner (1978) found that the return of menses did not show a simple relationship to weight or fatness. Also, the previously noted study by Hsu et al. (1979), in which 11 patients attained a normal body weight but were amenorrheic four to eight years after presentation, demonstrates the complexity of the situation. Similarly Richardson and Pieters (1977) described adolescent girls with amenorrhea in South Africa whose body fat was greater than 23%. These data emphasize that the critical fat/lean ratio is not the only factor which determines menses. Frisch and McArthur (1974) clearly state that

> . . . other factors such as emotional stress affect the maintenance or onset of menstrual cycles. Therefore, menstrual cycles may cease without weight loss and may not resume even though the minimum required weight is attained (pp. 950-951).

According to this theory, the minimum weight (fat) is necessary but not sufficient to support regular menstruation.

In this regard, it may be important to differentiate anorexic patients who lose weight entirely by carbohydrate restriction from those who engage in periodic bulimia. Those in the bulimic group have a higher basal metabolic rate (BMR) at a corresponding weight than do the restricting patients (Crisp, 1977) and a return of menses is more likely to occur at a lower weight in the bulimic patients, perhaps because of this increased BMR. For the restricting patients, Crisp has suggested that it is not only the attainment of a standard weight for age and height that is significant for resumption of menses but also that premorbid weight is an important indicator of this. Any hormonal assessments of anorexic patients should evaluate restricting and bulimic patients separately (Crisp, 1978).

Relatively little is known about the fertility of anorexic patients. However, there is no evidence to suggest they are not normally fertile after weight restoration and resumption of menses. Dally (1969) reported that about 50% of his married patients had children at the time of follow-up. Farquharson and Hyland (1966) found seven of their 15 patients had married and produced at least one child. Starkey and Lee (1969) reported that 27 of 28 recovered patients seen at least 10 years earlier and who attempted to become pregnant had conceived without difficulty. Ziegler and Sours

(1968) followed up 26 patients, of whom 12 had married. Nine of these had between one and five children. Beck and Brochner-Mortensen (1954) found that of 15 married patients, 13 had had between one and three pregnancies at the time of follow-up. There was no increased incidence of abortion or childhood illness. Similarly Theander (1970), in the longest follow-up to date, observed that 47 of his anorexic patients had married and of these 34 had borne at least one child. Only one had a tendency to habitual abortion. Of the remaining 13 married patients, four were just recently married, two married in their mid-40s, two were voluntarily sterile and five actively symptomatic. Theander also described one patient who became pregnant six times without resuming menses. De Carle (1962) also reported a patient who became pregnant while emaciated and amenorrheic.

Patients with anorexia nervosa who wish to have children should be counseled to wait until they have recovered. However, Hart, Kase and Kimball (1970) induced ovulation in three patients, who tolerated the subsequent pregnancy well. On the other hand, we have seen several patients in whom active symptomatology was exacerbated by pregnancy. While normal infants were delivered, the mothers remained seriously ill for many months. For this reason clomiphene or other fertility-inducing agents should not be used unless 1) the patient has gained weight to a level greater than 90% of average (see below); 2) her eating behavior and attitudes to her body have stabilized; and 3) she has maintained this state for one year. Most patients will not need clomiphene if these criteria are met. Sexually active patients may choose to use contraceptives. There is no evidence to suggest that anorexic patients have untoward responses to oral contraceptives. However, the use of such compounds in non-sexually active amenorrheic patients to produce withdrawal bleeding and therefore a semblance of normal hormonal function should be strongly discouraged, as this may foster the denial of illness and may prevent recognition of the natural return of menses.

## HYPOTHALAMIC FUNCTION

Patients with anorexia nervosa have been found repeatedly to display abnormal hypothalamic function. Possible pathogenic mechanisms underlying these disturbances include hypothalamic changes which: 1) reflect weight loss or caloric deprivation; 2) are secondary to emotional disturbance; and 3) are primary and responsible for both the emotional disturbance and the altered hormonal states. In the following review, we note that the various hormones are affected preferentially by weight, caloric intake, and emotional distress. These factors account for what is currently known about the origin of hypothalamic disturbances.

*Gonadotropins*

Studies in markedly underweight patients with anorexia nervosa demonstrate low plasma gonadotropins (Beumont, Carr and Gelder, 1973; Brown, Garfinkel, Jeuniewic, Moldofsky and Stancer, 1977; Hurd et al., 1977). A linear relationship of resting plasma LH with body weight has been shown with LH levels normalizing as weight is regained (Figure 1) (Beumont, Abraham, Argall and Turtle, 1978; Beumont, George, Pimstone and Vinik, 1976; Brown et al., 1977; Wakeling, DeSouza and Beardwood, 1977a). In contrast to weight, there is no relationship between resting

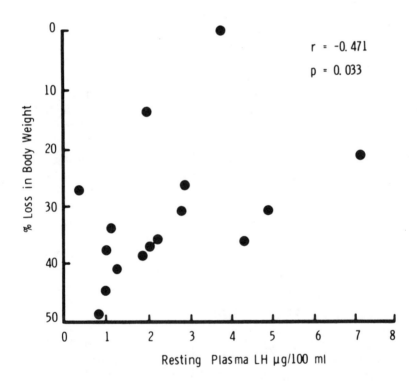

Relationship of resting morning plasma luteinizing hormone to weight loss. (from Brown et al, 1977 — reprinted with permission)

Figure 1

plasma LH levels and caloric intake or duration of amenorrhea (Brown et al., 1977). In addition, baseline FSH values are reduced and return to normal with weight gain (Beumont et al., 1976; Sherman and Halmi, 1977). One study, however, found no reduction in basal FSH and no relationship of FSH to body weight (Beumont et al., 1978). Several studies (Garfinkel, Brown, Stancer and Moldofsky, 1975; Halmi, Sherman and Zamudio, 1975; Warren and Vande Wiele, 1973) have found the reduction of LH to be more marked than that of FSH.

Studies of 24-hour secretory patterns of serum gonadotropins demonstrate that anorexic patients with weight loss have 24-hour patterns resembling those found in normal prepubertal or pubertal girls. These "immature" patterns are found in both restricting and bulimic groups of patients (Katz et al., 1978). They are characterized either by low LH levels throughout the 24 hours, as is normally found in prepubertal girls, or by decreased LH secretory activity during waking with higher mean LH concentration during sleep, as is found in early-to-mid-pubertal girls (Boyar, Katz, Finkelstein, Kapen, Weiner, Weitzman and Hellman, 1974; Brown, Kirwan, Garfinkel and Moldofsky, 1979; Katz, Boyar, Weiner, Gorzynski, Roffwarg and Hellman, 1976). The possibility that these developmentally inappropriate circadian patterns of LH secretion might be found in other types of amenorrhea has been thought to be unlikely because of studies on women with gonadal dysgenesis (Boyar, Finkelstein, Roffwarg, Kapen, Weitzman and Hellman, 1973), menopause (Yen, Tsai and Naftolin, 1972), and the polycystic-ovary syndrome (Yen, Vela and Rankin, 1970). These patients do not manifest immature circadian LH patterns, despite the amenorrhea they all have in common. Katz et al. (1976) have shown that an individual with an anorexia nervosa-like syndrome, secondary to schizophrenia, did not show an immature circadian LH pattern but this is contrasted by Pirke, Fichter, Lund and Doerr's (1979) report of a schizophrenic patient with weight loss and an immature circadian pattern. Kapen, Sternthal and Braverman (1981) have recently described a woman with amenorrhea secondary to a 20-pound weight loss due to dieting. But this individual displayed none of the features of anorexia nervosa. She had a pubertal pattern of LH secretion when underweight and this became an adult pattern after a 15-pound weight gain.

Pirke et al. (1979) found that the immature LH patterns were related to weight with adult patterns being observed when a body weight of greater than 80% of average was attained. Katz et al. (1978) reported that this immature circadian pattern persisted in women who had partially or totally achieved average weight, but who were otherwise symptomatic. They found that the degree of immaturity of the pattern did not correlate reliably with the duration of illness, the percent body fat, or the extent of the weight loss. However, those women who were restudied both when weight-recovered and when in clinical remission showed an adult LH pattern. It is possible that weight-recovered, but otherwise symptomatic, anorexics may persist in such abnormal dietary patterns that they maintain deficiencies in critical nutrients that may alter neurotransmitter function and secondarily the LH pattern. However, it is also plausible that the LH pattern is sensitive to the particular psychological distress of the anorexic rather than dietary factors. A third intriguing but unlikely (in view of the Pirke et al. [1979] results) possibility remains — that individuals who are at risk for anorexia nervosa do not develop normal adult circadian LH patterns as they pass through puberty and this may represent one constitutional predisposition to the disorder.

Several investigators have shown that the LH response to luteinizing hormone releasing hormone (LHRH) is greatly reduced in patients with anorexia nervosa (Figure 2). This response is also correlated with body weight so that those patients with the greatest loss in body weight have the smallest LH rise in response to LHRH (Akande, Carr, Dutton, Bonnar, Corker and Mackinnon, 1972; Brown et al., 1977; Isaacs, Leslie, Gomez and Bayliss, 1980; Mecklenburg et al., 1974; Palmer, Crisp, Mackinnon, Franklin, Bonnar and Wheller, 1975; Sherman and Halmi, 1977; and Sherman et al., 1975). Normal release of LH after LHRH can occur in patients with immature circadian patterns (Katz, Boyar, Roffwarg, Hellman and Weiner, 1977). While the LH response to LHRH can be greatly diminished at low body weights, the FSH response to LHRH appears to be regularly present even in severely underweight patients. Some authors have emphasized that there is a linear relationship of the LH response to LHRH with body weight (Beumont et al., 1976; Beumont et al., 1978; Brown et al., 1977; Jeuniewic, Brown, Garfinkel and Moldofsky, 1978). Other investigators have suggested an exponential relationship such that the LH responsiveness to LHRH increases dramatically at approximately 15% below ideal weight for height (Warren, Jewelewicz, Dyrenfurth, Ans, Khalaf and Vande Wiele, 1975; Warren, 1977). Whichever interpretation is more precise, it is clear that FSH responses to LHRH are normalized prior to the return of LH responses.

In some subjects, hyperresponsiveness of LH and FSH to LHRH has been observed during weight gain (Hirvonen, Seppala, Karonen and Allercreutz, 1977; Warren et al., 1975). Beumont et al. (1976) found the FSH response to LHRH was exaggerated at a lower body weight than the LH response, a phenomenon which is in accord with the increased FSH/LH ratio that has been noted in some anorexia nervosa patients stimulated with

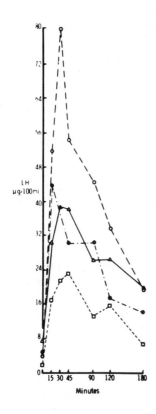

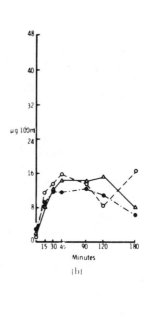

Luteinizing hormone response to LHRH: (a) <25% weight loss: (b) >25% weight loss (from Jeuniewic et al., 1978, reprinted with permission)

Figure 2

LHRH (Palmer et al., 1975). The reason for this is not clear. Changes in hormone clearance and/or catabolism may be responsible. Hyperresponsiveness to LHRH has been reported in other situations, e.g., children as they enter puberty (Roth, Kelch, Kaplan and Grumbach, 1972) and other types of secondary amenorrhea (Yen, Rebar, Vanderberg and Judd, 1973).

The repeated administration of LHRH will cause a return of the LH response toward normal (Sherman and Halmi, 1977). The pretreatment LHRH response in anorexia nervosa with minimal LH responses and normal FSH responses is comparable to that of a normal prepubertal child (Nillius and Wide, 1977). Repeated treatment with LHRH in patients with anorexia nervosa can restore normal ovarian steroid secretion and a normal ovarian cycle with follicular growth and maturation, ovulation, and corpus luteum formation (Nillius and Wide, 1977). During repeated LHRH therapy, there is a progressive increase in the LH response to LHRH together with a progressive decrease in the FSH response, with the prepubertal-like response pattern reverting to normal (Nillius and Wide, 1977). The results from treatment with prolonged LHRH strongly support the concept of a deficiency of endogenous LHRH secretion in low weight anorexia nervosa patients. In addition to alterations in the total response of gonadotropins to LHRH, some investigators have emphasized a delay in the time course of response of plasma LH and FSH to LHRH (Vigersky and Loriaux, 1977). Beumont et al. (1978) have studied the response to a four-hour infusion of LHRH rather than a single bolus as done in previous studies. In patients below 70% of average weight, maximal responses occurred only in the first hour, while in those with a higher weight the response was biphasic and maximal levels were achieved in the fourth hour (Beumont et al., 1978). This delay appears to be related to weight loss, since a similar delay is also found in patients with weight loss and secondary amenorrhea who do not have anorexia nervosa (Vigersky, Andersen, Thompson and Loriaux, 1977).

As for the LHRH results, data obtained from responses to clomiphene citrate suggest that the dysfunction is at the level of the hypothalamus. Clomiphene acts by blocking the negative feedback of estrogen on hypothalamic releasing factors; the LH response to clomiphene is impaired in anorexia nervosa. Clomiphene is effective in releasing LH only in those patients who have regained weight (Figure 3a and 3b) (Beumont, et al., 1973; Brown et al., 1977; Jeuniewic et al., 1978; Marshall and Fraser, 1971). After clomiphene, the occurence of menstruation has been unpredictable. Marshall and Fraser (1971) described four patients with their weight restored who had been amenorrehic but all menstruated following clomiphene. However, only two of these patients continued to have regular menses. Beumont et al. (1973) reported that five of six patients with LH responses to clomiphene menstruated between days 21 and 25 of treatment; two later menstruated spontaneously, but then these were not maintained in spite of weight maintenance. Jeuniewic et al. (1978) reported that two of four patients with LH responses to clomiphene menstruated regularly.

The regulation of normal menstruation depends upon an intact hypothalamic-pituitary gonadal axis. The cyclic pattern of pituitary gonadotropin release is determined in large part by the complex negative and positive feedback effects of the gonadal steroids, particularly estrogen, on the hypothalamic-pituitary unit (Jaffe and Keye, 1974; Kastin, Gual and

Schally, 1972; Wang and Yen, 1975). Estrogen levels in anorexia nervosa are very low when patients are underweight and gradually rise after weight restoration (Russell, Loraine, Bell and Harkness, 1965; Russell and Beardwood, 1968). Knobil, Dierschk, Yamaji, Hotchkiss and Weick (1972) have shown that the negative and positive effects of estrogen on gonadotropin release can be demonstrated experimentally by the administration of estro-

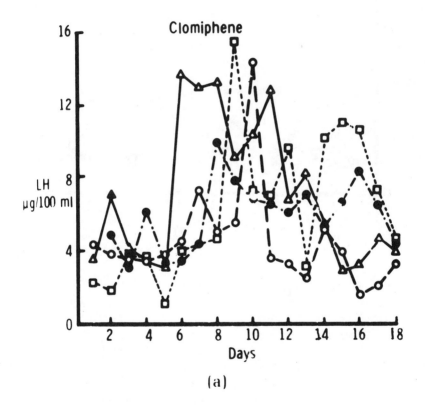

(a)

Luteinizing hormone response to clomiphene citrate: (a) ≤25% weight loss; (b) >25% weight loss. (from Jeuniewic et al., 1978, reprinted with permission)

Figure 3A

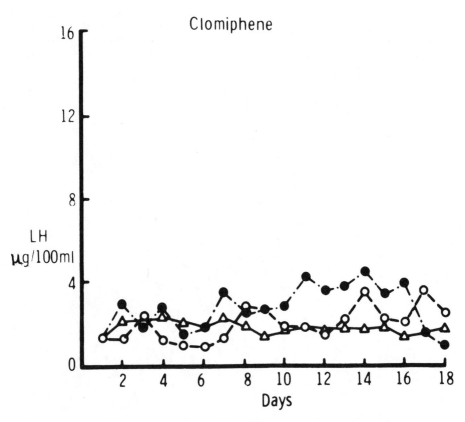

Figure 3B

gen during the follicular phase of the menstrual cycle. This, therefore, may be used as a tool for assessing the gonadotropin-releasing function of the complete hypothalamic-pituitary axis. Wakeling et al. (1977b) found that, in contrast to normal women, patients with anorexia nervosa failed to show feedback effects on LH after estrogen administration and prior to weight gain. Following weight restoration, there was an increase in LH resting levels to normal, and negative feedback effects of estrogen were then apparent. The positive feedback effects of estrogen, however, remained impaired in the majority of patients. Although the ability to respond to the positive feedback effect was delayed and more impaired than the negative feedback response, it was clearly weight-related.

Taken together, the above findings suggest that in recovery from anorexia nervosa, there is a return of hypothalamic-pituitary-gonadal activity in a definite sequence which recapitulates puberty (Donovan and Van Der Werfften Bosch, 1965). With marked weight loss there is amenorrhea associated with low circulating levels of gonadotropins and estrogens. At this time LH responses to LHRH are absent and FSH responses are reduced. With weight gain, the basal levels of LH and FSH rise and FSH responses to LHRH increase, in some cases in an exaggerated manner. With continued weight gain, responses normalize so that LH responses to LHRH increase, while FSH responses decrease. At about this time, the hypothalamus begins to respond normally to negative feedback effects of estrogen; subsequently, the capacity of the hypothalamus to respond to the positive feedback effects of estrogen returns. Clomiphene responses are also normalized. In some patients, however, return of menstruation is further delayed and occasionally may not occur even when normal weight is regained.

*Growth Hormone*

A number of investigators have reported that resting growth hormone (GH) levels are elevated in some patients with anorexia nervosa (Brown et al., 1977; Casper, Davis and Pandey, 1977; Frankel and Jenkins, 1975; Garfinkel et al., 1975; Landon, Greenwood, Stamp, and Wynn, 1966; Rappaport, Prevot and Czernichow, 1978). With recovery, plasma GH levels are normalized (Figure 4) (Brown et al., 1977; Frankel and Jenkins, 1975; Garfinkel et al., 1975). This fall in GH levels occurs prior to weight gain and is unrelated to body weight. Rather, it is more closely tied to the patient's caloric intake (Garfinkel et al., 1975). Changes in plasma LH and in plasma GH are therefore related to two different factors; plasma LH changes are related to loss of body weight and are reversed by an increase in body weight, while GH levels are altered by caloric intake. Elevated basal levels of GH are found in a variety of states in which there is decreased food intake, including protein-calorie malnutrition, kwashiorkor and marasmus (Pimstone, Becker and Hansen, 1973). In kwashiorkor, normalization of GH occurs after protein but not after carbohydrate refeeding. This observation, taken together with the lack of relationship of GH levels to the degree of weight loss or to the duration of amenorrhea (Brown et al., 1977) and the findings that GH levels in anorexics are elevated only in those with poor caloric intake, strongly supports the contention that the elevation in GH is secondary to starvation.

Following a glucose load, patients with elevated resting GH levels have been reported to show a drop in GH (Frankel and Jenkins, 1975; Garfinkel et al., 1975; Sherman and Halmi, 1977); however, a paradoxical rise following oral glucose has also been recorded (Alvarez, Dimas, Castro, Rossman, VanderLaan and VanderLaan, 1972; VanderLaan, Parker, Rossman and

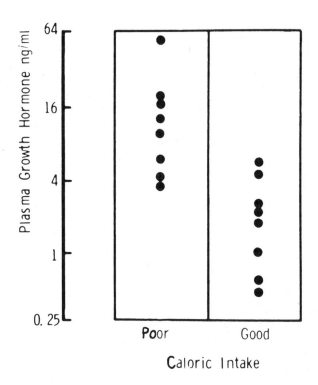

From Brown et al. (1977), reprinted with permission

Figure 4

VanderLaan, 1970). The reason for this discrepancy is not clear but may be related to the type of glucose solution used (Casper et al., 1977; Garfinkel et al., 1975). This paradoxical rise in GH does not occur after nutritional intake improves (Casper et al., 1977). Harrower, Yap, Nairn, Walton, Strong and Craig (1977) described that in anorexia nervosa as well as in acromegaly, bromocriptine reduces the raised GH concentrations that occur during an oral glucose tolerance test. A reduced growth hormone response to apomorphine has also been found in anorexia nervosa (Casper et al., 1977; Sherman and Halmi, 1977); this response returns to normal following weight restoration (Casper et al., 1977). However, the flattened response to L-dopa seen in anorexia nervosa may not revert to normal following weight gain (Sherman and Halmi, 1977). The GH response to insulin has also been described as attenuated in anorexia nervosa (Brauman and Gregoire, 1975; Devlin, 1975). On the other hand, normal GH responses to arginine have been reported (Neri, Ambrosi, Beck-Peccoz, Travaglini and Faglia, 1972; Sizonenko, Rabinovitch, Schneider, Paunier, Wollheim and Zhand, (1975).

In normal subjects, GH secretion is unaltered by the administration of thyrotropin releasing hormone (TRH), while in anorexia nervosa a prompt release of GH usually occurs (Gold, Pottash, Sweeney, Martin and Davies, 1980; Maeda, Kato, Yamaguchi, Chihara, Ohga, Iwasaki, Yoshimoto, Moridera, Kuromaru and Imura, 1976). This response, however, is not specific to anorexia nervosa. It has also been reported in acromegaly (Faglia, Beck-Peccoz, Ferrari, Travaglini, Ambrosi, and Spada, 1973) and depression (Maeda, Kato, Ohgo, Chihara, Yoshimoto, Yamaguchi, Kuromaru and Imura, 1975). A normal rise of GH has been reported during sleep in anorexia nervosa (Vigersky and Loriaux, 1977).

The data on GH in anorexia nervosa suggest that the raised basal levels are related directly to starvation. However, GH responses to provocative tests have been variable. Reasons for this are not clear, but may reflect studies of patients at various phases of the disorder or the clinical heterogeneity of patients, for example, with regard to bulimia. This area requires further investigation.

### PITUITARY-THYROID FUNCTION

Thyroxine (T4) levels in anorexia nervosa are usually within the normal range (Brown et al., 1977; Lundberg, Walinder, Werner and Wide, 1972) but may also be lower than normal (Miyai, Yamamoto, Azukizawa, Ishibashi and Kumahara, 1975; Wakeling, DeSouza, Gore, Sabur, Kingstone and Boss, 1979). While normal values are frequently obtained, they are usually at the low end of the normal scale (Hurd et al., 1977). Wakeling et al. (1979) did not find a rise in T4 levels after four-to-six weeks of weight gain. A correlation of resting T4 and cortisol levels has been noted (Brown et al., 1977). Thyroxine binding protein, as assessed by T3 resin uptake, is also normal (Brown et al., 1977).

Serum triiodothyronine (T3) levels are reduced in anorexia nervosa (Burman, Vigersky, Loriaux, Strum, Djuh, Wright and Wartofsky, 1977; Croxson and Ibbertson, 1977; Hurd et al., 1977; Miyai et al., 1975; Moshang and Utiger, 1977). This decrease in T3 is associated with an increase in the inactive reverse form of T3 (Burman et al., 1977). Absolute levels of T3 are linearly correlated with weight expressed as a percentage of ideal weight and both reduced T3 and elevated reverse T3 are normalized by weight gain (Leslie, Isaacs, Gomez, Raggatt and Bayliss, 1978; Wakeling et al., 1979). The identical alteration is seen in other forms of starvation (Vagenakis, 1977). Reversible changes in the levels of thyroid hormones occur with acute starvation and caloric deprivation (Chopra and Smith, 1975; Vagenakis, 1977) and with carbohydrate restriction (Spaulding, Chopra, Sherwin and Lyall, 1976). Moreover, Spaulding et al. (1976) have suggested that dietary carbohydrate is an important regulatory factor of T3 production. The alteration in T3 and reverse T3 is clearly related to fasting itself, as it also occurs in obese subjects during fasting (Vagenakis, Burger, Portnay, Rudolph, O'Brian, Azizi, Arky, Nicod, Ingbar and Braverman, 1975). Moshang and Utiger (1977) have proposed a teleological explanation for the low T3 and increased reverse T3 in states of starvation. They suggest that the target cells for thyroid hormones have regulatory mechanisms based upon metabolic needs. If conversion of T4 and T3 at the cellular level is regulated by need, then deprivation of calories would alter cellular mechanisms involved in the control of deiodination of T4. This would reduce production of T3 and increase reverse T3, which is a much less calorigenic hormone. If these mechanisms also exist within the pituitary, the pituitary thyrotroph might not interpret low levels of T3 as being insufficient for metabolic needs and TSH levels would not increase. Consistent with this interpretation, Gardner, Kaplan, Stanley and Utiger (1979) have recently reported that fasting is associated with a lower set point of the pituitary thyrotrophs.

Resting levels of thyrotropin (TSH) appear to be within normal limits (Beumont et al., 1976; Brown et al., 1977; Leslie et al., 1978; Lundberg et al., 1972; Moshang and Utiger, 1977; Vigersky and Loriaux, 1977; Wakeling et al., 1979), although there is one report that TSH is increased in anorexia nervosa (Aro, Lamberg and Pelkonen, 1975) and Hurd et al. (1977) found mean TSH levels to be less than the mean for control subjects. Wakeling et al. (1979) have recently shown that TSH levels are not related to body weight. Normal TSH levels demonstrate that the thyroid changes are not due to a primary failure of the thyroid gland.

Thyrotropin responses to thyrotropin releasing hormone (TRH) are of normal magnitude in anorexia nervosa (Beumont et al., 1976; Brown et al., 1977; Lundberg et al., 1972; Moshang, Parks, Baker, Vaidya and Utiger, 1975), thus again demonstrating that the pituitary is intact. As in normal subjects, the response correlates with the resting TSH level (Brown et al., 1977). The maximal response to TRH has also been correlated with body weight (Wakeling et al., 1979). A delay in the TSH response to TRH with normal magnitude has been noted by several investigators (Aro et al., 1975; Lundberg et al., 1972; Miyai et al., 1975; Vigersky and Loriaux, 1977; Wakeling et al., 1979). The delayed response occurs with simple weight loss (Vigersky et al., 1977) and returns to normal after weight gain (Leslie et al., 1978). Delayed thyrotropin responses to TRH have been suggested to indicate hypothalamic dysfunction or altered TSH clearance (Faglia, Beck-Peccoz, Ferrari, Ambrosi, Spada, Travaglini and Parocchi, 1973; Hall, Ormston, Besser, Cryer and McKendrick, 1972). The increase in serum T3 which normally follows TRH administration is not diminished (Burman et al., 1977).

Low values of T3 and T4, together with normal TSH concentrations, have been shown to occur in euthyroid patients with a variety of chronic illnesses (Carter, Corcoran, Eastman and Lazarus, 1974). In anorexia nervosa the changes in the hypothalamic-pituitary-thyroid axis are likely to occur as an adaptation to chronic illness and starvation, and are unlikely to be causally associated with the amenorrhea. Since these thyroid changes represent an adaptation to starvation, administration of thyroid hormone to correct these changes has no place in the management of anorexia nervosa.

## Pituitary-Adrenal Regulation

Morning plasma cortisol levels have generally been found to be elevated in most patients with anorexia nervosa (Alvarez et al., 1972; Brown et al., 1977; Casper, Chatterton and Davis, 1979; Hurd et al., 1977; Landon et al., 1966; Marks, Howorth and Greenwood, 1965; Swigar, Kolakowska and Quinlan, 1979; VanderLaan et al., 1970), although normal levels have also been reported (Vigersky and Loriaux, 1977). A correlation between resting plasma morning cortisol and plasma thyroxine has been reported. This may be related to alterations in binding globulins (Brown et al., 1977). Although the binding globulins for thyroxine and cortisol are not identical, it is likely that factors that affect one globulin could also affect another, resulting in similar changes in both hormones. Cortisol-binding globulin (CBG) capacities have been found to be normal (Boyar, Hellman, Roffwarg, Katz, Zumoff, O'Connor, Bradlow and Fukushima, 1977; Casper et al., 1979) and the apparent affinity constant of CBG for cortisol reduced (Casper et al., 1979). These tended toward normal after partial weight restoration but were not completely normalized (Casper et al., 1979). A decrease in cortisol-binding in serum has previously been demonstrated in kwashiorkor (Leonard, 1973).

The diurnal variation of plasma cortisol is flattened (Boyar and Katz, 1977; Garfinkel et al., 1975; Vigersky and Loriaux, 1977). Boyar et al. (1977) and Casper et al. (1979) found that the circadian rhythm for cortisol was preserved, but at a much higher level than that of normal controls. The absolute cortisol production rate (CPR) has been reported to be normal (Boyar et al., 1977), but is increased if cortisol production is calculated relative to body size (Walsh, Katz, Levin, Kream, Fukushima, Hellman,

Weiner ad Zumoff, 1978). There is indirect evidence that CPR is normally proportional to body size (Walsh et al., 1978) and therefore, in comparing the CPRs of emaciated patients to those of normal weight controls, it may be appropriate to express the CPR relative to body size. These results show an increased rate in cortisol secretion in anorexia nervosa. Twenty-four hour excretion of urinary-free cortisol is also increased in anorexia nervosa (Boyar et al., 1977; Walsh et al., 1978). The metabolic clearance rate of cortisol is significantly decreased and there is also a marked prolongation of the cortisol half-life (Boyar et al., 1977). These results are consistent with a moderate impairment of cortisol metabolism.

Studies relying on urinary steroid excretion have generally found that 17 ketosteroids are low (Danowski, Livstone, Gonzales, Jung and Khurana, 1972; Emanuel, 1956; Garfinkel et al., 1975; Seidensticker and Tzagournis, 1968; Warren and Vande Wiele, 1973), but 17-hydroxy and 17-ketosteroids have also been reported as normal (Bethge, Nagel, Solbach, Wiegelmann and Zimmerman, 1970). While responsiveness to dexamethasone may be normal (Warren and Vande Wiele, 1973), many patients display an incomplete failure of cortisol suppression (Danowski et al., 1972; Gerner and Gwirtsman, 1981; Walsh et al., 1978). Doerr, Fichter, Pirke and Lund (1980) reported that almost all patients with emaciation showed a failure of suppression or an early escape from suppression. This reverted to normal after weight gain. ACTH stimulation tests generally result in normal to hyperreactive adrenal responses (Danowski et al., 1972; Warren and Vande Wiele, 1973).

Response to metapyrone has been reported on small numbers of patients. These have been generally normal (Danowski et al., 1972; Warren and Vande Wiele, 1973) but Vanluchene, Aertsens and Vanderkerckhove (1979) found that, while quantitatively normal, the metapyrone response was delayed. Several possibilities may account for these observations. On the one hand, the observed impairment of cortisol metabolism may be responsible for these changes. For example, with cortisol synthesis blocked by metapyrone or dexamethasone, plasma levels will decrease more slowly because of the lowered metabolic clearance rate. Another possibility to explain the persistence of normal absolute rates of cortisol production in the face of elevated plasma cortisol levels, the increased urinary-free cortisol excretion, and the inconsistent responses to suppression/stimulation tests is that the hypothalamic-pituitary mechanisms regulating adrenal activity are less sensitive than normal to negative feedback from circulating corticosteroids (Walsh et al., 1978).

Several investigators (Boyar and Katz, 1977; Vanluchene et al., 1979) have found that emaciated anorexic patients have an increased excretion of the cortisol metabolite, tetrahydrocortisol relative to tetrahydrocortisone. These abnormalities are also found in patients with hypothyroidism (Boyar et al., 1977). As previously noted, starving anorexic patients show low T3, as do individuals with starvation from other causes. That these alternations in cortisol metabolism are likely related to the low levels of T3 has recently been demonstrated by Boyar et al. (1977) who administered T3 to anorexic patients and found that the cortisol abnormalities (both the cortisol half-life and the tetrahydrocortisol/tetrahydrocortisone ratio) were reversed.

Many of the changes in adrenal function seen in anorexia nervosa have also been described for starvation from other causes. For example, decreased urinary excretion of adrenal corticosteroids, diminished rates of cortisol metabolism, elevated levels of plasma cortisol and incomplete suppression by dexamethasone (Alleyne and Young, 1967; Rao, Srikantia, and Gopalan, 1968; Smith, Bledsoe and Chhetri, 1975) have all been described. However, unlike anorexia nervosa, in malnutrition, urinary-free cortisol is approximately normal and the cortisol production rate has been found to be reduced (Smith et al., 1975). It may be then that the elevation of cortisol production rate relative to body size and the increased urinary-free cortisol in anorexia nervosa indicate an increased activity of the hypothalamic-pituitary-adrenal system that is out of proportion to the emaciation. A variety of poorly understood factors, including the patient's emotional distress, increased physical activity and sleep disturbance, may account for these alterations in the hypothalamic-pituitary-adrenal axis.

*Prolactin*

Hyperprolactinemia is a common cause of secondary amenorrhea (Bohnet, Dahlen, Wuttke, and Schneider, 1976; Franks, Murray, Jequier, Steele, Nabarro, and Jacobs, 1975) and therefore studies have been directed to examining whether abnormal prolactin secretion plays a role in the amenorrhea of anorexia nervosa. A series of studies have reported normal resting prolactin levels (Beumont, Friesen, Gelder and Kolakowska, 1974; Isaacs et al., 1980; Mecklenburg et al., 1974; Vigersky, Loriaux, Andersen, Mecklenburg and Vaitukaitis, 1976; Vigersky and Loriaux, 1977; Wakeling et al., 1979). In addition, Wakeling et al. (1979) clearly demonstrated that there is no relationship between basal prolactin and body weight in anorexia nervosa. Similarly, there is no relationship between prolactin levels and those of the gonadotropins or estradiol (Wakeling et al., 1979). Chlorpromazine and other dopamine receptor-blockers are known to normally stimulate prolactin secretion (Beumont et al., 1974); Hafner, Crisp and McNeilly (1976) have shown that anorexic patients display a normal prolactin response to chlorpromazine. Moreover, TRH stimulation tests have resulted in reduced responses which altered with weight gain (Isaacs et al., 1980), normal increments in prolactin but a delayed response (Vigersky and Loriaux, 1977) and totally normal responses, not influenced by weight (Wakeling et al., 1979).

Normally in adults, plasma prolactin levels rise shortly after the onset of sleep at night. This is generally followed by a series of even larger secretory episodes resulting in progressively higher plasma concentrations during the night, with peak values occurring during the end of the sleep period (Weitzman, 1976). Kalucy, Crisp, Chard, McNeilly, Chen and Lacey (1976) found anorexic subjects to have low nocturnal prolactin levels. This absence of a sleep-induced rise in prolactin has been confirmed by Brown et al. (1979) and Tolis, Woods and Guyda (1979). Since TRH can normally stimulate prolactin in these patients, this suggests that the cause of the decreased prolactin secretion during sleep is of suprahypophyseal origin. This pattern of prolactin secretion may be due to dietary intake, since Hill and Wynder (1976) found that changing four healthy nonobese nurses from a western diet to a vegetarian diet resulted in a reduction in nocturnal release of prolactin.

The data available on prolactin in anorexia nervosa strongly suggest that basal prolactin secretion is essentially normal, and that prolactin responds to provocative tests normally. It is unlikely, therefore, that prolactin plays a role in the amenorrhea of these individuals. The failure of patients to resume menstruation and cyclical output of gonadotropins after weight restoration is clearly not associated with high circulating prolactin. The one consistent prolactin abnormality, low nocturnal levels, is likely to be the result of inadequate dietary intake.

*Melatonin*

Melatonin may be of interest in anorexia nervosa for two reasons: 1) It has a clearly defined diurnal rhythm and this may become altered as are LH and prolactin rhythms; and 2) it is known to influence the reproductive hormones. Clear-cut antigonadal and progonadal effects of the pineal have been demonstrated in the hamster (Hoffmann, 1973; Turek, Desjardins and Menaker, 1976; Orts, Kocan and Wilson, 1975; Reiter, Vaughan and Blask, 1974). In the adult human female, a relationship between melatonin and the gonadotropins has been reported. Morning melatonin levels fluctuate through the menstrual cycle, being highest early in the follicular phase and late in the progestational phase (Wetterberg, Arendt, Paunier, Sizonenko Van Donselaar and Heyden, 1976). A marked 24-hour rhythm in blood melatonin exists in adult humans, with levels higher at nighttime than in the day (Vaughan, Pelham, Pang, Loughlin, Wilson, Sandock, Vaughan, Koslow and Reiter, 1976). Jimerson, Lynch, Post, Wurtman and Bunney (1977) have shown that this melatonin rhythm is preserved in patients with affective disorder, even when undergoing one night's sleep deprivation in constant light. Their data seem to indicate a close link between melatonin rhythms and a relatively stable circadian clock. Recently Brown et al. (1979) assessed the circadian rhythm of melatonin secretion in five emaciated subjects with primary anorexia nervosa and a sixth with both anorexia nervosa and Turner's syndrome. All subjects showed a nocturnal rise in melatonin. By contrast, three of these subjects showed flattened nocturnal prolactin levels and all five primary anorexics displayed an immature circadian LH pattern.

*Testosterone*

Males with anorexia nervosa, especially of the restricting type, show complete impotence and absence of sexual activity and interest. Males with the bulimic variety are usually also impotent (Crisp, 1978). Following weight restoration there is a gradual return of normal sexual activity.

Reduced urinary testosterone in male patients (Beumont, 1970; Davidson, 1976; Frankel and Jenkins, 1975; Garfinkel et al., 1975; Ismail and Harkness, 1967), normal serum levels in females (Casper et al., 1979), and elevated serum levels (Baranowska and Zgliczynski, 1979) have been described. Both abnormalities tend to return to normal with weight restoration. In anorexia nervosa, the ratio of 5-alpha-reductase activity to 5-beta-reductase activity is significantly reduced such that the urinary metabolites of testosterone exhibit a preponderance of etiocholanolone at the expense of androsterone (Boyar and Bradlow, 1977). A similar alteration is seen in hypothyroidism; that the thyroid abnormality is responsible for the changes in androgen metabolism is evident from Boyar et al.'s (1977) work. This involves administration of exogenous T3 and noting a reversal of these changes.

*Carbohydrate Metabolism*

The presence of fasting hypoglycemia varies considerably, for example, from Mecklenburg et al.'s (1974) report in 100% of their patients to Vigersky et al.'s (1976) in 56%. Severe hypoglycemia, however, is uncommon. In response to a glucose load, anorexics who are starved display either a "flat" curve or a hyperglycemic response. This normalizes with proper nutrition.

A response similar to the anorexics can be seen after five days of carbohydrate deprivation in normal subjects (Hales and Randle, 1963) and also in obese subjects starved for 14 days (Beck, Koumans, Winterling, Stein, Daughaday and Kipnis, 1964). Similar curves are seen in individuals with chronic wasting diseases (Alvarez et al., 1972). Russell and Bruce (1964) have shown this impaired glucose tolerance in anorexia nervosa to be readily reversed by refeeding.

Fasting insulin levels have been reported to be both elevated and lowered in anorexia nervosa and the insulin response to a glucose load may be sustained (Crisp, Ellis and Lowy, 1967; Kanis et al., 1974; Vigersky et al., 1976; Wachslicht-Rodbard, Gross, Rodbard, Ebert and Roth, 1979). There is also an increase in insulin binding to erythrocytes which reverts to normal on refeeding (Wachslicht-Rodbard et al., 1979). The insulin resistance has been found to correlate with the severity of the weight loss (Vigersky et al., 1976). Similarly, insulin resistance has been reported in carbohydrate deprivation (Hales and Randle, 1963), in starvation (Unger, Eisentraut and Madison, 1963) and in starvation of obese individuals (Beck et al., 1964). Mecklenburg et al. (1974) by contrast reported insulin sensitivity in anorexia nervosa.

The insulin resistance in anorexia nervosa has been shown to persist after weight restoration and resumption of menses in spite of normalization of the impaired glucose tolerance curve (Crisp, 1968; Kanis et al., 1974). This has been the basis for suggesting an inherent insulin resistance in anorexia nervosa (Crisp et al., 1967; Kanis et al., 1974); however, it is important to note that Hales and Randle (1963) found a sustained insulin response in normal subjects for 14-35 days after carbohydrate deprivation. The occasionally high insulin levels, insulin resistance, and hypoglycemia seen in anorexia nervosa all suggest that insulin is not a useful treatment for anorexia nervosa.

*Thermoregulation*

Failure of individuals to respond normally to acute hypo- or hyperthermia has been described as constituting evidence for hypothalamic dysfunction (Mecklenburg et al., 1974) and is not related to amount of adipose tissue (Vigersky et al., 1977). There is a reduced basal temperature in anorexic patients (Wakeling and Russell, 1970). Normally, the response to acute hypothermia consists of an initial ("paradoxical") rise in core temperature due to peripheral vasoconstriction followed by shivering and then restabilization at basal temperature. Vigersky et al. (1976) reported that 69% of their anorexic patients did not display this paradoxical rise in temperature and none had observable shivering. Mecklenburg et al. (1974) demonstrated the paradoxical rise but none of their patients shivered in response to cold. The severity of this cold intolerance has been correlated with the degree of weight loss (Vigersky et al., 1976).

Normal individuals react to a heat stimulus with an initial ("paradoxical") fall in core temperature. This is due to increased heat loss, achieved by peripheral vasodilatation, stimulated by the induced increase in central temperature. Anorexic subjects generally do not display the paradoxical fall in core temperature and have been reported to show both an excess rise in core temperature in response to heat (Vigersky et al., 1976) and a significant delay in vasodilatation (Wakeling and Russell, 1970). Luck and Wakeling (1980) have recently found that the onset of vasodilatation and thermal sweating may occur at lower core and skin temperature in anorexics than in normal weight controls. Also anorexics were found to respond to a high calorie meal with an increase in core temperature and peripheral blood flow, unlike normals. Some of the responses to heat have been demonstrated to return to normal after weight gain (Wakeling and Russell, 1970) and the severity of the heat tolerance is significantly correlated with degree of weight loss (Vigersky et al., 1976). Moreover, Vigersky et al. (1977) have demonstrated abnormal thermoregulation in individuals with amenorrhea and simple weight loss without anorexia nervosa.

## Water Conservation (Vasopressin)

Several investigators have demonstrated that a significant proportion of anorexics display impaired ADH secretion as inferred from failure to concentrate their urine maximally (Mecklenburg et al., 1974; Russell, 1965; Russell and Bruce, 1966; Vigersky et al., 1976). Vigersky et al. (1976) found that abnormalities in water conservation were closely linked with those of thermoregulation. As for the abnormal thermoregulatory response, Vigersky et al. (1977) have observed partial diabetes insipidus in individuals with amenorrhea and simple weight loss without anorexia nervosa.

Recently investigators from the National Institute of Mental Health have measured arginine vasopressin (AVP) in both plasma and CSF (Gold, Kaye, Robertson, Goodwin and Ebert, 1980; Kaye, Ebert and Lake, 1980). They have reported an increase in the CSF to plasma ratio of AVP in anorexics, due to elevated CSF levels. These levels were further increased immediately on weight restoration. These findings may reflect alterations in catecholamine metabolism or they may be due to the fact that their weight-recovered patients were inducing vomiting: emesis is a potent stimulator of AVP.

*Hypothalamic Tumors Producing an Anorexia Nervosa-like Clinical State*

There is ample evidence from both humans and animals to document the fact that the hypothalamus is involved in regulation of eating and weight (Garfinkel and Coscina, 1982). Exactly how the hypothalamus organizes and integrates somatic sensory and environmental factors to regulate food intake is not known. Many factors are involved in this regulation and their significance is only partially understood. The hypothalamus and its closely connected limbic areas contain specific receptors controlling feeding. Some have suggested that a central receptor for lipid stores controls long-term changes in body weight and that CSF insulin levels may be involved in the regulation of these (Woods and Porte, 1975). Mayer has suggested that the known central glucoreceptors may be involved in regulating short-term food intake (Mayer, 1955) while others postulate that hepatic glucoreceptors, hypothalamic insulin or hepatic glycogen may be involved (Cahill, Aoki and Rossini, 1979; Debons, Krimsky and From, 1970; Russek, 1975). Recently the study of gastric and intestinal hormones has been pursued to determine their role in modulating satiety (Panksepp, Bishop and Rossi, 1979). The function of plasma amino acids in the regulation of intake has also become a new area of focus (Anderson, 1979). This topic has recently been reviewed by Garfinkel and Coscina (1982).

While a variety of somatic sensory stimuli modulate hunger and satiety, their integration occurs within the hypothalamus and its related areas. Traditionally, specific hypothalamic regions have been thought to be involved in the regulation of hunger and satiety. Thus, the ventromedial nuclear region of the hypothalamus has been termed the "satiety center" since lesions in this region in animals usually produce immediate hyperphagia and weight gain with the degree of gain proportional to the size of the lesion (Hoebel and Teitelbaum, 1966). On the other hand, stimulation of the lateral hypothalamus in animals induces feeding behavior and lesions in this area result in a temporary severe aphagia with slow partial recovery (Teitelbaum and Epstein, 1962). Because of these findings the lateral hypothalamus has traditionally been considered the "feeding center."

More recently, the notion that these discrete centers govern food intake has been partially modified to suggest that other tracts and areas may be as important (Panksepp, 1971). Recent observations have revealed that both hunger and satiety are substantially influenced by the functional states of neurochemically differing brain amine systems which are not exclusively located in the ventromedial or lateral hypothalamus. For example, many of the behavioral features historically labeled as the "lateral hypothalamic syndrome" can be ascribed to disruption of dopamine neurones which traverse the nigro-neostriatal pathway via the lateral hypothalamic area (Stricker and Zigmond, 1975; Ungerstedt, 1971). At the same time, damage to specific components of brain norepinephrine and/or serotonin systems may account for portions of the classic ventromedial hypothalamic syndrome (Coscina, 1977; Coscina and Stancer, 1977; Gold, 1973; Hoebel, 1976).

In view of the hypothalamic involvement in the regulation of eating behavior and weight, it is not surprising that both obesity and emaciation may be caused by a variety of lesions affecting the hypothalamus. However, the syndromes that have been described following hypothalamic damage generally, but not uniformly, do not correspond with typical anorexia nervosa. The vast majority of anorexics have no demonstrable anatomic hypothalamic abnormalities. Some patients, diagnosed in the literature as having anorexia nervosa, were later discovered to have hypothalamic tumors but the clinical picture differed from true anorexia nervosa. Thus, patients have been described as "anorexic" with emaciation in infancy (Kagan, 1958; Udvarhelyi et al., 1966) or in middle age following a prolonged psychosis (White and Hain, 1959) with none of the typical features necessary for the diagnosis. For example, Goldney (1978) reported on a 28-year-old woman with weight loss and "hysterical blindness" who was later found to have a craniopharyngioma. Although she had been diagnosed as having anorexia nervosa, she lacked a drive for thinness, a desire for self-starvation, hyperactivity, and other relevant clinical features.

On the other hand, there have been several case reports of patients with what appears to be typical anorexia nervosa, and later hypothalamic tumors have been discovered (Beeley, Daly, Timperley and Warner, 1973; Heron and Johnston, 1976; Lewin, Mattingly and Mills, 1972; Seidensticker and Tzagournis, 1968; Swann, 1977; White, Kelly and Dorman, 1977). These six case reports which have documented the definite coexistence of anorexia nervosa and hypothalamic tumor have represented a variety of pathologies (pinealoma, astrocytoma, glioma) and different locations, but in those where it was documented, sharing the involvement of the hypothalamus. While it is likely that these patients have had anorexic symptoms because of the destruction of neurones involved in regulation of eating, it is also quite feasible that this infrequent association is entirely due to chance.

## Monoamine Metabolism

The neurotransmitter monoamines (MA) are of interest in anorexia nervosa for several reasons: 1) they exert significant control over the release, or inhibition of release, of various neurohumors (Ettigi and Brown, 1977; Garfinkel, Brown, Warsh and Stancer, 1979); and 2) they exert significant regulatory control over eating behaviors as described briefly in the preceding section. Several investigators (Barry and Klawans, 1976; Mawson, 1974; Redmond, Swann and Heninger, 1976) have recently implicated abnormalities in MA function in the pathophysiology of anorexia nervosa. However, it must be stressed that the evidence for this is indirect and the speculations have been varied. Mawson (1974) suggested that the basis for anorexia nervosa may lie in a progressive depletion of subcortical brain norepinephrine and/or dopamine and that treatments which increase levels of these brain amines would be useful. He felt that ECT and chlorpromazine had proved useful because of their effects on these amines and further recommended L-dopa as a drug to correct the disorder. However, neither ECT nor chlorpromazine has actually been demonstrated to be superior to non-pharmacological therapies such as bedrest and high caloric diet, and both agents possess many other effects besides these on catecholamines. With regard to L-dopa, Johanson and Knorr (1977) also suggested a possible brain dopamine deficiency and therefore administered L-dopa to nine anorexic patients for up to four months. Five of the nine gained 3-6 kg and four failed to respond with significant weight gain. This brief uncontrolled study has methodological features which make its results questionable; still the findings are hardly supportive to a central dopamine deficiency. Redmond et al. (1976) focused on the abnormal satiety mechanism in anorexia nervosa and suggested that an increase in norepinephrine might be associated with this finding. In support of this, they described a single patient who was helped significantly by the adrenergic blocking agent phenoxybenzamine. Further investigation in this area is required.

In contrast, Barry and Klawans (1976) have postulated increased brain dopamine synthesis or receptor sensitivity in the production of many of the symptoms of anorexia nervosa. Again, the evidence for this is quite indirect. For example, amphetamine, which releases catecholamines at nerve endings, produces anorexia and hyperactivity (Baldessarini, 1972). Apomorphine is also a dopamine agonist and results in significantly reduced food intake which is reversed by dopamine receptor blockade (Barzaghi, Groppetti, Mantegazza and Muller, 1973). Chlorpromazine, a dopamine receptor blocker, results in weight gain. Barry and Klawans (1976) also linked the amenorrhea and decreased libido to a hyperdopaminergic state. Their hypothesis is based on indirect, largely psychopharmacological evidence.

There have been only a few direct evaluations of MA function in anorexic patients and those that are available have suffered from the methodological problems existing in other investigations in this field; in particular, the source of the measured amines (i.e., from the brain or the periphery) (Garfinkel, Warsh, Stancer and Sibony, 1976; Garfinkel, Warsh, Stancer and Godse, 1977), and the influence of diet, weight, and other factors must be taken into account, as well as the sensitivity and specificity of the methods used to measure the amines.

Halmi, Dekirmenjian, Davis, Casper and Goldberg (1978) have recently described reduced urinary 3, 4-methoxyhydroxyphenylglycol (MHPG) in anorexic patients; MHPG is an important end product of norepinephrine metabolism. They linked this finding to depressive symptomatology and reduced MHPG is not uncommon in bipolar depression (Garfinkel, Warsh and Stancer, 1979). However, their patients' MHPG levels increased with treatment so that it was not clear what effect reduced weight and low caloric intake play in this finding. Gerner and Gwirtsman (1981) also found reduced MHPG excretion in emaciated patients, but this was not related to depressed mood. Gross, Lake, Ebert, Ziegler and Kopin (1979) have confirmed this reduced urinary MHPG in emaciated anorexics but clearly documented its return to normal on weight gain. Urinary homovanillic acid, an index of dopamine metabolism, and plasma dopamine were similarly reduced only in the starvation state. Dopamine beta-hydroxylase was normal throughout. Darby, VanLoon, Garfinkel, Brown and Kirwan (1980) also found reduced plasma levels of dopamine and norepinephrine, which were weight-related (Figure 5).

Using the probenecid test, Kaye et al. (1980) reported reductions in both dopamine and serotonin turnover in emaciated anorexics. With weight restoration these tended to improve but CSF norepinephrine remained low, while patients were otherwise still symptomatic. Of importance, levels of neutral amino acids were normal even when patients were seriously underweight. Earlier, Yap, Hafkenscheid and van Tongeren (1975) had reported reduced plasma tryptophan and neutral amino acids in three patients. Plasma-free tryptophan, an important serotonin precursor, has been reported to be low in anorexia nervosa, even after weight gain (Coppen, Gupta, Eccleston, Wood, Wakeling and DeSousa, 1976), and we have also observed this but only in emaciated patients (Garfinkel and Warsh, unpublished). Also, possibly linked to MA abnormalities is the recent finding and characterization of a peptide in the urine of some anorexia nervosa patients which when injected into mice produced a reduction of food intake (Trygstad, Foss, Edminson, Johansen and Reichelt, 1978).

While reductions in plasma-free tryptophan and CSF, plasma, and urinary catecholamines have been documented, at present the mechanisms for these changes are not fully understood. In large measure they appear to

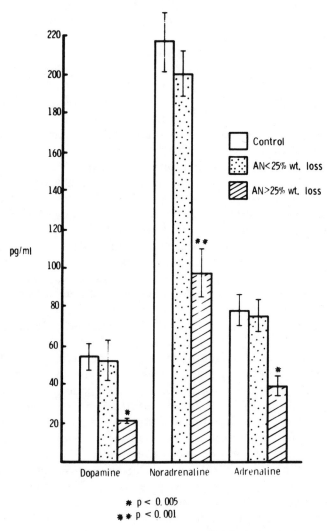

PLASMA CATECHOLAMINE LEVELS
IN ANOREXIA NERVOSA

* p < 0.005
** p < 0.001

from Darby et al., 1980,
reprinted with permission

Figure 5

be products of starvation. It is not yet known how these abnormalities relate to the changes in neuroendocrine secretion or anorexic symptoms.

## SUMMARY OF HYPOTHALAMIC-PITUITARY FUNCTION

There is considerable evidence to support the presence of disturbances in hypothalamic function in patients with anorexia nervosa. These occur through a variety of mechanisms and are generally reversible. Certain disturbances relate directly to the degree of weight loss. These include alterations in thermoregulation and water conservation, in TSH responses to TRH, in resting gonadotropin levels and LH responses to provocative tests. Other hypothalamic dysfunctions are secondary to caloric deprivation per se. These include alterations in resting plasma GH, plasma T3 and reverse T3 which all appear to be directly related to caloric intake. Some variations in adrenal steroid and testosterone metabolism reflect these thyroid changes. Many of these disturbances in hypothalamic function are therefore secondary either to weight loss or to caloric restriction. Others may in part reflect the emotional distress of the patient. The amenorrhea which may precede the weight loss may be partly related to this. The resumption of menses is largely, but not entirely, weight-related. Further studies are required to delineate the precise mechanisms underlying these findings. In addition, further investigations will help our understanding of the role of altered hypothalamic function in possibly contributing to the self-perpetuating nature of the syndrome.

## REFERENCES

Akande, E.O., Carr, P.J., Dutton, A., Bonnar, J., Corker, C.S. and Mackinnon, P.C.B.: Effect of synthetic gonadotrophin-releasing hormone in secondary amenorrhea. *Lancet,* 2:112-116, 1972.

Allbutt, T.C. and Rollesteon, H.D.: *A System of Medicine.* London: The Macmillan Company, 1910, p. 709.

Allison, R.S. and Davies, R.: The treatment of functional anorexia. *Lancet,* 1:902-907, 1931.

Alleyne, G.A. and Young, V.H.: Adrencocortical function in children with severe protein-calorie malnutrition. *Clin. Sci.,* 33:189-200, 1967.

Alvarez, L.C., Dimas, C.O., Castro, A., Rossman, L.G., VanderLaan, E.F., and VanderLaan, W.P.: Growth hormone in malnutrition. *J. Clin. Endocrinol. Metal.,* 43: 400-409, 1972.

Anderson, G.H.: Control of protein and energy intake: Role of plasma amino acids and brain neurotransmitters. *Can. J. Physiol. Pharmacol.,* 57:1043-1057, 1979.

Aro, A., Lamberg, B.A. and Pelkonen, R.: Letter: Dysfunction of the hypothalamic-pituitary axis in anorexia nervosa. *N. Engl. J. Med.,* 292:594-595, 1975.

Baldessarini, R.J.: Symposium: Behavior modification by drugs. I. Pharmacology of the amphetamines. *Pediatrics,* 49:694-701, 1972.

Baranowska, B and Zgliczynski, S.: Enhanced testosterone in female patients with anorexia nervosa: Its normalization after weight gain. *Acta Endocrinol.* (Copenh.), 90:328-335, 1979.

Barry, V.C. and Klawans, H.L.: On the role of dopamine in the pathophysiology of anorexia nervosa. *J. Neural. Transm.*, 38:107-122, 1976.

Barzaghi, F., Groppetti, A., Mantegazza, P. and Muller, E.F.: (Letter) Reduction of food intake by apomorphine: A pimozide-sensitive effect. *J. Pharm. Pharmacol.*, 25:909-911, 1973.

Bass, F.: L'amenorrhee au camp de concentration de Terezin. *Gynaecologica*, 123:211-213, 1947.

Beck, J.C. and Brochner-Mortensen, K.: Observations on the prognosis in anorexia nervosa. *Acta Med. Scand.*, 149:409-430, 1954.

Beck, P., Koumans, J.H.T., Winterling, C.A. Stein, M.H., Daughaday, W.H. and Kipnis, D.M.: Studies of insulin and growth hormone secretion in human obesity. *J. Lab. Clin. Med.*, 64:654-657, 1964.

Beeley, J.M., Daly, J.J., Timperley, W.R. and Warner, J.: Ectopic pinealoma: An unusual clinical presentation and a histochemical comparison with a seminoma of the testis. *J. Neurol. Neurosurg. Psychiatry*, 36:864-873, 1973.

Berkman, J.M.: Anorexia nervosa, anterior-pituitary insufficiency, Simmonds' cachexia and Sheehan's disease; including some observations in disturbances in water metabolism associated with starvation. *Postgrad. Med.*, 3:237-246, 1948.

Bethge, H., Nagel, A.M., Solbach, H.G., Wiegelmann, W. and Zimmerman, H.: Zentrale regulationsstorung der nebennierenrinden funkion bei der anorexia nervosa. *Mat. Med. Nordm.*, 22:204-214, 1970.

Beumont, P.J.V.: Anorexia nervosa: A review. *S. Afr. Med. J.*, 44:911-915, 1970.

Beumont, P.J.V., Abraham, S.F., Argall, W.J. and Turtle, J.R.: Plasma gonadotrophins and LHRH infusions in anorexia nervosa. *Aust. N.Z. J. Med.*, 8:509-514, 1978.

Beumont, P.J.V., Carr, P.J. and Gelder, M.G.: Plasma levels of luteinizing hormone and of immunoactive oestrogens (oetradiol) in anorexia nervosa: Response to clomiphene citrate. *Psychol Med.*, 3:495-501, 1973.

Beumont, P.J.V., Friesen, H.G., Gelder, M.G. and Kolakowska, T.: Plasma prolactin and luteinizing hormone levels in anorexia nervosa. *Psychol. Med.*, 4:219-221, 1974.

Beumont, P.J.V., George, G.C.W., Pimstone, B.L. and Vinik, A.I.: Body weight and the pituitary response to hypothalamic-releasing hormones in patients with anorexia nervosa. *J. Clin. Endocrinol. Metab.*, 43:487-496, 1976.

Bohnet, H.G., Dahlen, H.G., Wuttke, W. and Schneider, H.P.G.: Hyperprolactinemic anovulatory syndrome. *J. Clin. Endocrinol. Metab.*, 42:132-143, 1976.

Boyar, R.M. and Bradlow, H.L.: Studies of testosterone metabolism in anorexia nervosa. In: R. Vigersky (Ed.), Anorexia Nervosa. New York: Raven Press, 1977, pp. 271-276.

Boyar, R.M., Finkelstein, J.W., Roffwarg, H., Kapen, S., Weitzman, E.D. and Hellman, L.: Twenty-four-hour luteinizing hormone and follicle-stimulating hormone secretory patterns in gondal dysgenesis. *J. Clin. Endocrinol. Metab.*, 37:521-525, 1973.

Boyar, R.M., Hellman, L.D., Roffwarg, H., Katz, J., Zumoff, B., O'Connor, J., Bradlow, H.L. and Fukushima, D.K.: Cortisol secretion and metabolism in anorexia nervosa. *N. Engl. J. Med.*, 296:190-193, 1977.

Boyar, R.M. and Katz, J.: Twenty-four gonadotropin secretory patterns in anorexia nervosa. In: R. Vigersky (Ed.), *Anorexia Nervosa*. New York: Raven Press, 1977, pp. 177-187.

Boyar, R.M., Katz, J., Finkelstein, J.W., Kapen, S., Weiner, H., Weitzman, E.D. and Hellman, L.: Anorexia nervosa: Immaturity of the 24-hour luteinizing hormone secretory pattern. *N. Engl. J. Med.*, 291:861-865, 1974.

Brauman, H. and Gregoire, F.: The growth hormone response to insulin induced hypoglycaemia in anorexia nervosa and control underweight or normal subjects. *Eur. J. Clin. Invest.*, 5:289-295, 1975.

Brown, G.M., Garfinkel, P.E., Jeuniewic, N., Moldofsky, H. and Stancer, H.C.: Endocrine profiles in anorexia nervosa. In: R. Vigersky (Ed.), *Anorexia Nervosa*. New York: Raven Press, 1977, pp. 123-135.

Brown, G.M., Kirwan, P., Garfinkel, P. and Moldofsky, H.: Overnight patterning of prolactin and melatonin in anorexia nervosa. (Abstr.) 2nd International Symposium on Clinical Psycho-Neuro-Endocrinology in Reproduction. Venice, June, 1979.

Burman, K.D., Vigersky, R.A., Loriaux, D.L., Strum, D., Djuh, Y.Y., Wright, F.D. and Wartofsky, L.: Investigations concerning thyroxine deiodinative pathways in patients with anorexia nervosa. In: R. Vigersky (Ed.), *Anorexia Nervosa*. New York: Raven Press, 1977, pp. 255-262.

Cahill, G.F., Jr., Aoki, T.T. and Rossini, A.A.: Metabolism in obesity and anorexia nervosa. In R.J. Wurtman and J.J. Wurtman (Eds.), *Nutrition and the Brain*. New York: Raven Press, 1979, pp. 1-70.

Carter, J.N., Corcoran, J.M., Eastman, C.J. and Lazarus, L.: Effect of severe, chronic illness on thyroid function, *Lancet*, 2:971-974, 1974.

Casper, R.C., Chatterton, R.T. and Davis, J.M.: Alteration in serum cortisol and its binding characteristics in anorexia nervosa. *J. Clin. Endocrinol. Metab.*, 49:406-411, 1979.

Casper, R.C., Davis, J.M. and Pandey, C.N.: The effect of the nutritional status and weight changes on hypothalamic function tests in anorexia nervosa. In: R. Vigersky (Ed.), *Anorexia Nervosa*. New York: Raven Press, 1977, pp. 137-147.

Chopra, I.J., and Smith, S.R.: Circulating thyroid hormones and thyrotropin in adult patients with proten-calorie malnutrition. *J. Clin. Endocrinol. Metab.*, 40:221-227, 1975.

Coppen, A.M., Gupta, R.K., Eccleston, E.G., Wood, K.M., Wakeling, A. and DeSousa, V.F.A.: Letter: Plasma-tryptophan in anorexia nervosa. *Lancet*, 1:961, 1976.

Coscina, D.V.: Brain amines in hypothalamic obesity. In: R. Vigersky (Ed.), *Anorexia Nervosa*. New York: Raven Press, 1977, pp. 97-107.

Coscina, D.V. and Stancer, H.C.: Selective blockade of hypothalamic hyperphagia and obesity in rats by serotonin-depleting midbrain lesions. *Science*, 195:416-419, 1977.

Crisp, A.H.: Some aspects of the evolution presentation and follow-up of anorexia nervosa. *Proc. Roy. Soc. Med.*, 58:814-820, 1965.

Crisp, A.H.: Primary anorexia nervosa, *Gut*, 9:370-372, 1968.

Crisp, A.H.: Anorexia nervosa "feeding disorder," "nervous malnutrition" or "weight phobia"? *World Rev. Nutr. Diet*, 12:452-504, 1970.

Crisp, A.H.: Some psychobiological aspects of adolescent growth and their relevance for the fat/thin syndrome anorexia nervosa. *Int. J. Obes.*, 1:231-238, 1977.

Crisp, A.H.: Some aspects of the relationship between body weight and sexual behavior with particular reference to massive obesity and anorexia nervosa. *Int. J. Obes.*, 2:17-32, 1978.

Crisp, A.H., Ellis J., and Lowy, C.: Insulin response to a rapid intravenous injection of dextrose in patients with anorexia nervosa and obesity. *Postgrad. Med., J.*, 43:97-102, 1967.

Croxson, M.S. and Ibbertson, H.K.: Low serum triiodothyronine (T3) and hypothyroidism in anorexia nervosa. *J. Clin. Endocrinol. Metab.*, 44:167-174, 1977.

Dale, E., Gerlach, D.H., White, A.L.: Menstrual dysfunction in distance runners. *Obstet. Gynecol.*, 54:47-53, 1979.

Dally, P.: *Anorexia Nervosa*. New York: Grune and Stratton, 1969.

Danowski, T.S., Livstone, E., Gonzales, A.R., Jung, Y. and Khurana, R.C.: Fractional and partial hypopituitarism in anorexia nervosa. *Hormones*, 3:105-118, 1972.

Darby, P., VanLoon, G., Garfinkel, P.E., Brown, G.M. and Kirwan, P.: LH, growth hormone, prolactin and catecholamine responses to LHRF and bromocriptine in anorexia nervosa. Presented at the American Psychosomatic Society, New York, 1980.

Davidson, D.M.: Anorexia nervosa in a serviceman: Case report. *Military Medicine*, 617-619, Sept. 1976.

Debons, A.F., Krimsky, I. and From, A.: A direct action of insulin on the hypothalamic satiety center. *Amer. J. Physiol.*, 219:938-943, 1970.

De Carle, D.W.: Pregnancy associated with anorexia nervosa. Report of a case. *Surg. Clin. N. Am.*, 42:921-925, 1962.

Déjérine, J. and Gauckler, E.: *Les Manifestations Fonctionelles des Psychoneuroses*. Paris: Masson and Cie, 1911, p. 6.

Devlin, J.G.: Obesity and anorexia nervosa, a study of growth hormone release. *Ir. Med. J.,* 68:227-231, 1975.

Doerr, P., Fichter, M., Pirke, K.M. and Lund, R.: Relationship between weight gain and hypothalamic pituitary adrenal function in patients with anorexia nervosa (Abstr): Sixth International Congress of Endocrinology, Melbourne, 1980, p. 630.

Donovan, B.T. and Van Der Werfften Bosch, J.J.: Physiology of Puberty. Monographs of the Physiological Society. London: Edward Arnold, 1965.

Drew, F.L.: The epidemiology of secondary amenorrhea. *J. Chronic. Dis.,* 14:396-407, 1961.

Emanuel, R.W.: Endocrine activity in anorexia nervosa. *J. Clin. Endocrinol. Metab.,* 16:801-816, 1956.

Escamilla, R.F. and Lisser, H.: Testosterone therapy of eunuchoids. *J. Clin. Endocrinol.,* 1:633-642, 1941.

Ettigi, P.G. and Brown, G.M.: Psychoneuroendocrinology of affective disorders: An overview. *Am. J. Psychiatry,* 134:493-501, 1977.

Faglia, G.P., Beck-Peccoz, P., Ferrari, C. Ambrosi, B., Spada, A., Travaglini, P. and Parocchi, S.: Plasma thyrotropin-releasing hormone in patients with pituitary hypothalamic disorders. *J. Clin. Endocrinol. Metab.,* 37:595-601, 1973.

Faglia, G.P., Beck-Peccoz, P., Ferrari, C., Travaglini, P., Ambrosi, B. and Spada, A.: Plasma growth hormone response to thyrotropin-releasing hormone in patients with active acromegaly. *J. Clin. Endocrinol. Metab.,* 36:1259-1262, 1973.

Falta, W.: *Die Erkrankungen der Blutdrusen.* Berlin: Springer, 1928, p. 299.

Farquharson, R.F. and Hyland, H.H.: Anorexia nervosa; metabolic disorder of psychologic origin. *JAMA,* 111:1085-1092, 1938.

Farquharson, R.F. and Hyland, H.H.: Anorexia nervosa: The course of 15 patients treated from 20 to 30 years previously. *Can. Med. Assoc. J.,* 94:411-419, 1966.

Feicht, C.B., Johnson, T.S., Martin, B.J., Sparks, K.E. and Wagner, W.W., Jr.: (Letter) Secondary amenorrhoea in athletes (letter). *Lancet,* 2:1145-1146, 1978.

Frankel, R.J. and Jenkins, J.S.: Hypothalamic-pituitary function in anorexia nervosa. *Acta Endocrinol.,* 78:209-221, 1975.

Franks, S., Murray, M.A.F., Jequier, A.M., Steele, S.J., Nabarro, J.D.M. and Jacobs, H.S.: Incidence and significance of hyperprolactinaemia in women with amenorrhoea. *J. Clin. Endocrinol.,* 4:597-607, 1975.

Fries, H.: Studies on secondary amenorrhea, anorectic behavior, and body-image perception: importance for the early recognition of anorexia nervosa. In: R. Vigersky (Ed.), *Anorexia Nervosa.* New York: Raven Press, 1977, pp. 163-176.

Fries, H. and Nillius, S.J.: Dieting, anorexia nervosa and amenorrhoea after oral contraceptive treatment. *Acta Psychiatr. Scand.,* 49:669-679, 1973.

Frisch, R.E.: Food intake, fatness, and reproductive ability. In: R. Vigersky (Ed.), *Anorexia Nervosa.* New York: Raven Press, 1977, pp. 149-161.

Frisch, R.E. and McArthur, J.W.: Menstrual cycles: Fatness as a determinant of minimum weight for height necessary for their maintenance or onset. *Science,* 185:949-951, 1974.

Frisch, R.E., Wyshak, G. and Vincent, L.: Delayed menarche and amenorrhea in ballet dancers. *New Engl. J. Med.,* 303:17-19, 1980.

Gardner, D.F., Kaplan, M.M., Stanley, C.A. and Utiger, R.D.: Effect of triiodothyronine replacement on the metabolic and pituitary responses to starvation. *N. Engl. J. Med.,* 300:579-584, 1979.

Garfinkel, P.E., Brown, G.M., Stancer, H.C. and Moldofsky, H.: Hypothalamic-pituitary function in anorexia nervosa. *Arch. Gen. Psychiatry,* 32:739-744, 1975.

Garfinkel, P.E., Brown, G.M., Warsh, J.J. and Stancer, H.C.: Neuroendocrine responses to carbidopa in primary affective disorders. *Psychoneuroendocrinol.,* 4:13-20, 1979.

Garfinkel, P.E. and Coscina, D.V.: The biology and psychology of hunger and satiety. In: M.R. Zales (Ed.), *Eating, Sleeping and Sexuality: Treatment of Disorders in Basic Life Functions.* New York: Brunner/Mazel, 1982.

Garfinkel, P.E., Moldofsky, H. and Garner, D.M.: Prognosis in anorexia nervosa as influenced by clinical features, treatment and self-perception. *Can. Med. Assoc. J.,*

117:1041-1045, 1977.

Garfinkel, P.E., Moldofsky, H. and Garner, D.M.: The heterogeneity of anorexia nervosa: Bulimia as a distinct subgroup. *Arch. Gen. Psychiatry,* 37:1036-1040, 1980.

Garfinkel, P.E., Warsh, J.J. and Stancer, H.C.: Depression: New evidence in support of biological differentiation. *Am. J. Psychiatry,* 136:535-539, 1979.

Garfinkel, P.E., Warsh, J.J., Stancer, H.C. and Godse, D.: CNS monoamine metabolism in bipolar affective disorder. Evaluation using a peripheral decarboxylase inhibitor. *Arch. Gen. Psychiatry,* 34:735-739, 1977.

Garfinkel, P.E., Warsh, J.J., Stancer, H.C. and Sibony, D.: Total and free plasma tryptophan levels in patients with affective disorders. Effects of a peripheral decarboxylase inhibitor. *Arch. Gen. Psychiatry,* 33:1462-1466, 1976.

Garner, D.M. and Garfinkel, P.E.: Socio-cultural factors in the development of anorexia nervosa. *Psychol Med.,* 10:647-656, 1980.

Gerner, R.H. and Gwirtsman, H.E.: Abnormalities of dexamethasone suppression test and urinary MHPG in anorexia nervosa. *Am. J. Psychiatry,* 138:650-653, 1981.

Gold, M.S., Pottash, A.L.C., Sweeney, D.R., Martin, D.M. and Davies, R.K.: Further evidence of hypothalamic-pituitary dysfunction in anorexia nervosa. *Am. J. Psychiatry,* 137:101-102, 1980.

Gold, M.S., Kaye, W., Robertson, G., Goodwin, F.K. and Ebert, M.: Altered central vasopression in anorexia nervosa. (Abstr.) 133rd annual meeting of the American Psychiatric Association. Syllabus and Scientific Proceedings, 1980, p. 326.

Gold, R.M.: Hypothalamic obesity: The myth of the ventromedial nucleus. *Science,* 182:488-490, 1973.

Goldney, R.: Craniopharyngioma simulating anorexia nervosa. *J. Nerv. Ment. Dis.,* 166:135-138, 1978.

Gross, H.A., Lake, C.R., Ebert, M.H., Ziegler, M.G. and Kopin, I.J.: Catecholamine metabolism in primary anorexia nervosa. *J. Clin. Endocrinol. Metab.,* 49:805-809, 1979.

Gull, W.W.: The address in medicine delivered before the annual meeting of the BMA at Oxford. *Lancet,* 2:171, 1868.

Hafner, R.J., Crisp, A.H. and McNeilly, A.S.: Prolactin and gonadotrophin activity in females treated for anorexia nervosa. *Postgrad. Med.,* 52:76-79, 1976.

Hales, C.N. and Randle, P.J.: Effects of low-carbohydrate diet and diabetes mellitus on plasma concentrations of glucose, non-esterified fatty acid and insulin during oral glucose-tolerance tests. *Lancet,* 1:790-794, 1963.

Hall, R., Ormston, B.J., Besser, G.M., Cryer, A.R. and McKendrick, M.: The thyrotrophin-releasing hormone test in diseases of the pituitary and hypothalamus. *Lancet,* 1:759-763, 1972.

Halmi, K.A., Dekirmenjian, H., Davis, J.M., Casper, R. and Goldberg, S.: Catecholamine metabolism in anorexia nervosa. *Arch. Gen. Psychiatry,* 35:458-460, 1978.

Halmi, K.A., Sherman, B.M. and Zamudio, R.: LH and FSH response to gonadotropin-releasing hormone in anorexia nervosa: Effect of nutritional rehabilitation. *J. Clin. Endocrinol. Metab.,* 1:135-142, 1975.

Harrower, A.D.B., Yap, P.L., Nairn, I.M., Walton, H.J., Strong, J.A. and Craig, A.: Growth hormone, insulin, and prolactic secretion in anorexia nervosa and obesity during bromocriptine treatment, *Br. Med. J.,* 2:156-159, 1977.

Hart, T., Jr., Kase, N. and Kimball, C.P.: Induction of ovulation and pregnancy in patients with anorexia nervosa. *Am. J. Obstet. Gynecol.,* 108:580-584, 1970.

Heron, G.B. and Johnston, D.A.: Hypothalamic tumor presenting as anorexia nervosa. *Am. J. Psychiatry,* 133:580-582, 1976.

Hill, P. and Wynder, F.: Diet and prolactin release. *Lancet,* 2:806-807, 1976.

Hirvonen, E., Seppala, M., Karonen, S.L. and Allercreutz, H.: Luteinizing hormone responses to luteinizing hormone releasing hormone, and growth hormone and cortisol responses to insulin induced hypoglycemia in functional secondary amenorrhoea. *Acta Endocrinol.,* 84:225-236, 1977.

Hoebel, B.G.: Satiety: Hypothalamic stimulation, anorectic drugs and neurochemical substrates. In: D. Novin, W. Wyrwicka and G. Bray (Eds.), *Hunger: Basic Mechanisms and Clinical Implications.* New York: Raven Press, 1976, pp. 33-50.

Hoebel, B.G. and Teitelbaum, P.L.: Weight regulation in normal and hypothalamic hyperphagic rats. *J. Comp. Physiol. Psychol,* 61:189-193, 1966.

Hoffmann, K.: Influence of photoperiod and melatonin on testis size, body weight, and pelage color in djungarian hamster (Phodopus-Sungorus) *J. Comp. Physiol.,* 85:267-282, 1973.

Hsu, L.K.G., Crisp, A.H. and Harding, B.: Outcome of anorexia nervosa. *Lancet,* 1:61-65, 1979.

Hurd, H.P., 2nd, Palumbo, P.J. and Gharib, H.: Hypothalamic-endocrine dysfunction in anorexia nervosa. *Mayo Clin. Proc.,* 52:711-716, 1977.

Isaacs, A.J., Leslie, R.D.G., Gomez, J. and Bayliss, R.: The effect of weight gain on gonadotrophins and prolactin in anorexia nervosa. *Acta Endocrinol.,* 94:145-150, 1980.

Ismail, A.A. and Harkness, R.A.: Urinary testosterone excretion in men in normal and pathological conditions. *Acta Endocrinol.,* 56:469-480, 1967.

Jaffe, R.B. and Keye, W.R., Jr.: Estradiol augmentation of pituitary responsiveness to gonadotropin-releasing hormone in women. *J. Clin. Endocrinol. Metab.,* 39:850-855, 1974.

Jeuniewic, H., Brown, G., Garfinkel, P. and Moldofsky, H.: Hypothalamic function as related to body weight and body fat in anorexia nervosa. *Psychosom. Med.,* 40:187-198, 1978.

Jimerson, D.C., Lynch, H.J., Post, R.M., Wurtman, R.J. and Bunney, W.W.: Urinary melatonin rhythms during sleep deprivation in depressed patients and normals. *Life Sci.,* 20:1501-1508, 1977.

Johanson, A.J. and Knorr, N.J.: L-DOPA as treatment for anorexia nervosa. In: R. Vigersky (Ed.), *Anorexia Nervosa.* New York: Raven Press, 1977, pp. 363-372.

Josefson, A.: Three cases of progressive emaciation successfully treated with thyroid extract. *Nord. Med. Tidskr.,* 5:489-497, 1933 (Ger.).

Kagan, H.: Anorexia and severe inanition associated with a tumor involving the hypothalamus. *Arch. Dis. Child,* 33:257-260, 1958.

Kalucy, R.C., Crisp, A.H., Chard, T., McNeilly, A., Chen, C.N. and Lacey, J.H.: Nocturnal hormonal profiles in massive obesity, anorexia nervosa and normal females. *J.Psychosom. Res.,* 20:595-604, 1976.

Kanis, J.A., Brown, P., Fitzpatrick, K., Hibbert, D.J., Horn, D.B., Nairn, I.M., Shirling, D., Strong, J.A. and Walton, H.J.: Anorexia nervosa: A clinical, psychiatric, and laboratory study. *I.J. Med.,* 43:321-338, 1974.

Kapen, S., Sternthal, E. and Braverman, L.: A "pubertal" 24-hour luteinizing hormone (LH) secretory pattern following weight loss in the absence of anorexia nervosa. *Psychom. Med.,* 4:177-182, 1981.

Kastin, A.J., Gual, C. and Schally, A.V.: Clinical experience with hypothalamic releasing hormones. 2. Luteinizing hormone-releasing hormone and other hypophysiotropic releasing hormones. *Recent Prog. Horm. Res.,* 28:201-227, 1972.

Katz, J.L., Boyar, R.M., Roffwarg, H., Hellman, L. and Weiner, H.: LHRH responsiveness in anorexia nervosa: Intactness despite prepubertal circadian LH pattern. *Psychosom. Med.,* 39:241-251, 1977.

Katz, J.L., Boyar, R.M., Roffwarg, H., Hellman, L. and Weiner, H.: Weight and circadian luteinizing hormone secretory pattern in anorexia nervosa. *Psychosom. Med.,* 40:549-567, 1978.

Katz, J.L., Boyar, R.M., Weiner, H., Gorzynski, G., Roffwarg, H. and Hellman, L.: Toward an elucidation of the psychoendocrinology of anorexia nervosa: In: American Psychopathological Association, E.J. Sachar (Ed.), *Hormones, Behavior and Psychopathology.* New York: Raven Press, 1976, pp. 263-283.

Kay, D.W.K.: Anorexia nervosa: A study in prognosis. *Proc. Roy. Soc. Med.,* 46:669-674, 1953.

Kaye, W.H., Ebert, M.H. and Lake, C.R.: Central nervous system amine metabolism in anorexia nervosa. (Abstr.) 133rd annual meeting of the American Psychiatric Association. Syllabus and Scientific Proceedings 1980, p. 326.

Knobil, E., Dierschke, D.J., Yamaji, T., Hotchkiss, J. and Weick, R.F.: Roles of estrogen in the positive and negative feedback control of LH secretion during the menstrual cycles of the rhesus monkey. In: R.B. Saxena (Ed.), *Gonadotrophins*. New York: John Wiley and Sons, 1972, pp. 72-86.

Korbsch, R.: Die Magersucht im Gefolge Der akuten Magenschleimhautatrophie junger Madchen als eigenes Krankheitsbild. *Deutsche Med. Wchnschr.* 62:1948-1950, 1936.

Krause, F.: *Die Erkrankunger des Hypophysenvorderlappens. Klinische Fortbildung.* Berlin: Urban & Schwarzenberg, 1937.

Krause, F. and Muller, O.H.: Uber schwere Hypophysenvorderlappeninsuffizienz und ihre Behandlung. *Klin. Wchnschr.*, 16:118-122, 1937.

Kylin, E.: Die Simmondssche Kranheit. *Ergebn. d. in. Med. u. Kinderh.* 49:1-63, 1935.

Kylin, E.: Magersucht in der weiblichen spatpubertat. Eingentumliches Krankheitsbild suigenesis. *Deutsches Arch. F. Klin. Med.,* 180:115-152, 1937.

Landon, J., Greenwood, F.C., Stamp, T.C.B. and Wynn, V.: The plasma sugar, free fatty acid, cortisol, and growth hormone response to insulin, and the comparison of this procedure with other tests of pituitary and adrenal function. II. In patients with hypothalamic or pituitary dysfunction or anorexia nervosa. *J. Clin. Invest.,* 45:437-449, 1966.

Lasègue, C.: De l'anorexie hystérique. *Arch. Gen. de Med.,* 385, 1873. Reprinted in: R.M. Kaufman and M. Heiman (Eds.), *Evolution of Psychosomatic Concepts. Anorexia Nervosa: A Paradigm.* New York: International Universities Press, 1964.

Leeds, C.S.: Anorexia nervosa: hypoglycemia or hypoadrenia. *Northwest. Med.,* 27:233-238, 1928.

Leonard, P.J.: Cortisol-binding in serum in kwashiorkor: East African Studies, In: L.I. Gardner and P. Amacher (Eds.), *Endocrine Aspects of Malnutrition: Marasmus, Kwashiorkor and Psychosocial Deprivation.* Saint Ynex, CA: Kroc Foundation, 1973, pp. 355-362.

Leslie, R.D.G., Isaacs, A.J., Gomez, J., Ragatt, P.R. and Bayliss, R.: Hypothalamo-pituitary-thyroid function in anorexia nervosa: Influence of weight gain. *Br. Med. J.,* 2:526-528, 1978.

Levi, L.: Anorexie mentale et corps thyroide. *Encephale* (Paris), 17:507-515, 1922.

Lewin, K., Mattingly, D. and Mills, R.R.: Anorexia nervosa associated with hypothalamic tumor. *Br. Med. J.,* 2:629-630, 1972.

Luck, P. and Wakeling, A.: Altered thresholds for thermoregulatory sweating and vasodilatation in anorexia nervosa. *Br. Med. J.,* 2:906-908, 1980.

Lundberg, P.O., Walinder, J., Werner, I. and Wide, L.: Effects of thyrotropin-releasing hormone on plasma levels of TSH, FSH, LH and GH in anorexia nervosa. *Eur. J. Clin. Invest.,* 2:150-153, 1972.

Maeda, K., Kato, Y., Ohgo, S., Chihara, K., Yoshimoto, Y., Yamaguchi, H., Kuromaru, S., and Imura, H.: Growth hormone and prolactin release after injection of thyrotropin-releasing hormone in patients with depression. *J. Clin. Endocrinol. Metab.,* 40:501-505, 1975.

Maeda, K., Kato, Y., Yamaguchi, N., Chihara, K., Ohga, S., Iwasaki, Y., Yoshimoto, Y., Moridera, K., Kuromaru, S. and Imura, H.: Growth hormone release following thyrotrophin-releasing hormone injection into patients with anorexia nervosa. *Acta Endocrinol.* (Kbh), 81:8, 1976.

Marks, V., Howorth, N. and Greenwood, F.C.: Plasma growth-hormone levels in chronic starvation in man. *Nature,* 208:686-687, 1965.

Marshall, J.C. and Fraser, T.R.: Amenorrhea in anorexia nervosa: Assessment and treatment with clomiphene citrate. *Br. Med. J.,* 4:590-592, 1971.

Mawson, A.R.: Anorexia nervosa and the regulation of intake: A review. *Psychol. Med.,* 4:289-308, 1974.

Mayer, J.: Regulation of energy intake and the body weight: The glucostatic theory and the lipostatic hypothesis. *Ann. NY Acad. Sci.,* 63:15-43, 1955.

McCann, S.M. and Ojeda, S.R.: Synaptic transmitters involved in the release of hypothalamic releasing and inhibiting hormones. *Reviews of Neuroscience,* 2:91-110, 1976.

McCullagh, E.P. and Tupper, W.R.: Anorexia nervosa. *Ann. Int. Med.,* 14:817-838, 1940.

Mecklenburg, R.S., Loriaux, D.L., Thompson, R.H., Andersen, A.E., and Lipsett, M.B.: Hypothalamic dysfunction in patients with anorexia nervosa. *Medicine,* 53:147-159, 1974.

Miyai, K., Yamamoto, T., Azukizawa, M., Ishibashi, K. and Kumahara, Y.: Serum thyroid hormones and thyrotropin in anorexia nervosa. *J. Clin. Endocrinol. Metab.,* 40:334-338, 1975.

Morgan, H.G. and Russell, G.F.M.: Value of family background and clinical features as predictors of long-term outcome in anorexia nervosa: four-year follow-up study of 41 patients. *Psychol. Med.,* 5:355-371, 1975.

Morton, R.: *Phthisiologica: Or a Treatise of Consumptions.* London: Sam Smith and Benj. Walford, 1694.

Moshang, T., Jr., Parks, J.S., Baker, L., Vaidya, V., Utiger, R.D., Bongiovanni, A.M. and Synder, P.J.: Low serum triiodothyronine in patients with anorexia nervosa. *J. Clin. Endocrinol. Metab.,* 40:470-473, 1975.

Moshang, T., Jr. and Utiger, R.D.: Low triiodothyronine euthyroidism in anorexia nervosa. In: R. Vigersky (Ed.), *Anorexia Nervosa.* Raven Press, 1977, pp. 263-270.

Nemiah, J.C.: Anorexia nervosa: a clinical psychiatric study. *Medicine,* 29:225-268, 1950.

Neri, V., Ambrosi, B., Beck-Peccoz, P., Travaglini, P. and Faglia, C.: Growth hormone regulation and hypothalamic-pituitary-adrenal function in anorexia nervosa. *Folia Endocrinol.* (Roma), 25:143-152, 1972.

Nillius, S.J. and Wide, L.: The pituitary responsiveness to acute and chronic administration of gonadotropin-releasing hormone in acute and recovery stages of anorexia nervosa. In: R. Vigersky (Ed.), *Anorexia Nervosa.* New York: Raven Press, 1977, pp. 225-241.

Orts, R.J., Kocan, K.M. and Wilson, I.B.: Inhibitory action of melatonin on a pineal anti-gonadotropin. *Life Sci.,* 17:845-850, 1975.

Palmer, R.L., Crisp, A.H., Mackinnon, P.C.B., Franklin, M., Bonnar, J. and Wheller, M.: Pituitary sensitivity to 50 microg LH/FSH-RM in subjects with anorexia nervosa in acute recovery stages. *Br. Med. J.,* 1:179-182, 1975.

Panksepp, J.: Is satiety mediated by the ventromedial hypothalamus? *Physiol. Behav.,* 7:381-384, 1971.

Panksepp, J., Bishop, R. and Rossi, J.: Neurohumoral and endocrine control of feeding. *Psychoneuroendocrinology,* 4:89-106, 1979.

Pettersson, F., Fries, H. and Nillius, S.J.: Epidemiology of secondary amenorrhea. I. Incidence and prevalance rates. *Am. J. Obstet. Gynecol.,* 117:80-86, 1973.

Pimstone, B.L., Becker, D.J. and Hansen, J.D.L.: Human growth hormone in protein calorie malnutrition. In: A. Pecile and E.E. Muller (Eds.), *Growth and Growth Hormone.* Amsterdam: Excerpta Medica, 1973, pp. 389-401.

Pirke, K.M., Fichter, M.M., Lund, R. and Doerr, P.L.: Twenty-four hour sleep-wake pattern of plasma LH in patients with anorexia nervosa. *Acta Endocrinol.* (Copenh), 92:193-204, 1979.

Rakoff, A.E.: Psychogenic factors in anovulatory women. 1. Hormonal patterns in women with ovarian functions of psychogenic origin. *Fertil. Steril.,* 13:1-10, 1962.

Rao, K.S.J., Srikantia, S.G. and Gopalan, G.: Plasma cortisol levels in protein-calorie malnutrition. *Arch. Dis. Child,* 43:365-367, 1968.

Rappaport, R., Prevot, C. and Czernichow, P.: Somathormone et activité somatomédine plasmatique au cours des amaigrissements graves de l'anorexie mentale chez l'enfant. *Ann. Endocrinol.* (Paris), 39:259-260, 1978.

Redmond, D.E., Jr., Swann, A. and Heninger, G.R.: Letter: Phenoxybenzamine in anorexia nervosa. *Lancet,* 2:307, 1976.

Reiss, M.: Unusual pituitary activity in a case of anorexia nervosa. *J. Ment. Sci.,* 89:270-273, 1943.

Reiter, R.J., Vaughan, M.K., Blask, D.E. and Johnson, L.Y.: Melatonin: Its inhibition of pineal antigonadotrophic activity in male hamsters. *Science,* 185:1169-1171, 1974.

Richardson, B.D. and Pieters, L.: Menarche and growth. *Am. J. Clin. Nutr.,* 30:2088-2091, 1977.

Richardson, B.D.: Simmonds' disease and anorexia nervosa. *Arch. Intern. Med.,* 63:1-28, 1939.

Roth, J.C., Kelch, R.P., Kaplan, S.L. and Grumbach, M.M.: FSH and LH response to luteinizing hormone-releasing factor in prepubertal and pubertal children, adult males and patients with hypogonadotropic and hypertropic hypogonadism. *J. Clin. Endocrinol. Metab.,* 35:926-930, 1972.

Russek, M.: Current hypotheses on the control of feeding behavior. In: F.R. Mogenson and C.J. Calaresu (Eds.), *Neurol. Integration of Physiological Mechanisms and Behavior.* Toronto: University of Toronto Press, 1975, pp. 128-147.

Russell, G.F.M.: Metabolic aspects of anorexia nervosa. *Proc. Roy. Soc. Med.,* 58:811-814, 1965.

Russell, G.F.M. and Beardwood, C.J.: The feeding disorders, with particular reference to anorexia nervosa and its associated gonatrophin changes. In: R.P. Michael (Ed.), *Endocrinology and Human Behaviour.* London: Oxford University Press, 1968, pp. 310-329.

Russell, G.F.M. and Bruce, J.T.: Capillary-venous glucose differences in patients with disorders of appetite. *Clin. Sci.,* 26:157-163, 1964.

Russell, G.F.M. and Bruce, J.T.: Impaired water diuresis in patients with anorexia nervosa. *Am. J. Med.,* 40:38-48, 1966.

Russell, G.F.M., Loraine, J.A., Bell, E.T. and Harkness, R.A.: Gonadotrophin and estrogen excretion in patients with anorexia nervosa. *J. Psychosom. Res.,* 9:79-85, 1965.

Ryle, J.A.: Discussions of anorexia nervosa. *Proc. Roy. Soc. Med.,* 32:735-737, 1939.

Seidensticker, J.F. and Tzagournis, M.: Anorexia nervosa — clinical features and long term follow-up. *J. Chronic Dis.,* 21:361-367, 1968.

Sheehan, H.L. and Summers, V.K.: The syndrome of hypopituitarism. *Quart. J. Med.,* 18:319-378, 1949.

Sheldon, J.H.: Anorexia nervosa. *Proc. Roy. Soc. Med.,* 32:738-741, 1939.

Sherman, B.M. and Halmi, K.A.: Effect of nutritional rehabilitation on hypothalamic-pituitary function in anorexia nervosa. In: R. Vigersky (Ed.), *Anorexia Nervosa.* New York: Raven Press, 1977, pp. 211-223.

Simmonds, M.: Ueber embolische Prozesse in der Hypophysis. *Arch. Path. Anat., 217:226-239, 1914.*

Simmonds, M.: Uber Kachexic hypophysaren Ursprungs. *Deutsche Med. Wchnschr.,* 42:190, 1916.

Simmonds, M.: Atrophie des Hypophysisvorderlappens und hypophysare Kachexie. *Deutsche Med. Wchnschr.,* 44:852-854, 1918.

Sizonenko, P.C., Rabinovitch, A., Schneider, P., Paunier, L., Wollheim, C.B. and Zhand, G.: Plasma growth hormone, insulin and glucagon responses to arginine infusion in children and adolescents with idiopathic short stature, isolated growth hormone deficiency, panhypopituitarism and anorexia nervosa. *Pediatr. Res.,* 9:733-738, 1975.

Smith, P.E.: Hypophysectomy and replacement therapy in rat. *Am. J. Anat.,* 45:205-273, 1930.

Smith, S.R., Bledsoe, T. and Chhetri, M.K.: Cortisol metabolism and the pituitary-adrenal axis in adults with protein-calorie malnutrition. *J. Clin. Endocrinol. Metab.,* 40:43-52, 1975.

Spauding, S.W., Chopra, I.J., Sherwin, R.S. and Lyall, S.S.: Effect of caloric restriction and dietary composition on serum T3 and reverse T3 in man. *J. Clin. Endocrinol. Metab.,* 42:197-200, 1976.

Starkey, T.A. and Lee, R.A.: Menstruation and fertility in anorexia nervosa. *Am. J. Obstet. Gynecol.,* 105:374-379, 1969.

Stephens, L.: Fatal cases of anorexia nervosa. *Lancet,* 1:31, 1895.

Stricker, E.M. and Zigmond, M.J.: Brain catecholamines and the lateral hypothalamic syndrome. In: D. Novin, W. Wyrwicka and G.A. Bray (Eds.), *Hunger: Basic Mechanisms and Clinical Implications.* New York: Raven Press, 1975, pp. 19-32.

Swann, I.: Anorexia nervosa — a difficult diagnosis in boys. Illustrated by three cases. *Practitioner,* 218:424-427, 1977.

Swigar, M.E., Kolakowska, T. and Quinlan, D.M.: Plasma cortisol levels in depression and other psychiatric disorders: A study of newly admitted psychiatric patients. *Psychol. Med.,* 9:449-455, 1979.

Teitelbaum, P. and Epstein, A.M.: The lateral hypothalamic syndrome: Recovery of feeding and drinking after lateral hypothalamic lesions. *Psychol. Rev.,* 69:74-90, 1962.

Theander, S.: Anorexia nervosa. A psychiatric investigation of 94 female patients. *Acta Psychiat. Scand.* [Suppl], 214:1-194, 1970.

Tolis, G., Woods, I. and Guyda, H.: Absense of hyperprolactinemia during sleep in anorexia nervosa. (Abstr.) Proceedings of the Royal College of Physicians and Surgeons of Canada, 1979, p. 40.

Trygstad, O., Foss, I., Edminson, P.D., Johansen, J.H. and Reichelt, K.L.: Humoral control of appetite: A urinary anorexigenic peptide. Chromatographic patterns of urinary peptides in anorexia nervosa. *Acta Endocrinol.* (Copenh), 89:196-208, 1978.

Turek, F.W., Desjardins, C. and Menaker, M.: Melatonin-induced inhibition of testicular function in adult golden hamsters. *Proc. Soc. Exp. Biol. Med.,* 151:502-506, 1976.

Udvarhelyi, G.B., Adamkiewicz, J.J. and Cooke, R.E.: "Anorexia nervosa" caused by a fourth ventricle tumor. *Neurology,* 16:565-568, 1966.

Unger, R.H., Eisentraut, A.M. and Madison, L.L.: The effects of total starvation upon the levels of circulating glucagon and insulin in man. *J. Clin. Invest.,* 42:1031-1039, 1963.

Ungerstedt, U.: Stereotaxic mapping of the monoamine pathways in the rat brain. *Acta Physiol. Scand.* [Suppl], 367:1-48, 1971.

Vagenakis, A.G.: Thyroid hormone in prolonged experimental starvation in man. In: R. Vigersky (Ed.), *Anorexia Nervosa.* New York: Raven Press, 1977, pp. 243-252.

Vagenakis, A.G., Burger, A., Portnay, G.I., Rudolph, M., O'Brian, J.I., Azizi, R., Arky, R., Nicod, P., Ingbar, S.H., and Braverman, L.E.: Diversion of peripheral thyroxine metabolism from activating to inactivating pathways during complete feeding. *J. Clin. Endocrinol. Metab.,* 41:191-194, 1975.

VanderLaan, W.P., Parker, D.C., Rossman, L.G. and VanderLaan, E.F.: Implications of growth hormone release in sleep. *Metabolism,* 19:891-897, 1970.

Vanluchene, E., Aertsens, W. and Vanderkerckhove, D.V.: Steroid excretion in anorexia nervosa patients. *Acta Endocrinol.* (Copenh), 90:133-138, 1979.

Vaughan, G.M., Pelham, R.W., Pang, S.F., Loughlin, L.L., Wilson, K.M., Sandočk, K.L., Vaughan, M.K., Koslow, S.H. and Reiter, R.J.: Nocturnal elevation of plasma melatonin and urinary 5-hydroxyindoleacetic acid in young men: Attempts at modification by brief changes in environmental lighting and sleep and by autonomic drugs. *J. Clin. Endocrinol. Metab.,* 42:752-764, 1976.

Vigersky, R.A., Andersen, A.E., Thompson, R.H. and Loriaux, D.L.: Hypothalamic dysfunction in secondary amenorrhea associated with simple weight loss. *N. Engl. J. Med.,* 297:1141-1145, 1977.

Vigersky, R.A. and Loriaux, D.L.: Anorexia nervosa as a model of hypothalamic dysfunction. In: R. Vigersky (Ed.), *Anorexia Nervosa.* New York: Raven Press, 1977, pp. 109-122.

Vigersky, R.A., Loriaux, D.L., Andersen, A.E., Mecklenburg, R.S. and Vaitukaitis, J.L.: Delayed pituitary hormone response to LRF and TRF in patients with anorexia nervosa and with secondary amenorrhea associated with simple weight loss. *J. Clin. Endocrinol. Metab.,* 43:893-900, 1976.

Von Bergman, G.: Magerkeit und Magerschucht. *Deutsche Med. Wchnschr.,* 60:123, 1934.

Wachslicht-Rodbard, H., Gross, H.A., Rodbard, D., Ebert, M.H. and Roth, J.: Increased insulin binding to erythrocytes in anorexia nervosa: Restoration to normal with refeeding. *N. Engl. J. Med.,* 300:882-887, 1879.

Wakeling, A. and Russell, G.F.M.: Disturbances in the regulation of body temperature in anorexia nervosa. *Psychol. Med.,*1:30-39, 1970.

Wakeling, A., DeSouza, V.A. and Beardwood, C.J.: Assessment of the negative and positive feedback effects of administered oestrogen on gonadotrophin release in patients with anorexia nervosa. *Psychol Med.,* 7:397-405, 1977a.

Wakeling, A., DeSouza, V.A. and Beardwood, C.J.: Effects of administered estrogen on luteinizing hormone release in subjects with anorexia nervosa in acute and recovery stages. In: R. Vigersky (Ed.), *Anorexia Nervosa.* New York: Raven Press, 1977b, pp. 199-209.

Wakeling, A., DeSouza, V.A., Gore, M.B.R., Sabur, M., Kingstone, D. and Boss, A.M.B.: Amenorrhea, body weight and serum hormone concentrations, with particular reference to prolactin and thyroid hormones in anorexia nervosa. *Psychol. Med.,* 9:265-272, 1979.

Walsh, B.T., Katz, J.L., Levin, J., Kream, J., Fukushima, D.K., Hellman, L.D., Weiner, H. and Zumoff, B.: Adrenal activity in anorexia nervosa. *Psychosom. Med.,* 40:499-506, 1978.

Wang, C.F. and Yen, S.S.C.: Direct evidence of estrogen modulation of pituitary sensitivity to luteinizing hormone releasing factor during the menstrual cycle. *J. Clin. Invest.,* 55:201-204, 1975.

Warren, M.P.: Weight loss and responsiveness to LH-RH. In: R. Vigersky (Ed.), *Anorexia Nervosa.* New York: Raven Press, 1977, pp. 189-198.

Warren, M.P., Jewelewicz, R., Dyrenfurth, I., Ans, R., Khalaf, S. and Vande Wiele, R.L.: The significance of weight loss in the evaluation of pituitary response to LH-RH in women with secondary amenorrhoea. *J. Clin. Endocrinol. Metab.,* 40:601-611, 1975.

Warren, M.P. and Vande Wiele, R.L.: Clinical and metabolic features of anorexia nervosa. *Am. J. Obstet. Gynecol.,* 117:435-449, 1973.

Weitzman, E.D.: Circadian rhythms and episodic hormone secretion. *Annu. Rev. Med.,* 27:225-243, 1976.

Wetterberg, L., Arendt, J., Paunier, L., Sizonenko, P.C., Van Donselaar, W. and Heyden, T.: Human serum melatonin changes during the menstrual cycle. *J. Clin. Endocrinol. Metab.,* 42:185-188, 1976.

White, L.E. and Hain, R.F.: Anorexia in association with a destructive lesion of the hypothalamus. *AMA Arch. Path.,* 68:275-281, 1959.

White, J.H., Kelly, P. and Dorman, K.: Clinical picture of atypical anorexia nervosa associated with hypothalamic tumor. *Am. J. Psychiatry,* 134:323-325, 1977.

Woods, S.C. and Porte, D., Jr.: Insulin and the set-point regulation of body weight. In: D. Novin, W. Wyrwicka and G.A. Bray (Eds.), *Hunger: Basic Mechanisms and Clinical Implications.* New York: Raven Press, 1975, p. 273.

Yap, S.H., Hafkenscheid, J.C.M. and van Tongeren, J.H.M.: Important role of tryptophan on albumin synthesis in patients suffering from anorexia nervosa and hypoalbuminemia. *Am. J. Clin. Nutr.,* 28: 1356-1363, 1975.

Yen, S.S.C., Rebar, R., Vanderberg, G. and Judd, H.: Hypothalamic amenorrhea and hypogonadotropinism: Responses in synthetic LRF. *J. Clin. Endocrinol. Metab.,* 36:811-816, 1973.

Yen, S.S.C., Tsai, C.C. and Naftolin, F.: Pulsatile patterns of gonadotropin release in subjects with and without ovarian failure, *J. Clin. Endocrinol. Metab.,* 30:671-675, 1975.

Yen, S.S.C., Vanderberg, G. and Siler, T.M.: Modulation of pituitary responsiveness to LRF by estrogen. *J. Clin. Endocrinol. Metab.,* 39:170-177, 1974.

Yen, S.S.C., Vela, P. and Rankin, J.: Inappropriate secretion of follicle-stimulating hormone and luteinizing hormone in polycystic ovarian disease. *J. Clin. Endocrinol. Metab.,* 30:435-442, 1970.

Ziegler, R. and Sours, J.A.: A naturalistic study of patients with anorexia nervosa admitted to a university medical center. *Compr. Psychiat.,* 9:644-651, 1968.

# CHAPTER 5

# *Sociocultural Factors*

## EPIDEMIOLOGY OF ANOREXIA NERVOSA

Since Gull's and Lasègue's initial descriptions, it has been repeatedly noted that anorexia nervosa is more common in females, and usually develops during adolescence (see Bemis, 1978; Bruch, 1973; Crisp, 1970 for reviews). A century ago Fenwick (1880) commented that anorexia nervosa was more common in "the wealthier classes of society than amongst those who have to procure their bread by daily labour" (p. 107). Since then this overrepresentation in the upper social classes has frequently been observed (Bruch, 1973; Crisp, 1965; Crisp, Palmer and Kalucy, 1976; Morgan and Russell, 1975). These observations that anorexia nervosa occurs with a particular age, sex, and social class distribution suggest that sociocultural factors may be important determinants of the disorder in those who are otherwise vulnerable or predisposed to it. Furthermore, there is growing evidence that anorexia nervosa is increasing in frequency (Duddle, 1973; Jones, Fox, Babigan and Hutton, 1980; Halmi, 1974; Kendell, Hall, Hailey and Babigan, 1973; Sours, 1969).

It appears that anorexia nervosa has become more common, although an increased reporting of cases due to greater medical and public awareness of the disorder in the past ten years cannot be entirely discounted. Case registry studies have demonstrated an increase in patients presenting to psychiatrists. For example, Theander (1970) described and followed 94 female patients in southern Sweden over a 30-year period; he calculated the overall incidence for women to be 0.24 per 100,000 population per year. But there was a sharp rise in incidence in the final decade of the study

100

(1951-1960) to 0.45 per 100,000. This was reflected in an increase from an average of 1.1 to 5.8 new cases per year in the area of Sweden that he studied. Kendell et al. (1973), using case registries from three areas — Camberwell (London), Monroe County (New York) and North-East Scotland — found a comparable incidence (from 0.37 in Monroe County to 1.6 per 100,000 in North-East Scotland) and, like Theander, observed a significant increase in the second half of the period under study (43 cases vs. 25 in the first half).

More recently, Jones et al. (1980) used the psychiatric case register and hospital records from a major general hospital to estimate the incidence of anorexia nervosa in Monroe County, over two time periods, 1960-1969 and 1970-1976. They found that the number of diagnosed cases almost doubled (from 0.35 to 0.64 per 100,000) in the second time period. Moreover, the increase occurred among females but not males and it was most prominent in the 15-24-year-old group. Data from these studies cannot be utilized to reflect the real incidence of anorexia nervosa since the case registry method has severe limitations; it requires the individual's identification as a psychiatric or medical patient. Since many anorexics receive no treatment, or are treated by nonmedical personnel (psychologists, dietitians, clergy) or nonpsychiatric physicians, they escape detection.

Until a few years ago there had not been adequate investigations of the prevalence of anorexia nervosa. However, recently several studies have provided prevalence figures for selected populations. Crisp et al. (1976) conducted a detailed survey of nine schools in London. They discovered one severe case in every 100 girls over age 16 in private schools.The disorder was less common in public schools, once more emphasizing the preponderance of cases in the upper class. Overall, one serious new case was observed for every 250 girls over 15 years old. Because this study included only very severe cases and since they were dealing with high-school-age girls, these figures are, if anything, an underestimation of the magnitude of the problem. It has previously been shown that many patients develop the illness in their late teens or early twenties (Crisp and Stonehill, 1971; Garfinkel, Moldofsky and Garner, 1980) and therefore Crisp et al. (1976) might have observed a greater prevalence had they extended their studies to a slightly older group. It has been Crisp's impression (Crisp et al., 1976), as well as ours, that the disorder is even more common in university undergraduates.

Nylander (1971) has comprehensively studied dieting behavior among adolescents in Sweden. He found that most females "felt fat" and that this feeling increased with age. Fifty percent of 14-year-old females reported feeling fat and this figure reached 70% in the 18-year-olds. As would be expected, dieting behavior was also common, and increased in the late teens to reach its maximum in the 18-year-olds. By contrast, boys seldom reported feeling fat or dieting. Nylander reported a prevalence of serious cases of anorexia nervosa of one per 155 females surveyed while the prevalence of "mild cases" ("anorexic behavior") was approximately 10%. Nylander suggested that the difference between mild and severe forms was only one of degree.

Anorexia nervosa is not uncommon in women who present with behavior problems or amenorrhea. Although diagnostic criteria were not provided, Ikemi, Ago, Nakagawa, Mori, Takahashi, Suematsu, Sugita and Matsubara (1974) identified 13 cases of anorexia nervosa in a population of 230 (5.6%) Japanese adolescents with school maladjustment. Similarly, Carlson and Cantwell (1980) diagnosed anorexia nervosa in 9% of 102 children referred to a children's outpatient mental health facility in California. These are obviously not studies of a random sample of school-aged girls. In the investigation of 54 consecutive women with secondary amenorrhea, Holmberg and Nylander (1971) found that 41 (75%) patients described many symptoms of typical anorexia nervosa. Ninety-four percent were well below their ideal weights and some were cachexic. On average they had lost about 10 kg. Only three of the 41 patients had previously been diagnosed as having anorexia nervosa. Subsequently, a surprisingly high frequency (5-14%) of anorexia nervosa has been confirmed in women evaluated at amenorrhea clinics (Fries, 1977; Fries and Nillius, 1973; Jacobs, Knuth, Hull and Franks, 1977; Knuth, Pribilla, Marti and Winterhalter, 1979).

While it has been repeatedly noted that anorexia nervosa is overrepresented in the upper social classes (Crisp et al., 1976; Jones et al., 1980; Kendell et al., 1973; Morgan and Russell, 1975), Ushakov (1971) has described a similar association between socioeconomic background and anorexia nervosa in Russia. However, male patients tend not to display such social class skewing (Crisp and Toms, 1972; Marshall, 1978). We have also observed an upper social class preponderance in our referrals (Garfinkel et al., 1980) but we have found that in recent years the disorder is becoming more equally distributed through all social classes. Table 1 illustrates that

## TABLE 1

### Change in Socioeconomic Status in Anorexia Nervosa

|                  | Before 1975  | After 1976    |
|------------------|--------------|---------------|
| Social Class     |              |               |
| I - II           | 36 (70.6%)   | 103 (52.0%)   |
| III - VII        | 15 (29.4%)   | 95 (48.0%)    |

$X^2 = 7.09$, df $= 1$, $p < 0.01$

the proportion of our consultations from social classes I and II (Hollingshead, 1965) has decreased from 1970-75 to 1976-81. Kendell et al. (1973) recorded a similar finding in Monroe Country and North-East Scotland but failed to observe the spread to lower classes in London. The recent report by Jones et al. (1980) also did not find a higher working class representation in Monroe County.

Theander (1970) noted earlier that, as the disorder became more and more common, there would be a progressive rise in the proportion of patients from lower social classes. He attributed this change to improved case detection; however, it is equally plausible that attitudes concerning body weight, achievement, and control, which predispose to anorexia nervosa, are also becoming more evenly distributed throughout all socioeconomic sectors of society. For example, while previously almost unheard of in blacks or East Indians (Rowland, 1970), anorexia nervosa is now occurring in these groups (Jones et al., 1980; Kendell et al., 1973; Nwaefuna, 1981; Warren and Vande Wiele, 1973). Prior to 1979 no black patients presented to our consultation practices, but during the past two years, we have seen four black patients out of 120 patients (3.3%) and three of these were from upper class, professional families.

In addition to these changes, it has been our impression that anorexia nervosa may be developing more frequently in older women. While it remains true that it is overwhelmingly a disorder of adolescence, with bimodal risk ages of onset at 14 and at 18 (Halmi, Casper, Eckert, Goldberg and Davis, 1979) and a usual range from 12-25, 17% of our patients developed the illness when they were older than 20, 5% when they were over 25, and a few after being married. Comparing patients from our series seen from 1970-75 to those seen from 1976-81 there has been a trend toward increased average age of onset (Table 2). The fact that the age at presentation (Table 2) has significantly increased during this same period indicates that the interval between onset and referral has increased for our patients despite the recent public awareness of the disorder. It could be argued that the disorder has always been common in post-adolescence since earlier studies by Kay and Leigh (1954), and Halmi (1974) described 30% and 13%, respectively, of their patients were over age 25 at onset. There are also anecdotal case descriptions of women developing post-menopausal anorexia nervosa (Kellett, Trimble and Thorley, 1976; Launer, 1978), although one cannot be certain if these cases were presenting with the first onset or rather an exacerbation of a chronic disorder.

One epidemiologic finding that has endured over time is the sex distribution of the disorder. Studies of anorexia nervosa repeatedly note that 90-95% are female (see Bemis, 1978; Jones et al., 1980) and while Ushakov

## TABLE 2

### Age of Onset and Presentation:
### Patients Seen from 1970-75 Compared to 1976-81

|                      | N   | Mean | SD  | t     | df    | Signif.   |
|----------------------|-----|------|-----|-------|-------|-----------|
| Age of Onset         |     |      |     |       |       |           |
| 1970-75              | 59  | 17.0 | 3.7 |       |       |           |
|                      |     |      |     | 1.73  | 281   | p< 0.09   |
| 1976-81              | 224 | 18.0 | 4.2 |       |       |           |
| Age at Presentation  |     |      |     |       |       |           |
| 1970-75              | 59  | 19.3 | 3.6 |       |       |           |
|                      |     |      |     | 4.81* | 149.9 | p < 0.001 |
| 1976-81              | 228 | 22.2 | 6.0 |       |       |           |

* t-test (two tailed) with separate variance estimate because of a significant difference in between group variances (F = 2.73, p <0.001).

(1971) has estimated that the number of females hospitalized with the illness is only five times that of males in Russia, male cases remain infrequent in North America. For example, of 55 anorexics referred to us from 1970-75, only four were male (7.2%) and of the 221 patients* seen from 1976-81, seven (3.3%) have been male. While the disorder has increased among females, we continue to see males infrequently. Bruch (1978) also suggests that the proportion of male cases has not increased in frequency and this impression is confirmed in the Jones et al. (1980) study of Monroe County.

Hasan and Tibbetts (1977) reported that the proportion of males in their hospital record survey has increased from 3.1% prior to 1971 to 7% from 1971-1975. It would be interesting to determine if the proportion has decreased again during the last several years. The fact that the disorder appears to have increased in only one sex supports the idea that cultural factors play a role in producing the disorder in vulnerable adolescents. Specifically, pressures to achieve, to be successful, and to be slender may be significant in increasing the frequency of anorexia nervosa in women. The differential sex distribution of anorexia nervosa is probably also related to a variety of other factors. These include, as Crisp (1967) has noted, the rapid weight changes that occur during puberty in girls and other physical changes that occur in females during adolescence, as well as the need for increased self-control which may be associated with this period.

* The total N varies in some of our statistics since subjects on whom relevant data are missing have been excluded from the analyses.

## THE ROLE OF CULTURE IN PREFERRED APPEARANCES OF WOMEN

During other times in history cultural attitudes toward physical appearance have played a role in facilitating serious illness. In prerevolutionary China footbinding with its socially admired consequence, the clubbed "lily-foot," is one example of how social custom can result in serious physical disability and illness. This thousand-year-old custom required that young girls from families of higher social standing become physically deformed in pursuit of the dwarfed foot which represented the feminine ideal. The process involved the toes being gradually folded under the sole, while the heel and forefoot were contracted through a series of tight bindings. The foot-bound woman was a symbol of status for a husband since it showed that he was wealthy and that his wife was not required to work. Besides severely limiting the wife's mobility, it also served the purpose of restricting her extramarital social involvements. Foot-binding died out entirely only in the early twentieth century (Lyons and Petrucelli, 1978).

The wearing of corsets in the nineteenth century is another example of potentially unhealthy customs which derived from the expectation that women conform to an idealized appearance. In fact, corsets may be thought of as mechanical aids to achieve the thin look for which the anorexic strives and like self-starvation resulted in bodily harm. Apart from the extreme discomfort and interference with digestion, the corsets could cause serious injury due to the splitting of the steel stays. Even when these harmful consequences were recognized, corsets continued to be popular because of their association with beauty and "purity" (i.e., being uncorseted supposedly connoted promiscuity [Vincent, 1979]). Bodily comfort and health have been disregarded in other attempts to conform to cultural ideals related to physical appearance. Tattooing, scarification, cranial or other bone deformation, and decorative tooth filling are also examples of socially prescribed alterations of appearance (Polhemus and Procter, 1978).

At other times, particular illnesses have been romanticized and the look associated with them has become "desirable." Sontag (1978) graphically documents this phenomenon in her account of how the painful, agonizing wasting illness, tuberculosis (TB), was glamorized in the nineteenth century. TB was "one index of being genteel, delicate, sensitive. It became rude to eat heartily. It was glamorous to look sickly" (p. 28). The admiration of a tubercular appearance was not confined to artists but became widespread as a sign of a romantic personality. It was thought to afflict only sensitive people and it was believed to enhance creativity. TB was so closely associated with the creative process that it was even suggested that its disappearance was responsible for a decline in the arts (Sontag, 1978, p. 33). Because of the impact of this association, pallor became a fashionable attribute. Men sought out delicate, pale women and women used whitening powders rather than rouge. Some began to drink lemon juice and vinegar to destroy their appetites in order to maintain a pale appearance (Vincent, 1979). It is interesting that consumption, which was the original illness from which anorexia nervosa was differentiated ("nervous consumption" [Morton, 1694]), was glamorized to such a degree in the nineteenth century and that anorexia nervosa and "an anorexic look" has been similarly glamorized by the media in the twentieth century (e.g., Anorexia Nervosa: "The Golden Girl Disease," *Playgirl,* June 1975).

The idealized look or image for women has varied over time and across cultures and parts of the female body have acquired an almost fetishistic focus in various cultures and periods. More specifically, one has only to compare the full bodied women in Ruben's seventeenth century paintings with Modigliani's elongated women in the early twentieth century for examples of the shift as reflected through art. Ford and Beach (1952) have suggested that for the majority of societies, plumpness in females is admired and in some cultures it has been considered as a secondary sexual characteristic (Rudofsky, 1972). Obese women have symbolized fertility, strength and, where food is scarce, their body fat is an overt sign of one's wealth. When food is not abundantly available to all, overeating and obesity are viewed with admiration. It seems that only when food is plentiful can the luxury of dieting and slimness-consciousness develop.

During the twentieth century in Western society, there have been shifts of preferences with regard to the feminine form. Favor was shown for a buxom appearance in the early part of the century, followed by the "flat-chested" flappers of the 1920s and a return of bustiness and an hourglass figure in the 1950s. Recently preference has once more returned to thinness as attractive for females. The reasons for the recent trend are complex. To some degree, it may be a positive response to the increasing understanding that obesity does carry a risk for a variety of serious illnesses. However, just as in the last century, a "look" has evolved and it has come to be associated with other positive attributes. The media have capitalized upon and promoted this image and through popular programing have portrayed the successful and beautiful protagonists as thin. Thinness has thus become associated with self-control and success. Perhaps this may assume greater importance in a society where external controls and standards for behavior have become somewhat relaxed and individuals have responded by imposing greater self-control and discipline. One particularly popular form of self-control for women has been dieting. Dieting is then a security gesture, a device for asserting control — "at least my body is my domain, and I can resist the threatening chaos of a formless world in the narrow confines of my skin." In this hypothetical formulation, dieting is a form of counter-phobic behavior.

The currently idealized body form for women is for a bony thinness. Rakoff (1967) described it as best exemplified by those actresses "who resemble prepubertal girls onto whom the secondary sexual characteristics of mature women have been grafted." There is evidence that this image has further changed in the 15 years since Rakoff's observation. This shift in the idealized concept of feminine beauty during the 1970s can be illustrated by a survey conducted at Madame Tussaud's London Wax Museum (Wallechinsky, Wallace and Wallace, 1977) where visitors are polled annually for their choice of the most beautiful female figure on display. In 1970 Elizabeth Taylor was rated as the most admired figure. Since then, the emaciated model Twiggy has ascended in popularity and in 1976 she was considered to be the most elegant.

We have attempted to document and quantify the apparent shift in our culture's standard for the feminine beauty and the consequent pressure to diet, by collecting data from several sources including Playboy Magazine, Miss America Pageants, and diet articles from popular women's magazines (Garner, Garfinkel, Schwartz and Thompson, 1980). Height, weight, and measurement data were derived for all centerfolds over the past 20 years from Playboy Magazine. Figure 1 illustrates the mean percent of average weight (Build and Blood Pressure Study, 1959 of the Society of Actuaries) for centerfolds for each of the years surveyed. Percent of average weight for age and height decreased significantly over the 20 years ($r = 0.22$, $p < 0.001$). Other significant changes were that bust measurements have become smaller ($r = 0.18$, $p < 0.005$), waists larger ($r = 0.41$, $p < 0.001$) and hips smaller ($r = 0.12$, $p < 0.05$). The yearly means for these dimensions are shown in Figure 2. Because of increasing heights ($r = 0.22$, $p < 0.001$) absolute weight did not decline.

Garner et al. (1980) also collected height, weight, and age data for both the contestants (state representatives) and the winners of the Miss America Pageant from 1959 through 1978. Based upon national norms (Build and Blood Pressure Study, 1959), the absolute weights were converted to percent of average weight for age, height, and sex and Figure 3 illustrates both contestants' and Pageant winners' percent of average weight for each year. For all contestants, the correlation between year and percent of average weight was -0.83 ($p < 0.0001$) indicating an average decline in weight of 0.13 kg (0.28 lbs) per year for the contestants. For the Pageant winners the correlation between year and percent of average weight was -0.62 ($p < 0.003$) indicating an average yearly decline in weight of 0.17 kg (0.37 lb). The mean

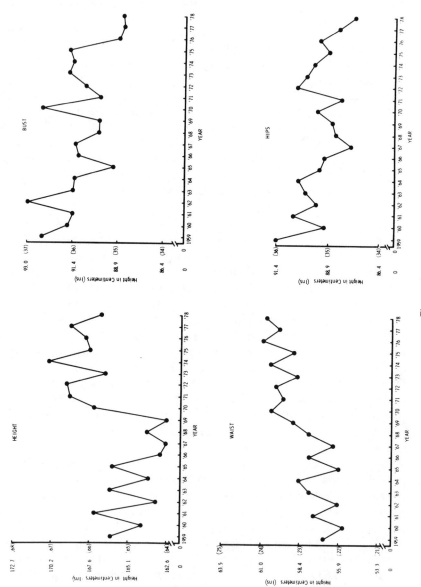

Figure 1

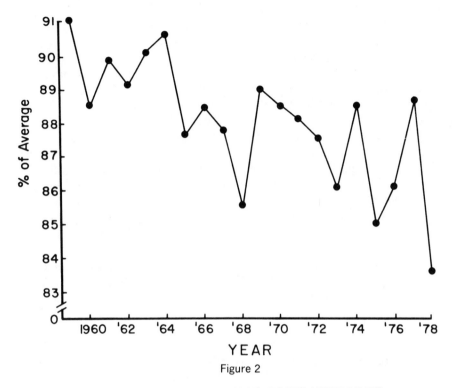

Figure 2

PERCENT OF AVERAGE WEIGHT* FOR MISS AMERICA PAGAENT
CONTESTANTS AND WINNERS

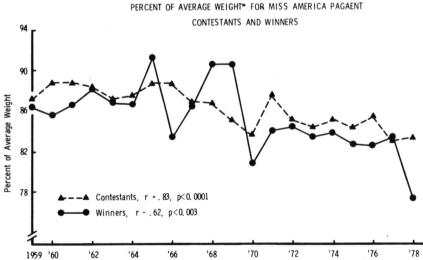

* Based upon the 1959 Build and Blood Pressure study of the Association of Life Insurance Medical Directors and Society of Actuaries.

Figure 3

weight for contestants before 1970 was 87.6% ± 0.4 of average compared to 84.6% ± 0.5 since 1970 ($p < 0.0001$). For pre-1970 the mean weight for Pageant winners was 87.7% ± 0.7 of average compared to 82.5% ± 0.7 since 1970 ($p < 0.001$). Although overall the Pageant winners have not weighed less than the average contestant, since 1970 the winners have weighed significantly less than the other contestants (contestants $m = 84.6\%$ ± 0.5; winners $m = 82.5\%$ ± 0.7, $p < 0.05$).

The Garner et al. (1980) findings support the idea that there has been a gradual but definite evolution in the preferred shape for women over the past 20 years. Particularly within the past ten years the shift in the ideal standard has been toward a thinner size. The Playboy bust, waist, and hip measurement data indicate a trend toward a more "tubular" or androgynous body form. Moreover, at least for Miss America Pageant contestants, winning over the last decade has been clearly associated with being thinner.

It has also been suggested that the movement toward a thinner shape for the ideal standard of beauty is more notable considering that recently revised actuarial statistics (Build and Blood Pressure Study, 1979) have indicated that the average female under 30 has become heavier over the past 20 years (Garner et al., 1980). This increase is due to improved nutrition and is evident in virtually all age and height categories for women under 30; it amounts to between 2.3 and 2.7 kgs (5-6 lbs) for most women between 17 and 24 years old. This can be translated into an average weight increase of 0.14 kg (0.3 lbs) per year over the last 20 years. Thus, while magazine centerfolds and Pageant participants have been getting thinner, the average woman of a similar age has been getting heavier. These findings demonstrate the tension between biological forces determining weight and the cultural ideal.

The impact of this conflict is shown by the pervasiveness of dieting among women. Huenemann, Shapiro, Hampton and Mitchell (1966) reported that between 63-70% of high school girls were dissatisfied with their bodies and wanted to lose weight; by contrast, males wanted to gain. For girls, "feeling fat" increased during high school and one-fifth were actively trying to diet. Dwyer, Feldman, Seltzer and Mayer (1969) studied the attitudes of high school seniors toward their weights and found that over 80% of the women but less than 20% of the men wanted to weigh less. Moreover, 30% of the women surveyed were actively dieting when questioned and 60% had dieted at some time by their senior year. This is in contrast to 6% of the men on diets and 24% who had ever dieted. Jakobovits, Halstead, Kelley, Roe and Young, (1977) reported that 11% of college women were on a diet and a further 75% were consciously trying to limit their food intake. Hawkins and Clement (1980) have reported that 79% of college females and 49% of males report bulimic episodes on a self-report "binge scale." Moreover, they found that approximately 3.5% of the 255 females studied had induced vomiting after a bulimic episode. Garner, Polivy and Olmsted (1981) have indicated that 7.6% of a sample of over 400 college females reported engaging in self-induced vomiting to control their weight and over 5% admitted depending on this strategy once a month or more often. Furthermore, almost 25% claimed to know personally someone else who resorted to this method of weight control. Thus, dieting and concern about weight control have reached major proportions among women on the university campus.

For North American women, thinness (Stunkard, 1975) and dieting (Dwyer and Mayer, 1970; Goldblatt, Moore and Stunkard, 1965) have been shown to be strongly related to higher social class. The association is encapsulated in the remark attributed to the Duchess of Windsor: "No woman can be too rich or too thin." We have recently documented the increased emphasis on dieting by examining five popular women's magazines from 1959 through 1978 (Garner et al., 1980). Diet articles were tabulated while advertisements and promotions were specifically excluded. A total of 385 diet articles appeared over the 20 years surveyed. The yearly mean for the first decade was 15.6 (S.D. = 5.5) compared to 22.9 (S.D. = 4.8) for the second decade ($p < 0.01$). This represents a significant increase in the number of diet articles appearing in the last ten years.

The diet citation results support the observation that there has been a growing emphasis on weight reduction that may be based on fashion's ideal figure, as well as for the rational goal of improved health. Garner et al. (1980) have indicated that the movement toward this ideal within the context of increasing population weights for females has several significant implications. These include significant biological and psychological consequences of chronic dieting. Symptoms such as irritability, poor concentration, anxiety, depression, apathy, lability of mood, and fatigue have been associated with prolonged caloric restriction (Bruch, 1973; Garner and Garfinkel, 1980; Keys, Brozek, Henschel, Mickelsen and Taylor, 1950; Nylander, 1971). Disturbances in sleep and mood have been related to undernutrition (Crisp, 1980). Dieting or "restrained eating" has been associated with increased emotionality and disinhibited eating in the presence of food (Herman and Polivy, 1975; Polivy, Herman and Warsh, 1978). Finally, it has been suggested that there is a critical body fat threshold (at which body fat comprises 23% or more of body mass) which is necessary for normal menstrual functioning (Frisch and McArthur, 1974) (see Chapter 4). Reduction of body weight below this level of fat has been associated with amenorrhea (Fries and Nillius, 1973). We have previously commented on the irony in the apparent gravitation of current symbols of "sexual attractiveness" closer to a weight which is at biological odds with this normal hormonal substratum (Garner et al., 1980).

## THE RELATIONSHIP BETWEEN CULTURAL VALUES AND ANOREXIA NERVOSA

Ryle (1939) first related a possible increase in the prevalence of anorexia nervosa to societal pressures: "The spread of the slimming fashion, now happily on the wane, and the more emotional lives of the younger generation since the War might have been expected to provide a general increase" (p. 735).

A number of contemporary writers have also linked recent sociocultural pressures for thinness to the apparent increased incidence of anorexia nervosa (Boskind-Lodahl, 1976; Bruch, 1973, 1978; Selvini Palazzoli, 1974). Bruch (1978) has referred to the increase as a "sociocultural epidemic" and has suggested that fashion's ideal form may indirectly affect vulnerable adolescents who come to believe that weight control is equal to self-control and will lead to beauty and success.

In an indirect examination of the hypothesis that increased cultural pressure to diet and be slim is one of the factors facilitating the development of anorexia nervosa, we studied a population of professional dance students and fashion models (Garner and Garfinkel, 1978, 1980). Both dancers and models represent groups who by career choice must focus increased attention and control over their body shapes. Thus, it was predicted that they should encounter, in a more intense and exaggerated form, the general social demand for dieting. It was predicted that anorexia nervosa and "anorexic behaviors" would be overrepresented in these dancers and models. Previous descriptive studies of professional ballet dancers have indicated disturbed body image perception, excessive dieting, vomiting to control weight, and frank cases of anorexia nervosa (Druss and Silverman, 1979; Vincent, 1979).

In our study we surveyed five independent groups totaling 423 female subjects. Ballet students (N = 183) from three national caliber professional dance schools and fashion students (N = 56) from a leading Canadian modeling school were compared to patients with anorexia nervosa (N = 68), female university students (N = 81), and a small group of students from a music conservatory (N = 35). The conservatory students were included as a comparison group who experience "high performance" expectations similar to the dance students but they are not required to maintain a thin body shape for their careers. This group was matched for age to a subgroup of the "high performance-oriented" dance students.

All subjects completed the Eating Attitudes Test (EAT) which is a 40-item, objective, self-report instrument designed to measure a broad rage of symptoms characteristic of anorexia nervosa (Garner and Garfinkel, 1979) (see Chapter 2 and Appendix). In addition, weight, age, and menstrual and weight histories were obtained on all subjects. The Hopkins Symptom Checklist (HSCL) (Derogatis, Lipman, Rickels, Uhlenhuth and Covi, 1974) was administered to a subgroup of dancers (N = 103) from the most competitive setting and to a subsample of anorexic (N = 31) and normal control (N = 55) subjects.

The dance and model groups had significantly higher mean EAT scores than did the normal control group (F = 135.5 $p < 0.001$; $p < 0.05$, Duncan's Multiple Range Test). The frequency distribution of the EAT scores for the subjects in the Garner and Garfinkel (1980) study is illustrated in Figure 4. There was little overlap between EAT scores of the anorexic group and normal control group. For the anorexic and normal groups, the EAT was efficient in correctly identifying group membership 91% of the time.

All normal subjects scoring 30 or over on the EAT (12%) were interviewed clinically and none met the modified Feighner et al. (1972) criteria for anorexia nervosa. Other normal controls were also interviewed because of past weight fluctuations or a history of amenorrhea; however, despite their being weight or diet conscious, they were not identified as cases of anorexia nervosa.

In the dance group, the 69 subjects (38%) who scored at or above the cut-off score on the EAT (i.e., >30) were interviewed and 11 cases of primary anorexia nervosa were identified. Similarly, other students with a suspicious menstrual and weight history were interviewed and this procedure revealed one additional case who had scored less than 30 on the EAT. Thus, 12 cases (6.5% of the total dance sample) of anorexia nervosa were detected. All but one of these subjects had developed anorexia nervosa after beginning to study dance. In the modeling student sample, four cases (7%) of anorexia nervosa were identified; however, two of these subjects had an onset prior to commencing the modeling course.

Forsyth and Kolenda (1966) have commented on the extreme competitiveness in preprofessional ballet training. Since two of the dance subsamples in the Garner and Garfinkel (1980) study were drawn from settings which were highly competitive, it could be argued that competitiveness alone was responsible for the higher prevalence of anorexia nervosa. Addressing this question, we studied a small group of students from a music conservatory who were closely matched for age to the students from one of

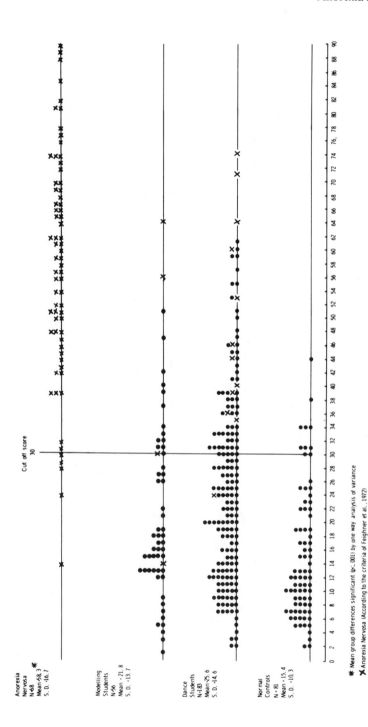

Figure 4

the dance schools. The mean EAT scores for the dance sample were significantly higher than those for the music students ($p < 0.001$); the music students' EAT scores were similar to the normal control group (Table 3). Only one music student scored greater than 30 on the EAT and no cases of anorexia nervosa were discovered. Thus it was concluded by Garner and Garfinkel (1980) that "a competitive environment alone did not lead to the greater expression of anorexia nervosa" (p. 653).

However, within the dance samples, students from the more competitive settings with higher performance expectations were found to have higher EAT scores. The high-achievement-setting group had significantly more individuals with EAT scores in the anorexic range (Table 4). Garner and Garfinkel (1980) found the prevalence of definite cases of anorexia nervosa developing in training was twice as high (7.6%) in the high-achievement-setting dance groups, as in the low-achievement-setting dancers (3.8%) or models (3.5%).

Another finding from this study was that the dancers from the highly competitive settings weighed significantly less than those from the less competitive settings. It could be argued that high EAT scores simply reflect starvation effects more common in dancers at a low weight. However, the findings of insignificant correlations within the dance sample between EAT score and weight ($r = 0.10$, N.S.) or EAT score and percent deviation from normal weight ($r = 0.09$, N.S.) did not support this contention.

Garner and Garfinkel (1980) did report that weight was related to the menstrual status of the dancers. Of the dancers from the competitive settings for whom menstrual data were available (N = 100), 28% were amenorrheic and another 11% menstruated only rarely (once every six months). Amenorrheic dancers weighed significantly less than dancers who menstruated. The finding is supported by Frisch, Wyshak and Vincent (1980) who found amenorrhea and irregular cycles to be related to leanness and occurring in 55% of their young ballet dancers.

Finally, Garner and Garfinkel (1980) reported that for both the dancers and anorexic patients psychological symptoms as measured by the HSCL were positively correlated with EAT scores (Table 5). Except for depression, this relationship was not evident in the normal comparison group.

Results of the Garner and Garfinkel (1980) study indicate that anorexia nervosa is more common in dance and modeling students than in women of a similar age and social class. The prevalence of 7% in these groups using rigorous diagnostic criteria is higher than in an earlier report (Garner and Garfinkel, 1978) and supports the hypothesis that individuals who must focus increased attention to a slim body are at risk for anorexia nervosa. Alternatively, it may also be that girls who are attracted to dance in the first

## TABLE 3

### EAT Scores for Groups Matched for Age and Competitive Environment

| | N | Age (years) mean* | % Deviation from Average Body Weight† (mean) | EAT Score (mean) | % with EAT Scores > 30‡ | Clinically Identified Anorexia Nervosa (%) |
|---|---|---|---|---|---|---|
| Dance students from high expectation setting | 49 | 15.4 | -17.9 | 25.9 | 43 | 8 |
| Music students from high expectation setting | 35 | 15.2 | -6.3 | 13.7 | 3 | 0 |

* N S.
† p < 0.001 t-tests (two-tailed)
‡ p < 0.001, chi square
Reprinted with permission from Garner and Garfinkel, 1980.

## TABLE 4

### Prevalence of Anorexia Nervosa and Symptoms of Anorexia Nervosa

| Group | N | % Deviation from Average Body Weight† | Mean EAT Score | Frequency of EAT ≥ 30 | Cases of AN Identified | Cases Developing AN while in Course of Study |
|---|---|---|---|---|---|---|
| Total dance group | 183 | -13.3 | 25.6 ± 1.1 | 69 (38%) | 12 (7%) | 11 (6%) |
| More Competitive Setting | 103 | -16.8 | 27.6 ± 1.5 | 46 (45%) | 8 (8%) | 8 (7.6%) |
| Less Competitive Setting | 80 | -8.6 | 23.2 ± 1.5 | 23 (29%) | 4 (5%) | 3 (3.8%) |
| Modeling students | 56 | -11.9 | 21.8 ± 1.8 | 19 (34%) | 4 (7%) | 2 (3.5%) |
| University and music students | 116 | -3.7 | 14.7 ± 0.9 | 11 (9%) | 0 | 0 |

† p < 0.001 (one-way analysis of variance)

## TABLE 5

### Correlations Between HSCL-58 and EAT Scores

| Groups | Somati-zation | Depression | Obsessive-Compulsive | Interpersonal Sensitivity | Anxiety | Total HSCL Score |
|---|---|---|---|---|---|---|
| Dance Students' EAT Score (N = 103) | r 0.22* | r = 0.48*** | r = 0.29** | r = 0.26 | r = 0.31*** | r = 0.41*** |
| Anorexia Nervosa Patients' EAT Score (N = 31) | r = 0.36* | r = 0.44** | r = 0.34* | r = 0.51** | r = 0.41** | r = 0.53*** |
| Normal Controls' EAT Score | r = 0.17 | r = 0.23* | r = 0.09 | r = 0.02 | r = 0.20 | r = 0.15 |

*** $p < 0.001$, Pearson correlation coefficients
** $p < 0.01$, Pearson correlation coefficients
* $p < 0.05$, Pearson correlation coefficients
Reprinted with permission from Garner and Garfinkel, 1980.

place (because of a drive for activity, for example) are those predisposed to anorexia nervosa. However, it was concluded that "it is unlikely that the results simply reflect selective enrollment of preexisting or incipient cases, since the majority of students at the school with the highest incidence (8%) were enrolled at 10-to-12 years of age and developed the disorder while actively studying ballet" (Garner and Garfinkel, 1980, p. 652). In addition, the preoccupation with the body, self-control, and perfection generated in the dancer's environment may be factors required for the disorder's expression and these factors may be characteristically different from more usual societal demands for slimness. The higher incidence of anorexia nervosa in the more competitive schools indicates that it may be important for future investigations to directly examine the role of perceived performance expectations.

If the pursuit of thinness in women plays a role in the development of anorexia nervosa, then the recent cultural shift in the aesthetic ideal for women toward a thinner body frame could be one factor accounting for the increased prevalence of the disorder. Bruch (1978) has suggested that one of the factors responsible for this shift is "the enormous emphasis Fashion places on slimness" (p. viii).

Other sociocultural factors affecting women and their changing role within society have been implicated in the development of anorexia nervosa. For example, there has also been an increased pressure on women for a wider range of roles for vocational achievement. Although this certainly represents a desirable transition for women, the dramatic shift in roles and expectations may pose adjustment problems for some. Selvini Palazzoli (1974) relates these new and often contradictory roles for women as a potential factor in the increase in anorexia nervosa. She feels women must maintain traditional standards for attractiveness while also rapidly assimilating the heightened demands for professional performance and success.

Boskind-Lodahl (1976) interprets the anorexic's symptoms as a reflection of contemporary women's often desperate striving to please others and validate their self-worth from external sources, often by controlling their appearance. Her viewpoint contrasts with that of some traditional psychoanalytic writers (e.g., Szyrynski, 1973) who have described the anorexic as rejecting the stereotype of femininity; rather, Boskind-Lodahl feels their pursuit of thinness constitutes "an exaggerated striving to achieve it" (p. 346). It is our opinion that both points of view are too simplistic in that the anorexic neither totally wants to revert to childhood nor does she simply mimic societal standards. More specifically, these individuals wish to be autonomous adults, but because of their ambivalence about their bodies they reject aspects of the feminine body which signify potential problems for them.

Bruch (1973, 1978) also has described the struggle to live up to perfectionist or unrealistic performance standards as a characteristic of people with anorexia nervosa and it may be an important predisposition to the disorder. Others have suggested that the family's overconcern with achievement, dieting, weight, and food may play a role in the disorder (Crisp, Harding and McGuinness, 1974; Selvini Palazzoli, 1974; see, also Chapter 7).

It is of course important to emphasize what might seem obvious — not all individuals exposed to these cultural pressures to perform, to be perfect, and to be slim develop anorexia nervosa. Cases of anorexia nervosa have been described throughout the past 100 years, while cultural standards for thinness have varied. Although we believe that the pressure toward thinness, within the context of high performance expectations, may be important factors in anorexia nervosa, the bulk of evidence suggests that the disorder is multidetermined. In addition to these sociocultural factors, particular deficits within the individual and her capacity for autonomy (Bruch, 1973) are also important. The confrontation with dramatic, rapid physical changes in body shape and sexual development during puberty has been emphasized by Crisp (1981). A premorbid tendency to obesity may be an important predisposition for some people. Particular personality traits and cognitive styles (Bruch, 1979) may also be risk factors. Relatively stable age-inappropriate perceptual disturbances are also likely to play a role (Bruch, 1973; Garner et al., 1978; see, also, Chapter 6). Finally, as yet poorly understood biological factors may contribute to the expression of the disorder. In addition to these predispositions within the individual, certain familial characteristics and interpersonal patterns may interact to facilitate the expression of the disorder (see Chapter 7). This concept of anorexia nervosa resulting from the interaction of a number of individual, familial, and cultural forces will be discussed further in Chapter 8.

## REFERENCES

Bemis, K.M.: Current approaches to the etiology and treatment of anorexia nervosa. *Psychol. Bull.,* 85:593-617, 1978.
Boskind-Lodahl, M.: Cinderella's step-sisters: A feminist perspective on anorexia nervosa and bulimia. *Signs: J. of Women in Culture and Society,* 2:342-356, 1976.
Bruch, H.: *Eating Disorders.* New York: Basic Books, 1973.
Bruch, H.: *The Golden Cage.* Cambridge, MA: Harvard University Press, 1978.
Bruch, H.: Anorexia Nervosa. In: R.J. Wurtman and J.J. Wurtman (Eds.), *Nutrition and the Brian Vol. 3.* New York: Raven Press, 1979, pp. 101-115.
Carlson, G.A. and Cantwell, D.P.: Unmasking masked depression in children and adolescents. *Am. J. Psychiatry,* 137:445-449, 1980.
Crisp, A.H.: Some aspects of the evolution, presentation and follow-up of anorexia nervosa. *Proc. Roy. Soc. Med.,* 58:814-820, 1965.
Crisp, A.H.: The possible significance of some behavioral correlates of weight and carbohydrate intake. *J. Psychosom. Res.,* 11:117-131, 1967.
Crisp, A.H.: Anorexia nervosa "feeding disorder," "nervous malnutrition" or "weight phobia"? *World Rev. Nutr. Diet,* 12:452-504, 1970.
Crisp, A.H.: Sleep, activity and mood. *Brit. J. Psychiatry,* 137:1-7, 1980.
Crisp, A.H.: Therapeutic outcome in anorexia nervosa. *Can. J. Psychiatry,* 26:232-235, 1981.
Crisp, A.H., Harding, B. and McGuinness, B.: Anorexia nervosa. Psychoneurotic characteristics of parents: Relationship to prognosis. A quantitative study. *J. Psychosom. Res.,* 18:163-173, 1974.
Crisp, A.H., Palmer R.L., and Kalucy, R.S.: How common is anorexia nervosa? A prevalence study. *Br. J. Psychiatry,* 218:549-554, 1976.
Crisp, A.H. and Stonehill, E.: Relationship between aspects of nutritional disturbance and menstrual activity in primary anorexia. *Br. Med. J.,* 3:149-151, 1971.
Crisp, A.H. and Toms, D.A.: Primary anorexia nervosa or weight phobia in the male: Report on 13 cases. *Br. Med. J.,* 1:334-338, 1972.
Derogatis, L., Lipman, R., Rickels, K., Uhlenhuth, E.G.H. and Covi, L.: The Hopkins Symptom Checklist (HSCL): A self-report symptom inventory. *Behav. Sci.,* 19:1-15, 1974.
Druss, R.G. and Siverman, J.A.: Body image and perfectionism of ballerinas: Comparison and contrast with anorexia nervosa. *Gen. Hosp. Psychiatry,* 2:115-121, 1979.
Duddle, M.: An increase of anorexia nervosa in a university population. *Br. J. Psychiatry,* 123:711-712, 1973.
Dwyer, J.T., Feldman, J.J., Seltzer, C.C. and Mayer, J.: Body image in adolescents: attitudes toward weight and perception of appearance. *Am. J. Clin. Nutrit.,* 20:1045-1056, 1969.
Dwyer, J.T. and Mayer, J.: Potential dieters: Who are they? *J. Am. Diet. Assoc.,* 56:510-514, 1970.
Feighner, J.P., Robins, E., Guze, S.B., Woodruff, R.A., Winokur, G. and Munoz, R.: Diagnostic criteria for use in psychiatric research. *Arch. Gen. Psychiatry,* 26:57-63, 1972.

Fenwick, S.: *On Atrophy of the Stomach and on the Nervous Affections of the Digestive Organs.* London: Churchill, 1880.

Ford, C.S. and Beach, F.A.: *Patterns of Sexual Behavior.* New York: Ace Books, 1952.

Forsyth, S. and Kolenda, P.M.: Competition, cooperation, and group cohesion in the ballet company. *Psychiatry,* 29:123-145, 1966.

Fries, H.: Studies on secondary amenorrhea, anorectic behaviour, and body image perception: Importance for the early recognition of anorexia nervosa. In: R. Vigersky (Ed.), *Anorexia Nervosa.* New York: Raven Press, 1977, pp. 163-176.

Fries, H. and Nillius, S.J.: Dieting, anorexia nervosa and amenorrhea after oral contraceptive treatment. *Acta Psychiatr. Scand.,* 49:669-679, 1973.

Frisch, R. and McArthur, J.W.: Menstrual cycles: Fatness as a determinant of minimum weight for height necessary for their maintenance or onset. *Science,* 185:949-951, 1974.

Frisch, R.E., Wyshak, G. and Vincent, L.: Delayed menarche and amenorrhea in ballet dancers. *New Eng. J. Med.,* 303:17-19, 1980.

Garfinkel, P.E., Moldofsky, H., Garner, D.M., Stancer, H.C. and Coscina, D.V.: Body awareness in anorexia nervosa: Disturbances in "body image" and "satiety." *Psychosom. Med.,* 40:487-498, 1978.

Garfinkel, P.E., Moldofsky, H. and Garner, D.M.: The heterogeneity of anorexia nervosa. *Arch. Gen. Psychiat.,* 37:1036-1040, 1980.

Garner, D.M. and Garfinkel, P.E.: Sociocultural factors in anorexia nervosa. *Lancet,* 2:674, 1978.

Garner, D.M. and Garfinkel, P.E.: The Eating Attitudes Test: An index of the symptoms of anorexia nervosa. *Psychol. Med.,* 9:273-279, 1979.

Garner, D.M. and Garfinkel, P.E.: Socio-cultural factors in the development of anorexia nervosa. *Psychol. Med.,* 10:647-656, 1980.

Garner, D.M., Garfinkel, P.E., and Moldofsky, H.: Perceptual experiences in anorexia nervosa and obesity. *Can. Psychiat. Assoc. J.,* 23:249-263, 1978.

Garner, D.M., Garfinkel, P.E., Schwartz, D. and Thompson, M.: Cultural expectation of thinness in women. *Psych. Rep.,* 47:483-491, 1980.

Garner, D.M., Polivy, J. and Olmsted, M.: Anorexia nervosa, obesity and dietary chaos: Common and distinctive features. Paper presented at the annual meeting of the American Psychological Association, Los Angeles, August, 1981.

Goldblatt, P.B., Moore, M.E., and Stunkard, A.J.: Social factors in obesity. *J. Am. Med. Assoc.,* 192:97-102, 1965.

Halmi, K.A.: Anorexia nervosa: Demographic and clinical features in 94 cases. *Psychosom. Med.,* 36:18-25, 1974.

Halmi, K.A., Casper, R.C., Eckert, E.D., Goldberg, S.C. and Davis, J.M.: Unique features associated with age of onset of anorexia nervosa. *Psychiat. Res.,* 1:209-215, 1979.

Hasan, M.K. and Tibbetts, R.W.: Primary anorexia nervosa (weight phobia) in males. *Postgrad. Med. J.,* 53:146-151, 1977.

Hawkins, R.C. and Clement, P.F.: Development and construct validation of a self-report measure of binge eating tendencies. *Addictive Behaviors,* 5:219-226, 1980.

Herman, C.P. and Polivy, J.: Anxiety, restraint and eating behavior. *J. Personality,* 84:666-672, 1975.

Hollingshead, A.B.: *Two Factor Index of Social Position.* New Haven, CT: Yale University Press, 1965.

Holmberg, N.G. and Nylander, I.: Weight loss in secondary amenorrhea. A gynaecologic, encodrinologic and psychiatric investigation of 54 consecutive clinic cases. *Acta Obstet. Gynecol. Scand.,* 50:241-246, 1971.

Huenemann, R.L., Shapiro, L.R., Hampton, M.C. and Mitchell, B.W.: A longitudinal study of gross body composition and body conformation and their association with food and activity in a teenage population. *Am. J. Clin. Nutr.,* 18:325-338, 1966.

Ikemi, Y., Ago, Y., Nakagawa, S., Mori, S., Takahashi, N., Suematsu, H., Sugita, M. and Matsubara, H.: Psychosomatic mechanism under social changes in Japan. *J. Psychosom. Res.,* 18:15-24, 1974.

Jacobs, H.S., Knuth, U.A., Hull, M.G.R. and Franks, S.: Post-"pill" amenorrhea — cause or coincidence? *Br. Med. J.,* 2:940-942, 1977.

Jakobovits, C., Halstead, P., Kelley, L., Roe, D.A. and Young, C.M.: Eating habits and nutrient intakes of college women over a thirty-year period. *J. Am. Diet. Assoc.,* 71:405-411, 1977.

Jones, D.J., Fox, M.M., Babigan, H.M. and Hutton, H.E.: Epidemiology of anorexia nervosa in Monroe County, New York: 1960-1976. *Psychosom. Med.,* 42:551-558, 1980.

Kalucy, R.S., Crisp, A.H. and Harding, B.: A study of 56 families with anorexia nervosa. *Brit. J. Med. Psychol.,* 50:381-395, 1977.

Kay, D.W.K. and Leigh, D.: The natural history, treatment and prognosis of anorexia nervosa based on a study of 38 patients. *J. Ment. Sci.,* 100:411-431, 1954.

Kellett, J., Trimble, M. and Thorley, A.: Anorexia nervosa after the menopause. *Br. J. Psychiatry,* 128:555-558, 1976.

Kendell, R.E., Hall, D.J., Hailey, A. and Babigan, H.M.: The epidemiology of anorexia nervosa. *Psychol. Med.,* 3:200-203, 1973.

Keys, A., Brozek, J., Henschel, A., Mickelsen, O. and Taylor, H.L.: *The Biology of Human Starvation, Vol. 1,* Minneapolis: University of Minnesota Press, 1950.

Knuth, A., Pribilla, W., Marti, H.R. and Winterhalter, K.H.: Hemoglobin Moabit: Alpha 86 (F7) Leu leads to Arg: A new unstable abnormal hemoglobin. *Acta Haematol.* (Basel), 61:121-124, 1979.

Launer, M.A.: Anorexia nervosa in late life. *Br. J. Med. Psychol.,* 51:375-377, 1978.

Lyons, A.S. and Petrucelli, R.J.: *Medicine: An Illustrated History.* New York: Harry N. Abrams, 1978.

Marshall, M.H.: Anorexia nervosa: Dietary treatment and re-establishment of body weight in 20 cases studied on a metabolic unit. *J. Hum. Nutr.,* 32:349-357, 1978.

Morgan, H.G. and Russell, G.F.M.: Value of family background and clinical features as predictors of long-term outcome in anorexia nervosa: Four year follow-up study of 41 patients. *Psychol. Med.,* 5:355-371, 1975.

Morton, R.: *Pthisiologica: Or a Treatise of Consumptions.* London: Sam Smith and Benj. Walford, 1694.

Nwaefuna, A.: Anorexia nervosa in a developing country. *Br. J. Psychiatry,* 138:270-271, 1981.

Nylander, I.: The feeling of being fat and dieting in a school population: Epidemiologic, interview investigation. *Acta Sociomed. Scan.,* 3:17-26, 1971.

Polhemus, T. and Procter, L.: *Fashion and Anti-fashion: An Anthropology of Clothing and Adornment.* London: Cox and Wyman, 1978.

Polivy, J., Herman, C.P. and Warsh, S.: Internal and external components of emotionality in restrained and unrestrained eaters. *J. Abnorm. Psychol.,* 87:497-504, 1978.

Rakoff, V.M.: Psychiatric aspects of obesity. *Mod. Treat.,* 4:1111-1124, 1967.

Rudofsky, B.: *The Unfashionable Human Body.* New York: Doubleday, 1972.

Rowland, C.V.: Anorexia nervosa — A survey of the literature and review of 30 cases. *Int. Psychiat. Clin.,* 7:37-137, 1970.

Ryle, J.A.: Discussion on anorexia nervosa. *Proc. Roy. Soc. Med.,* 32:735-737, 1939.

Selvini Palazzoli, M.P.: *Anorexia Nervosa.* London: Chaucer, 1974.

Smart, D.E., Beumont, P.J.V. and George, C.G.W.: Some personality characteristics of patients with anorexia nervosa. *Br. J. Psychiatry,* 128:57-60, 1976.

Society of Actuaries: Build and blood pressure study. Chicago, IL, 1959.

Society of Actuaries and Association of Life Insurance Medical Directors of America: Build and blood pressure study, Chicago, IL: Author, 1979.

Sontag, S.: *Illness as Metaphor.* New York: Farrar, Straus and Giroux, 1978.

Sours, J.A.: Anorexia nervosa: Nosology, diagnosis, developmental patterns and power control dynamics. In: G. Kaplan and L. Levovici (Eds.), *Adolescence: Psychosocial Perspectives.* New York: Basic Books, 1969, pp.185-212.

Stunkard, A.J.: From explanation to action in psychosomatic medicine: The case of obesity. Presidential address, 1974. *Psychosom. Med.,* 37:195-236, 1975.

Szyrynski, V.: Anorexia nervosa and psychotherapy. *American J. Psychother.*, 27:492-505, 1973.

Theander, S.: Anorexia nervosa. A psychiatric investigation of 94 female patients. *Acta Psychiat. Scand.* [Suppl.], 214:1-194, 1970.

Ushakov, G.: Anorexia nervosa. In: J.G. Howells (Ed.), *Modern Perspectives in Adolescent Psychiatry, Vol 4.* New York: Brunner/Mazel, 1971, pp. 274-289.

Vincent, L.M.: *Competing with the Sylph: Dancers and the Pursuit of the Ideal Body Form.* New York: Andrews and McMeel, 1979.

Wallechinsky, D., Wallace, I. and Wallace, A.: *Book of Lists.* New York: William Morrow, 1977.

Warren, M.P. and Vande Wiele, R.L.: Clinical and metabolic features of anorexia nervosa. *Am. J. Obstet. Gynecol.,* 117:435-449, 1973.

# CHAPTER 6

# Perceptual and

# Conceptual Disturbances

Bruch (1961, 1962, 1973, 1978) first described a group of three inter-related "perceptual and conceptual" disturbances in anorexia nervosa. These are: 1) *body image* disturbances; 2) *interoceptive* disturbances, such as an inability to accurately identify internal sensations such as hunger, satiety, or affective states; and 3) an overwhelming sense of personal *ineffectiveness*. According to Bruch, these disturbances evolve partly from faulty interactional patterns between the infant and mother (see Chapter 7 for her views on other determinants).

Bruch (1969) has distinguished between the use of the term "hunger" in its purely physiological sense from the recognition of particular sensations and cognitions (perceptual/conceptual components) that are experienced and associated with food deprivation. She has used the term "hunger" in the latter sense as a series of learned behaviors. According to Bruch, normal "hunger awareness" evolves when the mother's reactions to the child's state of food deprivation are congruent with his or her internal experiences. Initially the child requires clear signals from outside to know when to eat and when to stop. His or her labeling of internal experience needs to be confirmed by his/her environment. Faulty "hunger awareness" results in "perceptual/conceptual" confusion and is thought to occur when the mother does not respond to the child's own bodily needs but superimposes her perceptions of his/her needs. Bruch proposes that when this process is extended to other areas of functioning, the child becomes unable to differentiate between feelings and sensations originating from within from those that occur in response to external events. Although this is a gross simplification of Bruch's theory, it provides a sketch of her developmental model of anorexia nervosa.

Bruch's astute clinical observations over the past 40 years have stimulated a growing body of research exploring the perceptual and conceptual dimensions of anorexia nervosa (see Garner, Garfinkel and Moldofsky, 1978; Garner and Garkinkel, 1981, for earlier reviews). Investigations have been aimed largely at identifying abnormalities in these areas using precise and objective methods. While many studies have verified deficits in some patients, the results have not been conclusive. The specificity and exact role of these disturbances in the pathogenesis and perpetuation of the disorder and the mechanisms underlying their expression are issues that have not been adequately addressed.

The general organization of this chapter has followed Bruch's tripartite perceptual/conceptual model. But in the last section, in addition to examining the dimension of "ineffectiveness," we elaborate on this ego deficit and discuss a range of conceptual disturbances which are found in anorexia nervosa. It must be emphasized that while we depend heavily upon Bruch's paradigm, our interpretations may depart from her formulations. In fact, while the empirical research on body image, interoception, and conceptual deviations will be reviewed, we believe that a clear understanding of the development of these disturbances is not possible at present.

## BODY IMAGE DISTURBANCES

Body image is a complex construct which has been approached from many points of view. Its evolution can be traced from early descriptions of aberrant bodily perceptions of patients with neurological impairment or limb amputations (Kolb, 1975). It has been conceptualized as neural representation determining bodily experience (Head, 1920), as the mental image that one has of one's body (Traub and Orbach, 1964), as the feelings one has about one's body (Secord and Jourard, 1953) and as a personality construct (Fisher and Cleveland, 1958; Kolb, 1975; Schilder, 1935). While the term "body image" has been broadly applied, its specific meaning remains obscure. Shontz (1974), in particular, has been critical of the general use of the concept of body image as a "thing rather than an abstraction" which has little meaning because of inadequate attempts to link it with other theoretical constructs. In other words there is little advantage to the measurement of a "body image disorder" when this identification neither illuminates the cause nor prescribes a treatment. Shontz (1974) has attempted to clarify the body image construct by identifying different levels at which it may function. These range from sensory phenomena to personality features. A wide range of techniques of varying sensitivity have been used to measure these different aspects of body image. They include projective instruments, figure drawings, questionnaires, clinical interviews, and size estimation using visual and tactile cues. (For reviews see Fisher and Cleveland, 1958; Shontz, 1974; Swensen, 1957, 1968.)

## Clinical Manifestations

Despite the theoretical and practical limitations (Garner and Garfinkel, 1981), the body image concept seems to be clinically significant in anorexia nervosa. Bruch (1962) first recognized body image disturbance to be an essential characteristic of anorexia nervosa. While she considers it to be related to a more general misperception of internal states, specificially it involves the patient's inability to recognize her appearance as abnormal. The misperception reaches "delusional proportions" and is manifest in the lack of concern about, or stubborn defense of, an emaciated shape. Bruch (1973) considers correction of this body image misperception to be a "precondition to recovery" (p. 90).

If a broad definition of the body image construct is used, the disturbance in anorexia nervosa can be found to have different forms of expression. Two disturbed aspects of the body image phenomenon will be described. These may operate independently or conjointly. The first is "perceptual" and refers to the degree to which the patient is not able to assess her size accurately. The second involves cognitive and affective components without any obvious sign of "perceptual" mediators, and refers to some patients who assess their physical dimensions accurately but react to their bodies with extreme forms of disparagement or occasionally aggrandizement.

The most perplexing, yet most commonly described abnormality is the patient's apparent inability to recognize how thin she has become. Bruch (1973) refers to this as "disturbed size awareness" (p. 89). It is illustrated by a 23-year-old patient who explained:

> I look in a full length mirror at least 4 or 5 times daily and I really cannot see myself as too thin. Sometimes after several days of strict dieting, I feel that my shape is tolerable, but most of the time, odd as it may seem, I look in the mirror and believe that I am too fat.

When she made this statement she weighed 33 kg and was 168 cm tall. Eventually she gave up weighing herself because the numbers never agreed with her visual image. After two years of treatment, in which a positive therapeutic relationship had been established and her weight had increased considerably, she maintained this erroneous self-perception. She did recognize, however, that her self-perception had little to do with her actual weight. Another inpatient, weighing 32 kg, expressed disbelief when she learned that a patient whom she described as "very emaciated and sickly" was actually 10 kg heavier. She was also bewildered at the dissonance between numbers on the scale and her own experience of her body. Some patients may appear to be motivated to recover from their illness but find it difficult to maintain a normal weight because of this overestimation of their body dimensions. During psychotherapy the patient's first recognition of the distortion of her self-perception may intensify her overall sense of bodily mistrust and create a temporary crisis.

Some patients display a variation of this phenomenon in which their overestimation seems to be restricted to a particular part or parts of the body. Selected areas such as the stomach or thighs are magnified and seen as disproportionate to the rest of the body. These patients will acknowledge that in general they appear emaciated, but that further dieting is a necessary sacrifice to eliminate their "protruding stomach." These areas of the body are often subjected to rigid and bizarre "size standards," as indicated by such statements as: "I must be able to rest a ruler on both hipbones without it touching my abdomen" or "The inner surface of my thighs must not touch when I stand erect." This reliance on strict objective criteria demonstrates a profound mistrust of more conventional, subjective evaluations of size. The misperceived body region may have special psychological significance for the patient. For example, it may represent expectations for sexual or social maturity for which she feels unprepared.

Body image disturbance may be manifest in other patients who perceive their sizes relatively accurately according to objective or clinical assessment, but who exhibit an extraordinary loathing for all or parts of their body. This goes well beyond the dissatisfaction with their appearance common for Western women (Berscheid, Walster and Hohrnstedt, 1973), to the point of revulsion with one's shape. This body image disparagement has been described in obese individuals (Rand and Stunkard, 1978; Stunkard and Burt, 1967) but is usually not associated with anorexia nervosa. Although it may coexist with a body size estimation disorder, body image disparagement is fundamentally a conceptual disturbance. Some patients may at times feign "perceptual overestimation" in order to convince the clinician that weight gain is unnecessary. Although they see themselves as extremely thin, they defend this low weight for fear of the self-derogation which would result from the development of what are seen as repugnant deposits of body fat.

There is one further expression of body image disturbance which may occur either with normal size perception or with overestimation. This involves an exaggerated pleasure with, and overvaluation of, a thinner shape. Usually these patients do not seek treatment on their own but are conscripted by relatives. These patients see their low weight and thinness as an exceptional achievement earning them the distinction to which they have aspired. The emaciated shape may be viewed as a product of "oral asceticism" (Thoma, 1967) in which self-indulgence has been transcended. Galdston (1974) has commented on the cherished "60-pound ego ideal" which along with the fear of fatness is the motivation for some anorexics' pursuit of thinness. Others have noted the delight these patients take in inspecting their emaciated bodies while recording weight loss (Dally, 1969; King, 1963). Later the ecstacy with this "new shape" and its connotations for "self-control and beauty" is usually replaced by an intense fear of growing larger.

Thus, body image disturbance may involve the inability to assess one's size accurately as well as disturbed attitudes about one's body. Differentiating the various forms of body image disturbance is desirable since it may explain some of the disparate experimental findings to be discussed and may contribute to the development of effective treatment strategies.

## Empirical Studies of the Body Image

The objective measurement of body image in anorexia nervosa has involved the assessment of body size using three techniques. The first two methods involve estimation of the width of specific parts of the body and the third method requires the judgment of overall body size through manipulation of the width of one's own image. Disturbed "body image" has typically been defined as an overestimation of body parts or body size. Empirical studies using these techniques or variants of them are summarized in Table 1 and will be reviewed separately.

### Movable Caliper Technique

This method was originally used in anorexia nervosa by Slade and Russell (1973) and was based upon a technique described by Reitman and Cleveland (1964). It requires the subject to estimate the width or depth of specific body regions by adjusting movable calipers or beams of light from two reference points in space. Slade and Russell (1973) found that compared with normal controls, anorexic patients overestimated their body widths at specific regions (face, chest, waist, and hips). Overestimation decreased as the patients gained weight. Moreover, weight loss after discharge from hospital was related to in-hospital overestimation of body size. Crisp and Kalucy (1974) confirmed the finding that anorexic patients overestimated their sizes, particularly after ingesting a high carbohydrate meal, but they also reported that their control group overestimated to a similar degree.

## TABLE 1

### Summary of Body Image Investigations in Anorexia Nervosa

| Investigators | Criteria for Anorexia Nervosa (AN) | Sample Size | Average Age | Sex | Control Groups* | Assessment Method | Summary of Results |
|---|---|---|---|---|---|---|---|
| Gottheil et al. (1969) | + | 1 | 17 | F | None | Videotape | Viewing self, reduced denial of illness |
| Slade & Russell (1973) (1964) | + | 14 | 19.8 | 13 F 1 M | NC** (20) | Caliper device Reitman & Cleveland (1964) | AN overestimated compared to NC AN overestimation decreased with weight gain and was related to poor post-discharge prognosis |
| Crisp & Kalucy (1974) | Not specified | 6 | approx. 21 | 5 F 1 M | NC (5) | Caliper device | Both AN and NC overestimated Decreased overestimation related to good prognosis and weight gain Overestimation in AN but not NC effected by ingestion of high carbohydrate meal |
| Russell et al. (1975) | 1 | 14 | 19.8 | 13 F 1 M | NC** (20) | Caliper device | AN overestimated compared to NC AN overestimation decreased with weight gain and was related to poor post-discharge prognosis |
| Garner et al. (1976) | + | 18 | 20.7 | F | NC (16) Neurotic (16) Thin (16) | Caliper device Anamorphic lens | All groups overestimated size; not related to psychopathology Overestimation in AN, but not controls positively related to psychopathology |
| Garfinkel et al. (1977) | + | 28 | 20.4 | 27 F 1 M | None | Anamorphic lens | Overestimation related to poor clinical ratings and poor prognosis |

| Investigators | Criteria for Anorexia Nervosa (AN) | Sample Size | Average Age | Sex | Control Groups* | Assessment Method | Summary of Results |
|---|---|---|---|---|---|---|---|
| Goldberg et al. (1977) | + | 44 | 20.2 | F | None | Caliper device | Overestimation related to denial and resistance to weight gain in hospital |
| Fries (1977) | + | 21 | 20.8 | F | NC (22) Secondary amenorrhea (17) | Caliper device | AN and secondary amenorrhea groups overestimated compared to reported pilot studies where obese and schizophrenic subjects also overestimated |
| Button et al. (1977) | Not specified | 20 | 23.9 | F | NC (16) | Caliper device | No difference between AN and NC Rate of weight gain not related to estimates Overestimation related to vomiting and early relapse |
| Ben-Tovim et al. (1977) | Not specified | 1 (plus parents) | 19 | F | None | Caliper and generalized grid technique | Attitudes of parents of female AN— for both parents decreased width. leads to more favorable evaluation of their daughter |
| Garfinkel et al. (1978) | + | 26 | 20.8 | F | NC (16) | Anamorphic lens | AN self-estimates stable for one week and not affected by looking in mirror or ingestion of high calorie connotation meal |
| Casper et al. (1979) | Not specified | 79 | 20.1 | F | NC (103) | Caliper device | Overestimation in AN related to: 1) smaller weight gain over 5 weeks of treatment 2) lower pretreatment weight 3) less outpatient treatment 4) more previous hospitalization 5) greater denial 6) psychosexual immaturity |

TABLE 1
(continued)

| Investigators | Criteria for Anorexia Nervosa (AN) | Sample Size | Average Age | Sex | Control Groups* | Assessment Method | Summary of Results |
|---|---|---|---|---|---|---|---|
| Askevold (1975) | Not specified | 15 | ? | F | Physiotherapists (20) | "Pointing method" | Impressionistic results indicating that AN overestimate size |
| Pierloot & Houben (1978) | + | 31 | 20.9 (matched) (20) | | Psychoneurotic | Caliper and Askevold method | AN and controls overestimated AN significantly more overestimated. Decrease in over-estimation with light in room and mirror but not significantly No relation between overestimation and MMPI, or Barrier and Penetration scores or Rorschach. Askevold's method — overestimation in both groups, significantly greater in AN |
| Wingate & Christie (1978) | Not specified | 15 | 20.8 | F | 15 (normal controls) | Askevold method | AN had significantly lower E score on MMPI (ego strength). AN overestimated significantly greater than NC on shoulders, waist and hips NCs with lower E score tended to overestimate body width |
| Ben-Tovim et al. (1979) | Not specified | 8 | 19.7 | F | NC (11) NC mothers nurses (24) | Caliper device | All groups overestimated body width Overestimation was inversely related to actual width of body region |

| Investigators | Criteria for Anorexia Nervosa (AN) | Sample Size | Average Age | Sex | Control Groups* | Assessment Method | Summary of Results |
|---|---|---|---|---|---|---|---|
| Strober et al. (1979) | Not specified | 18 | 14.8 | F | Patient controls (24) | Askevold method, self-report of body distortions, figure drawings | Two testings, T-1 just after admission, T-2 6 months later<br>Both groups overestimated similarly<br>Only significant difference between groups was between AN and controls on self-report measure of body distortions at T-2 |
| Garfinkel et al. (1979) | Not specified | 16 | | F | NC (13) | Anamorphic lens | AN self-estimates stable on two testings one year apart<br>Body size estimation not related to weight gain in AN<br>Overestimation in AN related to lack of sucrose satiety |

*parentheses indicate N

**normal controls

+defined in terms corresponding in primary anorexia nervosa, presumably the same subjects as Slade and Russell (1973)

Subsequent investigations with this technique have yielded inconsistent findings. Fries (1977) and Pierloot and Houben (1978) reported a self-overestimation tendency in anorexic subjects when compared to controls. On the other hand, Garner, Garfinkel, Stancer and Moldofsky (1976) observed the self-overestimation of body regions to be as marked in controls as in anorexic subjects. When Button, Fransella and Slade (1977) repeated Slade and Russell's study with carefully matched controls, no differences were found between the two groups. However, it is significant that overestimation of size in the anorexic group was related to vomiting and early relapse. Casper, Halmi, Goldberg, Eckert and Davis (1979) found body size overestimation in both anorexic patients and age-matched controls indicating that "overestimation cannot be considered unique to anorexia nervosa." Indeed, it has been found in schizophrenics (Fries, 1977), thin and neurotic (Garner et al., 1976), obese (Fries, 1977; Garner et al., 1976), and pregnant women (Slade, 1977).

Ben-Tovim, Hunter and Crisp (1977) compared anorexics with control groups of young adolescents, their mothers, and nurses. Although group mean results were not presented, they concluded that overestimation of body width is a widespread phenomenon not confined to anorexia nervosa. An inverse relationship was found between accuracy of self-perception and the actual width of various body regions. However, the incomplete reporting of findings makes it impossible to determine the consistency of this trend. Although the movable caliper technique does not appear to differentiate regularly between groups, within the group of anorexic patients overestimation has been related to poor prognosis and psychopathology (Button et al., 1977; Casper et al., 1979; Goldberg, Halmi, Casper, Eckert and Davis, 1977; Slade and Russell, 1973).

Image-Marking Method

Askevold (1975) introduced a method for estimating perceived size which bears some resemblance to the movable caliper technique. The subject stands before a sheet of paper mounted on a wall and is asked to imagine that she is facing a mirror. With a pencil in each hand she is instructed to mark the place where she "sees" points which correspond to widths of specific body regions. Askevold (1975) recommended this method despite the absence of adequate control groups and statistical analysis of results. Pierloot and Houben (1978) and Wingate and Christie (1978) reported that the image-marking technique differentiated between anorexic patients and controls. In the latter study, lower ego strength (as measured by the E scale of the MMPI) was related to the anorexic's overestimation tendency. Furthermore, a group of controls selected for low E scale scores showed a tendency to self-overestimation which fell between the anorexia nervosa and first control groups. However, age differences between groups may have contributed to these results.

In a well-controlled study, Strober, Goldenberg, Green and Saxon (1979) assessed perception of body size with the image-marking method in anorexia nervosa patients and age-matched psychiatric inpatient controls. The patients were tested following admission and again six months later. Both groups overestimated body size to a similar degree on both occasions. Subjective experiences of body image distortion and differentiation of body concept in human figure drawings were also assessed. While anorexics exhibited somewhat greater deviation than controls, this only attained statistical significance on the second testing occasion with the body distortion questionnaire.

In summary, despite inconsistent findings, there is some evidence to suggest that anorexic patients overestimate body size using both methods designed to estimate the width of specific bodily regions. The majority of studies using the movable caliper technique indicate that both anorexics and age-matched controls overestimate, but that within the group of anorexic subjects the tendency may be related to prognostic and psychopathological features. Recent reports with the image-marking method have been similarly equivocal and its utility rests upon further studies of validity and reliability.

Distorting Photograph Technique

Glucksman and Hirsch (1969) introduced a method for assessing total body size perception. This involves the subject's estimation of her size using a projected photograph which can be distorted along the horizontal axis. The image can be made to look anywhere from 20% "thinner" to 20% "fatter" than its actual size. Glucksman and Hirsch (1969) initially found that six dieting obese subjects overestimated their body sizes in comparison with four controls. Garner et al. (1976) applied this technique (see Figure 1) to the study of body size perception in anorexic and obese patients.

Results from these weight-disordered groups are compared with three control groups in Figure 2. Approximately one-half of the anorexic patients showed a marked tendency toward body size overestimation and this was positively related to measures of introversion and lack of self-control. This tendency to overestimate body size applied only for the patient herself and did not extend to estimations of other people or objects. On clinical follow-up of the anorexic subjects, self-overestimation was a strong predictor of a poor prognosis (Garfinkel, Moldofsky and Garner, 1977). Moreover, overestimation in anorexic patients was found to be related to an interocep-

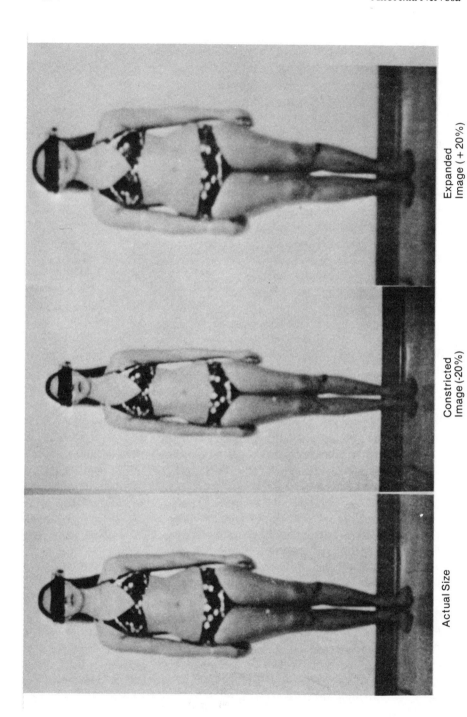

Figure 1. Range of images projected through the anamorphic lens.

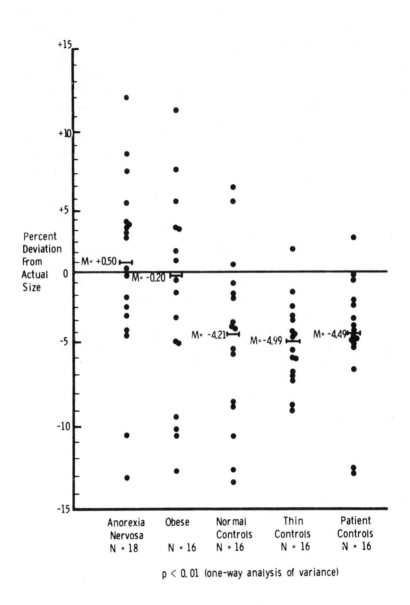

Figure 2. Self-estimation with the distorting photograph technique.

tive disturbance — the failure to develop an aversion to sucrose tastes (Garfinkel, Moldofsky, Garner, Stancer and Coscina, 1978). This last study also suggested that body size perception is a relatively stable phenomenon. In the anorexic group it was not significantly influenced by such visual cues as looking at one's image in a mirror or by the caloric connotation of a meal. Body size perception was also stable on separate testings one week (Garfinkel et al., 1978) and one year apart (Garfinkel, Moldofsky and Garner, 1979), irrespective of weight gain. Despite the reliability of body size estimation and its relationship to prognosis, it is essential to stress that not all anorexic patients overestimate body size. This raises a fundamental question related to the meaning and significance of body size misperception.

Previous studies (Garner et al., 1976; Garfinkel et al., 1978) have shown that there is a broad distribution of body size self-estimates across patients sampled. Some tend to overestimate while others underestimate. Figure 3 illustrates the distribution of body size self-estimates for the anorexic patients assessed on our unit from 1973 to 1981. The mean for all anorexic subjects is approximately +4.0% greater than actual size. This is significantly greater than the self-estimates of normal women of comparable age who as a group are quite accurate. Recently we have compared groups of anorexic

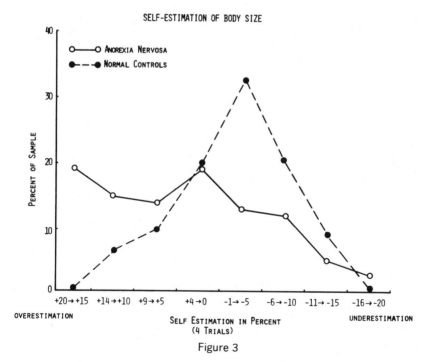

Figure 3

patients who display a marked tendency to overestimate body size with those who overestimate only moderately or underestimate their body size. The purpose of the comparison was to determine significant clinical and psychometric features which distinguish patients with severe overestimation tendencies. Subjects were patients seen in successive consultations at the Clarke Institute of Psychiatry who met a modified version of the Feighner, Robins, Guze, Woodruff, Winokur and Munoz (1972) criteria for anorexia nervosa (see Chapter 2). Approximately one-third of our patients overestimate their body size by + 10% or greater. This is very uncommon in normal women (Garner et al., 1976; Garfinkel et al., 1978). Therefore, the total group was divided using a mean self-estimate of + 10.0% as the partition. Table 2 illustrates the mean scores for the anorexic subjects on selected demographic and psychometric variables.

*Marked Overestimators Compared to Others with the Distorting Photograph Technique*

Overestimation of body size is related to a number of independent measures of psychopathology. It is associated with a greater presence of symptoms of anorexia nervosa as measured by the Eating Attitudes Test (EAT) (Garner and Garfinkel, 1979). Overestimators were more "external" on a locus of control measure (i.e., they felt they exerted less control over their lives). This has been used as an operational index of Bruch's (1962, 1973) "ineffectiveness" concept (Garner et al., 1976). Overestimators were more depressed as assessed by the Beck Depression Inventory (Beck, 1978) and the Hopkins Symptom Check List (HSCL) (Derogatis, Lipman, Rickels, Uhlenhuth and Covi, 1974). They were also more anxious (on the HSCL) and experienced greater physical anhedonia (Chapman, Chapman and Raulin, 1976) than others. While overestimators judged themselves to be larger, they preferred to be significantly smaller than their actual size. Subjects who overestimated also displayed more body image disturbance on an attitudinal measure of body satisfaction (Berscheid et al., 1973). There was a positive correlation (0.48, $p = 0.007$) between these two measures of "body image" despite the fact that they assess different aspects of the phenomenon. Therefore, marked overestimation both is a poor prognostic sign (Garfinkel et al., 1977) and is also associated with severity of psychopathology on a variety of parameters. It had been suggested that individual variability of body size estimates may be a meaningful factor in comparing groups (Pierloot and Houben, 1978). However, the variance in our subjects' four self-estimation trials (Table 2) did not significantly differ between the marked overestimators and other subjects.

## TABLE 2

### Clinical and Psychometric Features Comparing Marked Self-overestimators With Others on the Distorting Photograph Technique

| | Marked Overestimators ($\geq +10.0\%$) | | | Underestimators and Moderate Overestimators ($< +10.0\%$) | | | F Value | Significance Level |
|---|---|---|---|---|---|---|---|---|
| | (N) | mean | S.D. | (N) | mean | S.D. | | |
| **MANOVA on Demographic Variables** | | | | | | | | |
| OMNIBUS TEST | (38) | | | (87) | | | 1.36 | N.S. |
| Duration of illness | (38) | 47.9 | 63.6 | (87) | 41.4 | 42.3 | .46 | N.S. |
| Weight (kgs) | (38) | 45.6 | 11.0 | (87) | 42.3 | 9.2 | 2.97 | N.S. |
| Age | (38) | 21.1 | 5.5 | (87) | 21.6 | 4.9 | .30 | N.S. |
| Maximum premorbid weight (% average) | (38) | 104.8 | 20.8 | (87) | 103.1 | 19.5 | .20 | N.S. |
| **MANOVA on Psychometric Variables** | | | | | | | | |
| OMNIBUS TEST | (15) | | | (33) | | | 2.72 | $p < 0.03$ |
| Locus of control | (15) | 20.3 | 5.9 | (33) | 16.0 | 5.3 | 6.24 | $p < 0.02$ |
| Beck Depression Inventory | (15) | 31.4 | 13.0 | (33) | 21.0 | 15.6 | 5.03 | $p < 0.03$ |
| Depression (HSCL) | (15) | 30.1 | 8.4 | (33) | 23.5 | 7.4 | 7.29 | $p < 0.01$ |
| Physical anhedonia | (15) | 18.5 | 7.9 | (33) | 12.8 | 8.1 | 5.22 | $p < 0.03$ |
| Anxiety (HSCL) | (15) | 18.3 | 6.0 | (33) | 13.9 | 4.5 | 7.93 | $p < 0.07$ |
| Eating Attitudes Test (EAT) | (15) | 68.1 | 21.6 | (33) | 51.3 | 22.6 | 5.70 | $p < 0.02$ |
| **t-tests on other Body Image Parameters** | | | | | | | | |
| Self-estimates (variance — 4 trials) | (37) | 45.9 | 15.4 | (75) | 66.7 | 8.4 | 1.29 | N.S. |
| Ideal body size | (43) | -7.8 | 12.5 | (97) | +3.7 | 13.4 | 4.77 | $p < 0.001$ |
| Body dissatisfaction | (18) | 82.1 | 19.0 | (41) | 68.3 | 14.5 | 3.06 | $p < 0.005$ |

Reprinted with permission from Garner and Garfinkel, 1981.

Although the reliability and apparent utility of the distorting photograph technique have been supported by earlier studies and the above results, there is a disappointing lack of convergent data from other laboratories. This may relate to the complexity of the apparatus design. Recently Allen-beck, Hallberg, and Espmark (1976) suggested a method of assessing body size perception which involves adjusting one's own image on a TV video monitor. We trust that the technical advantages of this method will prompt others to explore overall body size estimation in anorexic patients.

## Methodological Issues in Body Image Assessment

Increased technological sophistication and improvements in psychometric instruments have greatly influenced psychological research in general. Research on body image disturbances in anorexia nervosa has also relied on more objective methods in an attempt to document and quantify clinically observed aberrations in body image. Despite the advantages of the more empirical measurement techniques, the recent literature on body image has been hampered by methodological shortcomings (Garner and Garfinkel, 1977, 1981; Garner, Garfinkel and Moldofsky, 1978). These will be addressed under the headings: 1) reliability; 2) validity; 3) selection of subjects; and 4) the experimental situation.

### 1) Reliability

Reliability refers to the internal consistency or stability (repeatability) of a procedure. A method is reliable if it consistently yields the same results under the same testing conditions, hypothetically holding all subject variables constant. Validity refers to the degree to which the measure accurately tests the concept. Reliability is especially critical since it sets an upper limit on the potential validity of the measure. If measurements are not repeatable, then they obviously cannot be accurate.

The reliability data for the measures of body size perception in anorexia nervosa indicate that they are relatively consistent and stable over time. On the same testing occasion with the caliper device, positive and usually significant intercorrelations (range = 0.25-0.93; mean = 0.64) between estimates of different bodily regions (face, chest, waist, hips) have been reported (Button et al., 1977; Halmi, Goldberg and Cunningham, 1977; Pierloot and Houben, 1978; Slade and Russell, 1973). There are similar findings with the image-marking method (range = 0.30-0.75; mean = 0.60) Pierloot and Houben, 1978; Strober et al., 1979). On a sample-wide basis with anorexic patients, self-estimation does not significantly change with weight gain using the caliper device (Button et al., 1977; Strober et al., 1979) and the image-marking method (Strober et al., 1979). Self-estimates with the distorting photograph method have been shown to be reliable over one week (anorexics, $r = 0.75$; controls, $r = 0.45$) (Garfinkel et al., 1978) and one year (anorexics, $r = 0.56$ and 0.70) irrespective of weight gain (Garfinkel el at., 1979). Thus, the recent literature seems to indicate that body size estimation is a relatively reliable phenomenon. What remains is the determination of its meaning and usefulness in understanding anorexia nervosa.

## 2) Validity

Estimates of validity may be determined in several different ways. Convergent validity is demonstrated by showing that measures under investigation correlate highly with other independent assessments of the same or a similar concept. In this regard, Garner et al. (1976) reported that mean self-estimates on the caliper device were correlated with those of the distorting photograph method for anorexic ($r = 0.50$, $p < 0.05$) and obese ($r = 0.44$, $p < 0.05$), but not for control subjects.

Pierloot and Houben (1978) found that anorexic patients overestimated body widths with both the caliper device and the image-marking method but they did not report the correlation between measures. Of interest, they found no relationship between either the size estimation task and the body "Barrier or Penetration" indices of the Rorschach test. Strober et al. (1979) addressed convergent validity by administering three different tests of "body image." The measures were (a) the image-marking method, (b) the Fisher Body Distortion Questionnaire (Fisher, 1970) and (c) a "draw a person" measure aimed at assessing the degree of differentiation of body concept. The correlations between measures were small, with none reaching statistical significance. Finally, with our large series of anorexic patients we have found a positive relationship between overestimation on the distorting photograph technique and body dissatisfaction from a self-report questionnaire (Table 2).

The preceding data seem to indicate that measures of body size perception are meaningfully related to one another. However, with the exception of the "body dissatisfaction" scale, there appears to be only a weak relationship between size perception and any of the more traditional measures of the body image construct.

Predictive validity is also an important consideration in evaluating measures of body size perception. Even if the mechanisms determining body size perception are not clearly understood, if the measure can meaningfully predict phenomena of interest, then it is useful. As indicated in the preceding review, body size estimation has been associated with a number of prognostic and psychopathological variables.

Finally, the most general and difficult form of validity to establish is construct validity. It refers to meaningfulness and conceptual integrity of the measure in relation to the theoretical construct that it is intended to reflect. The theoretical merit of the body image concept and the construct validity of the measures used to infer this phenomenon in anorexia nervosa will be explored in the section on theoretical issues.

## 3) Selection of Subjects

A major deficiency within the body image research relates to the composition and utilization of experimental and control groups. In many studies, diagnostic criteria for selection of patients are unclear (see Table 1). Furthermore, investigations often do not indicate how patients were selected, or fail to include relevant demographic characteristics such as current weight, duration of illness, or stage of treatment. The "patient uniformity assumption" (Kiesler, 1966) is inappropriately made by the failure of many studies to provide a detailed description of the characteristics of the patient population or to consider differences in the analysis of the results. This may be because the heterogeneity of anorexia nervosa has only recently been emphasized (Casper, Eckert, Halmi, Goldberg and Davis, 1980; Garfinkel et al., 1980). Characteristics such as vomiting (Button et al., 1977) and subject age (Button et al., 1977; Halmi et al., 1977) do influence estimation of body size and must be controlled for the results to be meaningful.

Control groups are another important consideration. While most recent studies have matched subjects on age, many have neglected such variables as socioeconomic status, dietary restraint, psychopathology and IQ. It is also becoming increasingly apparent that controls should be unaware of the hypotheses under investigation. Button et al. (1977) have suggested that publicity given to body image phemonema in anorexia nervosa could have affected the results of their study. Patients who are in hospital because of weight loss may also view the body estimation task very differently from non-patients or outpatients. They may have a vested interest in demonstrating to the experimenter that they really do see themselves as "fat." Differences in compliance, level of denial, or prior knowledge of expected findings have rarely been measured and may influence the results, although they may be irrelevant to the hypothesized origins of "body image disturbance."

The finding that self-overestimation occurs in normal controls, as well as in anorexia nervosa patients (Button et al., 1977; Casper et al., 1979; Crisp and Kalucy, 1974; Fries, 1977; Garner et al., 1976), raises the question of the precise meaning of overestimation. As with other psychological tests, intergroup comparisons may be of considerable interest, but it is not justified to assume that the norms for a test for a patient group have the same meaning in a quantitative or qualitative sense as those for a normal population. For example, a score of 20 on the Beck Depression Inventory (BDI) may indicate moderate depression in a normal sample, but for an anorexic group it could have an entirely different meaning. This is partially due to the fact that inflated scores on a number of items pertaining to concentration, weight loss, sleep disturbance, and sexual interest may result from starvation symptoms rather than from depressed affect. Therefore, intergroup comparisons of BDI scores could be quite misleading, especially if the two data distributions are assumed to be uniform. Anorexic patients who are sensitized to body shape may react to the task of self-estimation in a way completely different from their "normal" counterparts. Perhaps different mechanisms determine size estimation in patients versus controls. Casper et al. (1979) have pointed out that the "inaccurate appraisal of body dimensions constitutes a more serious disturbance in anorexia nervosa" when the patient is grossly underweight. Body image measures must be validated separately on an anorexic patient population. Investigations of the mechanisms responsible for self-overestimation must be conducted with these patients to determine their signficance.

## 4) The Experimental Situation

Additional areas of methodological concern relate to the laboratory setting, procedure, and apparatus utilized. For example, with the image-marking method (Askevold, 1975) the patient is required to estimate her size in the presence of prominent external referents within the experimental situation, the most obvious of which is her own body. Since her actual shape could be said to be visibly apparent, her purported "overestimating" may simply be a communication to the experimenter that she "feels fat" and does not want to gain weight. Nevertheless, the measure may be a useful nonverbal method for assessing the patient's attitudes about her body shape. This method is somewhat unappealing since it casts an illusion of objectivity despite such obvious sources of bias.

Button et al. (1977) reported different results on two patient samples who were tested on different body image machinery and under conditions of different lighting. They found significant group differences and greater overestimation among the anorexic subjects under conditions of greater illumination. Most studies have failed to report details of the lighting in the experimental situation. Other differences in the size estimation apparatus, such as whether its movement is manual or motorized, the numbers of light sources and the variable positioning of the experimenter, may significantly alter results. Even more critical are the experimenters themselves. Few studies indicate their gender or whether they were blind to the hypotheses. Given the evidence for the influence of experimenter expectancy effects (Barber, 1976), it would be desirable to provide controls for these sources of bias.

In summary, there are a variety of methodological pitfalls pervading research on body image in anorexia nervosa. While these do not necessarily negate the significance of previous reports, they may be responsible, in part, for the inconsistencies in the findings. It is desirable to control for many of the potential sources of bias in future studies, but where this is impossible, statistical control through covariance analyses is essential.

## Explanations of Faulty Size Awareness

Several theoretical explanations have been proposed for the mechanisms responsible for these disturbances in anorexia nervosa. They will be examined below.

### 1) Development Deviation

Bruch (1962, 1973, 1977) has suggested that body size misperception is related to the general concept of "hunger awareness" which includes both misperception of bodily sensations and cognitive disturbances. Using Piaget's model of cognitive development, Bruch postulates that anorexics experience a developmental arrest and do not progress past the concrete operational stage of development (Bruch, 1977). She suggests that they rely excessively on the process of accommodation, with a corresponding deficiency in the assimilation mode. This developmental conception of "body image" is supported by the Halmi et al. (1977) finding that accuracy of self-estimation increases as adolescent girls become older. Further, Modarressi and Kenny (1977) have reported that responses of young children to their images in a mirror follow a definite developmental pattern which correspond to their Piagetian stage of cognitive development. Exploration of conceptual development in anorexic patients using standard Piagetian measures could provide a more sophisticated means of testing the developmental hypothesis and link self-perception to other maturational cognitive styles.

A different developmental viewpoint has been favored by Crisp (1965, 1977). He maintains that anorexia nervosa involves an avoidance of biological maturity in vulnerable adolescents in response to the conflicts, demands, and expectations of adulthood. Menarche, and the body fat required for this, represent a developmental milestone which signifies changes associated with adulthood. The tendency for some anorexic patients to overestimate their body sizes in a manner that is similar to younger girls may indicate a form of "regression" that is extended to this particular area.

Evidence for the significance of menarche in relationship to body image comes from a study by Koff, Rierdan and Silverstone (1978). Using both a cross-sectional and longitudinal design, they studied three normal groups on two occasions six months apart: girls who were premenarchal on both test occasions, girls who were postmenarchal on both occasions, and girls who experienced menarche between the first and second testing. Postmenarchal girls produced more sexually differentiated human figure drawings and reported greater satisfaction with "female" body parts.

The results support the speculation by others (Kerstenberg, 1961, 1967; Whisnant and Zegans, 1975) that menarche is a pivotal event for the reorganization of the adolescent girl's body image and sexual identity. These changes in bodily experience may represent part of a more fundamental shift in thinking and feeling that is associated with the hormonal changes at menarche (Petersen, 1979; Petersen and Wittig, 1979). The amenorrhea of anorexia nervosa may be associated not only with age-inappropriate body size estimates, but also with similar changes in sexual identity, thinking, and feeling. Therefore, within the developmental deviation framework, self-overestimation may represent a regression to a premenarchal perception of "body image."

## 2) Adaptive Failure vs. Abnormal Sensitivity

Crisp and Kalucy (1974) observed that after weight recovery, anorexic patients persisted in their overestimation and that the degree of overestimation was related to the individual's premorbid weight. Moreover, the normal controls who showed the greatest overestimation were found to have lost weight prior to the experiment. Although these data were impressionistic, it was concluded that overestimation may reflect a "surviving perception of maximum-ever weight and size." Thus, the error may result from a failure to adapt one's perceptions to recent change in shape.

Slade (1977) offered an alternate hypothesis that attributes overestimation to "abnormal sensitivity" to body shape. He proposed a test of the "adaptive failure" explanation by measuring self-perception in pregnant women, since they experience a relatively rapid change in shape. Forty women, who were on average four months pregnant, were found to overestimate their sizes when compared to normal controls. Sixteen women were retested when about eight months pregnant and showed a reduction of their overestimation tendency, which Slade interpreted to be contrary to the adaptive failure hypothesis. Rather, increasing accuracy late in pregnancy may be due to heightened concern or "abnormal sensitivity." The implications of this finding are that a cognitively mediated sensitivity to one's actual size may underlie body image disturbances rather than the perceptual delay as suggested by the adaptive failure hypothesis. Slade's study did not, however, include any direct measure of sensitivity to body shape, which would have tested his preferred interpretation. Moreover, his assumption that the processes influencing size estimation in pregnancy are the same as those in anorexia nervosa may not be justified.

As indicated earlier (Table 2), marked self-overestimators report significantly more dissatisfaction with their bodies than the moderate overestimators or underestimators. Moreover, our results (Table 2) indicate that overestimators, as a group, prefer a smaller size. That is, although they view themselves as larger, they want to be considerably smaller than their actual size. These results support the idea that, at least for anorexic patients, overestimation is related to sensitivity about shape in that it is associated with dissatisfaction with one's body and a desire to be much thinner. However, they do not explain the observations by others of overestimation in some normal girls (Halmi et al., 1977), or in other groups with different assessment methods.

## 3) Denial of Illness

It has been reported that body size overestimation is associated with independent measures of denial of illness (Casper et al., 1979; Goldberg et al., 1977). Crisp and Kalucy (1974) found that patients substantially reduced their overestimation when told that their estimates were at least partially "a strategy designed to lend conviction to their insistence" that their weight was normal. It is unclear whether the "corrected" self-estimate represents a more authentic judgment or a compliant response to the experimenter's challenge. Pierloot and Houben (1978) employed a similar statement and found minimal changes in degree of patients' overestimation.

Our results argue against denial as a mediator since overestimation is associated with higher scores on a self-report measure of anorexic symptoms (EAT, Table 2). We and others (Bruch, 1973; Crisp, 1970) have found that denial may represent an initial posture of many patients, but this is reduced in most cases once a sound therapeutic alliance has been formed. Misperception of size tends to persist long past the initial phase of treatment.

4) Personality Characteristics as Mediators of Body Image

We have found that various measures of personality are related to anorexics' self-overestimation. However, their value in furthering the understanding of the mechanism responsible for body image disturbance is limited since the factors underlying most of these personality dimensions are as poorly understood as those influencing body image itself. For example, locus of control has been shown to correlate with overestimation tendencies (Garner et al., 1976; Pierloot and Houben, 1978). Thus, the degree to which one perceives life events as dependent upon luck, fate, or other factors outside one's personal control seems to be related to overestimation of body size; yet the exact connection between these two constructs is highly speculative. Although Bruch (1962) describes "a sense of ineffectiveness" as the core of the anorexic's perceptual/conceptual disturbance, precisely how this determines size overestimation is not understood. However, if the locus of control results are evaluated within the context of other personality findings, a more consistent picture begins to emerge.

Wingate and Christie (1978) have reported that overestimation in anorexic patients is negatively correlated with ego-strength as measured by the E scale of the MMPI. This relationship did not exist for a normal control group, but did for a second control group selected for low E scores. As indicated in Table 3, we have found a relationship between self-report measures of body dissatisfaction (Berscheid et al., 1973) and self-esteem (Janis and Field, 1959) as well as their association with self and ideal estimation with the distorting photograph technique. These data were collected on 25 consecutive anorexic subjects assessed on our unit. Self-esteem was positively correlated with body satisfaction and ideal body size. That is, patients with higher self-esteem were more satisfied with their bodies and preferred being larger. They also estimated their size as smaller. Others have emphasized the positive relationship between self-esteem and body satisfaction in normal subjects (Rosen and Ross, 1968; Secord and Jourard, 1953). The association between feelings about one's body and feelings about other, nonphysical aspects of self has been demonstrated by King and Manaster (1977). They reported that expectations for achieving job interview success were significantly related to body satisfaction, and even more to self-esteem. Further analyses revealed that virtually all of the predictive power accounted for by body satisfaction was due to features shared with self-esteem measures.

It could be argued that body satisfaction is subsumed under the more general concept of self-esteem. This is in agreement with self-esteem consistency theory (Wylie, 1968) which holds that expectations and perceptions

## TABLE 3

Intercorrelations of Self-estimates, Ideal Body Size, Self-esteem
and Body Satisfaction in Anorexia Nervosa (N = 25)

| | Self-estimates | Ideal Body Size | Self-esteem | Body Satisfaction |
|---|---|---|---|---|
| Self-estimates | | | | |
| Ideal Body Size | -0.63<br>p < 0.001 | | | |
| Self-esteem | -0.53<br>p < 0.003 | 0.51<br>p < 0.004 | | |
| Body Satisfaction | -0.48<br>p < 0.007 | 0.41<br>p < 0.02 | 0.65<br>p < 0.001 | |

Reprinted with permission from Garner and Garfinkel, 1981.

will be determined by one's self-evaluation of general, nonphysical attributes. It has been asserted that in anorexia nervosa, self-worth becomes concretized in the body shape (Bruch, 1973). Anorexics become highly sensitized to shape, and body fatness becomes an index by which non-physical qualities are evaluated. If an individual views the nonphysical aspects of herself negatively and if she also equates low self-worth with "fatness," she may see herself as larger than her actual size. In other groups, self-esteem has been shown to influence level of aspiration, school failure, intellectual functioning, athletic performance and industrial productivity (Cohen, 1959; Combs, Avila and Parkey, 1973; King and Manaster, 1977; Silverman, 1964; Wylie, 1968). Low self-esteem (and body dissatisfaction) may play a role in the misperception of size in anorexia nervosa, particularly when coupled with heightened shape concerns.

In summary, there has been recent interest in the objective measurement of body image in anorexia nervosa. However, many questions remain regarding both the basic mechanisms responsible for the findings and their precise meaning. Some questions are methodological in nature. For example, do the "whole body" measures assess the same underlying phenomenon as the "body part" methods? On a conceptual level it is unclear whether body image disturbances are pathogenic or a byproduct of a serious weight disorder. Also, how close is the association between the concept of body image identified clinically and that of body size estimation which has been measured objectively? Is body size misperception part of a general cognitive immaturity, "adaptive failure," or a cognitively mediated "abnormal sensitivity" to shape? The possible association between self-esteem and body satisfaction and the latter's relationship to size estimation suggests that, in line with self-esteem consistency theory, size perception may be closely tied to satisfaction with general aspects of self. Is overestimation a function of the general psychological disturbance in these patients, or is it related to a particular functional deficit of specific interest in the disorder? It is also not known how body size perception is affected by long-term treatment. The ways in which anorexic patients see themselves, as well as the cognitive and affective responses to this perception, remain an interesting and potentially fruitful area of study.

## DISTORTIONS IN INTERNAL PERCEPTIONS

According to Bruch (1962, 1973) the concept of "body awareness" or "body identity" is not limited to body image but extends to the perception and interpretation of interoceptive stimuli. More specifically, she postulates that anorexia nervosa and juvenile onset obesity are fundamentally related to disturbed awareness of inner processes which include misperception of hunger, satiety, and other bodily sensations. She considers the lack of responsiveness to fatigue, cold, and sexual feelings in anorexia nervosa to be examples of this disturbance. Accurately recognizing hunger, satiety, and other bodily sensations or feeling states is thought to be acquired by learning and, according to this viewpoint, people who develop anorexia nervosa have never learned the connection between basic drives and the appropriate biological or environmental stimulus situations which lead to drive reduction. While Bruch's etiological propositions are difficult to test empirically, the specific deficits that she has described are clinically evident in some patients and recently these have received some empirical support.

### Clinical Manifestations

Patients will often describe extreme confusion about their internal states early in treatment or will appear devoid of thoughts and feelings which reflect their personal experiences. When used to describe other psychosomatic disorders, this phenomenon has been termed alexithymia (Sifneos, 1973). These deficits range in depth from subtle confusion in affective labeling to complete mistrust of one's internal state. While variable in severity, this disturbance is very common in anorexia nervosa.

Anorexics have remarkable difficulty in focusing on, and accurately reporting, their emotional and physical states. When asked to describe their sensations of satiety they often respond with such incongruities as: "I feel like I have eaten"; "I don't like it"; "I feel guilty"; or they may describe bloating, discomfort, pain, or distension. Inquiries about their emotions may result in defensive or hostile responses to what is viewed as an intrusion into an area that they do not understand. Often they are evasive or vague about their sensations and feelings. At other times, their sincere attempts at self-reporting lack congruence or conviction and have a "parrot-like" quality. Apparently flippant comments, such as "I guess I should feel angry or maybe happy — take your pick," may reflect confusion rather than indifference. A common complaint is the feeling of emptiness, hollowness, or blankness inside. Because of this and the rigidity in expressed affect, the patient may be viewed as concrete, lacking insight or not psychologically-minded. The patient's description of her inner states may show inaccuracies in a broad range of self-perceptions. These may be related to core deficits in interoceptive awareness and/or to systematic cognitive distortions. The latter will be discussed further in the next section.

The anorexic's perceptions may be unduly influenced by external factors. These are used as the frame of reference for self-expression and experience because of the defects in internal experiences. Clinically, this may be apparent in the form of a symbiotic dependent relationship with one parent who is thought to know the patient better than she knows herself. For example, an anorexic patient, when asked about her own feelings in response to a relative's death, pointed to her mother and said, "Ask her — she can explain it better than I can." The anorexic's conviction that others are more attuned to her inner world than she is herself may be behind complaints of feeling controlled, dominated, and exploited by others. For example, another patient explained that, when others showed pleasure at her eating, she could not continue because she was not sure whether she was eating for herself or for them. It was as if eating were not intrinsically within her own area of influence.

This interoceptive confusion is most evident in relation to specific aspects of visceral functioning. It is expressed as a gross mistrust of the body to carry out automatic regulatory processes without conscious control. Some even consider their bodies to be like a foreign and defiant object which must be subdued. This control and hypervigilance are most obvious with food. Despite considerable intellectual data about caloric values and constituents of foods, these patients display little understanding of the body's capability in utilizing energy. Some patients believe that their bodies defy the laws of thermodynamics and gain or lose weight according to some mysterious and unreliable process. After eating they may experience the food as if a foreign substance were occupying their intestinal system. Normal satiety is impaired. Anorexics frequently report fearing that if they take one bite of food they are not going to be able to stop eating and will suddenly develop into grotesque obesity. This terrifying possibility is countered by rigid control of eating.

However, this bodily mistrust and fear of loss of control is not confined to eating. Many anorexics treat other bodily processes similarly. For example, patients will often show a preoccupation with bowel functioning. Laxative abuse is not only intended to promote weight loss but also to rigidly regulate bowel movements. One patient developed a marked dependence on a decongestant nasal spray because of her lack of trust in her body's own ability to reduce her nasal congestion. Stopping the spray produced fear and morbid concerns about suffocation which lasted several weeks. This patient experienced a fear of being overwhelmed or engulfed by her body which was viewed to exert an independent will. Some patients have had similar problems in attempting to regulate other natural functions such as micturition or sleep.

The anorexic's confused perception of her internal environment and her sense of helplessness in effectively dealing with people provides a core to her feelings of loss of control. These are countered by inordinate self-discipline and environmental control. Preoccupation with calories and control of eating are examples. There is a general attempt to impose orderliness and certainty. Regimented exercise, obsessive rituals, and the perpetual soliciting of reassurance from parents are all directed at obtaining constancy. Selvini Palazzoli (1974) has observed a disorder in the experience of time in some patients. It is as if time is feared because it is continually evolving and must be filled. Patients complain of boredom, restlessness, and occasionally terror in the absence of environmental structure which could provide cohesion and definition to experience.

Frequently, the only active reinforcements in the anorexic's life are the pleasures of weight loss, exercise, and self-control. When these are thwarted — for example, in hospital — there is an initial void which can lead to heightened anxiety. One patient engaged in rigorous exercise, studied relentlessly, and rigidly organized her daily activities while out of hospital. She found this an arduous lifestyle but was plagued with guilt when she altered the pattern. When she was forced to curtail her regimen in hospital, she complained of not knowing what to do with herself and being overwhelmed by boredom and aimlessness. However, it was a feeling that went beyond simple boredom. In the absence of self-imposed structure, she felt empty, isolated, and more helpless than ever before. She found it impossible to generate pleasureable activities by herself and complained of a growing sense of disorganization. Without the "self-definition" imposed by her parents and later by her robot-like activities, she began to recognize her lack of inner awareness of feelings, thoughts, and motives. Her previous constant activity had provided an appearance of self-involvement which was designed to fill up space and time.

The above examples illustrate distortions in interoception and confusion about the nature of one's affective states. The origin of these abnormalities is not known. Moreover, they are not unique to anorexia nervosa for they have been purported to occur in other psychosomatic disorders (Sifneos, 1973). It is not even known with certainty whether they are related to the pathogenesis of the disorder or are byproducts of it. Bruch (1973) has linked them to the core psychopathology of anorexia nervosa, which she feels is the lack of mastery or control these individuals experience. Deficits in self-esteem and self-trust may also be related to these interoceptive disorders. The lack of trust in internal experiences may be a manifestation of a more general lack of confidence in the validity of thinking, feeling, and perception.

Consistent with the clinical observations of interoceptive disturbances, several lines of experimental inquiry suggest that these patients may not experience their internal environment in the same way as individuals without eating disorders.

*Empirical Studies of Interoception*

In the early part of this century Cannon (1912) claimed that gastric contractions, measured by an intragastric balloon, could be related to hunger sensations in normal individuals. The relationship between gastric activity and "hunger" has not been supported by more recent investigations (Penick, Smith, Wieneke and Hinkle, 1967; Stunkard and Fox, 1971). However, the perception of gastric contractions in anorexia nervosa has been examined by Silverstone and Russell (1967) using an intragastric tube, and by Crisp (1967) using an intragastric pressure telemetry pill. Both studies found no significant differences in stomach motility between anorexic patients and normal subjects. The anorexic patients were capable of recognizing contractions, but interestingly, some did not interpret these as sensations of hunger.

Coddington and Bruch (1970) found that both anorexic and obese subjects were less accurate than normals in perceiving the amounts of food (Metrecal) that were directly introduced into their stomachs. While only three anorexic subjects were included in this study, it does support the hypothesized deficit in the recognition of internal state. Other studies have reported that subjects with juvenile onset obesity have difficulties appropriately responding to internal satiety cues (Cabanac and Duclaux, 1970; Campbell, Hashim and Van Itallie, 1971) or that their eating behavior may be largely determined by external circumstances such as the availability, salience, and palatability of food (Nisbett, 1972; Schachter, 1971; Schachter and Rodin, 1974). However, this external responsiveness may be a phenomenon of dieting, rather than obesity (Herman and Polivy, 1975) and therefore probably applies to anorexics as well as the obese.

The perception of hunger and satiety in anorexia nervosa was investigated by Garfinkel (1974) using several self-report questionnaires. Eleven anorexic patients reported distorted sensations of satiety compared with 11 control subjects. After fasting for 12 hours, all subjects were given a questionnaire inquiring about the experience of hunger. Subjects were then given a standard meal followed by another questionnaire assessing satiety. Except for an increased preoccupation with food and a fear of eating, anorexics did not differ from normals in their perception of hunger. However, in contrast to normals, the anorexic patients reported disturbed sensations of satiety including bloating, absence of stomach sensations, nausea, aches and pains. In a recent study, Dubois, Gross, Ebert and Castell (1979) have shown that anorexic patients display delayed gastric emptying compared with normal controls. After weight gain, the emptying rates for the anorexic patients studied tended to increase toward normal but were still significantly less than in controls. These results may partially explain the postprandial fullness, discomfort, and early satiety observed with most patients.

In a recent series of studies (Garfinkel et al., 1978, 1979), we have used taste perception as an index of satiety in anorexia nervosa. This procedure was derived from the work of Cabanac and Duclaux (1970), who found that obese subjects do not experience any difference in the rated pleasantness of sucrose tastes before versus after the ingestion of glucose. Normal subjects, in contrast, experience "satiety" or an aversion to the taste of sucrose after glucose preloading. On the basis of these results Cabanac and Duclaux (1970) suggested that obese subjects are less responsive than nonobese to internal cues related to nutritional requirements. A replication of the Cabanac and Duclaux study (Underwood, Belton and Hulme, 1973) reported an interesting but unanticipated finding. One of the normal subjects who displayed an absence of aversion to sucrose was later found to have anorexia nervosa.

Our first study of this demonstrated that disturbances in interoception as measured by the satiety-aversion-to-sucrose test were evident in anorexic patients in contrast to normal controls. A modified version of the Cabanac and Duclaux (1970) procedure was used — only a 20% sucrose solution was tasted since this had appeared to produce maximal differences between obese and controls in the Cabanac and Duclaux (1970) studies. Rather than using a 50 g glucose load, we used two test lunches which contained 400 Cal. One of these was designed to connote a high caloric content; it consisted of tuna salad, cole slaw, and a large chocolate sundae. The second lunch was identical in actual caloric content but was designed to connote a relatively low calorie content, tuna salad and cole slaw both supplemented with gluconal. Sweetness and pleasantness ratings were collected on all subjects every three minutes for one hour after lunch. Figure 4 illustrates the comparison between anorexics and controls and indicates that anorexics fail to develop an aversion to the sweet tastes.

Furthermore, in a larger sample of our anorexic patients this interoceptive disturbance was related to the tendency to overestimate body size (N = 72, $r = 0.26$, $p < 0.02$). Figure 5 compares overestimators vs. underestimators of body size on the satiety-aversion-to-sucrose test; it is the overestimators who fail to develop a normal aversion. In contrast to Crisp and Kalucy's (1974) earlier report, we did not find that the caloric connotation of the meal systematically influenced body size estimation in either patients or controls. The lack of satiety aversion was also independent of which meal was eaten. As in a previous report (Garfinkel, 1974), the results on a satiety questionnaire differentiated anorexics from normal subjects on various parameters. These were postprandial changes in mood, gastrointestinal sensations and willpower required to stop eating. Using a 10 cm analogue scale for "satiety," anorexics displayed greater pre-meal fullness and their fullness persisted longer after eating the meal that they believed to have more calories. This latter finding suggests a substantial cognitive influence in the satiety experience in anorexic patients.

In a follow-up one year later with 16 of the original patients and 13 controls, we found that the failure to develop an aversion to sucrose in the anorexics was stable over the two testing occasions. Moreover, normalization of weight in some patients did not alter this tendency. This suggests that the anorexic patients are less responsive than normal to internal cues related to nutritional requirements and thus they may be unable to habituate to repeated exposure to carbohydrate-containing foods. It also indicates that normalization of this apparent perceptual disturbance does not necessarily follow closely on weight restoration.

These findings support the suggestion that patients with anorexia nervosa have disturbed interoceptive experiences and specifically misperceive stimuli that lead to satiety in normal subjects. Their perception of satiety appears to be less influenced by internal state than by their cognitive expectations related to food intake. Therefore, they may possess a deficit in the internal

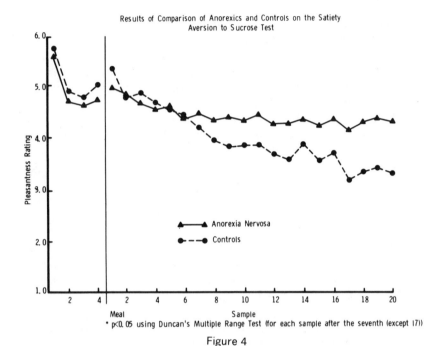

Figure 4

Figure 5

mechanisms for regulating carbohydrate ingestion, or the cognitive factors mediating intake may be sufficiently prominent that they prevail over the internal regulatory mechanisms. Two alternate explanations for the lack of satiety-aversion to sucrose are also possible: (a) anorexics may possess altered taste sensitivity or (b) their taste preference for carbohydrates is aberrant. Lacey, Stanley, Crutchfield and Crisp (1977) have reported heightened sucrose taste sensitivity as a consequence of carbohydrate avoidance in anorexia nervosa. After patients were refed with a normal diet they displayed diminished sensitivity to the taste of sucrose. Our findings with five patients, who were initially tested at a low weight and again after weight restoration, indicated that the weight gain did not significantly affect their responses to the sucrose solutions (Garfinkel et al., 1979). Thus, it appears that sucrose taste preferences are more transient and reversible through weight restoration than the sucrose satiety response. Further studies of the specific effects of chronic carbohydrate avoidance on the development of normal sucrose satiety are needed to clarify the mechanisms responsible for the abnormalities observed in anorexic patients.

In summary, several lines of experimental inquiry have suggested that patients with anorexia may misperceive internal experiences particularly related to satiety. It is not clear whether these perceptual disturbances are determinants or byproducts of the syndrome, and what their relationship is to complete recovery. Since the aberrant experience of satiety is clinically important with these patients, more detailed study of potential mechanisms may be of considerable value.

## CONCEPTUAL DISTURBANCES

A striking finding in our clinical contact with anorexia nervosa patients over the past ten years has been the prominence of persistent distorted attitudes and concepts which seem to affect almost every area of their lives. While these distorted thinking patterns obviously relate to food and body shape, they extend beyond these areas to the understanding of one's self and one's environment. Even patients who have regained their weight may have peculiar ideas about the value of attaining a minimal weight. Those thoughts are viewed by the patients as a logical extension from the central premise that thinness is a highly desirable state. This, and related assumptions, may play a role in the relapse of patients who manage to attain a relatively normal weight.

Bruch (1973, 1977, 1978) has recognized the significance of a broad range of conceptual deviations which characterize anorexia nervosa. She states that "disturbed hunger awareness, the frightening feeling of not being in control, is only a small fraction of the disturbances in conceptualization'' (1977, p. 5), which she links to faulty transactional patterns established in early childhood. The process of psychotherapy is the gradual but deliberate relabeling of "misconceptions and errors in the patient's thinking" (1973, p. 339).

Apart from Bruch, few authors have emphasized the role of cognitive factors in the development or maintenance of the disorder. However, one group (Ben-Tovim, Hunter and Crisp, 1977; Crisp and Fransella, 1972) has systematically assessed attitudes of anorexic patients. Ben-Tovim et al. (1977) used the repertory grid technique to evaluate the attitudes of an anorexic girl and her family towards body shape. Crisp and Fransella (1972) had earlier used the same method to explore changes in the personal constructs of two patients over the course of treatment.

Garner and Bemis (1982) have recently developed a model for the assessment and treatment of these conceptual disturbances through the use of cognitive-behavioral therapy techniques. Research on this to date has involved the assessment of cognitive distortions which are common in the disorder. Table 4 illustrates different processes with specific examples of faulty thinking. The categories are based on those proposed by Beck (1976) for depression and the anxiety disorders. Table 4 is not an exhaustive list and many of the examples reflect the contribution of more than one type of logical error. Many of the assumptions are values that the anorexic holds and they provide the support for her relentless dieting. They become the proximal "cause" of her behavior as distinguished from pathogenetic factors. Various predisposing factors (see Chapter 8) have been identified as potential determinants for the disorder. These antecedents follow a common cognitive pathway in that they lead to an unyielding pursuit of thinness and its associated fear of weight gain and of food. Once these themes become established, regardless of their determinants, they may become functionally autonomous.

Helping the anorexic patient examine her thinking is useful clinically, and it contributes to the understanding of how her avoidance of food can prevail over the profound effects of starvation and the social pressures to gain weight. The general cognitive characteristics of avoidance behavior are helpful in understanding its resistance to extinction. Bandura (1978) has identified how cognitive factors may become predominant in the regulation of avoidance behavior: "False beliefs activate avoidance responses that keep individuals out of touch with prevailing environmental conditions that might correct the erroneous concepts" (p. 346). Avoidance behavior becomes so controlled by an internal set of rules that it is little affected by the presence or absence of actual punishing environmental consequences.

# TABLE 4

**SELECTIVE ABSTRACTION,** or basing a conclusion on isolated details while ignoring contradictory and more salient evidence.

Examples:

> "I just can't control myself. Last night when I had dinner in a restaurant, I ate everything I was served, although I had decided ahead of time that I was going to be very careful. I am so weak."
> "The only way that I can be in control is through eating."
> "I am special if I am thin."

**OVERGENERALIZATION,** or extracting a rule on the basis of one event and applying it to other dissimilar situations.

Examples:

> "When I used to eat carbohydrates, I was fat; therefore, I must avoid them now so I won't become obese."
> "I used to be of normal weight, and I wasn't happy. So I *know* gaining weight isn't going to make me feel better."

**MAGNIFICATION,** or overestimation of the significance of undesirable consequent events. Stimuli are embellished with surplus meaning not supported by an objective analysis.

Examples:

> "Gaining five pounds would push me over the brink."
> "If others comment on my weight gain, I won't be able to stand it."
> "I've gained two pounds, so I can't wear shorts any more."

**DICHOTOMOUS OR ALL-OR-NONE REASONING,** or thinking in extreme and absolute terms. Events can be only black or white, right or wrong, good or bad.

Examples:

> "If I'm not in complete control, I lose all control. If I can't master this area of my life, I'll lose everything."
> "If I gain one pound, I'll go on and gain a hundred pounds."
> "If I don't establish a daily routine, everything will be chaotic and I won't accomplish anything."

**PERSONALIZATION AND SELF-REFERENCE,** or egocentric interpretations of impersonal events or overinterpretation of events relating to the self.

Examples:

> "Two people laughed and whispered something to each other when I walked by. They were probably saying that I looked unattractive. I *have* gained three pounds..."
> "I am embarrassed when other people see me eat."
> "When I see someone who is overweight, I worry that I will be like her."

**SUPERSTITIOUS THINKING,** or believing in the cause-effect relationship of non-contingent events.

Examples:

> "I can't enjoy anything because it will be taken away."
> "If I eat a sweet, it will be converted instantly into stomach fat."

Reprinted with permission from Garner and Bemis, 1982.

Beck (1970, 1976) has observed that, in avoidance behavior, cognitive sets may come to operate in an autonomous fashion. Over time a schema develops to which incoming data are shaped to fit. When anorexic patients follow their internal rules and avoidance, they are protected against information that could modify their beliefs.

The anorexic's avoidance differs from that of the phobic's in several ways. First, in the phobic, avoidance is triggered by specific external situations. In anorexia nervosa, the frightening stimulus is the self at undesirable weight levels; the fear of food is secondary to fears of one's increased size. Constant vigilance is required to monitor and control one's self in the face of prominent food cues which become even more tempting with dieting. Also, the phobic's behavior is *not* usually maintained by positive reinforcement. That is, phobics do not have a passion for the opposite of what they are trying to avoid. They do not feel euphoric in buildings without elevators. In contrast, while the anorexic has a "phobic" fear of weight gain or fat, she also derives pleasure and a sense of control from weight loss. Thus, the anorexic's behavior is maintained by both negative and positive reinforcement which may help to account for its resistance to change.

As can be seen from Figure 6, both positive (leading to approach) and negative (leading to avoidance) assumptions or expectations become determinants of the anorexic's behavior on a moment-to-moment basis. These assumptions are general principles that underlie and organize the more specific irrational ideas (Table 4). They are often not verbalized and cannot usually be assessed directly, but they can be inferred from patterns or inconsistencies in the patient's thinking. It is through these distortions that the anorexic patient is accessible in therapy.

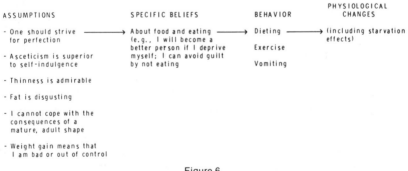

Figure 6

Reprinted with permission from Garner and Bemis, 1982.

In therapy, particular underlying assumptions begin to emerge with some consistency. A more complete discussion of these values and strategies for assisting patients has been presented elsewhere (Garner and Bemis, 1982) and is outlined in Chapters 9 and 10.

The following examples illustrate the kinds of assumptions that may underlie the thinking of many anorexic patients:

1) *The assumption that weight, shape, or thinness can serve as the sole or predominant basis for inferring personal value or self-worth.* This belief is particularly difficult to deal with because it is reinforced by the fashion industry and the media, who associate thinness with beauty, happiness, and success. This assumption's potency stems from the immediacy of reinforcement (or punishment) it provides, as well as its convenience in organizing often ambiguous or threatening life experiences around a single, familiar, and measurable standard. Here the anorexic patient seems to share the bias of behaviorists for objective and quantifiable measures. Weight then becomes the barometer of performance and self-worth.

2) *The assumption that complete self-control is necessary or even desirable.* This assumption is an exaggeration of a view which glorifies the attainment of complete skill mastery and self-discipline. It is often supported by perfectionistic families which overvalue achievement and foster excessive performance expectations.

3) *The assumption that "absolute certainty" is necessary in making decisions.* This assumption is manifest in different situations in which the individual dogmatically clings to moralistic, rigid principles where right and wrong are defined independent of the particular context. For example, the patient may believe that her emotions as well as her weight should be completely predictable. She will only allow herself to express anger if she is absolutely certain that the situation justifies this response. Another common example is the belief that social interactions may be attempted only if there is no chance of rejection. The requirement of absolute certainty in making decisions eliminates the possibility of taking even modest risks.

Other distorted assumptions, expectations, and beliefs may characterize the anorexic patient's mental life and a major task in therapy is to slowly and methodically help the patient to develop more functional ways of organizing her universe. These convictions are not only the product of philosophies promoted by our society and transmitted through the family, but also reflect the patient's idiopathic cognitive distortions of data from her outside world. Other distortions as well as clinical strategies aimed at their correction are described in Chapter 10.

## REFERENCES

Allenbeck, P., Hallberg, D. and Espmark, S.: Body image — an apparatus for measuring disturbances in estimation of size and shape. *J. Psychosom. Res.,* 20:583-589, 1976.

Askevold, E.: Measuring body image. *Psychother. Psychosom.,* 26:71-77, 1975.

Bandura, A.: The self-system in reciprocal determinism. *Am. Psychol.,* 33:344-358, 1978.

Barber, T.X.: *Pitfalls in Human Research: Ten Pivotal Points.* New York: Pergamon Press, 1976.

Beck, A.T.: Role of fantasies in psychotherapy and psychopathology. *J. Nerv. Ment. Dis.,* 150:3-17, 1970.

Beck, A.T.: *Cognitive Therapy and the Emotional Disorders.* New York: International Universities Press, 1976.

Beck, A.T.: Depression inventory. Philadelphia: Center for Cognitive Therapy, 1978.

Ben-Tovim, D.I., Hunter, M. and Crisp, A.H.: Discrimination and evaluation of shape and size in anorexia nervosa: An exploratory study. *Research Communications in Psychology, Psychiatry and Behavior,* 2:241-257, 1977.

Ben-Tovim, D.I., Whitehead, J. and Crisp, A.H.: A controlled study of the perception of body width in anorexia nervosa. *J. Psychosom. Res.,* 23:267-272, 1979.

Berscheid, E., Walster, E and Hohrnstedt, G.: The happy American body: A survey report. *Psychology Today,* November:119-131, 1973.

Bruch, H.: Conceptual confusion in eating disorders. *J. Nerv. Ment. Dis.,* 133:46-54, 1961.

Bruch, H.: Perceptual and conceptual disturbances in anorexia nervosa. *Psychol. Med.,* 24:187-194, 1962.

Bruch, H.: Hunger and instinct. *J. Nerv. Ment. Dis.,* 149:91-114, 1969.

Bruch, H.: *Eating Disorders: Obesity, Anorexia Nervosa, and the Person Within,* New York: Basic Books, 1973.

Bruch, H.: Psychological antecedents of anorexia nervosa. In: R. Vigersky (Ed.), *Anorexia Nervosa.* New York: Raven Press, 1977, pp.1-10.

Bruch, H.: *The Golden Cage.* Cambridge, MA: Harvard University Press, 1978.

Button, E.J., Fransella, F. and Slade, P.D.: A reappraisal of body perception disturbance in anorexia nervosa. *Psychol. Med.,* 7:235-243, 1977.

Cabanac, M. and Duclaux, R.: Obesity: Absence of satiety aversion to glucose. *Science,* 168:496-497, 1970.

Campbell, R.G., Hashim, S.A. and Van Itallie, T.B.: Studies of food intake regulation in man: Responses to variations in nutrive density in lean and obese subjects. *N. Eng. J. Med.,* 285:1402-1407; 1971.

Cannon, W.B. and Washburn, A.L.: An explanation of hunger. *Am. J. Physiol.,* 29:441-454, 1912.

Casper, R.C., Eckert, E.D., Halmi, K.A., Goldberg, S.C. and Davis, J.M.: Bulimia. *Arch. Gen. Psychiatry,* 37:1030-1035, 1980.

Casper, R.C., Halmi, K.A., Goldberg, S.C., Eckert, E.D. and Davis, J.M.: Disturbances in body image estimation as related to other characteristics and outcome in anorexia nervosa. *Br. J. Psychiatry,* 134:60-66, 1979.

Chapman, L.J., Chapman, J.P. and Raulin, M.L.: Scales for physical and social anhedonia. *J. Abnorm. Psychol.,* 85:4, 374-382, 1976.

Coddington, R.D. and Bruch, H.: Gastric perceptivity in normal, obese and schizophrenic subjects. *Psychosomatics,* 11:571-579, 1970.

Cohen, A.R.: Some implications of self-esteem for social influence. In: C.I. Houland and I.L. Janis (Eds.), *Personality and Persuasibility.* New Haven, CT: Yale University Press, 1959.

Combs, A., Avila, D.L. and Parkey, W.W.: *Basic Concepts for the Helping Professions.* Boston: Allyn and Bacon, 1973.

Crisp, A.H.: Clinical and therapeutic aspects of anorexia nervosa: A study of thirty cases. *J. Psychosom. Res.,* 9:67-78, 1965.

Crisp, A.H.: The possible significance of some behavioral correlates of weight and carbohydrate intake. *J. Psychosom. Res.,* 11:117-131, 1967.

Crisp, A.H.: Anorexia nervosa: "feeding disorder," "nervous malnutrition" or "weight phobia"? *World Rev. Nutri.,* 12:452-504, 1970.

Crisp, A.H.: Some psychobiological aspects of adolescent growth and their relevance for the fat/thin syndrome anorexia nervosa. *Int. J. Obes.,* 1:231-238, 1977.

Crisp, A.H. and Fransella, K.: Conceptual changes during recovery from anorexia nervosa. *Br. J. Med. Psychol.,* 45:395-405, 1972.

Crisp, A.H. and Kalucy, R.S.: Aspects of the perceptual disorder in anorexia nervosa. *Br. J. Med. Psychol.,* 47:349-361, 1974.

Dally, P.J.: *Anorexia Nervosa,* New York: Grune and Stratton, 1969.

Derogatis, L., Lipman, R., Rickels, K., Uhlenhuth, E. H. and Covi, L.: The Hopkins Symptom Checklist (HSCL): A self report symptom inventory. *Behav. Sci.,* 19:1-15, 1974.

Dubois, A., Gross, H.A., Ebert, M.H. and Castell, D.O.: Altered gastric emptying and secretion in primary anorexia nervosa. *Gastroenterology,* 77:319-323, 1979.

Feighner, J.P., Robins, E., Guze, S.B., Woodruff, R.A., Winokur, G. and Munoz, R.: Diagnostic criteria for use in psychiatric research. *Arch. Gen. Psychiatry,* 26:57-63, 1972.

Fisher, S. and Cleveland, S.E.: *Body Image and Personality.* New York: Dover Publications, 1958.

Fisher, S.: *Body Experience in Fantasy and Behavior.* New York: Meredith, 1970.

Fries, H.: Studies on secondary amenorrhea, anorectic behaviour and body image perception: Importance for early recognition of anorexia nervosa. In: R. Vigersky (Ed.), *Anorexia Nervosa.* New York: Raven Press, 1977, pp. 163-176.

Galdston, R.: Mind over matter: Observations on fifty patients hospitalized with anorexia nervosa. *J. Am. Acad. Child Psychiatry,* 13:246-263, 1974.

Garfinkel, P.E.: Perception of hunger and satiety in anorexia nervosa. *Psychol. Med.,* 4:309-315, 1974.

Garfinkel, P.E., Moldofsky, H. and Garner, D.M.: Prognosis in anorexia nervosa as influenced by clinical features, treatment and self-perception. *Can. Med. Assoc. J.,* 117:1041-1045, 1977.

Garfinkel, P.E., Moldofsky, H. and Garner, D.M.: The stability of perceptual disturbances in anorexia nervosa. *Psychol. Med.,* 9:703-708, 1979.

Garfinkel, P.E., Moldofsky, H. and Garner, D.M.: The heterogeneity of anorexia nervosa. *Arch. Gen. Psychiatry,* 37:1036-1040, 1980.

Garfinkel, P.E., Moldofsky, H., Garner, D.M., Stancer, H.C. and Coscina, D.V.: Body awareness in anorexia nervosa: Disturbances in body image and satiety. *Psychosom. Med.,* 40:487-498, 1978.

Garner, D.M. and Bemis, K.: A cognitive-behavioral approach to anorexia nervosa. *Cognitive Therapy and Research,* 6:1-27, 1982.

Garner, D.M. and Garfinkel, P.E.: Measurement of body image in anorexia nervosa. In: R. Vigersky (Ed.), *Anorexia Nervosa.* New York: Raven Press, 1977, pp. 27-30.

Garner, D.M. and Garfinkel, P.E.: The Eating Attitudes Test: An index of the symptoms of anorexia nervosa. *Psychol. Med.,* 9:1-7, 1979.

Garner, D.M. and Garfinkel, P.E.: Body image in anorexia nervosa: Measurement, theory and clinical implications. *Inter. J. Psych. Med.,* 11:263-284, 1981.

Garner, D.M., Garfinkel, P.E. and Moldofsky, H.: Perceptual experiences in anorexia nervosa and obesity. *Can. Psychiatr. Assoc. J.,* 23:249-263, 1978.

Garner, D.M., Garfinkel, P.E., Stancer, H.C. and Moldofsky, H.: Body image disturbances in anorexia nervosa and obesity. *Psychosom. Med.,* 38:227-336, 1976.

Glucksman, M.L. and Hirsch, J.: The response of obese patients to weight reduction. *Psychosom. Med.,* 31:1-7, 1969.

Goldberg, S.C., Halmi, K.A., Casper, R., Eckert, E. and Davis, J.M.: Pretreatment predictors of weight change in anorexia nervosa. In: R. Vigersky (Ed.), *Anorexia Nervosa.* New York: Raven Press, 1977, pp. 31-42.

Gottheil, E., Backup, C.E., and Cornelison, F.S., Jr.: Denial and self-image confrontation in a case of anorexia nervosa. *J. Nerv. Ment. Dis.,* 148:238-250, 1969.

Halmi, K.A., Goldberg, S.C. and Cunningham, S.: Perceptual distortion of body image in adolescent girls: Distortion of body image in adolescence. *Psychol. Med.,* 7:253-257, 1977.

Head, H.: *Studies in Neurology.* London: Hodder Stoughton, 1920.

Herman, C.P. and Polivy, J.: Anxiety, restraint and eating behavior. *J. Personal.,* 84:666-672, 1975.

Janis, I.L. and Field, P.B.: Sex differences and personality factors related to persuasibility. In: C.I. Houland and I.L. Janis (Eds.), *Personality and Persuasibility.* New Haven, CT: Yale University Press, 1959, pp. 55-68.

Kerstenberg, J.S.: Menarche. In: S. Lorand and H.I. Schneer (Eds.), *Adolescent Psychoanalytic Approach to Problems and Therapy.* New York: Paul B. Hoeber, 1961.

Kerstenberg, J.S.: Phases of adolescence, parts I and II. *J. Am. Acad. Child Psychiatry,* 6:426-463, 577-611, 1967.

Kiesler, D.J.: Some myths of psychotherapy research and the search for a paradigm. *Psychol. Bull.,* 65:110-136, 1966.

King, A.: Primary and secondary anorexia nervosa syndromes. *Br. J. Psychiatry,* 109:470-479, 1963.

King, M.R. and Manaster, G.J.: Body-images, self-esteem, expectations, self-assessments and actual success in a simulated job interview. *J. Applied Psychology,* 62:589-594, 1977.

Koff, E., Rierdan, J. and Silverstone, E.: Changes in representation of body image as a function of mencheal status. *Developmental Psychology,* 14:635-642, 1978.

Kolb, C.: Disturbances of body image. In: S. Arieti (Ed.), *American Handbook of Psychiatry.* Vol. 4. New York: Basic Books, pp. 810-831, 1975.

Lacey, J.H., Stanley, P.A., Crutchfield, M. and Crisp, A.H.: Sucrose sensitivity in anorexia nervosa. *J. Psychosom. Res.,* 21:17-21, 1977.

Modarressi, T. and Kenny, T.: Children's response to their true and distorted mirror images. *Child Psychiatry Hum. Dev.,* 8:94-101, 1977.

Nisbett, R.E.: Eating behavior and obesity in men and animals. *Adv. Psychosom. Med.,* 7:173-193, 1972.

Penick, S.B., Smith, G.P. Wieneke, K. Jr. and Hinkle, L.E., Jr.,: An experimental evaluation of the relationship between hunger and gastric motility. *Am. J. Physiol.,* 205:421-426, 1967.

Petersen, A.C.: Female pubertal development. In: M. Sugar (Ed.), *Female Adolescent Development,* New York: Brunner/Mazel, 1979, pp. 23-46.

Petersen, A.C. and Wittig, M.A.: Differential cognitive development in adolescent girls. In: M. Sugar (Ed.), *Female Adolescent Development.* New York: Brunner/Mazel, 1979, pp. 47-59.

Pierloot, R.A., and Houben, M.E.: Estimation of body dimensions in anorexia nervosa. *Psychol. Med.,* 8:317-324, 1978.

Rand, C.S. and Stunkard, A.J.: Obesity and psychoanalysis, *Am. J. Psychiatry,* 135:547-551, 1978.

Reitman, E.E. and Cleveland, S.E.: Changes in body image following sensory deprivation in schizophrenia and control groups. *Journal of Abnormal Social Psychology,* 68:168-176, 1964.

Rosen, G.M. and Ross, A.O.: Relationship of body image to self-concept. *J. Consult. Clin. Psychol.,* 32:100, 1968.

Russell, G.F.M.: Bulimia nervosa: An ominous variant of anorexia nervosa. *Psychol. Med.,* 9:429-448, 1979.

Russell, G.F.M., Campbell, P.G. and Slade, P.D.: Experimental studies on the nature of the psychological disorder in anorexia nervosa. *Psychoneuroendocrinology,* 1:45-56, 1975.

Schachter, S.: *Emotions, Obesity and Crime.* New York: Academic Press, 1971.

Schachter, S. and Rodin, I.: *Obese Humans and Rats.* Potomac, MD: Lawrence Erlbaum Associates, 1974.

Schilder, P.: *Image and Appearance of the Human Body*. London: Kegan, Paul, Trench, Trubner and Company, 1935.

Secord, P.F. and Jourard, S.M.: The appraisal of body cathexis: Body cathexis and the self. *Consult. Psychol.*, 17:343-347, 1953.

Selvini Palazzoli, M.: *Anorexia Nervoxa*. London: Chaucer Publishing Co., 1974.

Shontz, F.C.: Body image and its disorder. *Int. J. Psychiatry Med.*, 5(4):150-161, 1974.

Sifneos, P.E.: The prevalence of "alexithymic" characteristics in psychosomatic patients. *Psychother. Psychosom.*, 22:255-262, 1973.

Silverman, I.: Self-esteem and differential responsiveness to success and failure. *Journal of Abnormal Social Psychology*, 69:115-119, 1964.

Silverstone, J.T. and Russell, G.F.M.: Gastric hunger in contractions in anorexia nervosa. *Br. J. Psychiatry*, 13:257-263, 1967.

Slade, P.D.: Awareness of body dimensions during pregnancy: An analogue study. *Psychol. Med.*, 7:245-252, 1977.

Slade, P.D. and Russell, G.F.M.: Experimental investigations of bodily perception in anorexia nervosa and obesity. *Psychother. Psychosom.*, 22:259-363, 1973.

Sorlie, P., Gordon, T. and Kannell, W.B.: Body build and mortality. The Framingham study. *JAMA*, 243:1828-1831, 1980.

Strober, M., Goldenberg, I., Green, J. and Saxon, J.: Body image disturbance in anorexia nervosa during the acute and recuperative phase. *Psychol. Med.*, 9:695-701, 1979.

Stunkard, A.J. and Burt, V.: Obesity and body image, II: Age at onset of disturbances in the body image. *Am. J. Psychiatry*, 123:1443-1447, 1967.

Stunkard, A.J. and Fox, S.: The relationship of gastric motility and hunger: A summary of the evidence. *Psychosom. Med.*, 33:123-134, 1971.

Swensen, C.H.: Empirical evaluations of human figure drawings. *Psychol. Bull.*, 54:431-466, 1957.

Swensen, C.H.: Empirical evaluations of human figure drawings. *Psychol. Bull.*, 70:20-44, 1968.

Thoma, H.: *Anorexia Nervosa*, translated by G. Brydone. New York: International Universities Press, 1967.

Traub, A.C. and Orbach, J.: Psychological studies of body image: An adjustable body distorting mirror. *Arch. Gen. Psychiatry*, 11:53-66, 1964.

Underwood, P.J., Belton, E. and Hulme, P.: Aversion to sucrose in obesity. *Proc. Nutr. Soc.*, 32:94, 1973 (abstr.).

Whisnant, L. and Zegans, L.: A study of attitudes toward menarche in white middle-class American adolescent girls. *Am. J. Psychiatry*, 132:809-814, 1975.

Wingate, B.A. and Christie, M.J.: Ego strength and body image in anorexia nervosa. *J. Psychosom. Res.*, 22:201-204, 1978.

Wylie, R.: The present status of self-theory. In: E.G. Borgatta and W.W. Lambart (Eds.), *Handbook of Personality Theory and Research*. Chicago: Rand McNally, 1968.

# CHAPTER 7

# The Role of

# the Family

Both Gull and Lasègue recognized a contribution of the family to the anorexia nervosa syndrome. Lasègue (1873) in particular stressed:

> The relatives and friends begin to regard the case as desperate. It must not cause surprise to find me thus always placing in parallel the morbid condition of the hysterical subject and the preoccupations of those who surround her. These two circumstances are intimately connected, and we should acquire an erroneous idea of the disease by confining ourselves to an examination of the patient. . . . The moral medium amidst which the patient lives exercises an influence which it would be equally regrettable to overlook or misunderstand (p. 152).

Both Gull (1874) and later Charcot (1889) strongly recommended separation of the patient from her family for treatment to be successful. Similarly Stephens (1895) noted the fatal exacerbation of the disorder that closely followed a mother's frequent visits to her daughter while in hospital. While these physicians recognized a familial role in the disorder, this was either largely ignored in the later descriptive studies of the syndrome or described in terms of mother-daughter interactions by psychoanalytic investigators. In the past 20 years the study of familial predisposing factors has again received attention.

Before these factors are reviewed, it is important to stress a number of methodological problems and deficiencies relating to investigations in this area. First, all studies of anorexia nervosa have been retrospective; no one has yet examined a large group of families to determine predictive factors. While this is an extremely complex approach, with the new knowledge of high risk groups and the recent increase in prevalence of the disorder, a prospective study is not only possible, but necessary. The restrospective studies that exist are all marred by the fact that having an anorexic child will probably bring about significant changes in both the familial and also the marital relationships. Seeing one's child chronically and willfully starve herself would result in complex feelings and behavior in most normal individuals; rage, anxiety and guilt are common emotions.

As Lasègue (1873) noted, the troubled parents resort to "two methods . . . entreaties and menaces. . . . The anorexic becomes the sole preoccupation and conversation. The patient thus gets surrounded by a kind of atmosphere, from which there is no escape during the entire day." In this regard, one is reminded of erroneous early reports of the aloof parents of autistic children ("refrigerator parents"). Their aloofness was considered to be the pathogenic factor, rather than a possible consequence of this serious illness of infancy.

Many important familial issues may be observed in anorexia nervosa and these are often relevant to the treatment of the disorder. However, we must be careful to distinguish phenomena which predispose to the illness from those that are secondary elaborations of long-standing symptoms. It is not uncommon to observe struggles between parent and child for control if the child had been starving herself seriously for the previous five years; it would be wrong to infer that such a struggle necessarily represents the pathogenic substrate of the illness. Factors operating prior to, or at the onset of, the disease, or during the active phase of illness may differ significantly from those which may occur later. For example, Crisp, Harding and McGuinness (1974) have suggested that apparent psychopathology in parents may change over the course of treatment of the patient, e.g., some fathers may become more depressed as their daughters improve.

In addition to the retrospective nature of the studies, there are other serious problems of investigations in this field. There have been very few, if any, properly controlled studies. It is not sufficient to state that the parents have concerns about weight and eating. In order for this to be meaningful, it must be contrasted with such concerns in parents of non-anorexics, controlling for such significant variables as age and social class. Often there has been no measurement or quantification of the relevant variable being examined. For example, how have attitudes to achievement and success been measured in anorexics' parents? This has not been done by objective means but is usually a clinical description by a particular investigator who may be confirming the presence of a phenomenon for which he was searching. Clearly the biases introduced by such methodology are serious and they result in perpetuating myths about illnesses. For example, the domineering mother/passive father combination has been indiscriminantly applied to many psychiatric disorders, without unbiased verification. Furthermore, it is not uncommon to describe or report only those cases that conform to the stereotype, thereby perpetuating it. A case selection technique that involves a series of consecutive referrals is more likely to yield objective data.

There are several other problems in this area of investigation that relate more to the nature of anorexia nervosa as a syndrome than to the quality of the research design. In the first place anorexia nervosa is probably a heterogeneous syndrome. Given the significant differences that have been described between bulimic and restricting anorexics, it would not be surprising to observe marked familial differences between these groups. When the two groups are combined, these may be obscured and result in the overlooking of significant factors. It seems probable that in all likelihood there are other significant areas of heterogeneity between anorexic patients, for example with regard to maturation, ego functioning, and personality.

The maturational component itself is important as illness may often be associated with significant age-dependent changes in psychophysiological functioning (Weiner, 1977, p. 584). Weiner has suggested that while these are poorly understood, they may interact with familial or environmental events, resulting in disease at different times. The demands on a 14-year-old girl entering puberty and a 29-year-old married woman with a child will obviously be quite different, yet both may develop an anorexia nervosa syndrome. It would not be surprising then to find that events antecedent to the syndrome differ in these individuals and their families. This concept of heterogeneity in a clinical syndrome is common to other illnesses. For example, hypertension may be due to coarctation of the aorta, excess renin or aldosterone, or a pheochromocytoma (Weiner, 1977). Like hypertension or schizophrenia, anorexia nervosa is not a single illness caused by a single pathogen but is a syndrome and the clinical manifestations are a final common pathway, the distillation of a group of interacting forces.

The notion of variable aetiology and a final common pathway as the expression of illness is clarified by Weiner's concept of disease as the product of psychological and physiological limitation of the individual's capacity to adapt to specific situations (Weiner, 1977). These limitations may occur because of certain deficits within the individual, or as a response to particular environmental situations, or may be age-specific or because of delays in the development or maturation of mechanisms involved in the regulation of specific adaptations. This concept of anorexia nervosa as a result of multiple predisposing and initiating factors and the interaction of these with the individual's capacity to adapt at a specific time, will be further detailed in Chapter 8. For the understanding of the role of the family in anorexia nervosa it is important to recognize that there are multiple predisposing factors. While the familial characteristics that predispose to the disorder may be common in a population, it is their interaction with an individual's constitutional and psychological make-up and the cultural milieu that determine whether this predisposition will result in disease.

## DEMOGRAPHIC CHARACTERISTICS OF FAMILIES

As described in Chapter 5, a very common finding in many studies, until recently, has been that anorexia nervosa was overrepresented in upper middle class and upper class families (Bruch 1973; Crisp, Palmer and Kalucy, 1976; Dally, 1969; Fenwick, 1880; Hall, 1978; Morgan and Russell, 1975). Exceptions to this are cited by Rowland (1970) who reported 60% of his patients were lower class and Kay and Leigh (1954) who observed that the parents of their patients were from all social classes. However, these are unusual findings. More representative are studies such as that of Kalucy, Crisp and Harding (1977) who reported that 50% of their patients were from social classes 1 and 2 (and that upper social class was a good prognostic indicator) and our own findings that 59% of our patients have been from social classes 1 and 2 as were 70% of Hall's (1978) and 66% of Morgan and Russell's (1975). The latter estimated that only about 18% of the general population in England were in these social classes. Of importance is the impression of some, including ourselves, that as anorexia nervosa has become more common it is becoming more equally distributed through all social classes (Dally, 1969; Theander, 1970; Kendell, Hall, Hailey and Babigan, 1973). Theander's interpretation of this is that with better medical care for the lower social classes there is better case detection. However, it is also possible that factors in our culture which predispose to anorexia nervosa, attitudes about body weight, achievement and self-control, are becoming evenly distributed throughout society.

There has been no firm consensus that membership of a particular religious group predisposes to anorexia nervosa, particularly when social class and referral biases are controlled. Rowland (1970) found that 90% of his 30 patients were either Jewish (43%) or Roman Catholic (47%) but instead of this being due to particular religious attitudes to eating and weight, it may simply reflect New York City's population. Kalucy et al. (1977) described three Jewish families with "eating patterns which appeared to have some generic influence on the adoption of anorexia as the syndrome of choice" but this is far from clear, given the small numbers and lack of a control group. In the same city, Dally (1969) reported only seven Jews and 12 Roman Catholics among his sample of 140 patients. Most of his patients were from the Church of England. Ziegler and Sours (1968) felt the religious patterns of their patients did not differ from those expected in the general population. Hall (1978) reported that her patients' religious affiliation did not differ from the general New Zealand population. In our sample of 207 individuals with anorexia nervosa, about 18% were Jewish, 19% Catholic, and 41% Protestant, but again, we lack control figures for non-anorexic referrals from a similar social class, and 22% of our sample reported either another or no religion.

The patients come from a variety of family sizes and from any birth order (Hall, 1978). Some have speculated that for anorexia nervosa to occur there must be another sibling (Rowland, 1970) but this is clearly not so; indeed, Kay, Schapira and Brandon (1967) reported an overrepresentation (50%) of only children. However, Bruch (1973), Rowland (1970), Theander (1970) and our group found that 7-15% of patients were without siblings. There have been a few reports of a preponderance of first-born children (Bruch 1973). For example, Rowland (1970) observed 17 patients to be firstborn and only nine to be youngest. This was not so in Hall's (1978) study which reported 19 firstborn cases, 10 middle and 21 youngest children. Similarly, Theander (1970) found 37% were firstborn, 32% were second born children and 31% were third children or had been born later. These figures did not differ from a large sample of randomly selected Swedish families. Halmi, Goldberg, Eckert, Casper and Davis (1977) observed a similar birth distribution in their sample. These data strongly suggest that there has not been an overrepresentation of any particular birth order.

Cobb (1950) wrote that the family with an anorexic member might be "woman dominated," in the sense that there was a preponderance of female siblings in the families. Bruch (1973) reported that there were relatively few brothers of patients in her series — that is, her female patients has a total of 88 sisters and only 40 brothers. Moreover, this relationship was not observed in the families of male anorexics. Dally (1969) did not find such a marked preponderance of sisters: in 140 patients there were 137 sisters and 117 brothers. Similarly, Hall (1978) reported 62 sisters and 48 brothers of 50 female patients. We have found that the numbers of brothers and sisters in our series did not differ. Theander (1970) also found no differences either in total numbers of male versus female siblings or in numbers of families without either sisters or brothers.

Investigators have been impressed by the finding that many of the parents of anorexics are relatively elderly (Bruch, 1973; Dally, 1969; Hall, 1978; Jensen, 1968; Theander, 1970). For example, Theander (1970) compared the parents of anorexics with those of the general Swedish population for each of the decades he studied. Forty percent of mothers of probands born between 1921-1940 were less than 30 at the birth of the proband, but this occurred in the control group 55% of the time. This was not due to the patient being later in a sibline but to increased maternal age. Hall (1978) also reported that average age of both mothers (29) and fathers (32) of anorexics was greater than for the New Zealand population as a whole.

These findings closely correspond with the figures described by Halmi et al. (1977) in the United States. We found the average age of parents at the birth of our patients to be 33 for the fathers and 30 for the mothers. Seventeen percent of the mothers in our series were over 35 at the time of the patient's birth and 6% were over 40. Thirty-four percent of the fathers were over 35 and 17% over 40 at the time of the patient's birth. These figures are higher than national averages for parents in Canada. However, it must be stressed that in none of these studies has social class been controlled — that is, the relative increase in parental ages may be a phenomenon of being upper middle class and its characteristic pattern of delayed parenthood. Nevertheless, being a relatively older parent may impart a rigidity to parent-child relationships, or particular expectations on the child, or significant difficulties in separation, which may later facilitate the development of anorexia nervosa.

The marriages of the parents of anorexics appear to be stable in terms of the prevalence of separation or divorce. Bruch (1973) described only two instances of marital separation before the onset of the illness, and Halmi et al. (1977) observed only three of 44 parents were divorced. Ushakov (1971) also observed the high frequency of traditional family life in anorexia nervosa occurring in Russia. Hall (1978) described a rather high frequency (36%) of the parents themselves to be from families of "broken homes"; when the parents later marry they may exert greater effort to maintain the family. Only three of 50 were divorced in her series. Dally (1969) found 8% of his patients to be from divorced parents and 6% suffered the death of a parent before the patient was 15. Halmi (1974) reported 18% of 89 patients to be from broken homes, not significantly different from population norms. Thus, it would appear that the prevalence of loss of a parent through death or divorce is not different in anorexia nervosa from the general population.

To summarize the demographic characteristics of the families of anorexics, it is clear that two features have been regularly observed by many investigators. The families tend to be from the upper social classes and the parents are often somewhat older than the average. It has not clearly been determined whether or not the two variables are interrelated in these families.

## GENETIC FACTORS

There are a number of methods for determining whether a particular ill-ness has a genetic component. These include determining whether the disorder is more common in first degree relatives of an affected person than would be expected by chance; comparison of monozygous versus dizygous twins for concordance rates; comparison of twins reared together versus those reared apart for concordance rates; study of genetic markers and ex-amination of adopted away offspring of an affected individual (Kety, Rosenthal, Wender and Schulsinger, 1968; Wender, Rosenthal, Kety, Schulsinger and Welner, 1974). Few of these methods have provided data for anorexia nervosa.

Anorexia nervosa occurring in both a mother and child has been recorded but is uncommon. Halmi et al. (1977) reported it in three of 88 (3.4%) in their series. We have seen this in two of 207 patients. But these figures are unreliable since they are based on information volunteered by the parents and many parents may not readily admit to having suffered from the disorder. Hall (1978) reported that one mother of her 50 subjects had been anorexic. Crisp (1965) also described one such pair out of a series of 36. He has also reported two other patients with aunts who had anorexia nervosa. Cantwell, Sturzenberger, Burroughs, Salkin and Green (1977) and Ehrens-ing and Weitzman (1970) each also observed a mother and daughter with anorexia nervosa. However, there were no mother-daughter cases described in other large series, for example, by Theander (1970) or Dally (1969). While definite anorexia nervosa in the mother is quite uncommon, Kalucy et al. (1977) reported that 16% of the patients' mothers and 23% of the fathers had a definite history of "significantly low adolescent weight, often associated with very high levels of activity, pecularities of dietary habit and an overvaluation of the positive values of such low weight." That is, it was quite common to obtain a history of "anorexic-like" behavior without the development of the complete syndrome in the parents during their adolescence.

While mother-child concordance for anorexia nervosa is rare, the occur-rence of multiple cases in a single family is not. In Theander's (1970) series, seven sisters of six probands were reported to have anorexia nervosa; he calculated the morbidity risk among sisters of his sample to be 6.6%, con-siderably more than would be expected in the general population of adoles-cent girls. Similarly, Halmi et al. (1977) described four of 130 siblings (3.1%) in their series who had anorexia nervosa, a figure similar to that of Dally and Gomez's (1979). Hall (1978) found two of 50 patients and Thoma (1967) two of 30 patients had sisters with anorexia nervosa. We also (Garfinkel, Moldofsky and Garner, 1980) have found an increased prevalence of anorexia nervosa in sisters of patients; 6% of our patients have had at least one anorexic sister. In one family all three sisters have had the illness. Morgan and Russell (1975) have also described one family with three anorexic sisters.

However, this overrepresentation of anorexia nervosa in siblings in no way implies a genetic predisposition rather than a common environmental pathogenesis. While there have been no adopted away studies in anorexia nervosa, Crisp (1970) has reported an interesting family with two adopted anorexic girls. These patients were not related to each other but were brought up at different times in the same household. They were reared by a couple whose own marriage was not consummated. The father, who was a biscuit manufacturer, was thought to have had a mild case of anorexia nervosa. This case highlights the importance of environmental rather than hereditary factors.

There are a number of reports of anorexia nervosa in twins. These are described in Table 1 according to the author, zygosity, and concordance. It must be emphasized that in some cases zygosity has been determined roughly — by parental report and observation only — and is therefore subject to significant error. Similarly, whether a twinship is concordant for the disorder may be uncertain, since many of the co-twins have not been followed up beyond the age of risk — some described as discordant may actually turn out to be concordant if followed for a sufficient period. Because only 36 twin sets have now been described and because of these methodological issues, it is not possible to make a definite comment on monozygous versus dizygous differences in concordance rates. However, the monozygous concordance rate is 52% while there has been only one concordant dizygous twin pair (11.1%) described to date. Askevold and Heiberg (1979) arrived at a monozygous concordance rate of 38% in a more selective (by diagnostic criteria) earlier review. While both sets of figures are impressive and our monozygous versus dizygous differences approach a degree of significance suggesting a genetic predisposition, one must be cautious in the interpretation of the data since so few twins — especially dizygous ones — have been described and because, as we have said, of the potentially serious errors in reporting both zygosity and concordance.

There is little information about which member of a pair of twins will develop anorexia nervosa. Gifford, Murawski and Pilot (1970) suggested it occurred in the second-born with the lower birth weight but this has not been substantiated (Crisp, 1966; Halmi and Brodland, 1973). It has also been suggested that anorexia nervosa occurs in the more submissive, passive twin (Bruch, 1969; Crisp, 1966). This has been the case in our series of nine.

## TABLE 1

### Reports of Anorexia Nervosa in Twins

| Author and year | Monozygous vs Dizygous | Concordant vs Discordant |
|---|---|---|
| 1. Bom (1940) | M | C |
| 2. Duhrssen (1950) | M | C |
| 3. Meyer (1961) | M | C |
| 4. Koluch and Davidova (1962) | M | D* |
| 5. Ziolko (1966) | M | C |
| 6. Crisp (1966) | M | D |
| 7. Bruch (1969) | M | D |
| 8. Bruch (1969) | M | D |
| 9. Theander (1970) | M | C |
| 10. Gifford, Murawski and Pilot (1970) | M | D |
| 11. Dickens (1970) | D | D |
| 12. Mormont and Demoulin (1971) | M | D |
| 13. Halmi and Brodland (1973) | M | C |
| 14. Halmi and Brodland (1973) | M | C |
| 15. Debow (1975) | M | C |
| 16. Weiner (1976) | M+ | D |
| 17. Nemeth (1977) | D | D |
| 18. Werman and Katz (1975) | M | C |
| 19. Morgan and Russell (1975) | M | C |
| 20. Morgan and Russell (1975) | D | C |
| 21. Foster and Kupfer (1975) | M | C |
| 22. Neki, Mohan and Sood (1977) | M | C |
| 23. Beumont, Abraham, Argall, George and Glaun (1978) | M | D |
| 24. Beumont et al. (1978) | D | D |
| 25. Askevold and Heiberg (1979) | M | D |
| 26. Askevold and Heiberg (1979) | M | D |
| 27. Simmons and Kessler (1979) | M | C |
| 28. Garfinkel and Garner (previously unpublished) | M | D* |
| 29. Garfinkel and Garner | M | D |
| 30. Garfinkel and Garner | D | D |
| 31. Garfinkel and Garner | D | D |
| 32. Garfinkel and Garner | M | D§ |
| 33. Garfinkel and Garner | M | C |
| 34. Garfinkel and Garner | D | D |
| 35. Garfinkel and Garner | D | D§ |
| 36. Garfinkel and Garner | D | D |

§ co-twin was obese
* co-twin with conversion disorder
+ male

In our own sample, we have observed that there are more twins than one would expect by chance: Over 4% of our patients have been twins, while twinning occurs at a rate of about 1/88 in the population as a whole. This is surprising, since twins have not been overrepresented in other large series of anorexia nervosa. It may therefore be a spurious finding perhaps related to referral practices. Alternatively, twins *may* be at increased risk for anorexia nervosa. While this may be because of perinatal risks common to twins and to anorexics (Halmi et al., 1977), it may also be related to specific psychological issues: twins may be more vulnerable to problems of attaining a separate identity and increasing autonomy at puberty may increase the likelihood of anorexia nervosa. The fact that 75% of the twin sets reported have been monozygous rather than dizygous offers some support to this hypothesis.

There have been no studies of anorexia nervosa using the other techniques for determining genetic influence: There are no studies of adopted away offspring, crossfostering, genetic markers, or evaluations of twins reared apart. The reported increased risk (6%) for sisters of anorexics is as likely due to experiential as genetic factors. Of the 36 twins described in the literature about 75% are monozygous. The concordance rate for these have been considerably higher than for dizygous twins but the numbers are too small to permit a clear interpretation.

## OTHER ILLNESSES IN THE FAMILY

A number of investigators have recorded the frequency and types of mental and physical illnesses in the parents of anorexics. Emotional illness appears in the same proportion as in the general population (Theander, 1970). The prevalence of parental neurotic illness of various kinds is not different from other groups having a member with psychiatric illness (Kay and Leigh 1954). Kay and Leigh (1954) reported 34% and Dally (1969) 33% of parents were psychologically disturbed. Similarly there is no increased prevalence of parental schizophrenia. Theander (1970) reported that two mothers of 94 probands were schizophrenic, and Hall (1978) one of 50. Morgan and Russell (1975) reported paranoid or schizophrenic symptoms in two of the relatives of their 41 patients, whereas Kalucy et al. (1977) and Kay and Leigh (1954) found no cases in their series, so that the prevalence of schizophrenia in the nuclear family of the anorexic is similar to that of the general population.

However, the relationship between anorexia nervosa and family history of affective disorder is not as clear. But it appears that affective illness may be overrepresented in the parents. As we noted in Chapter 2, Cantwell et al.

(1977) have recorded an increased familial prevalence of depression; Kalucy et al. (1977) also found that 14% of the fathers in their series were suffering from manic depressive illness. The most recent study on this subject (Winokur, March and Mendels, 1980) noted a doubling of affective illness in the parents of anorexics in comparison with a control group. Hall (1978) found 10% of parents had suffered from depression, which is not out of keeping with population norms.

Several other studies have reported much lower rates. Beumont, Abraham, Argall, George and Glaun (1978) found only two cases in a sample of 34 patients. Theander (1970) reported the morbidity risk as 2.6% for parents and 8.8% for siblings, but only hospitalized depressives or suicides were included in his study. Kay and Leigh (1954) reported only one case in 38 patients. The extreme variability between studies may, in part, relate to variable definitions of affective illness. Because of these discrepant findings, it is not possible at present to know for certain the relationship between familial affective illness and anorexia nervosa. However, in view of the recent careful studies (Cantwell et al., 1977; Winokur et al., 1980) which have shown such an overrepresentation, a tentative conclusion would be that familial affective illness is one of the risk factors for anorexia nervosa. Whether this predisposition operates via genetic or environmental pathways is unknown.

Alcohol misuse may also be more common in the fathers of anorexics than in the general population. Halmi and Loney (1973) reported well-documented alcoholism in 13% of fathers and 2% of mothers; this is considerably higher than in the general population. Kalucy et al. (1977) found "excessive alcohol" use in 7% of mothers and 19% of fathers. Kay and Leigh (1954) reported a 5% prevalence of alcoholism in parents and Hall (1978) reported 12% in fathers and 2% in mothers.

Kalucy et al. (1977) have also commented on the increased prevalence of phobic avoidance in the mothers and obsessive compulsive characteristics of the fathers of anorexics. Again these findings are anecdotal. Crisp, Harding and McGuinness (1974) had previously reported on the marked obsessive traits of the fathers of bulimic anorexics. These fathers were considered to be particularly rigid in their high expectations and demands for self-control. Their daughters' poor impulse control was thought to be intolerable to them. It was this group of fathers that appeared more depressed following their daughters' weight recovery in the Crisp study.

Other studies have reported on the presence of physical illness in the parents. These do not seem excessive (Hall, 1978; Halmi et al., 1977; Kay and Leigh, 1954; Theander, 1970) with the possible exception of maternal migraine: Kalucy et al. (1977) found 30% of their patients' mothers suffered from migraine.

## THE FAMILY AS CULTURE BEARER

Families fulfill a variety of an individual's needs, including affectional, sexual, and material ones. In addition, the family represents the first and most significant force in adapting the growing child to his culture. In this regard, families may be regarded as important "culture bearers." An important question that arises from this is whether particular families magnify aspects of a culture and whether this may be a predisposition to illness. Some families will be more vulnerable than others to the slimness pressures and pressures for perfection and performance in the cultural climate. But as noted earlier in this chapter, there have been no controlled studies of anorexics' families examining these issues. However, accumulated anecdotal reports have repeatedly stressed certain family characteristics. These include weight and eating preoccupations, emphasis on appearance and youth and a heavy reliance on external standards for regulating self-worth and success.

Kalucy et al. (1977) have described a variety of "weight pathologies" in their clinical investigation of 56 families with an anorexic child. These included a prevalence of overweight in 23% of the mothers and 20% of the fathers; these figures do not differ from the population as a whole and are similar to the 18% frequency reported by Halmi et al. (1977). However, these studies have not differentiated bulimic from restricting anorexics. When we did separate bulimic from restricting anorexics (Chapter 3), an unusually high prevalence of maternal obesity was observed in the bulimic group, 49% versus 32% in the restricting group. This figure is extremely high when it is recalled that obesity in North America is inversely related to social class: upper middle class women are less likely to be obese (Stunkard, 1975). Obesity in fathers of our patients was less common, occurring in 20% of bulimics and 15% of restricting patients. Obesity in the siblings is not out of keeping with the population as a whole; for example, 13% of our patients' siblings were obese.

Other studies have not reported excessive parental obesity; for example, four of 30 mothers were obese in Rowland's (1970) study and seven of 140 were in Dally's (1969) study. Halmi, Struss and Goldberg (1978) compared height and weight data of 30 parents of anorexics with a similar number of controls, matched for age and social class. No differences were observed but they did not distinguish bulimic from restricting anorexics.

Kalucy et al. (1977) have suggested that there may be a number of other difficulties associated with weight in families with an anorexic member. Unfortunately, without control groups, it is difficult to comment on whether these difficulties are more common than might be expected in the population. Weight fluctuations or underweight in the parents were common in their study. For example, 11% of mothers demonstrated significant fluctuations in weight and 16% were underweight; the corresponding figures for fathers were 7% and 9%. These investigators also reported a high frequency of dieting behavior in the parents — in 27% of mothers and 16% of fathers. In an exploratory case study Ben-Tovim, Hunter and Crisp (1977) found that the parents of an anorexic girl approved of their daughter's slimness.

As for weight, a preoccupation with food has been described to be unduly prominent in many anorexics' families. Crisp (1967) and others believe that there is an overrepresentation of parental members in the food and nutrition industry or in nurturant professions (Beumont et al., 1978; Crisp, Harding and McGuinness, 1974). Kalucy et al. (1977) reported 27% of the mothers and 16% of fathers in their series to be chronically dieting with an "overvaluation of the importance of weight control." Twenty-three percent of the families had eating patterns which were grossly deviant and antedated the illness, leading Kalucy et al. to consider this to play a role in the onset of the illness. An example of this is a patient of ours whose family — when the girl was growing up — was never allowed by the mother to eat together. Dally (1969) described 18 families in his series to have given food unusual prominence; he cited nine vegetarian families and various "nature diets" in the others and suggested that these eating eccentricities indicated a poorer prognosis for the anorexic patient.

In addition to anecdotal reports of weight and eating concerns in these families, it has also been suggested that they are extremely involved in physical fitness. Exercise has become important to many in our society both for health reasons and for the sense of well-being that comes with regular exercise. However, it has been suggested that in these families activity and self-control go beyond the usual to become overvalued — "taking exercises has a very moral tone in these families" (Kalucy et al., 1977 p. 390). Associated with this, fear of aging in the parents and an undue emphasis on a youthful appearance has been described.

The fathers of anorexics, in particular, seem to be very concerned with external appearance (Bruch, 1973). Bruch has suggested that despite considerable personal success the fathers have tended to feel that they do not measure up in some way. She observed that they were very preoccupied with physical appearance, proper behavior, and performance, both in themselves and their children. While these characteristics are seen in many in our society, Bruch has suggested that these traits are more pronounced in the family with an anorexic member. Dally (1969), too, recognized the high ambition for external success in his patients' families.

## PSYCHODYNAMIC MODELS AND FAMLY INTERRELATIONSHIPS

There have been many reports documenting the presence of disturbed parent-child relationships in families with an anorexic individual. These have often been implicated in the genesis of the illness, despite the methodological problems that were discussed earlier in this chapter. It is our impression from the patients we have treated that there is no one family constellation nor a single type of mother-child relationship that will regularly be associated with anorexia nervosa. Rather, there are a variety of difficulties in families that may predispose to anorexia nervosa. But like Crisp (1970), we also feel that the illness is not always related to major earlier problems in the parent-child relationship. (Other investigators' estimates of the frequency of preexisting familial psychopathology are provided in Chapter 12.) However, by the time the family presents for treatment, hostility and dependency are often so magnified by the struggles of the previous months, or years, that the premorbid relationships may be obscured.

The familial relationships and intrapsychic models that have been described represent a variety of psychodynamic and interpersonal theoretical formulations. In our view, they fall into several categories: 1) They may be inaccurate; 2) they may reflect portions of the problem but not its central core; and 3) they may represent meaningful advances to the understanding of interrelationships that predispose to and perpetuate anorexia nervosa. The latter have often been unfortunately generalized to account for all cases of anorexia nervosa. This group of formulations tend to be procrustean and later reports are either squeezed in or cut off to fit the proposed model. Careful study will reveal that there is not a single family constellation, but rather a variety of familial interrelationships that are important.

There are several examples of the first two categories of formulations. Szyrynski (1973) summarized the families of anorexics with his statement, "Domestic life is dominated by the mother, with a rather passive and ineffectual father in the background." Cobb (1950) presented a similar view but these do not differ from models proposed earlier for so many psychiatric problems. Older psychoanalytic concepts of anorexia nervosa have relied "heavily on theories about fixation at the oral level of psychosexual development, on regression in instinctual drives from the genital level of development, and on symptom formation around oral conflicts" (Ross, 1977, p. 424) (Jessner and Abse, 1960; Moulton, 1942; Thoma, 1967; Waller, Kaufman and Deutsch, 1940).

Waller et al. (1940), for example, emphasized the role of symbolization of impregnation fantasies involving the gastrointestinal tract. These oral impregnation fantasies were presumed to be associated with marked guilt and the anorexia nervosa was thought to be a defense against these (Blitzer, Rollins and Blackwell, 1961; Sandler and Dare, 1970). Moulton (1942), Lorand (1943), and Szyrynski (1973) have all described cases in which similar symbolic distortions were purported to produce the desire for weight loss. Benedek (1936) described the analysis of a patient with oral aggression which was aimed at the mother's breast. Thoma (1967) is representative of this drive-related psychoanalytic viewpoint. He theorized that anorexia nervosa derives from the patient's abandonment of the genital stage of development with a predominance of "oral ambivalence." He emphasized that the primary defense is against drive representatives: The sexual fears are displaced by concerns about body size. These drive-dominated theories about the genesis of anorexia nervosa have been either totally erroneous or have focused on an aspect of the disorder, rather than on its central core.

More recent psychodynamic formulations have de-emphasized drive theory and have been focused on early object relations (Bruch, 1973; Ross, 1977; Selvini Palazzoli, 1974; Sours, 1974). These have been extremely useful observations, particularly when, as Kramer (1974) cautions, they don't overemphasize pathological mothering to the neglect of the child's role in the disturbed parent-child interaction. Of major importance in this regard have been Bruch's hypotheses about anorexia nervosa.

As described in Chapter 6, Bruch (1973) views anorexia nervosa as developing around three related ego disturbances — distortions of body image, internal perception, and a sense of ineffectiveness. Her central theme is that the search for self-mastery and autonomy is maladaptively pursued through control over one's body. Bruch's conception of this development involves familial and mother-child interactions as well as factors within the child herself. She feels that in these families there is also competition between parents about who is making a greater sacrifice to the child with the concomitant expectation that the child will accede obediently to the parents' extreme demands. These demands are for appearance, behavior, and success in achievements (Bruch, 1979). The mother-child interactions are significant from birth on. Bruch, like Piaget, differentiates two forms of behavior — those initiated by the individual and those that are in response to external stimuli. For healthy development, both are important. Bruch has suggested that anorexics have serious deficits in self-initiated behaviors. In part, these are related to a neglect of appropriate external responses to the child's inner states. Bruch (1973) has described the process of differentiating internal process thus:

If confirmation and reinforcement of his own, initially rather undifferentiated needs and impulses have been absent, or have been contradictory or inaccurate, then a child will grow up perplexed when trying to differentiate between disturbances in his biological field and emotional and interpersonal experiences, and he will be apt to misinterpret deformities in his self-body concept as externally induced. Thus he will become an individual deficient in his sense of separateness, with "diffuse ego boundaries," and will feel helpless under the influence of external forces (p. 56).

Bruch feels that the anorexic's fear of having no self-control can be related to these early experiences. "Such a child does not feel she is living her own life, but feels deprived of inner guideposts, helpless under the influence of internal urges and external demands, and like being the property of her parents" (1979, p. 107). In addition, Bruch feels that the pre-anorexic child's own conceptual development does not advance appropriately and this provides a further contribution to the development of the disorder. In Piaget's terms, anorexics do not pass into the abstract phase of development but remain with the style of thinking of earlier childhood, preconceptual, and concrete operations. The egocentrism that is characteristic of this phase is manifest behavior, morality, and relationships. It is this failure in conceptual development together with the confusion in the recognition of internal states that makes them both over-compliant in their pre-teen years and vulnerable to anorexia nervosa in adolescence, with its demands for autonomy and separation.

Selvini Palazzoli (1974) has independently evolved a similar formulation of the genesis of anorexia nervosa. Like Bruch, she avoids the emphasis on orality and focuses on the helplessness of the ego. According to this view, the individual perceives her body as not belonging to her; rather she concretely perceives her body as a threat which must somehow be controlled. Following Fairbairn's model of object relationships, Selvini Palazzoli (1974) suggests that the anorexic experiences her body as "the maternal object, from which the ego wishes to separate itself at all costs" (p. 90). The anorexic incorporates the feared maternal object in order to control it. Central to this model is the concept of a mother who rewards compliance to her wishes, is overprotective, and is unable to allow separation in the child.

While Sours (1974) acknowledges the heterogeneity of anorexia nervosa, his experience largely agrees with the findings of Bruch and Selvini Palazzoli. He emphasizes the need for the mother to have a submissive, perfect child as her own fulfillment. At the same time, Sours cautions against ignoring constitutional and familial factors that provide variations in the child's development. Taipale, Tuomi and Aukee (1971) have also described the mothers of anorexics as frustrated women with intellectual controls and high standards of performance who cannot tolerate independence in their children.

In Chapter 3, major clinical differences between bulimic and restricing anorexics were stressed. In particular, it was felt that many bulimic patients had borderline personality organizations. Specific hypotheses about parent-child interactions from object relations theories are relevant to this subgroup. These formulations have a close bearing on those just described. According to Mahler (1968), intrapsychic structure is thought to develop through the differentation of the self-representation from the object-representation. She has described this process as having four phases: autistic, symbiotic, separation-individuation and developing object constancy.

According to Masterson (1972, 1977), there is a developmental arrest in borderline individuals in the separation-individuation phase. This is presumed to be related to the mother's inability to tolerate the child's efforts to separate and eventually become autonomus, closely corresponding to the theories just described. The mother of the borderline patient is thought to reinforce the child's clinging dependency by withdrawing if the child attempts to separate. Through the preteen years such behavior may be quite acceptable and in fact it has been repeatedly noted how compliant anorexics have been in childhood. But when issues arise after puberty which tend to threaten this relationship (usually separation or autonomy), the child is exposed to her anxiety about separation and her fears of loss or withdrawal of the mother's love. Viewed in this light, the borderline individual's development of anorexia nervosa may be considered adaptive by preventing separation and by substituting obsessional mechanisms for behaviors that encourage individuation (Masterson, 1977). The symptoms may also represent a mechanism for expressing hostility to an ambivalently-regarded parent. These issues with separation-individuation, which to some extent correspond to Minuchin, Rosman and Baker's (1978) concept of the "enmeshed" family, help explain why borderline patients may be over-represented in an anorexic population.

We feel that the contributions from ego psychology of Bruch, Selvini Palazzoli and Masterson have been most important for understanding the psychology of anorexia nervosa. The experimental evidence supporting Bruch's hypotheses has been reviewed in the previous chapter. However, it is important to again stress that for anorexia nervosa, as a heterogeneous syndrome and with multiple predispositions, any one model will not fit all patients. Many individuals exist with these family backgrounds and parent-child relationships who do not develop anorexia nervosa and some patients with anorexia nervosa do not come from these developmental roots.

## SYSTEM MODELS

Selvini Palazzoli (1974) has gradually shifted her focus from a model which emphasized mother-daughter relationships to that of the entire family's interactions. Her group from Milan and Minuchin's group from Philadelphia have both evolved a systems approach in describing anorexia nervosa. According to Minuchin et al. (1978), the traditional linear model links together a variety of factors which converge on the individual and the locus of pathology is thought to be in the individual (p. 83). The systems model, by contrast, emphasizes the interdependence and circular interactions of forces:

> This model posits a circular movement of parts that affect each other. The system can be activated at any number of points. The activation and regulation of the system can be done by system members or by forces outside the system (Minuchin et al., 1978, p. 20).

According to this view, an individual's behavior is simultaneously caused and causative; a beginning and an end are defined only as arbitrary framing points.

Both Selvini Palazzoli and Minuchin have postulated that certain family relationships are closely related to the development and maintenance of psychosomatic syndromes in children and that the illness in turn plays an important role in maintaining the family homeostasis. As we noted earlier in this chapter, there is very little objective evidence for this, but a study by Crisp, Harding and McGuinness (1974) offers some support for the idea that the illness may be seen as protective to one or both parents. They compared the psychoneurotic status (using the Middlesex Hospital Questionnaire) of the parents of anorexics before and after in-hospital weight restoration, with a control group comparable in age, sex, and marital status. They found no differences between the controls and parents of anorexics initially. But after their daughters' weights had been restored, the parents of anorexics showed increased psychopathology. This was especially so for the subgroup with a bulimic individual.

Selvini Palazzoli and her colleagues developed an interest in the family of the anorexic through the work of Haley on communications in families of schizophrenics. In their clinical studies of families with an anorexic child, the Milan group have described certain predominant characteristics (Selvini Palazzoli, 1974, pp. 205-216):

1) Unlike families with a schizophrenic member, the families of anorexics are thought to communicate in a coherent manner. More disturbed pat-

terns of communication of a psychotic nature have been observed only in the families with a bulimic individual.

2) It is common for members of these families to reject messages sent by others. While contradiction is common, there is little resolution of the conflict.
3) The parents are thought to have difficulty in openly assuming the role of leaders in the family. No one is prepared to assume responsibility for things that go wrong.
4) The central family issue relates to the formation of "covert coalitions." While open alliances between parent and child are prohibited, the child is relegated to the role of secret ally to both father and mother. Selvini Palazzoli has referred to this triangle as "three-way matrimony" (1974, p. 211).
5) There is a spirit of "self-sacrifice."
6) The marital relationship is felt to be characterized by a facade of unity which generally conceals a profound underlying disillusionment. Each partner is thought to compete for a sense of moral superiority, i.e., for who has made the greater sacrifices for the sake of the family. Both this and the spirit of self-sacrifice have previously been emphasized by Bruch.

Like the Milan group, Minuchin et al. (1978) have emphasized a series of characteristics seen in families with a child who has a psychosomatic illness. Their work began with juvenile onset diabetes and gradually expanded to other disorders including anorexia nervosa and asthma. In this regard theirs is a nonspecific model that does not itself address the significant problem of symptom choice (Alexander, 1950). The characteristics they have identified are:

1) Family relationships are said to be characterized by an extreme form of proximity with weak boundaries between individuals. This has been termed an "enmeshed" family system. The Philadelphia group feel that there is often a poorly delineated boundary between the nuclear family and family of origin. Family members are considered to intrude on each other's thoughts and feelings. Excessive togetherness and sharing result in a lack of privacy. In this framework, loyalty and protection take precedence over autonomy and self-realization.
2) Overprotectiveness is viewed as the second characteristic of psychosomatic families. The Philadelphia group feel that these families become unduly concerned with each other's welfare. Because parents are so preoccupied with the child's behavior, the child becomes more conscious of herself and other people's expectations — she becomes a "parent watcher." The child's psychological and bodily functioning is said to become the subject of undue familial interest. The result of this intrusive concern is a retardation of the child's development of autonomy, competence, and involvement outside the family home. Because parental control is

maintained in a context of apparent concern, Minuchin et al. (1978) feel that it becomes very difficult for the child to protest. Family members are thought to make their wishes known indirectly and unselfishly, so that disagreement and initiative become acts of betrayal. The denial of self for another's benefit and indirect expression of one's wishes are very similar to Selvini Palazzoli's account of the family spirit of self-sacrifice and lack of leadership or personal responsibility for one's actions.

3) Rigidity or commitment to the maintenance of the status quo is considered to be a third feature of these families. In periods of change and growth, such as during the child's entrance into adolescence with its demands for increased age-appropriate autonomy, these families experience great difficulty in relinquishing their accustomed interpersonal behavior patterns. Extrafamilial stress such as a loss or change in occupation similarly may require adaptations that the family cannot make and these may precipitate illness.

4) Lack of conflict resolution is thought to be a further feature in the family transactional style. Harmony is highly valued and the family's threshold for conflict is low. Selvini Palazzoli has also emphasized this point.

5) Finally, the child's involvement in parental conflict is considered to be a key factor in the development and maintenance of psychosomatic symptoms. Minuchin et al. (1978) feel that parental conflict may be handled in several ways. One of these has been termed "triangulation." Here, the child may be openly encouraged to side with one parent against the other. She may switch sides from one parent to another depending on the circumstances. Alternatively, she may enter a more stable coalition with one parent against the other. A further pattern has been described and called "detouring." In this situation the parents are thought to submerge their conflicts in a posture of blaming or protecting their sick child who is defined by them as the only family problem. The child thus becomes an "avoidance circuit."

The child's involvement in the parental conflict was also observed by Selvini Palazzoli who saw the child as the arbitrator, mediator, or secret ally of mother or father. Piazza, Piazza and Rollins (1980) view the family with an anorexia member in a very similar fashion. They felt that the two pathological family structures which occurred most frequently were "a stable coalition between the anorectic and one parent, and a detouring of marital conflict through the anorectic child." However, they also suggest that the critical psychopathology is in the mother of the anorexic who is unconsciously reliving her own previous relationship with her mother. No data have been provided to support these assertions.

The systems approaches of both the Milan and Philadelphia groups share certain features. In particular, the ideas of covert coalitions, spirit of self-sacrifice, and intrusion into each others' affairs are common to both. Both emphasize how children reared in these settings may find the demands for autonomy in adolescence threatening. These formulations are similar to Crisp's (1967) view that the family constellations in anorexia nervosa are likely to prohibit adolescent maturation in the children.

It is our impression that several of these concepts quite appropriately describe the transactional patterns of many anorexic families. Nevertheless, these findings are anecdotal and have never been properly examined in a controlled investigation. While Minuchin et al. (1978) have presented an overview of the results of one study, no details or the methods are yet available, nor are its detailed results (p. 36). While common in families with an anorexic member, these characteristics are not seen in all. Moreover, while these patterns occur in families with an anorexic member, they are not specific to the disorder since they are stated to occur in other psychosomatic illnesses. If they are important they must interact with other variables within the individual to produce the specific disorder. Finally, it is important to stress that these characteristics may be present in many anorexics' families and may be important for treatment (as discussed in Chapter 10), but they may be perpetuating rather than predisposing factors to the illness.

## SUMMARY

The exact role of the family in the predisposition and perpetuation of anorexia nervosa is not clearly understood. This is partly due to methodological problems related to the few investigations that have been conducted in this area and partly due to the nature of anorexia nervosa, as a heterogeneous syndrome with multiple predispositions. Given the latter, no one family constellation will be uniformly observed in anorexia nervosa. The family's involvement may be viewed as important in two areas, as families represent and magnify aspects of a culture and as particular patterns may foster the development or elaboration of illness. With regard to the former, controlled studies have shown that the parents of anorexics tend to be older and from higher social classes. Anecdotal evidence has also implicated weight and eating pathologies, as well as the magnified performance expectations, in anorexic families. It is currently not known whether these are qualitiatively or quantitatively different from non-anorexic families. Further advances in understanding anorexia nervosa have evolved from both ego-psychology and general systems theory. While these formulations describe many individuals with anorexia nervosa and their families, it is not known whether they have been describing the psychology of the illness or its pathogenesis. Moreover, if these purported factors predispose an individual to anorexia nervosa, they must interact with other significant events to produce the illness.

REFERENCES

Alexander, F.G.: *Psychosomatic Medicine: Its Principles and Applications.* New York: W.W. Norton, 1950.

Askevold, F. and Heiberg, A.: Anorexia nervosa — Two cases in discordant MZ twins. *Psychother. Psychosom.,* 32:223-228, 1979.

Benedek, T.: Dominant ideas and their relation to morbid cravings. *Int. J. Psychoanal.,* 17:40-56, 1936.

Ben-Tovim, D.I., Hunter, M. and Crisp, A.H.: Discrimination and evaluation of shape and size in anorexia nervosa: An exploratory study. *Research Communications in Psychology, Psychiatry and Behavior,* 2:241-257, 1977.

Beumont, P.J.V., Abraham, S.F., Argall, W.J., George, G.C.W. and Glaun, D.E.: The onset of anorexia nervosa. *Aust. NZ. J. Psychiatry,* 12:145-149, 1978.

Blitzer, J.R., Rollins, N. and Blackwell, A.: Children who starve themselves: Anorexia nervosa. *Psychosom. Med.,* 23:369-383, 1961.

Bom, F.: Simmonds' disease (endogenous cachexia) in pair of uniovular twins. *Nordisk. Medicin.,* 8:2506-2510, 1940.

Bruch, H.: The insignificant difference: Discordant incidence of anorexia nervosa in monozygotic twins. *Am. J. Psychiatry,* 126:85-90, 1969.

Bruch, H.: *Eating Disorders: Obesity, Anorexia Nervosa, and the Person Within.* New York: Basic Books, 1973.

Bruch, H.: Anorexia Nervosa: In: J.J. Wurtman and R.J. Wurtman (Eds.), *Nutrition and the Brain.* New York: Raven Press, 1979, pp. 101-116.

Cantwell, D.P., Sturzenberger, S., Burroughs, J. Salkin, B. and Green, J.K.: Anorexia nervosa: An affective disorder? *Arch. Gen. Psychiatry,* 34:1087-1093, 1977.

Charcot, J.M.: *Diseases of the Nervous System.* London: The New Sydenham Society, 1889.

Cobb, S.: *Emotions and Clinical Medicine.* New York: Norton, 1950.

Crisp, A.H.: Clinical and therapeutic aspects of anorexia nervosa — A study of 30 cases. *J. Psychosom. Res.,* 9:67-78, 1965.

Crisp, A.H.: Anorexia nervosa in an identical twin. *Postgrad. Med.,* 42:86-92, 1966.

Crisp, A.H.: Anorexia nervosa. *Hosp. Med.,* 5:713-718, 1967.

Crisp, A.H.: Premorbid factors in adult disorders of weight, with particular reference to primary anorexia nervosa (weight phobia). A literature review. *J. Psychosom. Res.,* 14:1-22, 1970.

Crisp. A.H., Harding, B. and McGuinness, B.: Anorexia nervosa. Psychoneurotic characteristics of parents: Relationship to prognosis. A quantative study. *J.Psychosom. Res.,* 18:167-173, 1974.

Crisp, A.H., Palmer, R.L. and Kalucy, R.S.: How common is anorexia nervosa? A prevalence study. *Br. J. Psychiatry,* 218:549-554, 1976.

Dally, P.J.: *Anorexia Nervosa.* New York: Grune and Stratton, 1969.

Dally, P.J. and Gomez, J.: *Anorexia Nervosa.* London: William Heinemann Medical Books Ltd., 1979.

Debow, S.L.: Identical twins concordant for anorexia nervosa. A preliminary case report. *Can. Psychiatr. Assoc. J.,* 20:215-217, 1975.

Dickens, J.A.: Concurrence of Turner's syndrome and anorexia nervosa. *Br. J. Psychiatry,* 117:237, 1970.

Duhrssen, A.: Zum problem der psychogenen ess-storung. *Psyche* (Heidelberg), 4:56-72, 1950.

Ehrensing, R.H. and Weitzman, E.L.: The mother-daughter relationship in anorexia nervosa. *Psychosom. Med.,* 32:201-208, 1970.

Fenwick, S.: *On Atrophy of the Stomach and on the Nervous Affections of the Digestive Organs.* London: Churchill Foster, 1880.

Foster, F.G. and Kupfer, D.J.: Anorexia nervosa: Telemetric assessment of family interaction and hospital events. *J. Psychiatr. Res.,* 12:19-35, 1975.

Garfinkel, P.E., Moldofsky, H. and Garner, D.M.: The heterogeneity of anorexia nervosa: Bulimia as a distinct subgroup. *Arch. Gen. Psychiatry,* 37:1036-1040, 1980.

Gifford, S., Murawski, B.J. and Pilot, M.L.: Anorexia nervosa in one of identical twins. *Int. Psychiat. Clin.,* 7:139-228, 1970.

Gull, W.W.: Anorexia nervosa. *Trans. Clin. Soc.* (London) 7:22-28, 1974.

Hall, A.: Family structure and relationships of 50 female anorexia nervosa patients. *Aust. NZ. J. Psychiatry,* 12:263-268, 1978.

Halmi, K.A.: Anorexia nervosa: Demographic and clinical features in 94 cases. *Psychosom. Med.,* 36:18-25, 1974.

Halmi, K.A. and Brodland, G.: Monozygotic twins concordant and discordant for anorexia nervosa. *Psychol. Med.,* 3:521-524, 1973.

Halmi, K.A. and Loney, J.: Familial alcoholism in anorexia nervosa. *Br. J. Psychiatry,* 123:53-54, 1973.

Halmi, K.A., Struss, A. and Goldberg, S.C.: An investigation of weights in the parents of anorexia nervosa patients. *J. Nerv. Ment. Dis.,* 166:358-361, 1978.

Halmi, K.A., Goldberg, S.C., Eckert, E., Casper, R. and Davis, J.M.: Pretreatment evaluation in anorexia nervosa. In: R. Vigersky (Ed.), *Anorexia Nervosa.* New York: Raven Press, 1977, p. 43-54.

Jensen, L.: Anorexia nervosa. *Acta Psychiat. Scand.* [Suppl], 203:113-115, 1968.

Jessner, L. and Abse, D.W.: Regressive forces in anorexia nervosa. *Br. J. Med. Psychol.,* 33:301-312, 1960.

Kalucy, R.S., Crisp, A.H. and Harding, B.: A study of 56 families with anorexia nervosa. *Br. J. Med. Psychol.,* 50:381-395, 1977.

Kay, D.W.K. and Leigh, D.: The natural history, treatment and prognosis of anorexia nervosa, based on a study of 38 patients. *J. Ment. Sci.,* 100:411-431, 1954.

Kay, D.W.K., Schapira, K. and Brandon, S.: Early factors in anorexia nervosa compared with non-anorexic groups. *J. Psychosom. Res.,* 11:133-139, 1967.

Kendell, R.E., Hall, D.J., Hailey, A. and Babigan, H.M.: The epidemiology of anorexia nervosa. *Psychol. Med.,* 3:200-203, 1973.

Kety, S.S., Rosenthal, D., Wender, P.H. and Schulsinger, F.: The types and prevalence of mental illness in the biological and adoptive families of adopted schizophrenics. In: D. Rosenthal and S.S. Kety (Eds.), *The Transmission of Schizophrenia.* Proceedings of the Second Research Conference of the Foundations' Fund for Research in Psychiatry, Dorado, Puerto Rico, 26 June to 1 July 1967. Oxford, New York: Pergamon Press, 1968.

Koluch, J. and Davidova, M.: On the problem of anorexia nervosa. *Acta Paedopsychiat.,* 29:343-349, 1962.

Kramer, S.: A discussion of the paper by John A. Sours on 'The anorexia nervosa syndrome.' *Int. J. Psychoanal.,* 55:577-579, 1974.

Lasègue, C.: De l'anorexie hystérique. *Arch.Gen. de Med.,* 385 (1873). Reprinted in: R.M. Kaufman and M. Heiman (Eds.), *Evolution of Psychosomatic Concepts. Anorexia Nervosa: A Paradigm.* New York: International Universities Press, 1964.

Lorand, S.: Anorexia nervosa: Report of a case. *Psychosom. Med.,* 5:282-292, 1943.

Mahler, M.S.: *On Human Symbiosis and the Vicissitudes of Individuation.* Vol. 1. Infantile Psychosis. New York: International Universities Press, 1968.

Masterson, J.F.: *Treatment of the Borderline Adolescent: A Developmental Approach.* New York: Wiley, 1972.

Masterson, J.F.: Primary anorexia nervosa in the borderline adolescent — An object relations view. In: P. Hartocollis (Ed.), *Borderline Personality Disorders.* New York: International Universities Press, 1977, pp. 475-494.

Meyer, J.E.: The anorexia nervosa syndrome. Catemnestic research. *Arch. Psychiat. Nervenkr.,* 202:31-59, 1961.

Minuchin, S., Rosman, B.L. and Baker, L.: *Psychosomatic Families: Anorexia Nervosa in Context.* Cambridge, MA: Harvard University Press, 1978.

Morgan, H.G. and Russell, G.F.M.: Value of family background and clinical features as predictors of long-term outcome in anorexia nervosa: Four-year follow-up study of 41 patients. *Psychol. Med.*, 5:355-372, 1975.

Mormont, C. and Demoulin, C.: Le personalite d'une anorexique mentale et de sa jumelle monozygote. Etude comparative. *Acta. Psychiat. Belg.*, 71:477-487, 1971.

Moulton, R.: A psychosomatic study of anorexia nervosa including the use of vaginal smears. *Psychosom. Med.*, 4:62-74, 1942.

Neki, J.S., Mohan, D. and Sood, R.K.: Anorexia nervosa in a monozygotic twin pair. *J. Indian Med. Assoc.*, 68:98-100, 1977.

Nemeth, J.M.: Anorexia nervosa in one dizygotic twin. *The Psychiatric Forum*. Fall, 45-50, 1977.

Piazza, E. Piazza, N. and Rollins, N.: Anorexia nervosa: Controversial aspects of therapy. *Compr. Psychiat.*, 21:177-189, 1980.

Ross, J.L.: Anorexia nervosa: An overview. *Bull. Menninger Clin.*, 41:418-436, 1977.

Rowland, C.V., Jr.: Anorexia nervosa — A survey of the literature and review of 30 cases. *Int. Psychiat. Clin.*, 7:37-137, 1970.

Sandler, J. and Dare, C.: The psychoanalytic concept of orality. *J. Psychosom. Res.*, 14:211-222, 1970.

Selvini Palazzoli, M.: *Self-starvation*. London: Chaucer Publishing Co. Ltd., 1974.

Simmons, R.C. and Kessler, M.D.: Indentical twins simultaneously concordant for anorexia nervosa. *J. Am. Acad. Child Psychiatry*, 18:527-536, 1979.

Sours, J.A.: The anorexia nervosa syndrome. *Int. J. Psychoanal.*, 55:567-579, 1974.

Stephens, L.: Fatal case of anorexia nervosa. *Lancet*, 1:31, 1895.

Stunkard, A.J.: From explanation to action in psychosomatic medicine: The case of obesity: presidential address, 1974. *Psychosom. Med.*, 37:195-236, 1975.

Szyrynski, V.: Anorexia nervosa and psychotherapy. *Am. J. Psychother.*, 27:492-505, 1973.

Taipale, V., Tuomi, O. and Aukee, M.: Anorexia nervosa. An illness of two generations. *Acta Paedopsychiat.*, 38:21-25, 1971.

Theander, S.: Anorexia nervosa: A psychiatric investigation of 94 female cases. *Acta Psychiat Scand* [Suppl], 214:1-194, 1970.

Thoma, H.: *Anorexia Nervosa* (translated by G. Brydone). New York: International Universities Press, 1967.

Ushakov, G.K.: Anorexia nervosa. In: J.G. Howells (Ed.), *Modern Perspectives in Adolescent Psychiatry*, Vol. 4. Edinburgh: Oliver and Boyd, 1971, pp. 274-289.

Waller, J.V., Kaufman, M.R. and Deutsch, F.: Anorexia nervosa: Psychosomatic entity. *Psychosom. Med.*, 2:3-16, 1940.

Weiner, H.: *Psychobiology and Human Disease*. New York: Elsevier, North Holland, Inc, 1977.

Weiner, J.M.: Identical male twins discordant for anorexia nervosa. *J. Am. Acad. Child Psychiatry*, 15:523-534, 1976.

Wender, P.H., Rosenthal, D., Kety, S.S., Schulsinger, F. and Welner, J.: Cross-fostering. A research strategy for clarifying the role of genetic and experiential factors in the etiology of schizophrenia. *Arch. Gen. Psychiatry*, 30:121-128, 1974.

Werman, D.S. and Katz, J.: Anorexia nervosa in a pair of identical twins. *J. Am. Acad. Child Psychiatry*, 14:633-645, 1975.

Winokur, A., March, V. and Mendels, J.: Primary affective disorder in relatives of patients with anorexia nervosa. *Am. J. Psychiatry*, 137(6): 695-698, 1980.

Ziegler, R. and Sours, J.A.: A naturalistic study of patients with anorexia nervosa admitted to a university medical center. *Compr. Psychiat.*, 9:644-651. 1968.

Ziolko, H.U.: Anorexia nervosa. *Fortschr. Neuro. Psychiat.*, 34:353-396, 1966.

# CHAPTER 8

# *The Multidetermined Nature*

# *of Anorexia Nervosa*

In the preceding chapters we have reviewed how a variety of factors within the individual, family, and culture may play a role in anorexia nervosa. The overall theme has been that while the exact mechanisms of etiology are not known, anorexia nervosa is a syndrome that is the product of an interplay of a number of forces. In the present chapter we would like to develop this concept further both by describing a relevant model of illness and by reviewing what is known about anorexia nervosa as it applies to this model. Again, however, we must stress the obvious — a full understanding of the interactions that result in or perpetuate anorexia nervosa is not possible at the present time.

Two clinical investigators whose descriptions of illness models are relevant to understanding anorexia nervosa are Weiner (1977) and Kubie (1971). Weiner (1977) proposes a model encompassing multiple predisposing events and occurrence at particular times. He has related the onset to a failure of the individual's ability to adapt to specific internal and external demands. Kubie (1971) describes the manifestations and sequelae of illnesses as the result of continuous interaction between the individual, his symptoms and his environment, and his striving to overcome his symptoms.

The clinical descriptions of anorexia nervosa are generally similar; the descriptions of Morton (1694) or Gull (1868) fit the contemporary patient. Because of this similiarity clinically, people have erred in looking for a single pathogenesis to the illness. In the sense of shared symptomatology, anorexia nervosa is clearly a discrete psychiatric syndrome but, as for other syndromes, this does not necessarily imply a single pathogenesis. Rather, in any population there will be a group of individuals at risk for anorexia nervosa because of the presence of a specific combination of predisposing factors. It is the interaction and timing of these phenomena in a given individual which are necessary for the person to become ill. In this sense, anorexia nervosa is a final common pathway, the product of a group of interacting forces.

This is not unlike the situation for other syndromes, for example, jaundice, hypertension or depression. The depressive syndrome is a good example of illness as a final common pathway (Akiskal and McKinney, Jr., 1975). The forces that are of significance here may be quite diverse — genetic, neurochemical, interpersonal, and intrapsychic events. It is the interaction of these forces that generates a depressive syndrome; a single predisposing event is usually not sufficient. For example, the antihypertensive agent, reserpine, appears to precipitate a depressive syndrome in certain people, but by itself is highly unlikely to produce the disorder. It generally requires other predisposing factors, such as a previous personal or familial history of depression (Davis, 1977).

The best examples of predisposing and initiating forces interacting to produce illness come from the classic studies of Weiner and Mirsky and their colleagues. In their prospective studies of army inductees in the 1950s, they were able to predict the development of peptic ulcer in certain individuals under the stresses of being away from home and joining the army. In particular, the individuals who later developed peptic ulcer were identifiable by both psychologically conflictual material and also by the largely genetically determined pepsinogen level in serum. That is, 14 of 15 subjects who developed peptic ulcer had significantly elevated pepsinogen levels (Yessler, Reiser and Rioch, 1959). The investigators were also able to identify over 70% of the pepsinogen hypersecretors on the basis of a blind analysis of psychological test data. They were further able to predict the presence of an ulcer in seven of 120 subjects, with only three errors, solely on the basis of these psychological results (Weiner, Thaler, Reiser and Mirsky, 1957).

However, not everyone with the particular psychological profile and elevated pepsinogen secretion developed an ulcer. This emphasizes a further point — that is, of a group of individuals predisposed to an illness by particular characteristics, not everyone will develop the illness. Moreover, not everyone with a particular illness will be found to have all the predisposing factors. In this sense illnesses are quite heterogeneous. For example, in studies of large numbers of peptic ulcer patients, not all are found to have high levels of gastric acid secretion and pepsinogen (Weiner, 1977). Also, some people develop an ulcer in situations not associated with marked psychosocial demands and without apparently related intrapsychic conflict.

This clearly applies to anorexia nervosa. Many individuals are predisposed to the illness by virtue of certain characteristics — for example, ado-

lescent girls of upper social class, in Western society, under strong pressures
to be successful, and with certain personal and familial characteristics, may
be at risk for the illness. But certainly not all at risk will develop it. Of those
who develop the illness, only some risk factors may be present in any individual. For example, anorexia nervosa occurred, but was not common, 100
years ago when social pressures on young women were quite different. Anorexia nervosa, though rare, does occur in males, in women over the age of
25, and in individuals from lower social classes. Not everyone with the illness has demonstrable perceptual distortions and while certain personality
and family characteristics may increase the risk of illness, individuals with a
variety of personality types and family backgrounds develop anorexia nervosa.

Anorexia nervosa in males is a special example of this process. About 5%
of anorexics are male and for this group the disorder may be likely to have
an earlier age of onset (Bruch, 1977a). Not only is there no societal emphasis on thinness for males, but also the upper social class distribution that
is observed for females is absent (Crisp and Toms, 1972). The reduced
sociocultural influence in the predisposition to the disorder for males may
suggest more serious pathologies in other areas — in the individual and his
family in those who eventually develop the illness. For example, several authors have drawn attention to the presence of possibly significant homosex-
ual conflicts preceding the disorder in up to 50% of their male patients
(Crisp and Toms, 1972; Dally, 1969) and there may be abnormalities on
CTT scans indicative of cerebral atrophy in men (Nussbaum, Shenker,
Marc and Klein, 1980).

However, familial psychopathologies in males have been said to resemble
those of females (Crisp and Toms, 1972) and it has been our impression
from the few male patients we have treated and from examples in the literature (Beumont, Beardwood and Russell, 1972; Crisp and Roberts, 1962;
Hay and Leonard, 1979; Hogan, Huerta and Lucas, 1974; Roussounis,
1971; Taipale, Larkio-Miettinenk, Valanne, Moren and Aukee, 1972) that
many of the individual's psychopathological features resemble those of
female anorexics.

Only a proportion of individuals at risk ever become ill and of those who
do develop the illness, only a few risk factors will be present in any individual. Also, a particular predisposition to a disease may develop in different
ways. For example, an individual may be susceptible to depression because
of a sensitization to object loss which in itself may have arisen in various
ways, for example, either by earlier losses, or by particular qualities of his
earlier relationships. Both may result in his self-worth being highly regulated by external phenomena and therefore susceptible to depression. A bio-

chemical predisposition to illness may also develop in different ways. For example, a functional impairment in brain monoamines may play a role in depressive illnesses (Garfinkel, Warsh and Stancer, 1979). This may evolve through a problem in the transport of important precursor substances into neurons (e.g., tryptophan), or by defects in enzyme levels required to synthesize the neurotransmitter or by a defect in the receptor's ability to respond to the neurotransmitter amine. The net effect from each of these could be the same — a functional defect of an important substance.

One important predisposition to anorexia nervosa relates to problems in autonomous functioning. A number of different mechanisms may be responsible for this predisposition. For example, Bruch (1973) has stated that an individual who has never had her internal sensations validated will grow up without inner signals to help her develop a sense of self-control and then will feel helpless in functioning separately from her parents. But a child who, in spite of external validation of her feelings, still cannot recognize these will also have problems in autonomous functioning later. Similar difficulties will also be experienced by a child who grows up in a family with poor differentiation between members (e.g., Minuchin's "enmeshment") or in a family with particular coalitions between parent and child or in a family in which the homeostasis requires that parental conflict be expressed through a child. The biological phenomenon of an unusually early puberty, as suggested by Crisp (1970b), may expose the individual to demands which she is not yet capable of meeting. Twinning may represent a different problem in separation. Difficulty in autonomous functioning may result from each of these mechanisms, but once it occurs this may interact with other factors to produce anorexia nervosa in an individual.

To summarize, we can note, as Weiner (1977) has, that:

1) illness often results from an interplay of predisposing forces acting upon an individual;
2) of many people with the predisposition to an illness only some actually develop it;
3) for individuals with a disease the exact interaction of predisposing forces will vary; and
4) the same predisposing factors may actually develop in different people in different ways.

While knowledge of predisposing factors helps explain why a particular illness is "chosen," it does not account for the timing of the illness. It is well known that illnesses do not occur at random but coincide with events in an individual's life and with his emotional state (Petrich and Holmes 1977; Rahe, McKean and Arthur, 1967). According to Weiner (1977) the onset of illness is determined by the individual's failure to adapt to the demands in which he is placed. These demands may be highly varied: For example, infections, toxins, injury, bereavement, and conflict may all overwhelm the individual's adaptive capabilities and result in the onset of illness. The predisposing events to an illness, which determine the "type" of illness, can be quite different from the initiating events, which determine when the person falls ill. These in turn may be quite different from circumstances which perpetuate the disorder (Weiner, 1977, p. 13).

According to Kubie (1971) all illnesses are "processes." That is, there are continuous interactions between the individual and his external world, his symptoms and his attempts to deal with his symptoms, that result in an elaboration of the illness in a variety of forms. Whatever the origins of the symptom cluster may be, once it has evolved, the individual's attempts to deal with it may produce predictable changes in personality and behavior which account for many of the later symptoms that sustain or perpetuate the disorder. For example, there may be a variety of events which lead to an agoraphobia. However, once it has developed, the course of the illness may be greatly influenced by the individual's attempts to deal with the severe panic on being alone in public places. The individual will develop methods of attenuating the anxiety—for example, never going outside, or insisting that a spouse always be present—which in themselves will produce further problems (marked social isolation, marital disharmony, depression). These sustaining or perpetuating factors and their production of recurrences, chronicity, or further symptom development are important for a complete picture of the anorexia nervosa syndrome.

In the following sections we will review information about anorexia nervosa from this perspective. This will include discussion of factors that have been considered to predispose to anorexia nervosa within the individual, family and culture; initiating or precipitating factors; and factors associated with sustaining the illness and the elaboration of other symptoms.

## PREDISPOSING FACTORS IN THE INDIVIDUAL
## TO ANOREXIA NERVOSA

Factors suggested to play a predisposing role within the individual are summarized in Table 1. When these are reviewed, it becomes apparent that relatively little is actually known about the individual's vulnerability to anorexia nervosa. This is particularly so if clear lines are drawn between factors known to be involved in the genesis rather than the perpetuation of the illness.

## TABLE 1

*Factors Suggested to Predispose to Anorexia Nervosa*

A.  *Individual*

    1.  Autonomy, identity and separation concerns
- ego deficits
- maturation fears
- early puberty
- age and sex distribution
- twinning
    2.  Perceptual disturbances
    3.  Weight disturbance
    4.  Personality development
    5.  Cognitive processes
    6.  Perinatal trauma
    7.  Other illnesses
- Turner's syndrome
    8.  Unknown variables

B.  *Family* (see Chapter 7)

    1.  Demographic characteristics
- parental age
- social class
    2.  Magnification of the culture
- weight, eating, fitness
- performance expectations
    3.  Parental history of affective illness and possibly alcoholism
    4.  Family history of anorexia nervosa (in siblings)
    5.  Maternal obesity (for bulimic group)
    6.  Possible genetic component (see MZ vs DZ twin concordance)
    7.  Specific parent-child interactions (leading to difficulties in autonomy and separation)

C.  *Culture* (see Chapter 5)
    1.  Pressures for thinness
    2.  Performance expectations

1) *Autonomy and Identity*

A major predisposition to anorexia nervosa relates to difficulties in autonomous functioning and sense of personal identity and thus an impaired ability to function separately from one's family or other "guideposts." Several clinicians with differing theoretical orientations have emphasized these phenomena as predispositions to anorexia nervosa.

As we described more fully in Chapters 6 and 7, Bruch (1973) has related the core predisposition to anorexia nervosa to fundamental ego deficits in autonomy and mastery over one's body, which she has described as the overall sense of "personal ineffectiveness." Similarly, Selvini Palazzoli (1970) has emphasized "ineffectiveness" which she suggests derives from early interactions with parents. These interpersonal experiences "give rise to a paralyzing feeling of ineffectiveness that pervades every thought and activity of these patients" (p. 202).

Bruch conceives of this sense of ineffectiveness as a primary ego deficit which may antedate the development of body image or interoceptive disturbances. She states: "The two other characteristics, body image disturbance and misperception of bodily states, may well be subordinated, partial expressions of this overall sense of ineffectiveness" (1962, p. 191). She has provided vivid descriptions of what she means by ineffectiveness: "[anorexic patients] experience themselves as not being in control of their behavior, needs and impulses, as not owning their own bodies, as not having a center of gravity within themselves. Instead, they feel under the influence and direction of external forces. They act as if their body and behavior were the product of other people's influences and actions" (1973, p. 55). This feeling of ineffectiveness and subsequent lack of personal identity may often result in major difficulties when the individual is removed from the concrete guidelines of her parents or is placed in situations with new expectations.

Although he has approached the issue from a somewhat different perspective, Crisp has also described how unprepared the potential anorexic is for maturity and how many of the symptoms represent a means of avoiding adolescent concerns and responsibilities (Crisp, 1965, 1967, 1970a, 1978). Crisps feels that the "weight phobia" centers around the anorexic's desperate avoidance of the normal body proportions that are associated with puberty. The fact that some patients, but by no means all, experience very early puberty (Crisp, 1970a) may suggest that these individuals lack a psychological readiness for the demands that their biological development has forced upon them. While other investigators have not been able to confirm Crisp's assertion of early menarche in groups of anorexia nervosa patients

(Theander, 1970), this does not negate the importance of an early puberty as part of the predisposition for some individuals. More important may be the person's reaction to her physical maturation regardless of its relative timing with respect to peers.

Crisp has emphasized that the dieting and "weight phobia" have the effect of a "regression" to a prepubertal state (Crisp, 1965). The girl not only appears prepubertal but often rejects the female sexual role and adulthood, and becomes more closely drawn to her parents. There is some evidence for immature functioning in anorexia nervosa. For example, it was noted earlier that the luteinizing hormone patterns are immature (Chapter 4), that the visual perceptive aspects of body image characteristics are age-inappropriate (Chapter 6), and Bruch has commented on the immaturity of the individual's cognitive development in Piagetian terms (Bruch, 1979). Dr. M. Nakamura, working in Japan and on our unit in Canada, has also demonstrated that the neurophysiological cortical responses to sensory stimulation are age-inappropriate (Nakamura, personal communication, 1980). While this evidence for immature functioning beyond superficial appearance and behavior is quite striking, it is not known whether these actually represent regressive phenomena as Crisp suggests, or are due to selective lags in development in particularly important spheres which render the individual vulnerable to the development of anorexia nervosa.

These inabilities to deal with issues of autonomy and identity, due to either ego deficits, regression, or developmental delays, help explain the two strongest predisposing factors to the syndrome: the characteristic age and sex distribution. It has been suggested that adolescent girls are subject to specific pressures in our society. At a time when they are first becoming aware of developing into adulthood, their secondary sexual characteristics, and sexual feelings, they must assume an increased sense of responsibility for, and control over, their behavior (Crisp, 1970b).

Problems with autonomy and separation are not unique to individuals with anorexia nervosa, but rather are important issues of adolescence in general. There is no one explanation why particular adolescent girls or even young adults should have undue problems with autonomy and self-control. For some being a twin may hinder a developing sense of personal identity. For others, having Turner's syndrome may alter one's attitudes to emerging adulthood. For yet others, a particular family constellation may grossly hinder a sense of individuality. For many potential anorexics, deficits in ego functioning, and perhaps developmental lags in other key areas, may render them unable to master the adolescent issues of autonomy and self-control. However this predisposition evolves, once it is present, it may interact with other relevant factors to produce anorexia nervosa.

## 2) *Perceptual Disturbances*

Disturbances in self-perception of body size and of internal affective and visceral states are an important, but not universally demonstrable aspect of the syndrome. These have been reviewed in Chapter 6. As indicated there, demonstrable abnormalities in self-estimation are seen in a large group of anorexics. These are closely linked to abnormal responses on a satiety-aversion-to-sucrose test of interoception. In addition, these body image disturbances are stable over a one-year period, are highly correlated with certain measures of psychopathology, and are related to poor prognosis. There are close associations experimentally between disturbed body image and a sense of lack of self-control. Body image disturbances are not directly related to weight or premorbid obesity. Moreover, the body image characteristics of these anorexics are more comparable to normal young adolescent girls rather than late adolescent or young adult women; in this regard the body image may be viewed as partially immature. The affective component to body image, body satisfaction, is grossly disturbed and is closely related to a sense of low self-esteem (Garner and Garfinkel, 1981). At present, without prospective studies of normal young girls, it is not acutally known if these disorders are part of the predisposition or are sequelae of the illness. As Bruch (1973) has hypothesized, however, it is not unreasonable to speculate that such disturbances in self-perception might predispose an individual to relentless dieting, or to lack of recognition of the effects of dieting, particularly when the person is unable to rely accurately on internal sensations for when to stop eating and this is coupled with fears of losing control.

## 3) *Weight Pathologies*

A number of investigators have questioned whether anorexia nervosa may be related to attempts to control obesity (see Bemis, 1978). However, this is an area of considerable imprecision due to the retrospective recollection and recording of earlier data. Several groups have recorded the frequent occurrence of developmental obesity in girls who later develop anorexia nervosa. Crisp (1965, 1970a, 1978) has suggested that the natural evolution of anorexia nervosa is characterized by an accelerated rate of growth and premorbid development. He has reported that anorexia patients generally weigh more at birth than their siblings (Crisp, 1965, 1970b) and this finding has been confirmed (Halmi, 1974a). Others have commented on the frequency of premorbid obesity in the child. For example, in the series of Kay and Leigh (1954) nerly half of their patients had previous "weight deviation or major or minor difficulty connected with eating or digestion." Similarly, Theander (1970) reported over half of those on whom this information was available (33 of 64) had been overweight and Halmi (1974a and b) observed 31% were premorbidly overweight; she also found that premorbid obesity was associated with a relatively older age of onset. However, Fox (1976) reported that premorbid obesity, defined strictly as a weight greater than 20% above average for age and height, occurred in only 16%; a further 34% of his sample showed less marked degrees of overweight premorbidly. We found obesity (as defined by a weight greater than 15% above average) to be a common finding more often in the bulimic group (see Chapter 3). Crisp, Kalucy, Lacey and Harding (1977) have also noted that bulimic anorexics were more commonly obese premorbidly.

Dally (1969) used a different method of subclassifying anorexic patients (see Chapter 3). Eighty percent of his obese patients were in group O and 40% of group O patients had been premorbidly obese. Seventy-three percent of this group who later became bulimic had previously been overweight. These data correspond to our findings with bulimics. To summarize these findings, while a significant proportion of anorexic patients have been obese premorbidly, this is particularly evident for those with the bulimic form of the disorder.

In association with weight difficulties, there have been suggestions of different premorbid eating patterns in the potential anorexic. Crisp (1970b), for example, found that individuals who later developed anorexia nervosa were either not breastfed in infancy or were breastfed for longer periods than controls. This was not confirmed by Theander (1970). Some (Dally, 1969; Kay and Leigh, 1954; Kay, Schapira and Brandon, 1967) but not all (Blitzer, Rollins and Blackwell, 1961; Rowland, 1970) investigators have described early feeding difficulties to be common.

The higher birth weight and premorbid obesity may be significant predisposing factors for some individuals. As Crisp (1970a) has suggested, the earlier heightened nutritional state may lead to an earlier prepubertal growth spurt and accompanying sexual development. This requires an earlier confrontation with adolescent demands, for sexuality or autonomy, for which the potential anorexic may be unprepared. Alternatively, an individual who has previously been obese may be extremely aware of past humiliations that she attributes to her obesity. This may serve as a particularly potent factor in predisposing to relentless dieting, especially if her self-worth is largely determined by appearance.

## 4) *Personality*

Since most studies of personality features of anorexic patients have been based upon the analysis of clinical information or hospital files, the precise meaning of the personality constructs are usually not stated or operationally defined. Moreover, when individuals are described after they have been chronically ill, the basic personality may be intertwined with features of the illness itself and with the starvation state (see Chapter 1). Further, many patients develop anorexia nervosa when they are quite young and a full evolution of the personality has not yet occurred (Morgan and Russell, 1975). Because of these factors there has been considerable diversity of opinion regarding premorbid personality and anorexia nervosa. It has been the opinion of some that there is no characteristic personality structure in the disorder (Blitzer et al., 1961; Thoma, 1967). Morgan and Russell (1975), for example, reported "normal" personality development in 32% of their patients, obsessionality in 27%, social anxiety in 51%, and excessive dependency in 22% premorbidly. These are in contrast to the observations of others that obsessional or hysterical traits are unduly common in anorexic patients (Dally, 1969; Halmi, 1974a; Janet, 1929; King, 1963). For example, Fox (1976) singled out prominent obsessive-compulsive features in 30 of his 44 patients. King (1963) described his patients as having traits of egocentricity, sensitivity, shyness, introspection, and irritability; however, it is not clear whether these descriptions apply to premorbid or presenting features. Meyer (1961) and Du Bois (1949) also emphasized the obsessional personality traits of their patients, but like King seem to refer to the patient's behavior on presentation rather than premorbidly.

Bruch (1973) and Crisp (1965) have described the compliant, perfectionistic and dependent characteristics of many patients. Often they have been "model" children who excel at school only through great personal effort. They have presented few if any problems at home or at school prior to the illness. By contrast, Kay and Leigh (1954), King (1963), and Nemiah (1950) reported a high frequency of childhood neurotic traits. Halmi, Goldberg, Eckert, Casper and Davis (1977) quantified specific traits in 44 patients. There was some heterogeneity but 86% were "very well behaved," 61% perfectionistic, and 61% competitive and achieving. Recently Strober (in press) compared 22 young (12-16 years old) anorexic females with age-matched patients with affective or personality disorders. Of importance, the anorexic patients were all ill for less than 9 months (mean of 6.7 months), so the effects of chronicity on personality functioning were minimized. Strober compared these groups on a series of standard psychological tests, and the anorexics were tested before and after weight gain. The anorexic patients were found to score significantly higher on the Marlowe-Crowne Social Desirability Scale, confirming the notion that they display a great need to seek approval from others. Their tendency to conformity, conscientiousness, and lack of responsiveness to inner needs as observed on the California Psychological Inventory. Anorexics also were highly obsessional on the Leighton Inventory and Hopkins symptom checklist; the latter partially, but not completely, improved with weight gain.

In another study employing objective personality measures, Smart, Beumont and George (1976) administered a battery of psychological tests to 22 patients with anorexia nervosa and comparison groups of "normal" and "mixed neurotic" controls. The tests selected were the Eysenck Personality Inventory, 16 Personality Factor Questionnaire, Leyton Obsessional Inventory and the Raven's Standard Progressive Matrices measure of intellectual functioning. Results indicated that the anorexic patients were more neurotic, introverted, anxious, and independent when compared to normals. Although more "obsessional" than normal controls, the anorexic patients did not meaningfully differ from obsessional patients. Solyom, Miles and O'Kane (in press) have confirmed the highly obsessional nature of a group of chronically ill anorexic subjects.

In addition to these characteristics we have suggested that many, but certainly not all, patients with the bulimic form of anorexia nervosa may have borderline personality organizations (see Chapter 3). Masterson (1972) had earlier described anorexia nervosa as a continuation of the borderline's problems in adolescence and this has recently been emphasized by Stone (1980, p. 141).

The intelligence of anorexic patients has generally been described to be at least average. In the controlled study of Smart et al. (1976), patients scored in the high normal range. Others have emphasized that their scholastic excellence is the product of a need to please others rather than a generally high natural endowment (Bruch, 1973). We have observed anorexia nervosa in individuals with a range of intellectual capabilities. Three of our patients have been mentally retarded. This association has previously been described by Hurley and Sovner (1979), Morgan and Russell (1975) and Pierloot, Wellens and Houben (1975). The important issue is not the level of intelligence, but rather the degree of external expectation perceived by the individual.

It is difficult to make a meaningful comment on premorbid personality characteristics as they predispose to anorexia nervosa. Most reports are of limited value since it is very difficult to separate the psychopathological characteristics which are possible precursors of the disorder, from those which are byproducts of a serious illness or are secondary to starvation. However, it is clear that there is some variability in personality type among anorexic individuals, yet several characteristics are unduly prominent. These include a great need for approval from others, conformity, conscientiousness, and a lack of responsiveness to inner needs. These qualities suggest a group of individuals with extremely high personal expectations and a need to please others and conform in order to maintain a sense of self-worth.

## 5) *Cognitive or Conceptual Elements*

Bruch (1979) has emphasized that particular deficits in conceptual organization occur in anorexia nervosa. She feels that in spite of attaining adolescence, anorexics maintain the thinking styles of younger children. In Piaget's (1955) terminology, anorexics do not develop to the phase of abstract reasoning but remain in the preconceptual and concrete operational periods. This results in certain characteristic cognitive patterns. For example, "egocentrism" is characteristic of concrete operations and is evident in anorexia nervosa. The clinical correlates of this type of conceptualization include an inability to view situations in anything but extremes (i.e., dichotomous reasoning, "all or none"), personalization of many issues, rigid morality, viewing correlated events as causal, and highly superstitious thinking (see Chapters 6 and 10, and Garner and Bemis, 1982). Individuals who show these forms of thinking may be at risk for concrete interpretation of external events in a highly personalized form.

Bruch (1977b) has described how the anorexic concretely interprets society's demands for small proportions in an exaggerated manner with the belief that she will derive acknowledgement for her self-denial and extreme thinness. The anorexic also correlates unrelated events to changes in body size; in particular her low self-worth becomes concretized to body size. There is a literal belief in the idea that losing weight will satisfy the individual's extreme performance expectations for herself and also alleviate personal distress. The "dichotomous" thinking also presents serious problems in the area of self-control. The individual believes that if she eats anything more than her daily allotment she will be out of control; similarly she thinks that if she gains one pound this will become 100. Except for Crisp and Fransella (1972), there have been no attempts to systematically study cognitive characteristics in anorexia nervosa. The study of cognitive factors and how they change with weight gain would be particularly interesting.

## 6) *Perinatal Complications*

Halmi et al. (1977) have questioned whether early cerebral damage might either generate a predisposition to or sustain anorexia nervosa. There is evidence that prenatal and perinatal factors associated with damage to the central nervous system may "increase the vulnerability of an individual to childhood behavior problems" (Halmi et al., 1977, p. 53). Halmi et al. (1977) recorded pregnancy complications (bleeding, toxemia, infection, etc.) in 18%, and delivery complications (anorexia, prolonged labor, use of medication, etc.) in 30% of the births of their 44 patients. In a retrospective chart analysis, Halmi (1974a) had earlier found that 16% had incurred risks of brain damage due to perinatal complications. Theander (1970) obtained historical information on disease or accidents involving risks of cerebral injury in 20% of his sample and Morgan and Russell (1975) similarly found obstetric difficulties in 24%. In the only controlled study, Kay et al. (1967) reported an increase in birth complications in their anorexic sample in comparison with normal and neurotic women. More recently Halmi, Hamsher and Benton (1980) have described the persistence of subtle cognitive deficits, as measured by a neuropsychological battery, after weight restoration in some of their patients. The presence of these disturbances was related to a poor prognosis, as determined by weight, on one year follow-up.

These data on perinatal damage are obviously quite limited both by the general lack of controlled information and by the various problems in gathering this information. If such damage does present a vulnerability to anorexia nervosa, it likely is a minor contributor to the overall occurrence of the syndrome for most individuals, given the relative infrequency of the trauma (i.e., in <25% of patients). However, early trauma may be one factor that limits an individual's later coping abilities and thereby renders the evolution of anorexia nervosa more likely under stress. What is equally plausible, is that subtle birth damage may be a factor in sustaining the illness once it has evolved (Halmi et al., 1977).

## 7) *Other Illness*

Two other groups of illnesses have been purported to occur with increased frequency in anorexia nervosa. These are Turner Syndrome and congenital urogenital malformations. The relationship between these and anorexia nervosa has not yet been clearly defined.

Since Pitts and Guze (1963) first described the association of anorexia nervosa and Turner Syndrome, at least ten other such patients have been reported (Darby, Garfinkel, Vale, Kirwan and Brown, 1981; Margo and Hawton, 1978). In addition, we have treated a twelfth patient whose diagnosis was confirmed by laparoscopy and karyotyping, who has not been previously reported. Halmi and Rigas (1973) found one case of Turner Syndrome in a series of 59 anorexics studied; they concluded that the two disorders occurred together more often than by chance alone. Kron, Katz, Gorzynski and Weiner (1977) reported almost 10% of their anorexic patients had Turner Syndrome but felt it was premature to assume a significant concurrence of the two disorders.

We also karyotyped 20 consecutive patients referred to our unit and one was found to have Turner Syndrome (Darby et al., 1981). Thus, of anorexic patients karyotyped to date, between 2-10% have been found to have Turner Syndrome. Given the prevalence figures for Turner Syndrome to be one per 2500 (de Grouchy, 1978) and the recent increase in anorexia nervosa, it is quite possible that these associations are due to chance alone (Darby et al., 1981; Liston and Shershow, 1973). If the concurrence of the disorders eventually is shown to be greater than by chance, this may not necessarily be due to a common underlying genetic predisposition. Rather, it might indicate particular problems individuals with Turner Syndrome have with puberty, autonomy, body changes, or body image. However, there is no evidence for these at present.

Halmi and Rigas (1973) reported five cases of anorexia nervosa with associated urogenital abnormalities and a further case has been documented by Robertson and Hamberger (1979). Halmi and Rigas' cases represented 8% of their sample of anorexics; they suggested that the frequency of these congenital anomalies in anorexics was greater than would be expected by chance. However, Haller, Slovis, Baker, Berdon and Silverman (1977) have studied a large group of anorexics radiologically, including the use of intravenous pyelography. While this technique would not rule out all urogenital abnormalities, it is rather striking that no abnormalities at all were noted. Further documentation is required to ascertain whether such anomalies are overrepresented in anorexia nervosa.

## 8) *Other Variables*

There are likely other factors within the individual that may represent a predisposition to anorexia nervosa; we are just quite limited in our current knowledge. For example, can the early development of amenorrhea before any significant weight loss has occurred represent a possible predisposition, or, as Weiner has speculated, do female sex hormones and their changing levels at puberty somehow play a role in sensitizing the hypothalamus

(Weiner, 1977, p. 629)? Predisposing "congenital neuroendocrine vulnerability" and constitutional neuroendocrine deficiency have been postulated.
(Piazza, Piazza and Rollins, 1980; Ushakov, 1971). Clearly, further investigation is required to answer these questions and to determine the specific
protective factors which prevent most predisposed individuals from falling
ill.

## FAMILIAL AND CULTURAL PREDISPOSING FACTORS

The factors within the individual that predispose to anorexia nervosa interact with familial and cultural events. These are listed in Table 1. The familial and cultural predispositions to the illness were fully described in
Chapters 5 and 7 and will not be reviewed here.

## INITIATING OR PRECIPITATING EVENTS

The predisposing factors are responsible for the type of illness that
evolves and the precipitating events interact with these to determine the
onset of illness. There is no single precipitant of anorexia nervosa and, indeed, for some patients no particular precipitant can be identified. The frequency of identification of external precipitants varies widely; for example,
Theander (1970) identified specific causes in 50%, Halmi (1974a) in 55%,
Morgan and Russell (1975) in 65%, while Casper and Davis (1977) could
identify precipitating factors in all their patients. These figures will obviously depend on the criteria used to define a significant environmental
change. Moreover, it must be emphasized that for some people the lack of
an apparent environmental change is misleading, since with biological maturation the same environment may require new personal and social
behavior. The lack of external initiators has been reported to occur more
frequently in younger patients (Halmi, 1974b; Theander, 1970). But Halmi
et al. (1977) have also suggested that, when the illness develops in the absence of external stressors, there is a more severe underlying psychopathology and resistance to treatment. This is at variance with the frequent reports
of younger patients having a better prognosis (see Chapter 12) and requires
further investigation.

For many patients, an external initiating event or series of events can be
determined and these are varied, ranging, for example, from going to a
summer camp, to a pregnancy. Moreover, these precipitants do not differ
from those reported to be significant initiators for other psychiatric illnesses. This highlights the importance of the predisposing factors in the
"choice" of the syndrome. What the initators of anorexia nervosa do have

in common is that, whatever the event, the individual perceives personal distress in the form of 1) a threat of loss of self-control and/or 2) a threat or an actual loss of self-worth. Table 2 lists some of the frequent precipitants of anorexia nervosa. Their categorization is for convenience and is quite arbitrary.

Separations and losses have repeatedly been documented as precipitants of anorexia nervosa. Beumont, Abraham, Argall, George and Glaun (1978) noted that in 11 of 34 patients a bereavement had occurred. Kalucy, Crisp and Harding (1977) observed deaths within the family in 29% and events involving the patient leaving home in 34%. While actual parental separation occurred in only 7%, threats of separation were common. Similarly, Dally (1969) reported death or serious illness in a relative in 17%, Rowland (1970) "separation themes" in 43%, and Halmi (1974a) "family conflicts, including separation" in 36%. Others who have also stressed separations and deaths include Blitzer et al. (1961), Kay and Leigh (1954), Morgan and Russell (1975), and Theander (1970). The types of separations are extremely varied, from break-up of the parental home or death of a parent, to going away to college or a summer vacation. In addition, parental illness, a pregnancy in parent or a sibling, "family scandal," overt parental infidelities, or a sibling's promiscuity may all significantly alter the family balance and have been suggested to initiate the illness (Beumont et al., 1978; Kalucy et al., 1977; Theander, 1970). In all these situations the family homeostasis is disordered and the adolescent's lack of internal controls may then become more evident, when her external guidelines are disrupted.

## TABLE 2

### Common Initiating Factors to Anorexia Nervosa

*Predisposing Factors:*

Individual

Familial — — — — — — Initiating Factor----------DIET TO ENHANCE SELF-CONTROL & SELF-WORTH

Cultural

                  a) separation and losses
                  b) disruptions of family homeostasis
                  c) new environmental demands
                  d) direct threat of loss of self-esteem
                  e) personal illness

Another major group of precipitants include circumstances in which new demands or expectations confront the individual. Obviously these demands may occur following separations or object loss. They may also occur when the girl first enters an interpersonal relationship which involves some intimacy and sexual contact. These have been emphasized by most investigators who have recorded precipitating events to anorexia nervosa. For example, Beumont et al. (1978) described these in 47% of their patients, Dally (1969) in 36%, Rowland (1970) in 23% and Halmi (1974) in 16%. These sexual contacts may highlight the individual's fears of losing self-control and her helplessness in interpersonal settings. For a few patients, the initiator of the disorder may be a pregnancy (Lakoff and Feldman, 1972); this occurs within the context of fears of loss of self-control and, in the cases we have observed, severely disturbed maternal identification.

Situations requiring new accomplishments often highlight the extremely high personal expectations and competitiveness of some of these people. It is not uncommon for the illness to develop when the individual has experienced or has imagined personal failure; this was reported in 57% of Dally's (1969) series. Theander (1970), Rowland (1970) and Halmi (1974a) also felt this was an initiating factor for some of their patients. Beumont et al. (1978) described competitiveness and fears of failure at school, sports, or dance to be significant in 35%. Siblings' achievements (e.g., marriage, a pregnancy) may also be initiators of the illness for similar reasons.

These examples highlight the sensitivity of many anorexics to external events for the regulation and maintenance of their sense of self-worth. Self-esteem may be directly threatened in a variety of ways, for example, by academic or vocational failures as just described, or perceived social failures. In addition, for some patients the immediate period prior to the onset of illness is characterized by significant weight gain with perceived subsequent ridicule and rejection and heightened feelings of inadequacy.

For a small group of patients the anorexia nervosa is immediately preceded by a physical illness (Beumont et al., 1978; Dally, 1969). Often the illness itself is associated with a physiological anorexia and some weight loss. These patients often report that this weight loss helped them begin the relentless dieting they had previously contemplated.

Whatever the particular initiating event, the results are quite similar. The individual perceives a threat to her sense of worth and her control over her world. This leads to a heightened preoccupation with her body and the eventual conviction that she will feel better about herself and more in control if she continues to lose weight.

### FACTORS THAT SUSTAIN THE ILLNESS

The course of anorexia nervosa varies widely (see Chapters 11 and 12). Factors that relate to one patient's complete recovery versus another's becoming chronically ill are not yet properly understood. However, some of the factors that perpetuate the illness are known. These include:

1) *The Starvation Syndrome*

In Chapter 1, the psychological effects of starvation were described. Paradoxically, the symptoms of starvation intensify the anorexic's preoccupations with food. They also affect her self-concept and sense of self-control since impaired concentration, indecisiveness, obsessionality, mood lability, and sleep disturbance occur. Starving people may also tend to feel more hungry after they've eaten (Keys, Brozek, Henschel, Mickelsen, and Taylor, 1950); this will exacerbate the anorexic's fears of loss of control concerning food. The mechanisms for the production of the specific starvation-related symptoms are not properly understood. Zinc deficiency can greatly alter taste perception and this may play a role in the hypoguesis and bizarre food combinations seen in starving anorexics (Casper, Kirschner, Sandstead, Jacob and Davis, 1980). Recently, Gold, Kaye, Robertson, Goodwin and Ebert (1980) have demonstrated altered levels of central nervous system arginine vasopression (AVP) in a small number of anorexic patients. This same group have also shown that AVP is important for short-term memory and perhaps is associated with mood alterations (Ballenger, Post, Gold, Goodwin, Bunney and Robertson, 1980). Chronically elevated plasma cortisol levels in starvation may also play a role in some of the observed changes.

Many of the most serious effects of starvation from the point of view of chronicity are those on the individual's social and interpersonal functioning. Starvation produces both a reduction of interests and a marked social isolation. Over time, the person's friends grow further and further away and no longer share interests with her. If allowed to persist, these symptoms may result in serious deficits, particularly in self-concept and self-esteem, which the anorexic may inappropriately deal with by further attempts at self-control through dieting. Berkman (1948) and Russell (1977) had earlier commented on a self-perpetuating cycle due to starvation.

2) *Vomiting*

The presence of vomiting may considerably exacerbate the persistence of the overall syndrome and has been noted to be a poor prognostic sign (Crisp et al., 1977; Garfinkel, Moldofsky and Garner, 1977; see Chapter 12). While patients often express great shame or disgust about their vomiting, there is also another side to it; the vomiting may be viewed by the individual as adaptive — in allowing her to eat and yet maintain a thin body size. Since vomiting may represent a "solution" to the dilemma, its presence may often entrench the syndrome further.

## 3) *Gastrointestinal Physiology*

A major problem for the patient is her altered sense of satiety (Garfinkel, 1974). Feeling bloated, stuffed, or even nauseous after meals is common. Moreover, anorexics feel more full than normals before a meal, even if they haven't eaten for 12 hours (Garfinkel, Moldofsky, Garner, Stancer and Coscina, 1978). Dubois, Gross, Ebert and Castell (1979) and Saleh and Lebwohl (1980) have recently shown that there is a markedly delayed gastric emptying time in emaciated patients with anorexia nervosa; significantly, this was only partially improved shortly after weight gain. This delayed gastric emptying and the chronic constipation contribute to feelings of being full after meals; this may encourage an anorexic to begin cutting back on the size or frequency of her meals. Once she begins to cut back, for any reason, the likelihood of her once again relating her sense of worth to a particular look or a size is greatly increased.

## 4) *Body Perceptions*

While it is not certain whether disturbances in body image and interoception are determinants of or sequelae to the syndrome, when present they are significant perpetuating factors. Several investigators have shown that severe body image distortions are related to a poor prognosis (Crisp et al., 1977; Garfinkel et al., 1977). Patients who cannot accurately recognize their body sizes may feel more out of control after small weight increases and feel generally uncomfortable about their bodies, regardless of weight. Since these disturbances in body image are closely linked in the same individuals to the lack of developing an aversion for sucrose tastes, these individuals may experience further difficulties—they do not recognize an internal mechanism to help regulate quantities of carbohydrates ingested. They may be unable to habituate to carbohydrate-containing foods; this might lead to a sense of being out of control once they start to eat carbohydrates. Their way of overcoming this problem may be to curtail carbohydrates.

## 5) *Cognitive Factors*

As we have said, whatever predisposing or initiating factors have been present, all anorexics at some point begin to develop a similar attitude: Thinness is of great importance to their sense of well-being and all their efforts must be directed to maintaining their slimness. While initially highly bound to external phenomena for regulation of their self-worth, anorexics now turn inward to their personalized weight-related value system. It is at this time that the syndrome becomes self-perpetuating in another fashion—through positive self-reinforcement of successful weight loss and through phobic avoidance of weight gain (Garner and Bemis, 1982). The phobic avoidance secondarily affects particular foods which are believed to contain large amounts of calories. The phobic avoidance behavior is reinforcing, that is, whenever the individual's anxiety is increased by the presence of the feared object but then is reduced by avoiding the situation, the anxiety reduction itself is a reinforcer that perpetuates the behavior. Because of the dread about food, social behavior associated with eating is often avoided. Some patients avoid parties where food is being served, others movies (because of the smell of popcorn), and obviously luncheon dates with friends. So this phobic avoidance of foods helps perpetuate a serious social withdrawal. As we noted previously, the starvation syndrome, the individual's temperament, and concerns about self-esteem also contribute to this social isolation.

Russell, Campbell and Slade (1975) have shown the degree to which patients with anorexia nervosa are tied to "what the scales say." They found that anorexics, but not normals, increased their food intake and their weights when the scales were altered to record lower than actual weights. The opposite is also true. If the patient believes she is over some previously determined upper limit, she will begin to curtail her intake, again perpetuating the problem.

The previously described concrete and egocentric thinking patterns also help perpetuate the anorexic behavior. Particularly important here is the dichotomous thinking of extremes which does not allow for "in betweens." As long as it persists, it is difficult for the person to regulate her eating and her weight without swinging to extremes.

## 6) *Personality Features*

It was noted earlier in this chapter that there is no one personality type that is predisposed to anorexia nervosa but that certain features may be unduly common in many. Once it has evolved, certain personality features may be associated with sustaining the illness. Some have suggested that obsessionality may be a sustaining factor (see Chapter 12).

## 7) *General Level of Ego Functions*

The individual's ability to relate to others, her level of attainment in a career or school (Garfinkel et al., 1977), her ability to cope with stresses, and her level of impulse control will all affect the course of the illness (see also Chapter 12).

## 8) *Unresolved Predisposing Factors*

Significant familial or intrapsychic conflicts regarding maturation or autonomy will likely lead to chronicity or recurrences if they are not dealt with during and shortly after the period of weight restoration.

## 9) *Secondary Gain*

Ryle (1939) observed that "perpetuating factors include morbid enjoyment of the interest and anxiety aroused by the illness, the sense of power over the mother obtained thereby." Because the daughter's low weight assumes such obvious importance to the entire family's life, particular benefits may be derived from the symptom making change unlikely. An insecure young woman becomes "interesting" in the same way as a tubercular's appearance was supposedly "interesting" in the nineteenth century — a sentimental association with doomed romantic poets and dying operatic heroines.

## 10) *Cultural Emphasis on Slimness*

This may be an important perpetuating factor for many (Garner, Garfinkel, Schwartz and Thompson, 1980). This may be especially true for those who have been premorbidly obese and have memories of the personal devaluation associated with it or are engaged in occupations demanding unusual slenderness.

## 11) *Iatrogenic Factors*

Certain types of treatment may lead to an accentuation of a patient's lack of personal control. These include refeeding programs that emphasize rapid weight gain and neglect both provision for instituting external controls for the patient and attention to other psychosocial issues which have contributed to the illness. Psychological treatments that don't also take into account the need for weight gain to remove the starvation effects will also perpetuate the illness. Of crucial significance are doctor-patient relationships that further lower the patient's self-esteem by instituting humiliating punishment for failures to achieve treatment goals.

It is apparent from the overview of predisposing, precipitating, and perpetuating factors presented in this chapter that the precise circumstances leading to the development of anorexia nervosa in any one individual will be highly variable and consist of a complex interaction between contributing forces. At this time, the specific interaction between the factors necessary and sufficient for the expression of the disorder is not known. Furthermore, characteristics which protect some apparently vulnerable individuals have not been investigated. Nevertheless, it is our understanding that many people possess the "individual, family and cultural antecedents and these become pathogenic within the context of stressors which initiate dieting, weight loss and pursuit of thinness" (Garner and Garfinkel, 1980). Various precipitants may trigger the disorder, which lead to weight loss and the emergence of starvation effects, which in turn provide feedback perpetuating the anorexia nervosa syndrome. For this reason therapy for any patient must be individualized to fit her requirements at the time. These therapies are discussed in the next two chapters.

## REFERENCES

Akiskal, H.S. and McKinney, W.T., Jr.: Overview of recent research in depression. Integration of ten conceptual models into a comprehensive clinical frame. *Arch. Gen. Psychiatry,* 32:285-305, 1975.

Ballenger, J.C., Post, R.M., Gold, P.W., Goodwin, F.K., Bunney, W.E., Jr. and Robertson, G.: Endocrine correlates of personality and cognition in normals. Presented at 133rd Annual Meeting of the American Psychiatric Association, San Francisco, May 1980. Syllabus and Scientific Proceedings, p.144.

Bemis, K.M.: Current approaches to the etiology and treatment of anorexia nervosa. *Psychol. Bull.,* 85:593-617, 1978.

Berkman, J.M.: Anorexia nervosa, anterior-pituitary insufficiency, Simmonds' cachexia and Sheehan's disease. *Postgrad. Med.,* 3:237-246, 1948.

Beumont, P.J.V., Beardwood, C.J. and Russell, G.F.M.: The occurrence of the syndrome of anorexia nervosa in male subjects. *Psychol. Med.,* 2:216-231, 1972.

Beumont, P.J.V., Abraham, S.F., Argall, W.J., George, G.C.W. and Glaun, D.E.: The onset of anorexia nervosa. *Aust. N.Z. J. Psychiatry,* 12:145-149, 1978.

Blitzer, J.R., Rollins, N. and Blackwell, A.: Children who starve themselves: Anorexia nervosa. *Psychosom. Med.,* 23:369-383, 1961.

Bruch, H.: *Eating Disorders.* New York: Basic Books, 1973.

Bruch, H.: Psychological antecedents of anorexia nerovsa. In: R.A. Vigersky (Ed.), *Anorexia Nervosa.* New York: Raven Press, 1977a.

Bruch, H.: Anorexia nervosa. In: E.D. Wittkower and H. Warnes (Eds.), *Psychosomatic Medicine, Its Clinical Applications.* New York: Harper and Row, 1977b, pp. 229-237.

Bruch, H.: Anorexia nervosa. In: R.J. Wurtman and J.J. Wurtman (Eds.), *Nutrition and the Brain,* Vol. 3. New York: Raven Press, 1979, pp. 101-115.

Casper, R.C. and Davis, J.M.: On the course of anorexia nervosa. *Am. J. Psychiatry,* 134:974-978, 1977.

Casper, R.C., Kirschner, B., Sandstead, H.H., Jacob, R.A. and Davis, J.M.: An evaluation of trace metals, vitamins, and taste function in anorexia nervosa. *Am. J. Clin. Nutr.,* 33:1801-1808, 1980.

Crisp, A.H.: Some aspects of the evolution presentation and follow-up of anorexia nervosa. *Proc. Roy. Soc. Med.,* 58:814-820, 1965.

Crisp, A.H.: Anorexia Nervosa: 'Feeding disorder,' 'nervous malnutrition' or 'weight phobia'? *World Rev. Nutr. Diet,* 12:452-504, 1970a.

Crisp, A.H.: Premorbid factors in adult disorders of weight, with particular reference to primary anorexia nervosa (weight phobia). A literature review. *J. Psychosom. Res.,* 14:1-22, 1970b.

Crisp, A.H.: Some aspects of the relationship between body weight and sexual behavior with particular reference to massive obesity and anorexia nervosa. *Int. J. Obes.,* 2:17-32, 1978.

Crisp, A.H. and Fransella, K.: Conceptual changes during recovery from anorexia nervosa. *Br. J. Med. Psychol.,* 45:395-405, 1972.

Crisp, A.H. and Roberts, F.J.: A case of anorexia nervosa in a male. *Postgrad. Med.,* 38:350-353, 1962.

Crisp, A.H., and Toms, D.A.: Primary anorexia nervosa or weight phobia in the male: Report on 13 cases. *Br. Med. J.,* 1:334-338, 1972.

Crisp, A.H., Kalucy, R.S., Lacey, J.H., and Harding, B.: The long-term prognosis . In: R.A. Vigersky (Ed.), *Anorexia Nervosa.* New York: Raven Press, 1977, pp. 55-56.

Dally, P.: *Anorexia Nervosa.* New York: Grune and Stratton, 1969.

Darby, P.L., Garfinkel, P.E., Vale, J.M., Kirwan, P.J. and Brown, G.M.: Anorexia nervosa and "Turner syndrome:" Cause or coincidence? *Psychol. Med.,* 11:141-145, 1981.

Davis, J.M.: Central biogenic amines and theories of depression and mania. In: W.E.Fann, I. Karacan, A.D. Pokorny and R.L. Williams (Eds.), *Phenomenology and Treatment of Depression.* New York: Spectrum Publications, 1977, pp. 17-32.

de Grouchy, J.: Organization of the primate genome: A comparative approach. In: S. Cermendares and R. Lisker (Eds.), *Human Genetics.* Amsterdam: Exerpta Medica, 1978, pp. 98-105.

Du Bois, F.S.: Compulsion neuroses with cachexia (anorexia nervosa). *Am. J. Psychiatry,* 106:107-115, 1949.

Dubois, A., Gross, H.A., Ebert, M.H. and Castell, D.O.: Altered gastric emptying and secretion in primary anorexia nervosa. *Gastroenterology,* 77:319-323, 1979.

Fox, K.C. and James, N.M.: Anorexia nervosa: A study of 44 strictly defined cases. *N.Z. Med. J.,* 84:309-312, 1976.

Garfinkel, P.E.: Perception of hunger and satiety in anorexia nervosa. *Psychol Med.,* 4:309-315, 1974.

Garfinkel, P.E., Moldofsky, H. and Garner, D.M.: The outcome of anorexia nervosa: Significance of clinical features, body image and behavior modification. In: R.A. Vigersky (Ed.), *Anorexia Nervosa.* New York: Raven Press, 1977, pp. 315-329.

Garfinkel, P.E., Moldofsky, H., Garner, D.M., Stancer, H.C. and Coscina, D.V.: Body awareness in anorexia nervosa: Disturbances in "body image" and"satiety." *Psychosom. Med.,* 40:487-498, 1978.

Garfinkel, P.E., Warsh, J.J. and Stancer, H.C.: Depression: New evidence for biological differentiation. *Am. J. Psychiatry,* 136:535-539, 1979.

Garner, D.M. and Bemis, K.: A cognitive-behavioral approach to anorexia nervosa. *Cognitive Therapy and Research,* 6:1-27, 1982.

Garner, D.M. and Garfinkel, P.E.: Socio-cultural factors in the development of anorexia nervosa. *Psychol. Med.,* 10:647-656, 1980.

Garner, D.M. and Garfinkel, P.E.: Body image in anorexia nervosa: Measurement, theory and clinical implications. *Intl. J. Psychiatry in Med.,* 11:263-284, 1981.

Garner, D.M., Garfinkel, P.E., Schwartz, D. and Thompson, M.: Cultural expectations for thinness in women. *Psychol. Rep.,* 47:483-491, 1980.

Gold, P.W., Kaye, W., Robertson, G., Goodwin, F.K. and Ebert, M.: Altered central vasopressin in anorexia nervosa. Presented at the 133rd Annual Meeting of the American Psychiatric Association San Francisco, May 1980. Syllabus and Scientific Proceedings, p. 326.

Gull, W.W.: The address in medicine delivered before the annual meeting of the BMA at Oxford. *Lancet,* 2:171, 1868.

Haller, J.O., Slovis, T.L., Baker, D.H., Berdon, W.E. and Silverman, J.A.: Anorexia nervosa — The paucity of radiologic findings in more than fifty patients. *Pediat. Radiol.,* 5:145-147, 1977.

Halmi, K.A.: Anorexia nervosa; demographic and clinical features in 94 cases. *Psychosom. Med.,* 36:18-25, 1974a.

Halmi, K.A.: Comparison of demographic and clinical features in patient groups with different ages and weights at onset of anorexia nervosa. *J. Nerv. Ment. Dis.,* 158:222-225, 1974b.

Halmi, K.A., Hamsher, K. and Benton, A.L.: Neuropsychological predictors in anorexia nervosa. Presented at the 133rd annual meeting of the American Psychiatric Association, San Francisco, May 1980. Syllabus and Scientific Proceedings, p. 327.

Halmi, K.A., Goldberg, S.C., Eckert, E., Casper, R. and Davis, J.M.: Pretreatment evaluation in anorexia nervosa. In: R.A. Vigersky, (Ed.), *Anorexia Nervosa.* New York: Raven Press, 1977, pp. 43-54.

Halmi, K.A. and Rigas, C.: Urogenital malformations associated with anorexia nervosa. *Br. J. Psychiatry,* 122:79-81, 1973.

Hay, G.G. and Leonard, J.C.: Anorexia nervosa in males. *Lancet,* 2:574-575, 1979.

Hogan, W.M., Huerta, E. and Lucas, A.R.: Diagnosing anorexia nervosa in males. *Psychosomatics,* 15:122-126, 1974.

Hurley, A.D. and Sovner, R.: Anorexia nervosa and mental retardation: A case report. *J. Clin. Psychiat.,* 40:480-482, 1979.

Janet, P.: *The Major Symptoms of Hysteria:* New York: MacMillan, 1929.

Kay, D.W.K. and Leigh, D.: The natural history, treatment and prognosis of anorexia nervosa, based on a study of 38 patients. *J. Ment. Sci.,* 100:411-431, 1954.

Kay, D.W.K., Schapira, K. and Brandon, S.: Early factors in anorexia nervosa compared with non-anorexic groups. *J. Psychosom. Res.,* 11:133-139, 1967.

Kalucy, R.C., Crisp, A.H. and Harding, B.: A study of 56 families with anorexia nervosa. *Br. J. Med. Psychol.,* 50:381-395, 1977.

Keys, A., Brozek, J., Henschel, A., Mickelsen, O. and Taylor, H.L.: *The Biology of Human Starvation.* Minneapolis: University of Minnesota Press, 1950.

King, A.: Primary and secondary anorexia nervosa syndromes. *Br. J. Psychiatry,* 109:470-479, 1963.

Kron, L., Katz, J.L., Gorzynski, G. and Weiner, H.: Anorexia nervosa and gonadal dysgenesis, *Arch. Gen.Psychiatry,* 34:332-335, 1977.

Kubie, L.S.: Multiple fallacies in the concept of schizophrenia. *J. Nerv. Ment. Dis.,* 153:331-342, 1971.

Lakoff, K.M. and Feldman, J.D.: Anorexia nervosa associated with pregnancy. *Obstet. Gynecol.,* 39:699-701, 1972.

Liston, E.H. and Shershow, L.W.: Concurrence of anorexia nervosa and gonadal dysgenesis. *Arch. Gen. Psychiatry,* 29:834-836, 1973.

Margo, J.L. and Hawton, L.E.: Anorexia nervosa and Turner's syndrome. *Br. Med. J.,* 2:15-16, 1978.

Masterson, J.F.: *Treatment of the Borderline Adolescent: A Developmental Approach.* New York: John Wiley & Sons, 1972.

Meyer, J.E.: The anorexia nervosa syndrome. Catemnestic research. *Arch. Psychiat. Nervenkr.,* 202:31-59, 1961.

Morgan, H.G. and Russell, G.F.M.: Value of family background and clinical features as predictors of long-term outcome in anorexia nervosa: Four year follow-up study of 42 patients. *Psychol. Med.,* 5:355-371, 1975.

Morton, R.: *Phthisiologica: Or a Treatise of Consumptions.* London: Sam Smith and Benj. Walford, 1694.

Nemiah, J.C.: Anorexia nervosa; a clinical psychiatric study. *Medicine*, 29:225-268, 1950.

Nussbaum, M., Shenker, R., Marc, J. and Klein, M.: Cerebral atrophy in anorexia nervosa. *J. Pediatr.*, 96:867-869, 1980.

Petrich, J. and Holmes T.H.: Life change and onset of illness. *Med. Clin. of N. America*, 61:825-838, 1977.

Piaget, J.: *The Child's Construction of Reality.* London: Routledge and Kegan, 1955.

Piazza, E., Piazza, N. and Rollins, N.: Anorexia nervosa: Controversial aspects of therapy. *Compreh. Psychiat.*, 21:177-189, 1980.

Pierloot, R.A., Wellens, W. and Houben, M.E.: Elements of resistance to a combined medical and psychotherapeutic program in anorexia nervosa. An overview. *Psychother. Psychosom.*, 26:101-117, 1977.

Pitts, F.N., and Guze, S.B. Anorexia nervosa and gonadal dysgenesis (Turner's syndrome). *Am. J. Psychiatry*, 119:1100-1102, 1963.

Rahe, R.H., McKean, J.D. Jr. and Arthur, R.J.: A longitudinal study of life-change and illness patterns. *J. Psychosom. Res.*, 10:355-366, 1967.

Robertson, M.M. and Hamberger, A.S.: A case of anorexia nervosa with an associated urogenital malformation. *Psychol. Med.*, 9:775-776, 1979.

Roussounis, S.H.: Anorexia nervosa in a prepubertal male. *Proc. R. Soc. Med.*, 64:666-667, 1971.

Rowland, C.V., Jr.: Anorexia nervosa — A survey of the literature and review of 30 cases. *Int. Psychiat. Clin.*, 7:37-137, 1970.

Russell, G.F.M., Campbell, P.G. and Slade, P.D.: Experimental studies on the nature of the psychological disorder in anorexia nervosa. *Psychoneuroendocrinology*, 1:45-56, 1975.

Russell, G.F.M.: The present status of anorexia nervosa. *Psychol. Med.*, 7:363-367, 1977.

Ryle, J.A.: Discussions on anorexia nervosa. *Proc. Roy. Soc. Med.*, 32:735-737, 1939.

Saleh, J.W. and Lebwohl, P.: Metoclopramide-induced gastric emptying in patients with anorexia nervosa. *Am.J. Gastroenterol.*, 74:127-132, 1980.

Selvini Palazzoli, M.D.: Anorexia nervosa. In: S. Arieti (Ed.), *The World Biennial of Psychiatry and Psychotherapy*, Vol. 1. New York: Basic Books, 197-218, 1970.

Smart, D.E., Beumont, P.J.V. and George G.C.W.: Some personality characteristics of patients with anorexia nervosa. *Br. J. Psychiatry*, 128:57-60, 1976.

Solyom, L., Miles, J.E. and O'Kane, J.: Comparative study of anorexia nervosa. *Can. J. Psychiatry* (in press).

Stone, M.H.: *The Borderline Syndromes: Constitution, Personality and Adaptation.* New York: McGraw-Hill, 1980.

Strober, M.: A cross-sectional and longitudinal (post weight restoration) analysis of personality and symptomalogical features in young, nonchronic anorexia nervosa patients (submitted for publication).

Taipale, V., Larkio-Miettinenk, Valanne, E.H., Moren, R. and Aukee, M.: Anorexia nervosa in boys. *Psychosomatics*, 13:236-240, 1972.

Theander, S.: Anorexia nervosa: A psychiatric investigation of 94 female cases. *Acta Psychiat. Scand.* [Suppl], 214:1-194, 1970.

Thoma, H.: *Anorexia Nervosa* (translated by G. Brydone). New York: International Universities Press, 1967.

Ushakov, G.: Anorexia nervosa. In: J.G. Howells (Ed.), *Modern Perspectives in Adolescent Psychiatry*, Vol. 4, Edinburgh: Oliver and Boyd, 1971.

Weiner, H., Thaler, M., Reiser, M.F. and Mirsky, I.A.: Etiology of duodenal ulcer. 1. Relation of specific psychological characteristics to rate of gastric secretion (serum pepsinogen). *Psychosom. Med.*, 19:1-10, 1957.

Weiner, H.: *Psychobiology and Human Disease.* New York: Elsevier, North Holland, Inc., 1977.

Yessler, P.G., Reiser, M.F. and Rioch, D.: Etiology of duodenal ulcer II. Serum pepsinogen and petptic ulcer in inductees. *JAMA*, 169:451-456, 1959.

# CHAPTER 9

# *The Hospital Management*

Many management plans have been advocated for treating anorexic patients. These have been largely based on the theoretical orientation of the physician and the mechanisms presumed to be responsible for the illness. For example, according to some, anorexia nervosa reflected a hormonal deficiency disease (Kylin, 1937) or a primary "love" deficiency (Groen and Feldman-Toledano, 1966) and treatment was focused on replacing these. The diversity of treatments that have been recommended is exemplified by the overview provided in Table 1; this is by no means an exhaustive list. We agree with Russell's (1973) statement that at present, in the absence of controlled prospective studies describing clear-cut benefits for a particular treatment, no particular mode of treatment may be regarded as definitive for anorexia nervosa. As more outcome data become available, the comparative effectiveness of different therapies may be meaningfully evaluated.

In the meantime, we have evolved a management plan for our patients, based on our understanding of the disorder as described in the preceding chapters, and based on the writings of several physicians (Bruch, Crisp, Russell, Selvini Palazzoli) whose approach to therapy has appeared most valuable to our patients over time. It must also be emphasized that the treatment needs of different patients can vary widely and therefore within the overall framework there must be considerable flexibility on the part of the physician. In this chapter we will review the initial and inhospital management of the patient. In the following chapter we will discuss the long-term psychotherapy aimed at minimizing sequelae. Naturally there is considerable overlap between the two, especially since patients may have to be readmitted and since principles of the psychotherapy apply to inhospital management.

214

## TABLE 1

## Therapies That Have Been Suggested for Anorexia Nervosa

| Type of Treatment | References* |
|---|---|
| **SOMATIC TREATMENTS** | |
| Nurturance | |
| Refeeding | Crisp, 1965; Russell, 1977 |
| Forced feeding | Quaeriteur, 1971; Janet, 1926 |
| I.V. feeding | Finkelstein, 1972 |
| Parenteral hyperalimentation | Maloney, 1980 |
| Tube feeding | Silverman, 1974; Williams, 1958 |
| Bedrest | Crisp, 1965; Dally and Sargant, 1966 |
| Pharmacotherapies | |
| Anticonvulsants | Green and Rau, 1974 |
| Appetite stimulants | Benady, 1970 |
| Anabolic steroids | Finkelstein, 1972 |
| Insulin | Dally and Sargant, 1960 |
| Chlorpromazine | Crisp, 1965 |
| Chlorpromazine plus insulin | Dally and Sargant, 1960 |
| Tricyclic antidepressants | Needleman, 1976 |
| L-Dopa | Johanson and Knorr, 1977 |
| Lithium | Barcai, 1977 |
| Surgery | |
| Leucotomy | Crisp and Kalucy, 1973 |
| Pituitary transplants | Theander, 1970 |
| Implantation of a calf's hypophysis | Kylin, 1937 |
| Other | |
| ECT | Wall, 1959; Bernstein, 1964 |
| Periodic fasts | Allison and Davies, 1931 |
| Gastric lavage | Allison and Davies, 1931 |
| **PSYCHOLOGICAL TREATMENTS** | |
| Psychoanalytic | Gifford, Murawski, & Pilot, 1970; Silverman, 1974 |
| "Superficial" — supportive psychotherapy | Farquharson and Hyland, 1966 |
| Fact-finding psychotherapy | Bruch, 1973; Frazier, 1965 |
| Family therapy | Barcai, 1971; Minuchin et al., 1973 Rosman et al., 1976 |
| Dream analysis | Szyrynski, 1973 |
| Playback of videotaped therapy | Gottheil, Backup and Cornelison, 1969 |
| Providing "substitute parents" in the hospital | Groen and Feldman-Toledano, 1966 |
| Psychoeducation | Cotugno, 1980 |
| Behavior therapy | |
| Systematic desensitization | Hallsten, 1965; Lang, 1965 |
| Operant conditioning | Agras et al., 1974; Azerrad and Stafford, 1969; Bachrach et al., 1965; Garfinkel et al., 1973, Halmi et al., 1975 |
| Aversive counter-conditioning | Kenny and Solyom, 1971 |

* References for various treatments are not exhaustive but merely provide examples for treatments cited.

In the previous chapter we described anorexia nervosa as a syndrome with characteristic signs and symptoms. However, within the syndrome there is considerable heterogeneity between patients, in such areas as maturation, ego strengths, some personality features, and level of premorbid functioning. Similarly, we have emphasized that there is no one pathogenesis but that several predisposing and precipitating factors are observed in different patients. In spite of this heterogeneity, several issues are important to most anorexic patients. Briefly these are:

1) Difficulty in feeling in control of her body and her life, impaired recognition of internal bodily states and revulsion at physical bodily functions.
2) Difficulty in autonomous functioning and in emotional separation from the family or particular individuals.
3) A sense of personal mistrust. Rather than trust her body, the anorexic fears it.
4) Feelings of self-worth that are closely bound to external standards for appearance and performance; personal identity and goals are confused.
5) Starvation perpetuates many of the psychological symptoms and enhances the urge to diet by increasing concerns with self-esteem and self-control.

Because of these issues a few general rules apply to the management of the anorexic patient. These are:

1) The effects of starvation must be reversed if the patient is to benefit meaningfully from psychotherapy
2) The patient must always be dealt with openly and honestly, and with particular attention to her disordered self-esteem, even though much of her overt behavior may appear to be stubbornly defiant or mistrusting
3) Psychotherapies must be directed at the specific predisposing and perpetuating factors operating in any individual to prevent recurrences and to minimize sequelae.
4) A relationship type of psychotherapy with a slowly evolving sense of trust is a useful context for facilitating the above.

As with psychotherapeutic treatment in general the management of an anorexic patient begins with the initial interview, with an emphasis on slowly beginning to develop a working alliance and mutual trust. Once a tentative diagnosis has been made through a review of the history, physical examination, and appropriate laboratory investigations, the patient and her parents are given a detailed explanation of the disorder, its uncertain etiology, and the factors which are thought to contribute, its possible consequences and how to formulate treatment goals. Specific laboratory investigations as described in Chapter 1 may be indicated and their purpose is reviewed for the patient.

Care must be taken to elicit the initial cooperation of the patient and her family and to avoid blaming one particular family member for the presence of the illness. By the time a physician is consulted, the parents have usually spent months in a bitter struggle with their daughter and, in addition to their rage, they generally share a strong sense of guilt over their presumed role in the disorder. Care must be taken not to blame the parents or one individual both because there is no one thing that has caused the illness and because it is likely the scapegoated individual may flee and prevent further meaningful treatment.

Generally the parents share many misconceptions about the illness, through poorly written "glamorizing" articles in the lay press and through their own soul-searching for a particular cause. Clarification and some education about the disorder are indicated. It is usually helpful to recommend selected reading materials which augment the physician's discussion and which further answer questions about anorexia nervosa. This also reduces the denial. We generally encourage family members to read Bruch's (1978) *The Golden Cage* if they have not already done so. In addition, we often provide the patient with summaries of the Keys, Brozek, Henschel, Mickelsen and Taylor (1950) studies of the effects of starvation on psychological functioning to help her begin to understand why starvation symptoms further contribute to her current battle with self-control.

Many patients deny their illness; they feel there would be nothing wrong with them if only others would leave them alone. At times parents collude with the denial, for example by saying their emaciated daughter cannot be admitted to hospital for fear of missing her exams or a holiday. In the initial contact attempts must be made to obviate the denial by pointing out the serious nature of the disorder and its sequelae. For the patient, it is not effective simply to indicate how thin she is, because she does not view her reduced weight as a problem. It is more useful to emphasize particular symptoms which the patient herself views as distasteful — for example, her food preoccupations, fears of losing control, irritability, lowered self-worth, or social isolation — and for which she may appreciate help.

The establishment of an effective working relationship takes time. Anorexic patients mistrust themselves and also mistrust physicians who are generally thought to be interested only in weight gain or to represent parental authority. It is within this setting of general mistrust and the patient's often somewhat negative approach to treatment that the physician must begin to develop an alliance with the patient; this is the most difficult and yet the most critical aspect of the management. "The most important factor in treatment is to gain the patient's confidence. . . . Fortunately, this is often made possible by a warm, friendly attitude and by spending sufficient time to get to know her" (Farquharson and Hyland, 1966, p. 419). This alliance slowly develops through the demonstration of a patient, yet firm, noncritical approach, through consistency and a sensitivity to the patient's needs and through a demonstration that the problem and its treatment do not only revolve around her weight.

For each patient, treatment goals should be formulated at the end of the initial sessions. These may be initially to develop a collaborative working alliance, to explore factors related to the illness and to perform investigations to determine the presence of complications. From the beginning the emphasis must be not only on the weight restoration but also on the recognition that weight loss is a maladaptive solution to specific life problems that also need to be solved. The treatment goals must be individualized and they cannot be only those of the physician or the parents; the patient must share in the treatment goals. For most patients overall goals include an enhanced sense of self-worth, ease in interpersonal relationships, and a sense of more natural self-control. In addition to the obvious need for weight restoration, it may also be a specific treatment goal to increase an awareness of the factors leading to the illness and its sequelae.

### HOSPITALIZATION

Few will deny that the severe weight loss of anorexia nervosa requires attention. However, controversy has surrounded almost every means of weight restoration. The issue of hospitalization is perhaps the least controversial. Yet Selvini Palazzoli has felt that hospitalization is to be avoided if at all possible since these patients view "all hospitals as places of torture, humiliation and oppression" (Selvini Palazzoli, 1974, p. 116). Similarly, in a review of 36 patients treated over 25 years, Browning and Miller (1968) concluded that hospitalization did little to alter the long-term course of the disorder. But Bruch (1973) has pointed out that these authors have probably overlooked the life-saving value of hospitalization for some emaciated patients. In their emphasis on the psychological management of the family and the patient, these workers who abjure hospitalization ignore the physical dangers of the condition. In severe cases the cachexia and potential starvation are most appropriately treated in a medical setting.

Historically, hospital admission has been advocated in order that the physician control the situation (Gull, 1874). Others have recommended the use of hospital to separate the patient from her parents (Allison and Davies,

1931); Janet (1926) advised that treatment "must forbid the presence of other members of the family" (p. 1066). Farquharson and Hyland (1938) maintained that the patient had to be in hospital to carry out a thorough investigation so that both the physician and the patient have confidence in the treatment. Others have recommended hospital admission to have the physician assume control over a serious situation, to help break through the denial, and to begin rapid treatment of significant complications (Beumont, 1970; Crisp, 1965; Farquharson and Hyland, 1966; Galdston, 1974; Garfinkel, Moldofsky and Garner, 1977a; Lucas, Duncan and Piens, 1976; Moldofsky and Garfinkel, 1974; Russell, 1970; Sours, 1969).

Hospital admission should be considered for specific indications. These are:

1) When weight loss has reached significant proportions, both the patient's and parents' helplessness require intervention to break the cycle and curtail the starvation. (Rather than rely on an absolute weight or a percentage weight loss we feel this depends on several variables — including the rate of loss, severity of the starvation symptoms, and the degree of inflexibility the patient manifests. In general when weight loss is > 25% it is very difficult for the patient to gain significant weight on her own.) Mayer (1963) has written that when weight loss is 40% or more from the ideal, emergency action is required.
2) Hospitalization is often necessary to break an unending cycle of starvation and bulimic-vomiting in non-emaciated patients (for example, patients who vomit several times per day or more without interruption generally require the external controls of a hospital setting in order to initiate treatment).
3) Brief hospital admission may be indicated occasionally for diagnostic observation, treating complications, transient crises, confronting the patient's denial, and the initiation of individual and family psychotherapies (Garfinkel, Moldofsky and Garner, 1977a).

Using these criteria in an earlier evaluation we found that 62% of our patients required admission to hospital (Garfinkel, Moldofsky and Garner, 1977b). Russell (1970) has observed that once considerable weight loss has occurred outpatient treatment is rarely successful, and Dally (1977) felt hospital admission was indicated in 80% of his patients. Those who do not require hospital admission should be treated directly with psychotherapy as described in Chapter 10.

There is no one type of hospital setting uniquely suited to treating patients with anorexia nervosa (Russell, 1981). Silverman (1977) has suggested that there are advantages to a general medical ward, with its milieu of emotionally healthier patients, in comparison with a psychiatric unit. However, we feel that the medical specialty of the physician managing the inpatient is not as important as the attitudes, facilities, and philosophy of the staff. What is required is an atmosphere of consistency, understanding, and firm limits. In this regard it is generally helpful to have patients in hospital units where the staff are familiar with the management of anorexia nervosa and have a clear and consistent philosophy and understanding of the disorder and its treatment (Bruch, 1973, p. 328). This enables the treatment team dealing with the patient to act in uniform fashion and minimizes staff "splitting," patients' manipulations, and concomitant crises.

There are of course problems in having several anorexic patients together. They may group together as common adversaries of the staff and help each other in various manipulations. Even more pernicious is the competition that develops among them — who is on the least amount of calories, who has the lowest target weight. However, we feel that the advantages of an "anorexic unit" — staff expertise and the spirit of working together for recovery that may grow among the patients — outweigh these disadvantages.

While it is usually warranted to admit the anorexic patient to hospital, it is not uncommon for her initially to refuse. This is often due to the severity of the denial, the ego-syntonic nature of the weight loss, or fears of separation from her parents (Russell, 1973). Many patients will, however, agree to a hospital admission if the physician focuses on symptoms that the patient herself finds distressing, if the family are cooperative and if the goals and plans of a hospital stay are outlined fully. We have found pre-hospital interviews, in which the patient meets various members of staff and receives an explanation of their role in her treatment, to be useful. In addition, the interview can be an effective mechanism for describing the details and rationale of the hospital treatment and for eliciting an initial commitment from the patient to be an active collaborator in treatment. For some patients, without this initial introduction and assessment of her suitability for hospital, the hospital period may be spent negotiating with staff over every detail of hospital management or the hospital stay may be terminated prematurely because of the enormous expectations of the treatment program.

Some patients may refuse to be admitted to hospital even after this assessment period. They should be encouraged to gain weight over several weeks and if this fails, it will provide further evidence to the individual that she is no longer in control of her weight. If she again refuses hospital treatment, it may be warranted to continue to see her for supportive care out of the hospital. But *she and her family should clearly understand that meaningful psychotherapy cannot occur until the starvation symptoms have been alleviated.* The general support she would be receiving should not be misconstrued as a psychotherapy aimed at prevention of relapse. Rarely, it may be necessary to admit a severely emaciated patient to hospital involuntarily because of the risk of death (Russell, 1981; Whipple and Manning, 1978). This may confront the patient therapeutically, perhaps for the first time. While this may be necessary, it is generally preferable to see the patient several times in order to determine if she will agree to inpatient treatment since involuntary hospitalization has a negative effect on the individual's sense of trust and willingness to comply with therapy (Russell, 1977).

## WEIGHT RESTORATION

Weight restoration must occur if the psychological treatment is to be meaningful (Russell, 1981). There are two reasons for this. First, the effects of starvation must be removed for the patient to truly benefit from psychotherapy. Starvation symptoms have been described in detail in Chapters 1 and 8 and need not be repeated here. Weight gain is associated with significant psychological changes (Maloney and Farrell, 1980; Stonehill and Crisp, 1977; Strober, 1980) which would make the patient more amenable to psychotherapy. Second, the patient has developed a phobic posture toward weight (Crisp, 1965) and she must learn to face her phobia — her increased body size — as a precondition to dealing with underlying psychological issues. As long as a low weight is maintained through rigid dieting, the phobia is being reinforced, as is the avoidance of dealing realistically with significant life problems. While weight gain is necessary, every effort should be made to do this humanely and with as much cooperation as possible from the patient. A variety of methods have been advocated; there are no convincing studies demonstrating the advantages of one particular method.

While there is general agreement on the need to remove starvation symptoms via increased calorie intake and weight gain, a variety of methods are currently being recommended. These include:

1) tube feedings;
2) parenteral hyperalimentation;
3) behavioral modification techniques;
4) general supportive nursing care with high calorie diet;
5) bedrest with high calorie diet and support; and
6) various pharmacotherapies either alone or as adjuncts to treatment.

These will be reviewed, highlighting the advantages and disadvantages of each.

*Tube Feedings*

Williams (1958) strongly recommended nasogastric feedings after a review of 53 anorexic patients treated at the London Hospital between 1897-1953. He observed that those patients who were tube fed gained an average of 10 kg versus 6.4 kg for the remainder. In addition, ten of the sample had died, eight solely from malnutrition. These two factors together led him to advocate tube feedings for all inpatients. Wall (1959) also recommended routine tube feedings. More recently Thoma (1977) described "frequently" using tube feeding for serious weight loss, and the threat of I.V. or tube feedings is often presented to a patient as a consequence of not gaining sufficient weight (Galdston, 1974; Groen and Feldman-Toledano, 1966; Lesser, Ashenden, Debuskey and Eisenberg, 1960; Silverman, 1977).

There are several serious disadvantages to tube feeding:

1) It represents a direct intrusion into the gastrointestinal tract of someone who is already preoccupied and misguided about bodily functions (Stafford-Clark, 1958).
2) It may be perceived as an assault or act of hostility which the patient attributes to her worthlessness.
3) It may be done with minimal patient cooperation and as such leads to increased mistrust.
4) The physiological side effects are not insignificant (Browning and Miller, 1968).
5) It is almost always unnecessary (Russell and Gillies, 1964).

Moldofsky and Garfinkel (1974) and others (Dally, 1969; Russell, 1970) have viewed the use of tube feedings as a maneuver of desperation or anger on the part of the physician who feels pressured by the need to do something. When faced with an extremely ill patient who is not responding to conventional therapies, however, either nasogastric feedings or parenteral hyperalimentaion can be life-saving. Their use should be restricted to such infrequent emergency situations.

*Intravenous Feedings, Parenteral Hyperalimentation*

Total parenteral hyperalimentation (TPN) has evolved over the past 15 years as a very useful means of supplying essential nutrients by peripheral or central veins to surgical patients or those with gastrointestinal illnesses who cannot absorb food (Dudrick, Wilmore, Vars and Mullen, 1969; Fisher, 1976). Recently, several physicians have recommended its use for severely ill, intractable anorexic patients (Abbott, 1976; Bruch, 1978; Finkelstein,

1972; Hirschman, Rao and Chan, 1977; Sours, 1980).

Maloney and Farrell (1980) described four patients who had resisted all previous efforts to gain weight and yet gained from 5-12.5 kg with TPN; this weight was maintained over a follow-up of almost one year. More recently they have expanded this series to eight patients with good results (Maloney, 1980). Pertschuk, Forster, Buzby and Mullen (1980) have also described 11 patients treated with TPN and compared them with a group of patients treated by other means. While presumably the most resistant, the TPN-treated patients gained weight more rapidly (2 kg/week) and most continued to gain after the TPN had been discontinued. These patients did not resist the treatment possibly because TPN removes sensations of hunger and satiety and also removes the responsibility of eating from the patient, thus alleviating significant anxiety. However, this study also documents the disadvantages of using TPN. Frequent complications were: Four of the 11 suffered significant untoward effects — two had marked hypophosphatemia, one of whom died; one developed a pneumothorax; and one developed arthritis. Also, five experienced transiently increased serum transaminase.

TPN may be considered a potentially life-saving technique for the rare patient with serious weight loss unresponsive to other measures. We used it only once, for a young woman who had lost over 50% of her body weight and who was capable of exercising vigorously while on bedrest and receiving relatively high doses of chlorpromazine. TPN should not be considered a routine weight-restoring technique because of the prevalence of significant complications.

## BEHAVIORAL THERAPIES

Procedures derived from learning theory have grown in popularity in the last 15 years. These involve both respondent and operant paradigms. The operant techniques have been utilized both individually and within a family framework. Their efficacy has been difficult to evaluate because many descriptions have lacked adequate control groups, have had insufficient follow-up periods, and have often relied on weight gain as a sole determinant of clinical change. These are summarized in Table 2. Most procedures have combined behavioral methods with other individual and family therapies. In addition, little attention has been focused on the heterogeneity of patients with anorexia nervosa and how this may relate to the effects of various treatment modalities.

A few case reports have described systematic desensitization, based on Pavlovian principles, to relieve the fear associated with eating (Hallsten, 1965; Lang, 1965; Ollendick, 1979; Schnurer, Rubin and Roy, 1973).

## TABLE 2

### Descriptions of Operant Conditioning in Anorexia Nervosa

| Investigator | Sample Size | Definition of Anorexia Nervosa | Control Group | Description of Procedure | Method of Assessing Change | Results | Duration of Follow-up |
|---|---|---|---|---|---|---|---|
| 1. Bachrach et al. (1965) | 1 | + | none | praise and a variety of hospital reinforcements for both eating and weight gain | weight and ability to work | patient's weight was increased by 11.5 kg and she was functioning as a student | |
| 1a. Erwin (1977) | same patient | | | as for Bachrach et al. | eating and weight | improved social functioning; gradual weight loss to previous emaciated state | 16 years |
| 2. Leitenberg et al. (1968) | 2 | + | subjects served as their own controls | a) baseline followed by attempt at extinction and then by various rewards for weight gain b) nonreinforcement reinforcement schedule | weight, caloric intake, school or vocational performance | a) weight of 44 kg and attending school b) weight of 41 kg and working | a) 9 mos. b) 4 mos. |

| Investigator | Sample Size | Definition of Anorexia Nervosa | Control Group | Description of Procedure | Method of Assessing Change | Results | Duration of Follow-up |
|---|---|---|---|---|---|---|---|
| 3. Stumphauzer (1969) | 1 | not provided | none | attention from uncle and passes were rewards for eating "regular" meals | weight | weight gain of 5 kg | 10 days |
| 4. Azerrad and Stafford (1969) | 1 | not provided | none | tokens awarded for food eaten; tokens exchanged for privileges | weight | weight gain of 12 kg | 5 mos. |
| 5. Blinder et al. (1970) | 6 | + | none | variable reinforcements for weight gain; these were selected according to patients' behavior | weight, menses and social relationships | 1 patient well; 1 patient suicide; 1 patient readmitted with delirium and 3 no follow-up | 0-10 mos. |
| 6. Bianco (1972) | 2 | + | none | as for Blinder et al. | weight | both patients well | 2 years |
| 7. Lobb and Schaefer (1972) | 1 | criteria of Bruch (1970) but also "depressive neurosis and alcoholism" | none | token system and cigarettes as reward for weight gain | weight | weight normal and decreased drinking | 4 mos. |
| 8. Brady and Rieger (1972) | 16 | + | none | reinforcement contingent on weight gain | weight and adjustment | average weight gain of 5.4 kg. Two deaths and 3 patients with poor adjustment | 4-59 mos. |

| Investigator | Sample Size | Definition of Anorexia Nervosa | Control Group | Description of Procedure | Method of Assessing Change | Results | Duration of Follow-up |
|---|---|---|---|---|---|---|---|
| 9. Garfinkel et al. (1973) | 5 | + | none | as for Blinder et al. | weight | 4 patients doing well and 1 re-admitted | 0-10 mos. |
| 10. Elkin et al. (1973) | 1 | + | subject served as his own control | comparison of effects of feedback, reinforcement and varying diet | weight and caloric intake | total weight gain 3 kg; presentation of high calorie meals most important | no follow-up |
| 11. Agras et al. (1974) | 5 | + | subjects served as their own control | comparison of effects of positive and negative reinforcement, information feedback and size of meals | weight and caloric intake | avg. weight gain 8 kg; information feedback most important and augments effects of positive reinforcement | no follow-up |
| 12. Bhanji and Thompson (1974) | 11 | not provided | none | variety of rewards for eating | weight, eating, menses and mental functioning | all but 1 gained weight; follow-up on 7 of 11 patients — 3 were doing poorly on global score | 2-72 mos. |
| 13. Takayama (1974) | 1 | not provided | none | tokens and parental attention for eating | weight and social adjust-ment | weight gain of 10 kg and good social adjustment | 10 mos. |

| Investigator | Sample Size | Definition of Anorexia Nervosa | Control Group | Description of Procedure | Method of Assessing Change | Results | Duration of Follow-up |
|---|---|---|---|---|---|---|---|
| 14. Halmi et al. (1975) | 8 | + | none | variety of social reinforcements for weight gain | weight, menses and social-vocational adjustment | patients' weights at 84-111% of standard; one-half with "good" adjustment | 2-13 mos. |
| 14a. Halmi (1977) | 15 | + | none | variety of social reinforcements for weight gain | weight, menses and social-vocational adjustment | average gain of 8 kg | maintained over 6-30 mos. |
| 15. Werry and Bull (1975) | 1 | prior grand mal epilepsy | none | variety of reinforcements for weight gain | weight | weight gain of 8.5 kg | no follow-up |
| 16. Neumann and Gaoni (1975) | 1 | + | none | various rewards for eating | weight and social functioning | weight gain of 12 kg; on follow-up weight normal, and improved socially | 30 mos. |
| 17. Kehrer (1975) | 8 | + | none | token system for food eaten | weight and social functioning | weight gains ranged from 3-13 kg; all were socially adapted | 2-6 mos. |
| 18. Wulliemier et al. (1975) | 9 of 17 | not provided | yes | comparison of operant reinforcement with isolation, appetite stimulating drugs and supportive psychotherapy | weight gain | weight gain three times as great with operant conditioning | none |

| Investigator | Sample Size | Definition of Anorexia Nervosa | Control Group | Description of Procedure | Method of Assessing Change | Results | Duration of Follow-up |
|---|---|---|---|---|---|---|---|
| 19. Geller (1975) | 1 | + | none | combination of social rewards for weight gain, educational feedback and high calorie meals | weight and social functioning | weight regained to ideal; socially active | 1 year |
| 20. Rosman et al. (1976) | 50 | not provided | none | operant conditioning in the context of family therapy | remission of "anorexic symptoms" and psychosocial functioning | 86% complete reccvery | 3-48 mos. |
| 21. Garfinkel et al. (1977) | 17 of 42 | + | yes | comparison of various rewards for weight gain with a variety of psychotherapies and pharmaco-therapies | global scale of weight, eating, menses, psychosocial and vocational adjustment | no difference between the two groups on outcome | at least 1 year following treatment ($M \pm SE = 31 \pm 3$ mos.) |
| 22. Pertschuk (1977) | 29 | + | none | various rewards for weight gain | weight readmission, return of menses, additional symptoms, social adjustment | 12 were hospitalized, 6 for weight loss, 4 made suicide attempts, 10 became bulimic, 12 had made a gooc adjustment | 3-45 mos. |
| 23. Parker et al. (1977) | 10 | + | none | variable rewards for weight gain | weight | all patients gained weight | — |

| Investigator | Sample Size | Definition of Anorexia Nervosa | Control Group | Description of Procedure | Method of Assessing Change | Results | Duration of Follow-up |
|---|---|---|---|---|---|---|---|
| 24. Agras and Werne (1977) | 25 | + | none | reinforcement for weight gain | weight | average gain of 7.3 kg | — |
| 24a. Agras and Werne (1978) | 15 | + | none | reinforcement for weight gain | global scale | 4 recovered, 3 markedly improved, 7 improved and 1 unchanged | 11-29 mos. |
| 25. Pertschuk et al., (1978) | 7 | + | subjects served as their own controls | multiple baseline approach privileges for weight gain | weight | average gain of 2-4 kg/week, greater than control period, 1 required re-admission | 3-28 mos. |
| 26. Poole and Sanson (1978) | 5 | + | none | individualized reforcers for weight gain | weight | all gained at least 10 kg. 3 readmitted | 3-11 mos. |
| 27. Vandereyeken and Pieters (1978) | 32 | + | comparison of 2 behavioral treatments | group A — rewards for weight gain, group B — as for A but also allowed visits by relatives, information about weights and graded exercises | weight | group B gained at a more rapid rate, but no significant differences in overall gains (13 vs 16 kg) | — |

| Investigator | Sample Size | Definition of Anorexia Nervosa | Control Group | Description of Procedure | Method of Assessing Change | Results | Duration of Follow-up |
|---|---|---|---|---|---|---|---|
| 28. Blue (1979) | 1 | not provided | none | as for Bachrach, Erwin and Mohr (1965) and use of punishment | weight, social adjustment | patient reported to be well | 12 mos. |
| 29. Eckert et al. (1979) | 40 of 81 | + | yes — 40 patients treated with milieu therapy random, prospective study | 35 days involving initial restriction and earning or withdrawing privileges based on weight, every 5 days | weight | no significant differences between groups (5 kg vs 4.1 kg) | — |
| 30. Fichter and Kessler (1980) | 1 | + | none | token reinforcement for attending meals in dining room, decreasing speed of eating, proper sequencing of dishes and not playing with food | weight and behavioral change | weight unchanged but other behaviors deteriorated | 7 mos. |

+ appear to meet general criteria of anorexia nervosa

In addition, Kenny and Solyom (1971) treated one patient's compulsive vomiting with aversive counterconditioning. This involved administering an electric shock while the patient imagined herself engaged in self-induced vomiting. A three-month follow-up revealed no resumption of vomiting; however, she continued erratic eating patterns with no weight gain.

Operant techniques have become popular for weight restoration because they are associated with rapid weight gain while avoiding the unpleasant effects of drugs and tube feedings. Prior to 1970, five investigators reported on an operant paradigm in treating anorexic patients (Azerrad and Stafford, 1969; Bachrach, Erwin and Mohr, 1965; Blinder and Ringold, 1967; Leitenberg, Agras and Thomson, 1968; Stumphauzer, 1969). Since 1970, there has been a steady stream of articles supporting these weight gain statistics.

In 1972, Stunkard reviewed the use of behavior therapies in eating disorders. Behavior modification was portrayed as a creative approach which requires individual tailoring of each patient's program to the specific variables which maintain that patient's behavior. This flexible approach is illustrated by Lobb and Schaefer's (1972) treatment of one patient with a sequence of new reinforcers when older ones became ineffective.

Activity was the reinforcer of choice in another study reported by Bianco (1972). He described the successful treatment and two-year follow-up of two patients whose access to ward and off-ward privileges was the reward for consistent weight gain. Garfinkel, Kline and Stancer (1973) applied this type of approach with five patients by varying the reinforcement program to the specific interests expressed by the patients. Rapid weight restoration was achieved with all patients. Preliminary follow-up of seven patients treated in this manner revealed that two had relapsed (Moldofsky and Garfinkel, 1974). Several more recent studies have verified the impressive short-term effects of operant conditioning on weight. These are summarized in Table 2. However, there has been only one prospective controlled study with randomization of subjects assigned to behavioral or non-behavioral groups (Eckert, Goldberg, Halmi, Casper and Davis, 1979). This study found no significant differences between behavioral treatment and milieu therapy alone, in terms of weight gain over 35 days. But these results may have been due to the particular operant methodology used, i.e., rewarding every five days (rather than daily as is usually recommended), not individualizing rewards, and only studying the groups for one month.

Several studies have attempted to separate the effects of different variables within the operant treatment framework. Elkin, Hersen, Eisler, and Williams (1973) sequentially examined the effects of feedback, reinforcement, and size of the meal in an anorexic patient. The combination of all three variables produced the greatest weight gain and caloric consumption; however, when reinforcement and feedback were held constant, dramatic effects were observed simply by increasing the amount of food presented. Agras and Werne (1977) also found that caloric intake was related to the amount of food being offered.

In a similar series of single-case experiments, Agras, Barlow, Chaplin, Able and Leitenberg (1974) explored the effects of the above variables plus the introduction of negative reinforcement. This study was aimed at clarifying the surprising results obtained in an earlier experiment (Leitenberg et al., 1968) in which the removal of reinforcement did not cause the expected decrease in caloric intake. As in the previous study, Agras et al. (1974) found that withdrawal of reinforcement did not diminish eating. They speculated that eating was still being unwittingly reinforced (negatively) by the hospital environment. Specifically, patients became aware that discharge from hospital was dependent on weight gain. A second experiment in this series confirmed this and demonstrated that removal of positive reinforcement produced the predicted decrement in eating when the patient was informed that weight gain would not result in discharge. The remaining experiments in the series suggested that information feedback was the most influential variable in promoting weight gain.

The long-term benefits of operant conditioning are not as impressive as the immediate gains. Blinder, Freeman and Stunkard (1970) described the treatment of six patients using a variety of reinforcers. For three patients, physical activity was made contingent upon one half-pound of daily weight gain. A fourth patient's dosage of chlorpromazine was reduced if she gained weight. Two other patients were treated simply by specifying the target weight required for discharge. However, at follow-up one patient had required readmission and one had committed suicide.

Bhanji and Thompson (1974) described 11 patients who, with just one exception, achieved rapid weight gain in treatment. Follow-up data were available on seven of the original 11 patients, obtained from questionnaire information. Using global ratings, three patients had a poor outcome, three had achieved a fair adjustment, and one was in complete remission. Despite the small sample and questionable reliability of the follow-up measure, these results cast some skepticism on the long-term effectiveness of the popular operant techniques. Halmi, Powers, and Cunningham (1975) described the treatment of eight patients using individualized positive reinforcement programs in the hospital and after discharge. Other therapies were not used concurrently with behavior therapy, thus allowing an independent assessment of the positive reinforcement method. Short-term adjustment was assessed after an average period of seven months. One-half of the patients were rated as achieving "good" adjustment, while three others maintained "adequate" stabilization, and one displayed only "fair" or marginal functioning. Similarly, Pertschuk (1977) followed 29 patients for an average of two years. While 12 had adjusted well, six were unimproved and 12 required rehospitalization. Agras and Werne (1978) reported somewhat more favorable results in 15 patients.

Recently a group at the Philadelphia Clinic have deviated from traditional inpatient treatment programs and emphasized the value of family therapy (Liebman, Minuchin and Baker, 1974a, 1974b; Minuchin, Baker, Liebman, Milman, Rosman and Todd, 1973; Minuchin, Baker, Rosman Liebman, Milman and Todd, 1975; Rosman, Minuchin, Liebman and Baker 1976). They have claimed unusual success using a combination of family therapy and operant conditioning requiring an average of less than two weeks in hospital. Their regimen consists of:

1) hospitalization for investigation to rule out organic factors;
2) informal lunches to assess the patient's negativism;
3) initiation of operant procedures to achieve weight gain;
4) family therapy lunch sessions; and
5) weekly outpatient family therapy.

The procedure is aimed at elimination of confrontations around food while focusing upon weight gain rather than eating. The outpatient phase entails redefinition of the parents' conception of the "presenting problem" by emphasizing the total family's responsibility for maladaptive eating patterns in their child.

The Philadelphia Clinic group report that after three-month to four-year follow-up they have successfully treated 43 of 50 patients and families (Rosman et al., 1976). Clearly, the results reported with the family therapy approach are impressive and warrant independent controlled evaluations. One partial explanation for the success rates may be that patients seen at the Philadelphia Clinic were young and first seen very early in the illness (median time of six months from onset of weight loss) and early age of onset and a short duration of illness have been found to be correlated with a good prognosis (see Chapter 12).

Garfinkel et al. (1977b) assessed the clinical outcome of 42 patients with anorexia nervosa treated at least one year previously. Of these, 40% had been treated using an inhospital operant conditioning approach that rewarded weight gain (Garfinkel et al., 1973). The remainder had been treated by a variety of pharmacological, dietary and psychotherapeutic means. Outcome was determined using a global scale, weight gain, and return of menses. Their data indicate that patients treated with behavior therapy were no different at outcome from those treated with somatic or alternate psychotherapies. Both groups showed equal improvement on all parameters. Behavior modification, while not harmful, does not imply a better prognosis. Following operant conditioning, patients have the same difficulty as others in regulation of eating and weight and in interpersonal relationships. Behavior modification in no way prevents recurrence, for six of the 17 patients required repeat admission to the hospital for weight loss.

Behavior modification has been criticized by Bruch (1974) as a "potentially . . . dangerous method" of treatment in anorexia nervosa (p. 1419). She has claimed that the technique aggravates the anorexic's feelings of helplessness and ineffectiveness by coercing the patient into eating in spite of intense fear. She described nine patients who had been exposed to behavior modification while in hospital. All initially gained weight but later relapsed and complained of adverse psychological reactions to their behavior therapy programs. Although Bruch's skepticism is warranted from her cases, it may be an overstatement of the position, given the acknowledged selectivity of her cases. Behavior modification, per se, may not be responsible for poor results. The application of behavior modification or any other procedure, without adequate consideration to the patient's feelings and concerns, may produce devastating consequences.

To summarize the role of behavioral modification, we can note that most patients gain weight with this treatment and that while not proving harmful, there is no evidence to suggest that it is superior to other conventional therapies in the long run. Not all patients with anorexia nervosa require or benefit from behavioral modification. Only when weight gain is an immediate concern should it be considered, and then maximal attention must be paid to enlisting the patient's cooperation and participation in setting up a reward program which she does not find excessive. While we have used traditional operant reinforcement procedures on our unit, we follow this format of highly individualized reinforcers for specified weight gains only occasionally, depending on the patient's needs. When such a procedure is utilized we are careful to focus on the overall treatment of the person, so that weight gain does not become the overriding issue of management. At other times, while the operant conditioning contract is not formally specified, behavioral techniques using rewards for weight gain may still be part of inhospital management when we allow patients off bedrest as their weight is being restored.

It is evident from a review of the literature on treatment of anorexia nervosa that therapists often recommend a variety of therapeutic methods, which unintentionally rely on operant conditioning principles. For example, Silverman (1974) has advocated psychoanalytic treatment but explains "as the child begins to relate to hospital staff . . . and to commence eating, she begins to earn privileges such as possession of her own pyjamas or clothing" (p. 72). Whether employing formal or informal behavioral programs, it is impossible to avoid rewarding therapeutic gains such as weight gain or greater social appropriateness. In promoting weight gain, several words of caution are warranted. Because operant techniques appear to be simple and thus appealing methods, they may be applied mechanically without regard for individual differences between patients or for theoretical issues specific to anorexia nervosa. They can parallel the anorexic's pre-hospital perceptions of the world as controlling and unresponsive to her personal needs. For example, there are reports of treating anorexics by rewarding patients for counting and increasing the mouthfuls of food eaten (Agras and Werne, 1978). This is hardly conducive to promoting eating as a natural process. There is no need for locked rooms, depriving patients of baths, radios, etc. (Quaeritur, 1971), as this destroys the therapeutic alliance. Similarly, Blue's (1979) recommended "treatment" with a "switch" as punishment by the patient's mother can never be condoned.

## MODIFIED BEDREST, HIGH CALORIE DIET WITH SUPPORTIVE NURSING CARE

The combination of general support in a controlled environment together with a high calorie diet has often been recommended either by itself (Berkman, 1948; Lucas, Duncan and Piens, 1976; Russell, 1970) or in conjunction with bedrest (Crisp, 1965; Dally, 1969; Fox and James, 1976; Hall, 1975; Hurst, 1939; Ryle, 1939; Stafford-Clark, 1958). We find this approach to be a safe, efficacious and nonpunitive method of facilitating weight gain and it is associated with few untoward effects. On our unit, the following principles are incorporated into the general management regimen:

1) controlled weight gain in a setting of emotional support;
2) information feedback and dietary reeducation;
3) a graduated level of activity, often beginning with bedrest;
4) emphasis that weight gain is necessary but only one part of treatment;
5) occupational and group therapies;
6) a relationship type of individual psychotherapy; and
7) family therapy.

On admission to hospital patients agree to be on bedrest and are begun on a regular diet. Bedrest early in the hospitalization has several advantages: It enables the patient to recognize that she will not be allowed to be out of control; it prevents excessive activity; and serves to confront the patient's denial by signifying to her the serious nature of the illness. In view of the potential dangers of having people on total bedrest for long periods (i.e., two-to-three months), we prefer a system of modified bedrest whereby patients are initially totally in bed but are then gradually allowed up as their weight increases. The rate at which this is allowed is highly variable, depending on each patient and her degree of emaciation, but on average we might allow one hour out of bed for each kilogram gained. As patients are slowly restored to a healthy weight, further activities and often eventually exercises are permitted. This portion of the treatment relies on operant conditioning, since weight gain allows the patient more time out of bed and, as she progresses, other activities.

However, others (Crisp, 1965; Crisp, 1970; Fox and James, 1976) have found that total bedrest for six-to-eight weeks, until the patient reaches her weight goal, is associated with good results and no untoward effects provided it occurs within the context of a psychotherapeutic relationship. This is preferable to modified bedrest on a general medical or psychiatric unit where the whole team are not fully conversant with the total management of the anorexic patient (Day, 1974).

The patient's "target" weight should be specified and agreed upon at the onset of treatment. This helps reassure her that her weight gain will not be allowed to continue indefinitely. The patient should be reassured that she won't be forced, or even permitted, to become too heavy. Staff must not be manipulated into a promise of keeping her weight at an abnormally low level (Beumont, 1970), and the target weight must be one the patient can maintain without undue emphasis on dieting. There are several ways to determine a target weight. Arbitrarily choosing a weight that is 90% of average for the patient's age and height is acceptable to most patients, when it is explained that this is associated with maximal health (Sorlie, Gordon and Kannel, 1980) and allows them to be thin in a healthy sense. It also serves to further reinforce that the staff's purpose is not to refeed them to an obese state. This level of weight is above the "magic" number patients have arbitrarily constructed and also above the weight for normal biological function, so that by achieving and maintaining this weight, the patient can break through the phobic nature of her fear of fatness and she is physiologically able to resume normal hormonal production. Alternatively, following Crisp's (1970) suggestion, the target weight can be a matched population weight, but matched to the time of onset of her illness. This emphasizes for the patient the idea that she has not matured since her illness began and underscores the importance of the developmental arrest created by the disorder.

Others simply choose a weight previously attained by the patient when she was healthy and was menstruating (Hall, 1975). If the patient was premorbidly obese or if the anorexia nervosa has had a late developmental onset (> 25) the first arbitrary formula may be preferable. The important issues concerning the target weight are:

1) It must be above the previously tolerable upper limit for the patient in order for her to overcome her irrational fears about a larger size; and it allows her to separate out "what the scales say" from her sense of self-worth;
2) it must be one the patient can maintain without undue dieting; and
3) while there is a minimum specified weight, a range of 3-4 lbs should be the goal rather than a single "ideal" weight.

A desirable rate of weight gain should be specified. It appears to be important not to allow the patient to gain weight too quickly as this fosters her sense of being out of control. It is necessary to explain to the patient that while about 1 kg gained per week is reasonable, gaining more than 2 kg per week will not be tolerated. While some recommend weighing the patient each morning (Agras and Werne, 1978; Maxmen, Siberfarb and Farrell, 1974), this is often not necessary and may further the patient's preoccupation with fractions of a kilogram (Pardee, 1941). Weighing the patient twice weekly keeps her informed of weight changes without furthering this preoccupation (Day, 1974). However, patients are often offered their preference for frequency of weighing.

The duration of the weight restoration period is variable using the regimen, but on average lasts 8-12 weeks. While this is a relatively lengthy hospital period, it is important not to discharge the patient immediately after her weight is restored; it is preferable to keep her in hospital for a further three weeks, as a maintenance period. During this latter stage the emphasis should be on reeducating the patient to more normal eating habits, thus making eating a somewhat more automatic activity. As she becomes more comfortable with her prescribed diet, and more confident in selecting foods, the patient is entrusted with the responsibility for her own diet. Educational sessions are begun with the dietitian. The patient may be requested to plan her meals for three days. Following this, food models may be used to demonstrate the sizes of the planned meals. Any foods that are still feared are discussed and both the nutritional value and the fears of these foods explored. Similarly, if some patients fear eating out, they will be initially accompanied to restaurants by staff, prior to their going with family, friends, or on their own. During this maintenance period the patient soon chooses her own meals and is fully involved with the community at large; however, a minimum acceptable weight must be agreed upon and if there is a recurrence of weight loss, these privileges may be revoked.

An important part of the management involves providing the patient with as much information feedback as possible. Experimentally this has been associated with the most consistent weight gain (Agras et al., 1974). This includes having the patient know how her weight changes over time, but also learning to ignore the day-to-day variations that naturally occur (and to avoid cutting back calories in response to one day's gain). It also includes the patient's knowing her caloric intake during the various stages and what levels are associated with weight gain versus weight maintenance. When the patient's weight is restored, during the maintenance period, the feedback should include meal planning, reeducation about serving portions and at times cooking, and information about new clothing sizes, grooming, etc., as is required.

While one component of anorexia nervosa involves a weight or body size phobia, food may secondarily become a phobic object. Most patients have followed inflexible diets, often for years. Most often carbohydrates have become feared objects which are strictly avoided. Hospitalization provides the opportunity for the patient to learn to overcome specific fears by eating a variety of foods and then observing that they are not immediately transformed into large quantities of body fat.

In this regard, it is important for the medical team not to foster "anorexic" eating patterns. Rather than allow the patient a diet of 2500 calories made up largely of lettuce and cottage cheese, she must learn to eat a well-balanced diet that includes carbohydrates. Patients may be allowed one exchange daily from the general menu, but they should not be allowed to recreate the familial situation whereby they and their families treated her food as though it were special.

With extremely emaciated patients, gastric dilatation is a potentially serious complication of rapid refeeding (Jennings and Klidjian, 1974). For this reason starting the patient on a 1200-1500 calorie diet is recommended. This should be gradually increased to 2500 calories per day over the first week or two. After that the caloric content may be individualized, depending on the patient's rate of weight gain. Most patients will gain weight quite satisfactorily on 3000-3600 calories per day. However, the daily caloric requirement for individuals can vary greatly. In general, it has been found that about 7500 excess calories will result in 1 kg weight gain in anorexics (Russell and Mezey, 1962; Walker, Roberts, Halmi and Goldberg, 1979); but those who have been previously obese may gain weight more readily on the same caloric intake (Stordy, Marks, Kalucy and Crisp, 1977).

It is important for the patient to develop control over her eating. This means initially eating all her meals in bed and later in the ward dining room. Food should be available only at meal and snack times. Patients are not allowed to bring food on the unit but as they become more normal in weight

they are permitted more time to eat off the ward. While some may encourage unlimited accessibility to food (Galdston, 1974), we are concerned
about the possible iatrogenic contribution to the development of bulimia
when external controls are not provided during the weight restoring period.
Similarly the family should not be allowed to bring foods into hospital as
this tends to recreate earlier confrontations over foods (Crisp, 1977). While
on the weight restoration regimen, patients are expected to eat their meals
with a nurse in attendance (Hurst, 1939; Russell, 1977) and they are expected to finish their entire meal before they leave the table. Not completing
meals may reintroduce the avoidance behavior. Patients will usually eat
what is prescribed without coercion if they sense attention is being paid to
their other problems and that there is some control over their rate of gain.
Nevertheless, at least initially they may experience severe anxiety prior to
and during meals. This may be dealt with in a variety of ways.

The emotional support and encouragement of staff are important. Also
helpful is the awareness that the anxiety is a necessary part of overcoming
the phobia to weight. It is only by experiencing the panic of weight gain that
the patient begins to learn to deal with these feelings more appropriately.
This is similar to the "therapeutic encirclement" of the borderline patient
described by Sadavoy, Silver and Book (1979). Many patients also benefit
from help in dealing with the reality of eating, its effects on the body, and
their excessive guilt at eating when inactive. Some patients also derive
benefit from such anxiety-reducing techniques as deep-muscle relaxation exercises and others may temporarily require anxiolytic medication to enable
them to begin to eat. Gross (1980) has suggested that hypnosis may be
useful to reduce anxiety. To overcome patients' fears of loss of control he
recommends self-hypnosis. Some patients may not initially be able to complete their prescribed meals in spite of these efforts. They may be allowed to
make up the caloric differences by a high caloric drink (e.g., Ensure,
Sustagen) (Miesem and Wann, 1967; Whipple and Manning, 1978).
However, this should not be permitted indefinitely; rather the drinks should
gradually be tapered and replaced with a balanced solid diet.

Patients who vomit after meals should not be allowed to use the
washrooms without staff accompaniment for one to two hours after eating.
This is preferable to denying them general use of the washrooms. While this
may seem intrusive and dehumanizing, the patients are usually quite
amenable to this if supervision is explained properly to them. However, if a
patient continues to vomit even while in hospital, it may be necessary to
have her on total bedrest using a commode for elimination until she is able
to control her eating. It should be explained to the patient that although
vomiting originally began as a means to achieve control, the symptom is

now out of control and she has become a slave to it. Patients should be encouraged to talk to staff whenever they feel the urge to vomit. Preventing the vomiting for two or three weeks generally reduces the urge to vomit considerably. Thereafter the urges may be less frequent but on occasion they may be very intense. The patient can gradually be reintroduced to previously avoided anxiety-provoking foods in accordance with desensitization procedures. Hersen and Detre (1980) have used flooding and response prevention to reduce the physiological arousal which occurs in the presence of avoided foods.

Anorexic patients often engage in deception, such as surreptitious disposal of food or exercising when on bedrest. These actions are not signs of malice, but of the extreme fear of weight gain. Nevertheless, a certain level of nursing vigilance is required. The attitude of the nursing staff is important. Staff must continually convey an understanding that the illness makes the patient do things which are out of her character when she is fearful of gaining weight, but that she will not be allowed to behave in these self-defeating ways (Russell, 1973). Throughout, the staff must be understanding and supportive, but firm. A punitive and angry approach will merely increase the patient's resistance and destroy the alliance. If a patient has been deceptive about hiding foods, excessive exercising, or vomiting, she must be confronted in a nonjudgmental manner.

The entire treatment team must be aware of, and sensitive to, the initial demands on the patient: They are asking her to cooperate in an area in which she does not truly wish to change, in which she is extremely fearful of losing control, and with people whom she does not yet trust. Nursing staff must recognize and then discuss with the patient her realistic and irrational fears. They should repeatedly, but gently, introduce elements of reality to the patient — about her appearance, her behavior, and her means of responding to anxiety-laden situations. They help in the very early clarification of different affective states and in evaluating mechanisms that may be used to cope with these. They should constantly explain why nutritional rehabilitation is an essential precondition for dealing effectively with other problems. Nurses often have the difficult task of dealing directly with most food-related issues, yet they must convey the attitude that their relationship with the patient is not based solely on weight or food and that they are responding to a unique individual, not merely to an abstract concept (Miesem and Wann, 1967).

The staff must recognize that the initial weight-restoring period may be associated with increased patient anxiety, bodily preoccupation, and guilt. Physical complaints may become common. Ambivalence about proceeding with the treatment and thoughts concerning leaving the hospital prematurely may occur. The staff must act sympathetically, with a great deal of support and understanding, yet always with recognition of the reality of the situation. They must not change the treatment plan merely because they are sympathetic. The treatment may be jeopardized if one member of the staff feels it is wise to bend the rules a little and win the patient's favor by being less firm. The patient's attempts to split and project onto the staff may at times be interpreted, but of greater importance is the entire staff's ability to recognize and not to respond to these defenses (Sadavoy et al., 1979).

This mixture of firmness with support may produce a variety of responses in the staff. If the staff do not have a sense of understanding and direction in the management of the patient, they become helpless and inconsistent in dealing with the resistant, deceitful behavior. This usually produces frustration, followed by anger, which is directed at the patient or her physician. This often results in a variety of approaches which punish the patient for her resistance to treatment and totally negate the therapeutic alliance. At other times some staff may not feel comfortable with being firm, often out of a desire to be liked by the patient or a wish to deal only with psychological issues. This facilitates the patient's manipulations and again treatment may break down. Other responses common in these situations are feelings of inordinate power over the patient, or a desire to infantilize her, facilitated by the patient's small size and at times regressive behavior. These feelings in the staff can be minimized if there is a clear understanding of the treatment philosophy and the rationale upon which it is based. Regular staff seminars are important in this regard, as is a sense of open communication within the treatment team (Book, Sadavoy and Silver, 1978).

Free time may be quite frightening for patients who have been inflexible in all their behavior for the months or years prior to admission. As they are gradually off bedrest they may be introduced to a variety of activities. However, it is wise not to structure every moment; rather, patients should gradually learn to accept and enjoy relaxing times when they don't have to be "productive." Some emphasis should be placed on occupational therapies, not merely to pass the time but to encourage the development of individual skills that compete with the sense of helplessness experienced by most patients. Crafts may be utilized for self-expression. Often patients enjoy sewing clothes, not in their emaciated sizes but rather in their anticipated healthy sizes. This may, in a small way, help them to accept the inevitable changes in their body shape while indicating that there is a rational limit to the weight gain. Similarly, they may be encouraged to give their old clothes away to a children's hospital to emphasize how juvenile they were. Cooking lessons with the dietician may be appropriate for some, but this should only be attempted in the maintenance phase when starvation symptoms are no longer present. Once the patient has achieved her target weight there may be benefit in interpretive dance classes or yoga to help promote positive bodily perceptions and acceptance of a new shape. Throughout, the patient must be viewed as an individual whose unique skills will be enhanced, not someone who is slotted for all programs that are available.

We encourage some patients to begin a program of graded exercises after weight restoration. If begun prior to discharge, they may demonstrate to the patient that she can appropriately control her exercise rather than become a slave to it. Some patients, however, are not able to tolerate this and would be better off deferring any exercise program until they have recovered.

Decisions about continuing schooling while in hospital must be considered carefully. While these are people who place great emphasis on scholastic achievements and who have succeeded academically, this is often within the area of their psychopathology regarding excess performance. It may be necessary to de-emphasize academic achievement as a counterbalance to the patient's preoccupations. However, there is a realistic element in the patient's anxiety about falling behind in schooling. For this reason it may be wise for many patients to continue their studies from the hospital, after the starvation symptoms have cleared, and provided firm limits are set on the amount of time spent studying. For some older patients with concerns regarding career plans, the maintenance phase may be utilized for initiating vocational rehabilitation.

Some patients benefit from group therapy. This should be instituted when the starvation symptoms have begun to be reduced (Hedblom, Hubbard and Andersen, in press; Sclare, 1977). We have found assertive training groups to be useful. They allow the patients to display a more direct expression of appropriate affect in a controlled setting as a preparation to such situations in their lives out of the hospital. Progress in these group may enable them to have more confidence in acting on their own internal demands, rather than merely in response to others (Grossniklaus, 1980). We have also encouraged the formation of other groups for specific anorexic patients, as adjuncts to their ongoing therapies (Polivy, 1981). In general, these groups have been for the more verbal, psychologically-minded patients who are not excessively competitive or regressed. The main purpose of these groups is to provide a setting in which patients may discuss their feelings connected with the disorder and how it has affected them, in a setting where they can be accepted and understood. The groups provide support, models of coping, peer feedback and education. While we have felt these groups to be useful, they must be led by skilled therapists or there is danger in fostering patients' identities as "anorexics." They are never substitutes for individual therapies but may be useful additions to ongoing therapy, particularly in helping the individual to deal with the transition period from hospital to home.

According to Sclare (1977), Hamilton and Hamill have described a similar group therapy program. In addition to this group for patients, they developed concurrent group therapies for the parents. Rose and Garfinkel (1980) have described the use of parents' groups in anorexia nervosa; these were supportive, educational groups for those in whom family therapy was not possible. Piazza, Piazza and Rollins (1980) have used a weekly parents' group for hospitalized patients for support and also to help the parents in working with the inpatient staff.

Contact with the patient's family has usually begun at the time of the initial assessment. This is maintained through the hospitalization period. When the patient is in hospital a number of rules should be established to keep the family removed from day-to-day inpatient management. The family should not be allowed to bring foods into the hospital or to phone during meal periods. They should not be involved in specific details of the girl's treatment, for example what she ate for lunch. However, they should be seen regularly to inform them of general issues in management. Similarly, unless there is a specific reason for forbidding it, visiting should be allowed. Once the patient has settled into the hospital the family are generally seen in regular therapy by a family therapist who may, or may not, also be the individual therapist. The timing of family therapy must be individualized but usually can begin once the patient has started to gain weight and developed some control over her eating. The specific issues that are dealt with will vary from family to family, but often will focus on emotional separation and the need to enhance boundaries between family members while permitting effective parenting. These are dealt with in greater detail in Chapter 10. In our program individual psychotherapy remains the cornerstone of treatment for the anorexic patient. While this begins in hospital, for convenience this aspect of treatment will be discussed in Chapter 10.

## THE ROLE OF MEDICATIONS

Many drug therapies have been tried either as the major focus of treatment or as adjuncts to general support and psychological therapies. While some medications may prove beneficial to individual patients, it must be stressed that their value is rather limited and in our opinion should never constitute the only therapeutic endeavor.

Probably the most widely used medications, particularly in the United Kingdom, have been the phenothiazines, especially chlorpromazine. Chlorpromazine was first recommended in the late 1950s by Sargant (Dally, Oppenheim and Sargant, 1958; Dally and Sargant, 1960; Dally and Sargant, 1966), and then adapted by others (Ghafoor and Ravindranath, 1969). Dally and Sargant (1960) compared the use of high doses of chlorpromazine, together with insulin, bedrest and high caloric diet, with other methods (in patients treated by other physicians). They found both a greater and more rapid gain associated with the former treatments. While it is impossible to sort out which factors were responsible for these results, Dally and Sargant (1960) originally felt it was the combination of chlorpromazine with insulin that was particularly useful but later suggested the chlorpromazine itself was equally successful (Dally and Sargant, 1966). They administered very high doses of the neuroleptic, beginning with oral doses of 150 mg per day and increasing to the patient's tolerance, often to 1-1.5 g. Crisp (1965) too has recommended chlorpromazine but felt it to be merely an adjunct to psychotherapy and he used much smaller doses (400-600 mg/day).

Chlorpromazine has several advantages:

1) It reduces the patient's initial anxiety and resistance to eating and weight gain;
2) its sedating effect may help the patient tolerate bedrest or other reduced activity; and
3) its use results in weight gain (Robinson, McHugh and Folstein, 1975), possibly through its effects on catecholamines (Leibowitz, 1976).

However, there are also serious problems with chlorpromazine, including:

1) It further lowers the patient's blood pressure, often to levels where she may be symptomatic when standing.
2) it may aggravate the leukopenia that is often seen in anorexia nervosa.
3) it may reduce body temperature (Russell, 1970).
4) it reduces the convulsive threshold (Dally [1969] reported that about 10% of his patients had a grand mal seizure within two weeks of starting treatment).
5) Dally and Sargant (1966) observed an increased frequency of post-discharge bulimia in their chlorpromazine-treated patients. Equal numbers (33%) of their chlorpromazine- and non-chlorpromazine-treated patients required readmission to hospital. More recently Dally (1977) has suggested that only about half of his patients require chlorpromazine.

Because of these problems, we use chlorpromazine only for the minority of patients who show marked anxiety to foods and inability to eat after the general supportive measures have been attempted. We begin with small doses (50-75 mg qhs) and rarely more than 300 mg/day have been required. As patients overcome their resistance, the medication is gradually reduced and almost all are off it at discharge. There may be advantages to using a less sedating high potency neuroleptic like haloperidol, but here the advantage of having the patient less obtunded is offset by the increased frequency of extrapyramidal effects. The neuroleptic medications do not seem to improve the patient's beliefs about her body; they merely reduce her tension. Plantey (1977) and Hoes (1980) have each reported single patients who responded to pimozide; this is of some interest and should be pursued given the reports by Munro (Munro, 1977; Riding and Munro, 1975) of pimozide's efficacy in hypochondriacal monosymptomatic psychosis and given the superficial similarity of this condition to anorexia nervosa. Some patients with borderline personality organization may also benefit from long-term use of a neuroleptic but this has not been clearly demonstrated (Klein, 1977).

As an alternative to neuroleptics some have recommended minor tranquilizers for their anxiolytic effects (A. Andersen, personal communication, 1980; Hall, 1975). In a survey of consultant internists and  psychiatrists, Bhanji (1979) found the psychiatrists to be more likely to prescribe major tranquilizers, antidepressants, and insulin and the internists to use minor tranquilizers for anorexia nervosa. Benzodiazepines are said to have several advantages. In particular, their anxiolytic properties are excellent, patients display less slowing of their mental processes, and the above-noted untoward effects associated with neuroleptics are not encountered. However, they have one significant disadvantage, a high potential for dependency in a group of individuals with considerable risk for addiction. For this reason, use of a short-acting minor tranquilizer (lorazepam 1-2 mg) one hour before each meal can be a good substitute for chlorpromazine to help some patients begin to eat, provided its use is limited to just a few weeks. However, we suggest that lorazepam should not be used in bulimic patients who as a group have a great addiction potential. Gross, Ebert, Goldberg, Kaye, Caine, Faden, Hawks and Zinberg (1980) recently conducted a four-week crossover trial of delta-9-tetrahydrocannabinol (THC) versus diazepam in anorexia nervosa. This was based on THC's tendency to stimulate appetite and promote weight gain. However, THC was not found to be superior to diazepam and had significant untoward effects; three patients experienced severe dysphoria with feelings of loss of control and paranoid ideation on the THC. This did not occur with the diazepam.

Because of the depressive features that may be seen in anorexia nervosa and the frequency of a family history of affective disorder, it has been suggested that anorexia nervosa is a variant of affective illness (see Chapter 2). As a result, both tricyclic antidepressants and lithium carbonate have been recommended. Needleman and Waber (1976, 1977) have described six pediatric patients referred to them consecutively, who responded to amitriptyline in doses between 75-150 mg/day. They felt that behavioral and other psychotherapies had been minimized and ascribed the significant weight responses (gains of 7-16 kg) to the tricyclic medication. White and Schnaultz (1977) described two adolescent anorexics with depressed mood; they responded well to imipramine in conjunction with ongoing psychotherapy. Moore (1977), Katz and Walsh (1978), and Cuixart and Conill (1979) have each reported favorable responses to antidepressants in individual cases, although the response of Katz and Walsh's (1978) patient who tripled her weight (from 30-90 kg) and became hypomanic can hardly be considered a desirable outcome. Kendler (1978) also reported a single patient who responded to amitriptyline and later developed obesity. Mills, Wilson, Eden and Lines (1973) and Mills (1976) have reported less favorable but unclear results in a larger sample of patients.

At present, in the absence of controlled studies using adequate doses of the tricyclic drugs, we must conclude that their efficacy has not been demonstrated. Moreover, amitriptyline has been shown to produce carbohydrate cravings in a non-anorexic population (Paykel, Mueller and De La Vergne, 1973) and therefore there may be a significant risk of precipitating bulimia in patients who are in any event predisposed to it. Because of their unproven benefits and potential for untoward effects, we reserve the use of these medications for those with major depressive features which have persisted after weight restoration. It is our experience that few patients require tricyclics.

Lithium carbonate has been studied even less and its risks are greater in anorexic patients. Barcai (1977) has cautiously recommended its use for some adult anorexic patients, based on two patients who gained 12 kg and 9 kg on the drug and had concomitant improvement in their mental state. The patients he chose were hyperactive and displayed affective lability and pressure of speech. Reilly (1977) also reported on the use of lithium in a single patient. Hsu, Crisp and Harding (1979) reported one patient whose severe mood swings responded to lithium but she remained intensely preoccupied with weight loss. Patients on lithium generally gain some weight. However, the risks of lithium intoxication are great in a population that frequently indulges in dieting, sodium restriction, vomiting, and laxative and diuretic misuse. Spring (1974) described an anorexic patient with near fatal lithium intoxication. Freeman (personal communication) described two patients on lithium carbonate. One developed signs of serious intoxication and the second developed some lithium side effects without perceived benefit. While there may be some patients with anorexia nervosa who share clinical features with a hypomanic syndrome, we do not recommend lithium's use unless the mood swings are severe and there has been a family history of beneficial response to lithium. If so, lithium may be administered only if the patient is fully cooperative and is capable of minimizing the risks of intoxication. We have tried this in two patients; one has responded to the medication and remains on it.

Electroconvulsive therapy (ECT) has occasionally been recommended (Wall, 1959; Bernstein, 1964). Laboucarié and Barres (1954) treated a large number of anorexic patients with ECT and found it useful occasionally. Dally (1969), however, found that while many patients had depressive symptoms, they were not improved after ECT and if anything the relationship with the patient was impaired. Russell (1970) correctly suggested that it is of very limited value and should be used only for severe depression that has proved refractory to general and pharmacological measures. A few intractable patients have been described before and after leucotomy (Altschule, 1953; Carmody and Vibber, 1952; Crisp, 1967; Crisp and Kalucy, 1973; Dally, 1969; Glazebrook, Matas and Prosen, 1956; Morgan and Russell, 1975; Sargant, 1951; Sifneos, 1952). On occasion the results have been good, particularly, according to Dally (1969), for those with highly obsessional features. Often there is weight gain but there may also be a release of impulsive behaviors including bulimia and suicide attempts. The results appear unpredictable and leucotomy should probably not be used, but if it is it should be used only as a last resort, and then only with the full understanding and agreement of the patient.

Johanson and Knorr (1977) have recommended the use of L-dopa to stimulate weight gain in anorexic patients, based on two erroneous assumptions: 1) many patients present with an akinetic (weakness, inactivity) syndrome reminiscent of Parkinsonism; and 2) 6-hydroxy-dopamine-induced adipsia and aphagia in rats may be a model for anorexia nervosa. In fact, anorexic patients are generally neither "anorexic" nor inactive. Moreover, their lowered plasma dopamine levels are due to weight loss and respond to weight gain (Darby, Van Loon, Garfinkel, Brown and Kirwan, 1980). Johanson and Knorr (1977) treated nine patients with low doses of L-dopa and observed five to gain small (3-5.5 kg) amounts of weight in hospital. One relapsed shortly after discharge. These results cannot be interpreted as supportive of L-dopa therapy. In a carefully controlled case study, Redmond, Swann and Heninger (1976) reported that phenoxybenzamine, an $\alpha$ - adrenergic blocking agent, induced weight gain but further studies are required here.

Cyproheptadine, a serotonin and histamine antagonist, has been noted to produce weight gain in patients with a variety of illnesses, including asthma (Lavenstein, Dacaney, Lasagna and Van Metre, 1962), tuberculosis (Shah,

1968) and "essential anorexia" (Pawlowski, 1975). Benady (1970) described the successful treatment of a single patient with anorexia nervosa with cyproheptadine. Since then two placebo-controlled double blind studies of cyproheptadine have been reported. Vigersky and Loriaux (1977) described 24 patients, 13 treated with cyproheptadine and 11 with placebo for eight weeks. Four drug-treated (31%) and two placebo-treated (18%) patients responded with weight gain; these differences were not statistically significant and the overall results could hardly be considered encouraging to the use of cyproheptadine.

In a multi-center project, Goldberg, Halmi, Eckert, Casper and Davis (1979) randomly assigned 81 patients to one of four treatment combinations of cyproheptadine or placebo with behavior therapy or no behavior therapy. They found that both drug and placebo groups gained between 4-5 kg over the 35 days. While there were no differences between cyproheptadine and placebo in stimulating weight gain they felt that there was a subgroup of patients characterized by a history of delivery complications who were drug responders. However, these results must be considered in light of the retrospective method of estimating delivery complications. In a further description of this study on a larger sample, Goldberg, Eckert, Halmi, Casper, Davis and Roper (1980) found that cyproheptadine tended to produce some non-weight-related benefits, as measured by rating scales.

Other agents have been recommended either to stimulate appetite or to induce more rapid weight gain; notable in this regard has been insulin (Wall, 1959) which is still used. As we described previously, Dally and Sargant (1960) recommended regular insulin administration in conjunction with chlorpromazine. We feel strongly that insulin has no place in the management of anorexia nervosa. Patients are not without appetite but are frightened and anxious about losing control over their hunger; to increase appetite increases these fears and, as Crisp (1965) and Dally (1969) note, may lead to bulimia. Thoma (1967) has also suggested that they may have a particular sensitivity to the drug, given their relative hypoglycemia, and this may lead to hypoglycemic coma. In fact, many patients have low circulating insulin levels and insulin resistance (see Chapter 4).

Many other hormone preparations have been tried, including cortisone, anterior pituitary extracts and implants, ACTH, testosterone, and ovarian extracts (Greenblatt, Barfield and Clark, 1951; Decourt and Michard, 1953; Schwartzman, 1954; see also Chapter 4). None are useful and all are based on the erroneous assumption that the various metabolic deficiencies that are demonstrable are related to the etiology of the illness. In this regard, thyroxine is still frequently prescribed (12 of our patients had been placed on it prior to seeing us and 33 of Theander's (1970) patients received thyroid preparations), based on the laboratory evidence of thyroid hypofunction. As noted in Chapter 4, the thyroid changes that occur in anorexia nervosa are a conservation response to the starvation state, and exogenous thyroxine is definitely not required to correct this. Thyrotropin-releasing hormone has also been administered and no behavioral or mood-elevating effects were observed (Amsterdam, Winokur, Caroff and Mendels, 1981).

There have been several reports on the use of anticonvulsants in the treatment of patients with eating disorders, including anorexia nervosa (Greenway, Dahms and Bray, 1977; Green and Rau, 1977; Weiss and Levitz, 1976; Wermuth, Davis, Hollister, and Stunkard, 1977). This followed Green and Rau's (1974) original favorable report of clinical improvement in nine out of ten patients on diphenylhydantoin. Their hypothesis was that eating disorders were a heterogenous group, but that for some there was an underlying neurophysiologic basis (Rau and Green, 1975). Four of their patients had anorexia nervosa; three of these responded to the medication with normal eating patterns. They followed this with a report of an expanded uncontrolled series (Green and Rau, 1977). Twenty-six patients were treated with diphenylhydantoin; nine patients responded positively but 17 either failed to respond or had an inadequate trial. Twelve patients had abnormal electroencephalograms (EEG); of these, six were drug responders. Of the total group, seven were considered to have anorexia nervosa and four of these patients responded to diphenylhydantoin. These individuals all displayed abnormal EEGs and non-food-related impulsive behaviors. Wermuth et al. (1977) followed this with a placebo-controlled study of phenytoin in the "binge-eating syndrome." Of their 20 patients, seven displayed some abnormality of the EEG using nasopharyngeal leads and a sleep/wake state. In only three of these was the EEG definitely abnormal. While about 40% of the subjects appeared to show some improvement with phenytoin versus placebo, the two patients with anorexia nervosa displayed no improvement. Weiss and Levitz (1976) also described one anorexic patient who failed to respond to diphenylhydantoin.

We agree with Russell (1977) that laxatives generally have no place in the management of anorexic patients; rather, constipation should be managed by dietary means. Enemas are generally to be avoided. In a report of a double blind study, Moldofsky, Jeuniewic and Garfinkel (1977) found metoclopramide to be more effective than placebo in relieving the postprandial dyspepsia in a small number of patients. However, this study was stopped after the medication precipitated depressive features in several. In an open study, Saleh and Lebwohl (1980) reported that metoclopramide reduced the delayed gastric emptying of seven anorexic patients and also decreased their subjective gastrointestinal discomfort after meals. In view of metoclopramide's potential for precipitating depression, perhaps another dopamine blocking agent which does not cross the blood brain barrier, domperidone, might be useful for the satiety-related symptoms and not alter the affective state.

Potassium supplements may be required for patients who persistently vomit or misuse laxatives and diuretics. About 4% of our patients have been prescribed or have somehow obtained diuretics and have then gone on to misuse them to reduce a subjective sense of bloating. It is not uncommon for women to believe that diuretics are a recommended means of reducing body fat; Cho and Fryer (1974) reported that 25% of female physical education students stated this.

Some anorexic patients may be given a diagnosis of idiopathic edema, after they have started the diuretic. MacGregor, Markandu, Roulston, Jones and de Wardener (1979) recently described ten women on long-term (three to 13 years) diuretics for idiopathic edema. Yet five of them had originally been placed on a diuretic because of their weight concerns and not the edema. Once on the medication all patients report the development of transient (MacGregor et al., 1979) or persistent edema (Edwards and Dent, 1979) on drug withdrawal. This makes it difficult to stop the drug. It is likely that idiopathic edema is a heterogenous syndrome in which lowered dopamine excretion (Edwards, Besser and Thorner, 1979) or microscopic capillary leaks (Streeten, 1978) may play a role. It is clearly not always the result of diuretic therapy, as it has been described prior to the introduction of diuretics (Streeten, 1978). Most patients with idiopathic edema respond to conservative measures and do not require diuretics. For those few that do, care should be taken to rule out anorexia nervosa. We emphasize this because it has been our experience that it may be difficult for patients to stop using diuretics once they have started.

The initial management of the anorexic patient serves two purposes: 1) to restore the patient's nutritional state to normal not only to reduce concern about possibly serious complications, but also to remove the starvation symptoms which perpetuate the diet cycle and which block progress in psychotherapy; and 2) to begin to develop a working alliance with some mutual trust. Both are necessary to prepare for the long-term treatment, whose goals are to reduce the morbidity and prevent relapses.

### REFERENCES

Abbott, W.M.: Indications for parenteral nutrition. In J.E. Fisher (Ed.), *Total Parenteral Nutrition.* Boston: Little Brown and Co., 1976.

Agras, W.S., Barlow, D.H., Chaplin, N.H., Able, G.G. and Leitenberg, H.: Behavior modification of anorexia nervosa. *Arch. Gen. Psychiatry,* 30:279-286, 1974.

Agras, S. and Werne, J.: Behavior modification in anorexia nervosa: Research foundations. In: R.A. Vigersky (Ed.), *Anorexia Nervosa.* New York: Raven Press, 1977, pp. 291-303.

Agras, S. and Werne, J.: Behavior therapy in anorexia nervosa: A data-based approach to the question. In: J.P. Brady and H.K.H. Brodie (Eds.), *Controversy in Psychiatry*. Philadelphia: Saunders, 1978, pp. 655-675.

Allison, R.S. and Davies, R.P.: The treatment of functional anorexia. *Lancet,* 1:902-907, 1931.

Altschule, M.D.: Adrenocortical function in anorexia nervosa before and after lobotomy. *New England J. Med.,*248:808-810, 1953.

Amsterdam, J., Winokur, A., Caroff, S. and mendels, J.: Thyrotropin-releasing hormone's mood-elating effects in depressed patients, anorectic patients and normal volunteers. *Am. J. Psychiatry,* 138:115-116, 1981.

Azerrad, J. and Stafford, R.L.: Restoration of eating behavior in anorexia nervosa through operant conditioning and environmental manipulation. *Behav. Res. Ther.,* 7:165-171, 1969.

Bachrach, A.J., Erwin, W.J. and Mohr, J.P.: The control of eating behavior in an anorexic by operant conditioning techniques. In: L.P. Ullman and I. Krasner (Eds.), *Case Studies in Behavior Modification.* New York: Holt Rinehart and Winston, 1965.

Barcai, A.: Lithium in anorexia nervosa: A pilot report on two patients. *Acta Psychiat. Scand.,* 55:97-101, 1977.

Benady, D.R.: Cyproheptadine hydrochloride (periactin) and anorexia nervosa: A case report. *Br. J. Psychiatry,* 117:681-682, 1970.

Berkman, J.M.: Anorexia nervosa, anterior-pituitary insufficiency, Simmonds' cachexia and Sheehan's disease: Including some observations on disturbances in water metabolism associated with starvation. *Postgrad. Med.,* 3:237-246, 1948.

Bernstein, I.C.: Anorexia nervosa treated successfully with electroshock therapy and subsequently followed by pregnancy. *Am. J. Psychiatry,* 120: 1023-1025, 1964.

Beumont, P.J.V.: Anorexia nervosa: A review. *S. Afr. Med. J.,* 44:911-915, 1970.

Bhanji, S.: Anorexia nervosa: Physicians' and psychiatrists' opinion and practice. *J. Psychosom. Res.,* 23:7-11, 1979.

Bhanji, S. and Thompson, J.: Operant conditioning in the treatment of anorexia nervosa: A review and retrospective study of 11 cases. *Brit. J. Psychiatry,* 124:166-172, 1974.

Bianco, F.J.: Rapid treatment of two cases of anorexia nervosa. *Journal of Behavior Therapy and Experimental Psychiatry*, 3:223-224, 1972.

Blinder, B.J., and Ringold, A.L.: Rapid weight restoration in anorexia nervosa. *Clin. Res.,* 15:473 (abstract), 1967.

Blinder, B.J., Freeman, D.M.A. and Stunkard, A.J.: Behavior therapy of anorexia nervosa: Effectiveness of activity as a reinforcer of weight gain. *Am. J. Psychiatry,* 126:77-82, 1970.

Blue, R.: Use of punishment in treatment of anorexia nervosa. *Psychol. Rep.,* 44:743-746, 1979.

Book, H.E., Sadavoy, J. and Silver, D.: Staff countertransference to borderline patients on an inpatient unit. *Am. J. Psychother,* 32:521-532, 1978.

Brady, J.P. and Rieger, W.: Behavior treatment of anorexia nervosa. In: T. Thompson and W.S. Dockens, III (Eds.), *Proceedings of the International Symposium on Behavior Modification.* New York: Appleton-Century-Crofts, 1972.

Browning, C.H. and Miller, S.I.: Anorexia nervosa: A study in prognosis and management. *Am. J. Psychiatry,*124:1128-1132, 1968.

Bruch, H.: *Eating Disorders.* New York: Basic Books, 1973.

Bruch, H.: Perils of behavior modification in treatment of anorexia nervosa. *JAMA,* 230: 1419-1422, 1974.

Bruch, H.: *The Golden Cage.* Cambridge: Harvard University Press, 1978.

Carmody, J.T.B. and Vibber, F.L.: Anorexia nervosa treated by prefrontal lobotomy. *Ann. Int. Med.,* 36:647-652, 1952.

Cho, M. and Fryer, B.A.: Nutritional knowledge of collegiate physical education majors. *J. Am. Diet. Assoc.,* 65:30-34, 1974.

Cotugno, A.J.: A psychoeducational approach in the treatment of anorexia nervosa. *Psychology in the Schools,* 17:222-240, 1980.

Crisp, A.H.: Clinical and therapeutic aspects of anorexia nervosa — a study of thirty cases. *J. Psychosom. Res.,* 9:67-78, 1965.

Crisp, A.H.: The possible significance of some behavioral correlates of weight and carbohydrates intake. *J. Psychosom. Res.,* 11:117-131, 1967.

Crisp, A.H.: Premorbid factors in adult disorders of weight, with particular reference to primary anorexia nervosa (weight phobia). A literature review. *J. Psychosom. Res.,* 14:1-22, 1970.

Crisp, A.H.: Diagnosis and outcome of anorexia nervosa: The St. George's view. *Proc. Roy. Soc. Med.,* 70:464-470, 1977.

Crisp, A.H. and Kalucy, R.S.: The effect of leucotomy in intractable adolescent weight phobia (primary anorexia nervosa). *Postgrad. Med. J.,* 49-833-893, 1973.

Cuixart, P.C. and Conill, V.T.: Anorexie mentale juvenile traitée par antidepresseurs et psychothérapie sans necessité d'isolement. *Neuropsychiat. de L'Enfance,* 27:135-138, 1979.

Dally, P.J.: *Anorexia Nervosa.* New York: Grune and Stratton, 1969.

Dally P.J.: Anorexia nervosa: Do we need a scapegoat? *Proc. Roy. Soc. Med.,* 70:470-474, 1977.

Dally, P.J. and Sargant, W.: A new treatment of anorexia nervosa. *Brit. Med. J.,* 1:1770-1773, 1960.

Dally, P.J. and Sargant, W.: Treatment and outcome of anorexia nervosa. *Brit. Med. J.,* 2:793-795, 1966.

Dally, P.J., Oppenheim, G.B. and Sargant, W.: Anorexia nervosa. *Brit. Med. J.,* 2:633-634, 1958.

Darby, P.L., Van Loon, G., Garfinkel, P.E., Brown, G.M. and Kirwan, P.: LH, growth hormone, prolactin and catecholamine responses to LHRF and bromocriptine in anorexia nervosa. *Psychosom. Med.,* 41:585 (abstract), 1980.

Day, S.: Dietary management of anorexia nervosa. *Nutr. Lond.,* 28:289-295, 1974.

Decourt, J. and Michard, J.P.: Les amenorrhees de cause psychique. *Rev. Prat.,* 3:27-34, 1953.

Dudrick, S.J., Wilmore, D.W., Vars, H.M. and Mullen, J.L.: Can intravenous feeding as the sole means of nutrition support growth in the child and restore weight loss in an adult? An affirmative answer. *Ann. Surg.,* 169:974-984, 1969.

Eckert, E.D., Goldberg, S.C., Halmi, K.A., Casper, R.C. and Davis, J.M.: Behavior therapy in anorexia nervosa. *Brit. J. Psychiatry,* 134:55-59, 1979.

Edwards, C.R.W., Besser, G.M. and Thorner, M.O.: Bromocriptine-responsive form of idiopathic edema. *Lancet,* 2:94, 1979.

Edwards, O.M. and Dent, R.G.: Idiopathic oedema. *Lancet,* 1:670, 1979.

Elkin, M., Hersen, M., Eisler, R.M. and Williams, J.G.: Modification of caloric intake in anorexia nervosa: An experimental analysis. *Psychol. Reports,* 32:75-78, 1973.

Erwin, E.: *Behavior Therapy.* New York: Cambridge University Press, 1977.

Farquharson, R.F. and Hyland, H.H.: Anorexia nervosa; Metabolic disorder of psychologic origin. *JAMA,* 111:1085-1092, 1938.

Farquharson, R.F. and Hyland, H.H.: Anorexia nervosa: The course of 15 patients treated from 20 to 30 years previously. *Can. Med. Assoc. J.,* 94:411-419, 1966.

Fichter, M.M. and Kessler, W.: Behavioral treatment of an anorexic male: Experimental analysis of generalization. *Behav. Anal. Med.,* 4:152-168, 1980.

Finkelstein, B.A.: Parenteral hyperalimentation in anorexia nervosa. *JAMA,* 219:217, 1972.

Fisher, J.E.; *Toral Parenteral Nutrition.* Boston: Little Brown and Co., 1976.

Fox, K.C. and James, N.M.: Anorexia nervosa: A study of 44 strictly defined cases. *N.Z. Med. J.,* 84:309-312, 1976.

Frazier, S.H.: Anorexia nervosa. *Dis. Nerv. Syst.,* 26:155-159, 1965.

Freeman, R.J.: Lithium in the treatment of anorexia nervosa: A cautionary note. (Personal communication, 1980).

Galbraith, H.F.: Clinical experience with glibenclamide. *Postgrad. Med. J.,* [Suppl] 46:95-97, 1970.

Galdston, R.: Mind over matter: Observations on 50 patients hospitalized with anorexia nervosa. *J. Am. Acad. Child Psychiat.,* 13:246-263, 1974.

Garfinkel, P.E., Kline, S.A. and Stancer, H.C.: Treatment of anorexia nervosa using operant conditioning techniques. *J. Nerv. Ment. Dis.,* 157:428-433, 1973.

Garfinkel, P.E., Moldofsky, H. and Garner, D.M.: The role of behavior modification in the treatment of anorexia nervosa. *Journal of Pediatric Psychology,* 2:113-121, 1977a.

Garfinkel, P.E., Moldofsky, H. and Garner, D.M.: The outcome of anorexia nervosa: Significance of clinical features, body image and behavior modification. In: R.A. Vigersky (Ed.), *Anorexia Nervosa,* New York: Raven Press, 1977b, pp. 315-329.

Geller, J.L. Treatment of anorexia nervosa by the integration of behavior therapy and psychotherapy. *Psychother. Psychoso.,* 26:167-179, 1975.

Ghafoor, P.K.A. and Ravindranath: Treatment of anorexia nervosa with chlorpromazine and modified insulin therapy. *J. Ass. Physicians* (India), 17:369-372, 1969.

Gifford, S., Murawski, B.J. and Pilot, M.L.: Anorexia nervosa in one of identical twins. *Inter. Psychiat. Clin.,* 7:139-228, 1970.

Glazebrook, A.J., Matas, J. and Prosen, H.: Compulsive neurosis with cachexia. *Can. Med. Assoc. J.,* 75:40-42, 1956.

Goldberg, S.C., Halmi, K.A., Eckert, E.D., Casper, R.C. and Davis, J.M.: Cyproheptadine in anorexia nervosa. *Br. J. Psychiatry,* 134:67-70, 1979.

Goldberg, S.C., Eckert, E.D., Halmi, K.A., Casper, R.C., Davis, J.M. and Roper, M.: Effects of cyproheptadine on symptoms and attitudes in anorexia nervosa *Arch. Gen. Psychiatry,* 37:1083, 1980.

Gottheil, E., Backup, C.E. and Cornelison, F.S., Jr.: Denial and self-image confrontation in a case of anorexia nervosa. *J. Nerv. Ment. Dis.,* 148:238-250, 1969.

Green, R.S. and Rau, J.H.: Treatment of compulsive eating disturbances with anticonvulsant medication. *Am. J. Psychiatry,* 131:428-432, 1974.

Green, R.S. and Rau, J.H.: The use of diphenylhydantoin in compulsive eating disorders: Further studies. In: R.A. Vigersky (Ed.), *Anorexia Nervosa.* New York: Raven Press, 1977, pp. 377-382.

Greenblatt, R.B., Barfield, W.E. and Clark, S.L.: The use of ACTH and cortisone in the treatment of anorexia nervosa. *J. Med. Assoc. Ga.,* 39:482-487, 1951.

Greenway, F.L., Dahms, W.T. and Bray, G.A.: Phenytoin as a treatment of obesity associated with compulsive eating. *Curr. Therap. Res.,* 21:338-342, 1977.

Groen, J.J. and Feldman-Toledano, Z.: Educative treatment of patients and parents in anorexia nervosa. *Br. J. Psychiatry,* 112:671-681, 1966.

Gross, H.A., Ebert, M., Goldbert, S., Kaye, W., Caine, E., Faden, V., Hawks, R. and Zinberg, N.: A trial of delta-9-THC in primary anorexia nervosa. 133rd Annual Meeting of the American Psychiatric Association, San Francisco. Syllabus and Scientific Proceedings. 1980, pp. 327-328.

Gross, M.: Anorexia nervosa: Differing treatment interventions, efficacy and economics. Annual Meeting of the American Orthopsychiatric Association, Inc. Toronto, April, 1980.

Grossniklaus, D.M.: Nursing interventions in anorexia nervosa. *Perspectives in Psychiatric Care,* 18:11-16, 1980.

Gull, W.W.: Anorexia nervosa. *Transactions of the Clinical Society of London,* 7:22-28, 1874. Reprinted in R.M. Kaufman and M. Heiman (Eds.), *Evolution of Psychosomatic Concepts. Anorexia Nervosa: A Paradigm.* New York: International Universities Press, 1964.

Hall, A.: Treatment of anorexia nervosa. *N.Z. Med. J.,* 82:10-13, 1975.

Hallsten, E.A., Jr.: Adolescent anorexia nervosa treated by desensitization. *Behav. Res. Ther.,* 3:87-91, 1965.

Halmi, K.A., Powers, P. and Cunningham, S.: Treatment of anorexia nervosa with behavior modification. *Arch. Gen. Psychiatry,* 32:93-96, 1975.

Halmi, K.A.: Effectiveness of behavioral therapy in anorexia nervosa. *Psychiat. Drug Mar.,* 19-24, 1977.

Hedblom, J.E., Hubbard, F.A. and Andersen, A.E.: A treatment program for anorexia nervosa: The unique contributions of a multidisciplinary team. (In press)

Hersen, M. and Detre, T.: The behavioral psychotherapy of anorexia nervosa. In: T.B. Karasu and L. Bellak (Eds.), *Specialized Techniques in Individual Psychotherapy.* New York: Brunner/Mazel, 1980.

Hirschman, G.H., Rao, D.D. and Chan, J.C.: Anorexia nervosa with acute tubular necrosis treated with parenteral nutrition. *Nutr. Metab.*, 21:341-348, 1977.

Hoes, M.J.: Copper sulfate and pimozide for anorexia nervosa. *J. Orthomolecular Psychiatry*, 9:48-51, 1980.

Hsu, L.K., Crisp, A.H. and Harding, B.: Outcome of anorexia nervosa. *Lancet*, 1(8107): 61-65, 1979.

Hurst, A.: Discussion on anorexia nervosa. *Proc. Roy, Soc. Med.*, 32:744-745, 1939.

Janet, P.: *Psychological Healing* Vol. 2. New York: Allen and Unwin, 1926.

Jennings, K.P. and Klidjian, A.M.: Acute gastric dilatation in anorexia nervosa. *Br. Med. J.*, 2:477-478, 1974.

Johanson, A.J. and Knorr, N.J.: L-Dopa as treatment for anorexia nervosa. In: R.A. Vigersky (Ed.), *Anorexia Nervosa*. New York: Raven Press, 1977, pp. 363-372.

Katz, J.L. and Walsh, B.T.: Depression in anorexia nervosa. *Am. J. Psychiatry*, 135:507, 1978.

Kehrer, H.E. Behandlung der Anorexia Nervosa mit Verhaltenstherapie. *Medizinische Klinik*, 70:427-432, 1975.

Kendler, K.S.: Amitriptyline-induced obesity in anorexia nervosa: A case report. *Am. J. Psychiatry*, 135:1107-1108, 1978.

Kenny, F.T. and Solyom, L.: The treatment of compulsive vomiting through faradic disruption of mental images. *Can. Med. Assoc. J.*, 105:1071, 1971.

Keys, A., Brozek, J., Henschel, A., Mickelsen, O. and Taylor, H.L.: *The Biology of Human Starvation*. Minneapolis: University of Minnesota Press, 1950.

Klein, D.F.: Psychopharmacological treatment and delineation of borderline disorders. In: P. Horticollis (Ed.), *Borderline Personality Disorders*. New York: International Universities Press, 1977, pp. 365-383.

Kylin, E.: Magersucht in der weiblichen spatpubertat. *Deutsches Arch. Klin. Med.*, 180:115-152, 1937.

Laboucarié, J. and Barres, P.: Les aspects cliniques, pathogéniques et thérapeutiques de l'anorexie mentale. *L'Evolution Psychiat.*, 1:119-146, 1954.

Lang, P.: Behavior therapy with a case of anorexia nervosa. In: L.P. Ullman and L. Krasner (Eds.), *Case Studies in Behavior Modification*. New York: Holt, Rinehart and Winston, 1965.

Lavenstein, A.F., Dacaney, E.P., Lasagna, L. and Van Metre, T.E.: Effect of cyproheptadine on asthmatic children. Study of appetite, weight gain, and linear growth. *JAMA*, 180:912-916, 1962.

Leibowitz, S.F.: Brain catecholaminergic mechanisms for control of hunger. In: D. Novin, W. Wyrwicka and G.A. Bray (Eds.), *Hunger: Basic Mechanisms and Clinical Implications*. New York: Raven Press, 1976, p. 1.

Leitenberg, H., Agras, W.S. and Thomson, L.E.: A sequential analysis of the effect of selective positive reinforcement in modifying anorexia nervosa. *Behav. Res. Ther.*, 6:211-218, 1968.

Lesser, L.I., Ashenden, B.J., Debuskey, M. and Eisenberg, L.: Anorexia nervosa in children. *Amer. J. Orthopsychiat.*, 30:572-580, 1960.

Liebman, R., Minuchin, S. and Baker, L.: An integrated treatment program for anorexia nervosa. *Am. J. Psychiatry*, 131:432-436, 1974a.

Liebman, R., Minuchin, S. and Baker, L.: The role of the family in the treatment of anorexia nervosa. *J. Am. Acad. Child Psychiatry*, 13:264-274, 1974b.

Lobb, L.G. and Schaefer, H.H.: Successful treatment of anorexia nervosa through isolation. *Psychol. Reports*, 30:245-246, 1972.

Lucas, A.R., Duncan, J.W. and Piens, V.: The treatment of anorexia nervosa. *Am. J. Psychiatry*, 133:1034-1038, 1976.

MacGregor, G.A., Markandu, N.D., Roulston, J.E., Jones, J.C. and de Wardener, H.E.: Is "idiopathic oedema idiopathic?" *Lancet*, 1:397-400, 1979.

Maloney, M.J.: Hyperalimentation in severe anorexia nervosa. New Research Abstract. Presented at the American Psychiatric Association Annual Meeting. San Francisco, May 7, 1980.

Maloney, M.J. and Farrell, M.K.: Treatment of severe weight loss in anorexia nervosa with hyperalimentation and psychotherapy. *Am. J. Psychiatry,*137:310-314, 1980.

McCullagh, E.P. and Tupper, W.R.: Anorexia nervosa. *Ann. Inter. Med.,* 14:817, 1940.

Maxmen, J.S., Siberfarb, P.M. and Farrell, R.B.: Anorexia nervosa. Practical initial management in a general hospital. *JAMA,* 229:801-803, 1974.

Mayer, J.: Anorexia nervosa. *Postgrad. Med.,* 34:529-534, 1963.

Miesem, M.L. and Wann, F.: Care of adolescents with anorexia nervosa. *Am. J. Nurs.,* 67: 2356-2359, 1967.

Mills, H.: Amitriptyline therapy in anorexia nervosa. *Lancet,* 2:687, 1976.

Mills, I.H., Wilson, R.J., Eden, M.A. and Lines, J.G.: Endocrine and social factors in self-starvation amenorrhea. In: R.F. Robertson and A.T. Proudfoot (Eds.), *Symposium: Anorexia and Obesity.* Royal College of Physicians of Edinburgh, 1973, pp. 31-43.

Minuchin, S., Baker, L., Liebman, R., Milman, L., Rosman, B. and Todd, T.: Anorexia nervosa: Successful application of a family therapy approach. *Pediatr. Res.,* 7:294 (abstract), 1973.

Minuchin, S., Baker, L. Rosman, B., Liebman, R., Milman, L. and Todd, T.: A conceptual model of psychosomatic illness in children: Family organization and family therapy. *Arch. Gen. Psychiatry,* 32:1031-1038, 1975.

Moldofsky, H. and Garfinkel, P.E.: Problems of treatment of anorexia nervosa. *Can. Psychiatr. Assoc. J.,* 19:169-176, 1974.

Moldofsky, H. Jeuniewic, N. and Garfinkel, P.E.: Preliminary report on metoclopramide in anorexia nervosa. In: R.A. Vigersky (Ed.), *Anorexia Nervosa.* New York: Raven Press, 1977, pp. 373-375.

Moore, D.C.: Amitriptyline therapy in anorexia nervosa. *Am. J. Psychiatry,* 134:1303-1304, 1977.

Morgan, H.G. and Russell, G.F.M.: Value of family background and clinical features as predictors of long-term outcome in anorexia nervosa: Four-year follow-up study of 41 patients. *Psychol. Med.,* 5:355-371, 1975.

Munro, A.: Delusions of parasitosis [Letter]. *Br. Med. J.,* 1:1219, 1977.

Needleman, H.L. and Waber, D.: [Letter] Amitryptiline therapy in patients with anorexia nervosa. *Lancet,* 2:580, 1976.

Needleman, H.L. and Waber, D.: The use of amitryptiline in anorexia nervosa. In: R.A. Vigersky (Ed.), *Anorexia Nervosa.* New York: Raven Press, 1977, pp. 357-362.

Neumann, M. and Gaoni, B.: Preferred food as the reinforcing agent in a case of anorexia nervosa. *J. Behav. Ther. & Experimental Psych.,* 6:331-333, 1975.

Ollendick, T.H., Behavioral treatment of anorexia nervosa: A five-year study. *Behav. Mod.,* 3:124-135, 1979.

Pardee, I.: Cachexia (anorexia) nervosa. *M. Clin. North America,* 25:755-773, 1941.

Parker, J.B., Jr., Blazer, D. and Wyrick, L.: Anorexia nervosa: A combined therapeutic approach. *South Med. J.,* 70:448-452, 1977.

Pawlowski, G.J.: Cyproheptadine: Weight-gain and appetite stimulation in essential anorexic adults. *Curr. Ther. Res.,* 18:673-678, 1975.

Paykel, E.S., Mueller, P.S. and De La Vergne, P.: Amitriptyline, weight gain and carbohydrate craving: A side effect. *Br. J. Psychiatry,* 123:501-507, 1973.

Pertschuk, M.J.: Behavior therapy: Extended follow-up. In: R.A. Vigersky (Ed.), *Anorexia Nervosa.* New York: Raven Press, 1977, pp. 305-313.

Pertschuk, M.J., Edwards, N. and Pomerleau, O.F.: A multiple-baseline approach to behavioral intervention in anorexia nervosa. *Behav. Ther.,* 9:368-376, 1978.

Pertschuk, M., Forster, J., Buzby, G. and Mullen, J.L.: Total parenteral nutrition in anorexia nervosa. Syllabus and Scientific Proceedings of the American Psychiatric Association Annual Meeting, San Francisco, 1980, pp. 206-207.

Piazza, E., Piazza, N. and Rollins, N.: Anorexia nervosa: Controversial aspects of therapy. *Compr. Psychiat.,* 21:177-189, 1980.

Plantey, F.: [Letter] Pimozide in treatment of anorexia nervosa. *Lancet,* 1:1105, 1977.

Polivy, J.: Group therapy for anorexia nervosa. *J.Psychiatr. Res. Treatment Eval.,* 3:279-283, 1981.

Poole, A.D. and Sanson, R.W.: A behavioral programme for the management of anorexia nervosa. *Aust. N.Z. J. Psychiatry,* 12:49-53, 1978.

Quaeriteur: [Letter] Treatment of anorexia nervosa. *Lancet,* 1:908, 1971.

Rau, J.H. and Green, R.S.: Compulsive eating: a neurophysiologic approach to certain eating disorders. *Compr. Psychiatry,* 16:223-231, 1975.

Redmond, D.E., Jr., Swann, A. and Heninger, G.R.: [Letter] Phenoxybenzamine in anorexia nervosa. *Lancet,* 2:307, 1976.

Reilly, P.P: Anorexia nervosa. *R.I. Med. J.,* 60:419-422, 1977.

Riding, B.E.J. and Munro, A.: [Letter] Pimozide in monosymptomatic psychosis. *Lancet,* 1: 400-401, 1975.

Robinson, R.G., McHugh, P.R. and Folstein, M.F.: Measurement of appetite disturbances in psychiatric disorders. *J. Psychiatr. Res.,* 12:59-68, 1975.

Rose, J. and Garfinkel, P.E.: A parents' group in the management of anorexia nervosa. *Can. J. Psychiatry,* 25:228-233, 1980.

Rosman, B.L., Minuchin, S., Liebman, R. and Baker, L.: Input and outcome of family therapy in anorexia nervosa. In: J.L. Claghorn (Ed.), *Successful Psychotherapy.* New York: Brunner/Mazel, 1976.

Russell, G.F.M.: Anorexia nervosa. In: J.H. Price (Ed.), *Modern Trends in Psychological Medicine.* London: Butterworths, 1970, pp. 131-164.

Russell, G.F.M.: The management of anorexia nervosa. In: *Symposium on Anorexia Nervosa and Obesity.* Royal College of Physicians in Edinburgh, 1973, p. 43.

Russell, G.F.M.: General management of anorexia nervosa and difficulties in assessing the efficacy of treatment. In: R.A. Vigersky (Ed.), *Anorexia Nervosa.* New York: Raven Press, 1977, pp. 277-289.

Russell, G.F.M.: The current treatment of anorexia nervosa. *Br. J. Psychiat.,* 138:164-166, 1981.

Russell, G.F.M. and Gillies, C.: Investigation and care of patients in a psychiatric metabolic ward. *Nurs. Times,* 60:852-854, 1964.

Russell, G.F.M. and Mezey, A.G.: An analysis of weight gain in patients with anorexia nervosa treated with high calorie diets. *Clin. Sci.,* 23:449-461, 1962.

Ryle, J.A.: Discussion on anorexia nervosa. *Proc. Roy. Soc. Med.,* 32:735-737, 1939.

Sadavoy, J., Silver, D. and Book, H.E.: Negative responses of the borderline to inpatient treatment. *Am. J. Psychother.,* 33:404-417, 1979.

Saleh, J.W. and Lebwohl, P.: Metoclopramide-induced gastric emptying in patients with anorexia nervosa. *Am. J. Gastroenterol.,* 74:127-132, 1980.

Sargant, W.: Leucotomy in psychosomatic disorders. *Lancet,* 2:87-94, 1951.

Schnurer, A.T., Rubin, R.R. and Roy, A.: Systematic desensitization of anorexia nervosa seen as a weight phobia. *J. Behav. Ther. Exptl. Psychiat.,* 4:149-153, 1973.

Schwartzman, J.: Testosterone: A study of its effect on anorexia and underweight in children. *Arch. Paediat.,* 71:99-110, 1954.

Sclare, A.B.: Group therapy for specific psychosomatic problems. In: E.D. Wittkower and H. Warner (Eds.), *Psychosomatic Medicine in Clinical Applications.* Hagerston, Maryland: Harper and Row, 1977, pp. 107-115.

Selvini Palazzoli, M.: *Self-starvation.* London: Chaucer Publishing Co. Ltd., 1974.

Shah, N.M.: A double-blind study on appetite stimulation and weight gain with cyproheptadine as adjunct to specific therapy in pulmonary tuberculosis. *Curr. Med. Pract.,* 12:861-864, 1968.

Sifneos, P.E.: A case of anorexia nervosa treated successfully by leucotomy. *Am. J. Psychiatry,* 109:356-360, 1952.

Silverman, J.: Anorexia nervosa: Clinical observations in a successful treatment program. *J. Pediatr.,* 84:68-73, 1974.

Silverman, J.A.: Anorexia nervosa: clinical and metabolic observations in a successful treatment plan. In: R.A. Vigersky (Ed.), *Anorexia Nervosa.* New York: Raven Press, 1977, pp. 331-339.

Sorlie, P., Gordon, T. and Kannel, W.B.: Body build and mortality: The Framingham study. *JAMA,* 243:1828-1831, 1980.

Sours, J.A: Anorexia nervosa: Nosology, diagnosis, developmental patterns and power-control dynamics. In: G. Caplan and S. Lebovici (Eds.), *Adolescence: Psychological Perspectives.* New York: Basic Books, 1969, pp. 185-212.

Sours, J.A.: *Starving to Death in a Sea of Objects: The Anorexia Nervosa Syndrome.* New York: Jason Aronson, 1980.

Spring, G.K.: Hazards of lithium prophylaxis. *Dis. Nerv. Syst.,* 35:351-354, 1974.

Stafford-Clark, D.: [Letter] Anorexia nervosa. *Br. Med. J.,* 2:446, 1958.

Stonehill, E. and Crisp, A.H.: Psychoneurotic characteristics of patients with anorexia nervosa before and after treatment and at follow-up 4-7 years later. *J. Psychosom. Res.,* 21:189-193, 1977.

Stordy, B.J., Marks, V., Kalucy, R.S. and Crisp, A.H.: Weight gain, thermic effect of glucose and resting metabolic rate during recovery from anorexia nervosa. *Am. J. Clin. Nutr.,* 30: 138-146, 1977.

Streeten, D.H.P.: Idiopathic edema: Pathogenesis, clinical features and treatment. *Metabolism,* 27:353-383, 1978.

Strober, M.: Personality and symptomatological features in young, non-chronic anorexia nervosa patients. *J. Psychosom, Res.,* 24:353-359, 1980.

Stumphauzer, J.S.: Application of reinforcement contingencies with a 23-year-old anorexia patient. *Psychol. Reports,* 24:109-110, 1969.

Stunkard, A.: New therapies for the eating disorders: Behavior modification of obesity and anorexia nervosa. *Arch. Gen. Psychiatry,* 26:391-398, 1972.

Szyrynski, V.: Anorexia nervosa and psychotherapy. *Am. J. Psychother.,* 27:492-505, 1973.

Theander, S.: Anorexia nervosa: A psychiatric investigation of 94 female patients. *Acta Psychiat. Scand.* [Suppl.], 214:1-194, 1970.

Thoma, H.: *Anorexia Nervosa* (Translated by G. Brydone). New York: International Universities Press, 1967.

Thoma, H.: On the psychotherapy of patients with anorexia nervosa. *Bull. Menninger Clinic,* 41:437-452, 1977.

Vandereyeken, W. and Pieters, G.: Short-term weight restoration in anorexia nervosa through operant conditioning. *Nord. Tids. Beteendet,* 7:221-236, 1978.

Vigersky, R.A. and Loriaux, D.L.: The effects of cyproheptadine in anorexia nervosa: A double-blind trial. In: R.A. Vigersky (Ed.), *Anorexia Nervosa.* New York: Raven Press, 1977, pp. 349-356.

Walker, J., Roberts, L., Halmi, K.A. and Goldberg, S.C.: Caloric requirements for weight gain in anorexia nervosa. *Am. J. Clin. Nutr.,* 32:1396-1400, 1979.

Wall, J.H.: Diagnosis, treatment and results in anorexia nervosa. *Am. J. Psychiatry,* 115: 997-1001, 1959.

Weiss, T. and Levitz, L.: Diphenylhydantoin treatment of bulimia. *Am. J. Psychiatry,* 133: 1093, 1976.

Wermuth, B.M., Davis, K.L., Hollister, L.E. and Stunkard, A.J.: Phenytoin treatment of the binge-eating syndrome. *Am. J. Psychiatry,* 134:1249-1253, 1977.

Werry, K.S. and Bull, D.: Anorexia nervosa: A case study using behavior therapy. *J. Am. Acad. Child Psychiatry,* 14:646-651, 1975.

White, J.H. and Schnaultz, N.L.: Successful treatment of anorexia nervosa with imipramine. *Dis. Nerv. Sys.,* 38:567-568, 1977.

Williams, W.: Anorexia nervosa: A somatic disorder. *Br. Med. J.,* 2:190-195, 1958.

Whipple, S.B. and Manning, D.E.: Anorexia nervosa. Commitment to a multifaceted treatment program. *Psychother. Psychosom.,* 30:161-169, 1978.

Wulliemier, F.: Anorexia nervosa: Gauging treatment effectiveness. *Psychosomatics,* 19:497-499, 1975.

# CHAPTER 10

# *Psychotherapy*

Abnormal attitudes toward food and weight may persist in many patients, at times even after a normal weight has been maintained (Hsu, Crisp and Harding, 1979; Morgan and Russell, 1975; Warren, 1968). Dally and Gomez (1979) have observed that these attitudes are "one of the most distressing and long-lasting features of anorexia nervosa . . . and are likely to continue or to recur in situations of crisis for many years" (p. 134-135). Further, social impairment and psychiatric sequelae are not uncommon (see Chapter 12). Even in patients who have had periods of good adjustment, the potential for relapse in a concern (Bemis, 1978; Dally, 1969; Erwin, 1977; Kay and Schapira, 1965; Rowland, 1970; Theander, 1970; Van Buskirk, 1977; Warren, 1968). Results from follow-up reports stress the need for post-hospital treatment and it is generally agreed that psychotherapy is the cornerstone of long-term management of the disorder (Bruch, 1973; Crisp, 1965b; Dally and Gomez, 1979; Goodsitt, 1969; Russell, 1973; Selvini Palazzoli, 1978 and others). However, controlled studies which would conclusively demonstrate the role of such long-term therapies have not yet been conducted.

Many types of psychotherapy have been recommended. Classical psychoanalytic psychotherapy has provided rich formulations for understanding anorexia nervosa (Lorand, 1943; Nicolle, 1939; Waller, Kaufman and Deutsch, 1940) and has continued to be employed by some (Meyer, 1971; Silverman, 1974; Sours, 1974; Szyrynski, 1973; Thoma, 1967), despite opinions that it may be ineffective (Blinder, Freeman and Stunkard, 1970; Bruch, 1973; Dally, 1969; Garner and Bemis, 1982; Moldofsky and Garfinkel, 1974; Ross, 1977; Selvini Palazzoli, 1978; Thoma, 1967). More recent models have been derived from object relations theory and have emphasized ego structural deficits which interfere with separation, individuation, and autonomous functioning (Ehrensing and Weitzman, 1970; Goodsitt, 1969, 1977; Masterson, 1977; Selvini Palazzoli, 1978; Sours, 1969, 1980; Story, 1976). Based on this viewpoint, Bruch (1973) has described a "fact-finding" relationship psychotherapy which emphasizes the development of trust. Simple supportive approaches have been advocated (Farquharson and Hyland, 1966; Frazier, 1965; Groen and Feldman-Toledano, 1966; Russell, 1973; Ryle, 1936) and some have suggested that anorexia nervosa is a relatively innocuous disorder disposed to spontaneous remission (Lesser, Ashenden, Debuskey, Eisenberg, 1960; Farquharson and Hyland, 1966; Ziegler and Sours, 1968). Family therapy has become increasingly popular and has been particularly useful with younger patients (Caille, Abrahamsen, Girolami and Sorbye, 1977; Conrad, 1977; Minuchin, Rosman and Baker, 1978; Selvini Palazzoli, 1978). Russell (1973) has suggested that the most precise approach to an individual patient would be "based on knowledge of the causes of abnormal mechanisms underlying the illness" but at this time the "causation of anorexia nervosa remains unknown" (p.44).

While there is an extensive literature on anorexia nervosa, there have been few detailed descriptions of what is actually done in psychotherapy. Several prominent clinicians have been exceptions in that they have provided valuable insights into the conduct of their therapy of anorexia nervosa (Bruch, 1973, 1978; Crisp, 1970; Masterson, 1977; Minuchin et al., 1978; Selvini Palazzoli 1978). More commonly, the approach by a therapist may be tied to a conventional model of psychotherapy, with no emphasis on the anorexic patient's special problems, such as her unwilling participation in therapy or food and weight issues. It is our impression that the orthodox practice of many traditional methods without attention to these special areas may alienate the patient, frustrate the therapist, and result in treatment failure. At times, the method of treatment of an individual may be more related to the therapist to whom she is referred and the therapist's rigid reliance on a single theoretical framework, than to the needs of the individual. In a timeless analogy, Maslow (1966) has cautioned against operating from a single orientation by observing, "If the only tool you have is a hammer [you tend] to treat everything as if it were a nail" (pp. 15-16).

Consistent with a multidetermined view of the disorder, we will describe a multifaceted approach which considers the divergent needs of a wide range of patients. This approach selectively incorporates elements from existing models (Bruch, Minuchin, Masterson, Selvini Palazzoli) and introduces methods that have evolved within our hospital. It is related to the observation that the "uniformity myth" (Kiesler, 1966) has been applied to anorexic patients, when they are a diverse group for whom no single therapeutic method will prove effective. From a clinical standpoint we have found a treatment approach that incorporates principles from differing therapies most useful when specific strategies are systematically applied to particular problem areas. There has been a growing consensus among psychotherapy researchers and clinicians that the application of several strategies may be preferable to operating from an exclusive theoretical model. Goldfried (1980) has documented this recent trend and has argued that a more powerful psychotherapy results from empirically derived clinical strategies without exclusive allegiance to one theoretical position. This is done by finding meaningful "points of commonality among different orientations" (p. 994).

There have been a few recent reports of the efficacy of combining behavioral, individual, family, and drug therapies in the treatment of anorexia nervosa (Geller, 1975; Hersen and Detre, 1980; Parker, Blazer and Wyrick, 1977). It is our impression that a multidimensional psychotherapy may be extended to the integration of varied theoretical and management principles. A synergistic effect may be obtained when these methods are systemically applied to diverse problem areas. A methodological compatibility is achieved if it is recognized that issues contributing to the disorder vary across this heterogeneous group. Further, each patient experiences many forms of psychological, social, behavioral, and physical dysfunction. As therapy proceeds, new issues may emerge which require a shift in one's clinical approach. While this psychotherapy utilizes concepts from several models, its foundation is a relationship type of psychotherapy, with an emphasis on the evolution of trust, as Bruch (1973) has advocated.

## GENERAL PSYCHOTHERAPEUTIC PRINCIPLES

Before proceeding to the specific components of the psychotherapy, several therapist characteristics and general parameters of treatment will be discussed.

### 1) *Flexibility*

Alexander and French (1946) attributed the "principle of flexibility" to all skilled therapists. The therapist must adapt his therapeutic style to accommodate different patients. As with other disorders, patients with anorexia nervosa differ in maturation, intelligence, ego strengths, personality, level of premorbid functioning and social context. These factors must be considered and reassessed periodically in the determination of the most suitable approach to treatment. Versatility with different treatment methods is a distinct asset. Strategies which are effective in resolving psychological disturbances may be ineffective in promoting weight gain. It is naive, and perhaps dangerous, to assume that simply exposing major psychological conflicts will resolve the eating and weight-related behavior which have come to occupy so much of the anorexic's life. They may have become functionally autonomous or may have taken on new meaning once the starvation syndrome begins to interact with the patient's thoughts and feelings. Moreover, the patient may later develop complaints which differ from the major themes originally responsible for her weight loss. These include anxiety, phobias, social difficulties, depression, sexual dysfunction, and compulsive rituals, among others. Different strategies may be necessary for managing these diverse complaints.

Finally, the therapist's flexible style can be beneficial to the anorexic patient who approaches therapy encased in rigidity. Some patients report benefit from the simple observation that someone, whom they have come to respect, lives without mechanically controlling every aspect of existence.

## 2) *The Sex and Background of the Therapist*

There has been some debate about the preferred sex of the therapist. Selvini Palazzoli (1978) appears to favor a female therapist with whom the patient can develop a "symbolic erotic bond" which she feels can aid in detachment from the mother and acceptance of heterosexuality. Moreover, a female can be a role model for "complete womanhood with whom the patient can identify herself" (p. 126). Selvini Palazzoli (1978) contends that as therapy progresses, the male therapist may come to be seen as "a substitute for a weak and neglectful father figure endowed with negative attributes" (p. 125). Boskind-Lodahl (1976) also recommends a female therapist, based on a feminist perspective that traditional sex-role stereotyping of women is one determinant of the disorder and resolution of this can be inhibited by a man. On the other hand, Rampling (1978) and Szyrynski (1973) both recommend male therapists. Rampling (1978) suggests that the anorexic's "realization that she can attract a man and can gain pleasure from his attentions" is a major force in bringing about therapeutic change. Similarly, Szyrynski (1973) claims that "a male therapist may be probably more effective than a woman" since he may "replace . . . her inadequate father figure" and will not be identified with the patient's "hostile mother" (p. 502). It is our impression that there is no evidence for these generalizations regarding the intrinsic benefits for a particular sex of the therapist. However, for any specific patient it may be important to take the sex of the prospective therapist into consideration when planning a referral.

Selvini Palazzoli (1978) has also specified that the therapist must be a physician since "non-medical psychotherapists . . . are prone to panic at signs of deterioration that would leave the medical man quite unruffled" (p. 125). Clearly, anyone treating an anorexic patient must be closely allied with a physician and an inpatient facility. A physician must be responsible for a consultation and for ongoing evaluation of the patient's physical condition. Non-physician psychotherapists may be responsible for the ongoing psychotherapy. Panic may be avoided if the psychotherapist has some familiarity with the treatment of anorexia nervosa and a clear set of guidelines for the minimum weight and degree of "dietary chaos" which warrant immediate hospitalization. The experience and understanding of the therapist in treating the disorder and a reliable medical liaison eliminate the need for the psychotherapist to be a physician. In any event, both physical and psychological aspects of the disorder must be addressed in therapy.

3) *Duration of Therapy*

The therapist undertaking treatment of an anorexic patient should be prepared to see the patient over a long period of time, often for several years. While some clinicians have reported the success of brief therapies (Minuchin et al., 1978), this has been with younger patients who are less seriously ill. The general consensus is that, while the response to hospitalization is usually favorable (Morgan and Russell, 1975), the subsequent years are difficult and require continuing help (Bruch, 1973; Crisp, 1970; Dally and Gomez, 1979; Russell, 1981). Early in therapy the patient may be overwhelmed by the severity of her emotional difficulties which have been hidden by her weight disturbance. She will require the therapist's reassurance that the commitment to therapy is for as long as it is required. This will be helpful in countering the often unexpressed concern of patients that they will be prematurely abandoned after their weight has been restored. Since they frequently view themselves as emotionally and characterologically without substance, they may not understand why the therapist would choose to engage in psychotherapy once the tangible weight and eating symptoms have been ameliorated. This can lead to a protracted dependence upon concrete symptoms to "legitimize" continued treatment. Complications may be avoided by a realistic appraisal of the duration of therapy with an understanding that other symptoms may emerge when the patient achieves a normal weight.

## THE THERAPEUTIC RELATIONSHIP

A fundamental aspect of psychotherapy is the formation of a significant relationship between therapist and patient. It has been argued that improvement in therapy is predominantly a function of nonspecific factors, such as this positive relationship, rather than the particular orientation and techniques of the clinician (Frank, 1973; Greben, 1977; Marmor, 1971, 1976). Whether it is the relationship and personal qualities of the therapist or specific components of treatment which contribute more to outcome is the subject of debate (Greben, 1977; Parloff, Waskow and Wolfe, 1978; Strupp, 1978).

Freud (1910) had observed the necessity of establishing a "working alliance" in which the therapist was experienced as an understanding and benevolent person. Later he observed the favorable effects of the patient's developing warm and positive feelings toward the therapist (Freud, 1912). The decisive role of establishing a sound therapeutic relationship has been further recognized in approaches as diverse as psychoanalytic psychotherapy (Masterson, 1977), cognitive-behavioral therapy (Beck, Rush, Shaw and Emery, 1979) and behavioral treatment (Rhoads and Feather, 1972; Wilson and Evans, 1978). It is an error to consider that the formation of such a trusting relationship is all there is to therapy. But this relationship is necessary in order for other aspects of the psychotherapy to be effective. The factors which facilitate the development of a positive relationship with an anorexic are not different from those required for other patients. However, there are several points which must be emphasized in approaching these reticent patients.

### 1) *Warmth and Genuineness*

A caring attitude and a genuine concern for the patient are necessary. The anorexic patient must understand that the therapist is not in collusion with family or friends who may simply want her to gain weight. Concern may be conveyed by the therapist's awareness that the problems extend beyond the issues of food and weight. At the same time, the patient's feelings about eating and shape must be acknowledged and openly discussed. A kind, firm but non-authoritarian approach is helpful in inspiring the patient's confidence that the interest is in her own experience and not just her dramatic symptoms. This is where the therapeutic style may be important. Formality and sternness should be avoided since they will elicit anger and fear. Moreover, it is important for the therapist to communicate in clear language and to avoid jargon or simplistic interpretations of symptoms.

On the other hand, inappropriate warmth will be seen by the patient as an insincere attempt to manipulate her into compliance. As observed by Beck et al. (1979), when the degree of warmth is too intense, patients may react negatively by believing that they are "undeserving of such caring" or that they have deceived the therapist since "he appears to like me and I know I am worthless" (p. 46). Excessive warmth may be interpreted by some as seductiveness or deep affection. This would likely evoke panic from a patient who is terrified by far less intense commitments.

## 2) *Understanding and Acceptance*

The therapist must convey a sense of understanding of the patient's experiences. The anorexic usually enters therapy with the conviction that her experiences are idiosyncratic to her and that no one (especially someone without the disorder) could possibly appreciate life from her point of view. The therapist must be aware of the phenomenology of the disorder. As the patient's private world of immediate food and weight fears recedes, more substantive concerns about control and competence emerge. If they are openly acknowledged and understood, the patient is no longer alone in her vigil. An accepting relationship allows the patient to form a meaningful attachment to the therapist which in turn can be the conduit for the development of autonomy.

The idea that the therapeutic attachment is an integral component in the patient's development of a sense of self may initially appear paradoxical. However, when ill, the patient's ability to function independently has generally been prevented by: 1) a sense of ineffectiveness; 2) an inability to identify or trust her own experiences, 3) inappropriate dependence on family; or 4) fears of the expectations of biological maturity. Within an accepting therapeutic relationship, the patient is able to develop confidence in her abilities and self-perceptions, and excessive family bonds become weaker. Thus the accepting atmosphere of the therapeutic relationship ultimately promotes independence. According to Rogers (1967, 1975), the expression of empathic understanding facilitates the development of therapeutic collaboration. It is often difficult to be accepting of a patient who is withdrawn and uncooperative. However, it must be emphasized that the initial hostility or denial is usually a veneer masking overwhelming feelings of inadequacy, fears of engulfment, or fears of one's own rage.

## 3) *Openness and Honesty*

The patient's development of a sense of trust in the therapist and treatment is a central aspect of psychotherapy. This in turn is related to the therapist's being truthful about every detail of the proposed therapy. Anorexics are particularly sensitive to what they view as the inevitable purpose of therapy which is to make them "lose their will" and become fat by whatever means possible. Selvini Palazzoli (1978) notes that:

> The therapist must therefore be perfectly frank and open with them from the start, for only in this way can they gradually be persuaded to collaborate with him. They are extremely sensitive to the least sign of insincerity and circumlocutions; they are always afraid of hidden motives . . . (p. 112).

While this sensitivity may represent a protective reaction to perceived assaults on valued symptoms, it may also denote a more basic vulnerability.

People with anorexia nervosa are usually reluctant to enter any relationship. In previous relationships they have often felt dependent, insignificant, and excessively prone to influence. The structure of the "doctor-patient" interaction invites a recapitulation of earlier relationships in which the anorexic has felt incompetent or subjugated. Whether the fear is envelopment or control, the therapeutic relationship is seen initially as a threat. Since most patients are fearful of interpersonal closeness, they may attempt to incur the therapist's rejection by various sabotaging behaviors. These may take the form of precipitous weight loss, increased vomiting, self-harm, or castigation of the therapist.

The more overt or disruptive behavior is typical of the bulimic subgroup of anorexic patients who experience difficulties with impulse control. Their logic seems to be, "It will be less painful if you reject me now for my unacceptable behavior than later when you realize my intrinsic inadequacy." The rejection resolves fears of both abandonment and of engulfment. The therapist must be tolerant in these instances, while simultaneously establishing limits. Occasionally, genuine but "dramatic" expressions of concern such as scheduling an emergency appointment or responding to a late evening telephone call will have impact on the patient and provide early signs of the therapist's trustworthiness. These may be followed by the gradual establishment of more firm limits.

While there are numerous obstacles interfering with the patient's willingness to enter the therapeutic relationship, there are also pitfalls from the therapist's perspective. Cohler (1977) has suggested that psychotherapy with anorexic patients "leads to intense emotional reactions in the therapist; perhaps the most intense encountered in a therapeutic relationship" (p. 353). He has viewed the capacity of the therapist to bear the feelings of "hopelessness, manipulation and powerlessness" to be important aspects of the therapeutic process.

Similarly, Selvini Palazzoli (1978) has observed that the anorexic's behavior can arouse "strong feelings of aggression in the therapist" and that these become manifest as "therapeutic pessimism" or even punitive forms of treatment. This is not unlike the feelings used to describe the therapist's reaction to the "borderline" patient (Book, Sadavoy and Silver, 1978; Masterson, 1977). Anorexics have been repeatedly described as manipulative (Amdur, Tucker, Detre and Markhus, 1969; Frazier, 1965; Maxmen, Siberfarb and Farrell, 1974; Rowland, 1970; Schlemmer and Barnett, 1977; Story, 1976) or even as malingerers (Hawkings, Jones, Sim and Tibbetts, 1956), which no doubt has led to the malevolent treatment occasionally reported (Blue, 1979; Quaeritur, 1971). Indeed, they display considerable ingenuity in subverting efforts of others to help.

The therapist should not interpret this as a personal insult since it reflects the patient's terror at weight gain and her unwillingness to accept or trust other people. The therapist must be able to tolerate these interactions and patiently wait for the more authentic expressions of the patient's confusion and helplessness. Recognition that the patient's behavior is an attempt at self-protection and not a personal attack can provide the therapist with some solace. Following the advice of Chessick (1968) and Sadavoy, Silver and Book (1981) with borderline patients, it is important for the therapist to become aware of potentially destructive feelings toward the patient and the possible need to make a referral or to deal with the matter in supervision.

## THE INITIAL PHASE OF PSYCHOTHERAPY

Psychotherapy has been defined by Strupp (1978) as "an interpersonal process designed to bring about modifications of feelings, cognitions, attitudes and behavior which have become troublesome to the person seeking help" (p. 3). Accordingly, the circumstances surrounding the initiation of treatmeant of anorexia nervosa differ from those of the more typical psychiatric patient who readily admits to psychological discomfort. It is usually not the anorexic patient but her relatives who define the "problem" and seek professional help. The period preceding the initial meeting has generally been filled with family conflict in which the patient has ultimately been outvoted. Thus, the prospective patient arrives for this appointment under considerable duress and responds by remaining unconcerned, negativistic, or defiant (Bemis, 1978; Bruch, 1973; Crisp, 1970; Goldberg et al., 1977; King, 1963; Thoma, 1972; Warren, 1968.) The therapist is often viewed as the executor of the familial wishes and the patient is usually prepared to resist. Details of this initial consultation have also been described in Chapter 9.

Initially the task is to understand as much as possible about the patient and her family, while also conveying the attitude that the patient's beliefs and feelings are genuine for her at the time (Garner and Bemis, 1982). They should not be dismissed as senseless or bizarre but rather viewed as manifestations of problems that have to be solved. It is often useful to begin by taking a complete weight history to determine the patient's current position in her "weight range." This should usually be conducted with the patient alone in order to emphasize the recognition that her particular problems are separate and unique. When the denial of symptoms or resistance is marked, the consultant must proceed slowly in gathering information about the general circumstances in the patient's life. Extending the discussion to issues other than weight helps the patient to see that the therapist's interests extend beyond the immediate concerns shared by friends and relatives. At the end of this initial session, the patient should be seen with her parents or spouse, and both familial concerns related to the patient and general patterns of functioning can be discussed.

If the patient is quite emaciated but relatively cooperative, it may be useful to describe in detail the effects of starvation (see Chapter 1) derived from studies with normal volunteers (Keys, Brozek, Henschel, Mickelsen and Taylor, 1950). Many of these symptoms may have been quite distressing, including dry skin, hair loss, lanugo, paresthesiae, sensitivity to noise, and hypothermia. Psychological disturbances such as anxiety, depression, labile moods, feelings of inadequacy, fatigue, food preoccupations, poor concentration, episodes of bulimia, and social withdrawal are also heightened by starvation and are felt to be unpleasant by the patient.

Patients usually do not associate these symptoms with a common cause and the description of the "starvation state" helps them integrate their experiences. Moreover, describing these symptoms as "physiologically derived" may in part relieve the patient of guilt surrounding the development of what she may have seen as unacceptable "psychiatric symptoms." Finally, the therapist's sympathetic acknowledgement of the patient's suffering in other areas reassures her that his interests are for her general well-being and not simply her weight. Slowly a collaborative atmosphere is created in which both the patient and therapist are allies against symptoms of the disorder itself rather than opponents over the single issue of eating.

As Crisp (1970) advises, it is often appropriate in an initial interview to discuss in a general manner the meaning of a "sub-pubertal" weight, as a means of avoiding frightening issues associated with a normal adolescence. The patient is often able to identify vague experiences of adolescence as a major threat which somehow appeared to be "resolved" (although replaced by conflicts of a different variety) once her weight fell below her critical "menstrual weight" threshold. This can be illustrated by posing a hypothetical question: "Although I understand that you would prefer not to gain weight, if you were to gain, at what point would you begin to experience panic?" Most patients have not considered the question in this way but are able to identify that they would begin to panic at a particular weight. This weight may often represent the threshold for return of menses and the normalization of their hypothalamic-pituitary function.

In responding to the question, some patients seize the opportunity to elaborate upon fears of "growing up," an event for which they feel unprepared. The interpretation of this phobic response to demands of adulthood and the avoidance of maturity through the reversal of its hormonal substrate is a concept that many patients readily appreciate as having personal meaning. However, this is not at the core of every patient's psychopathology, and is by no means a useful exercise for all.

Once the patient displays some confidence in the relationship, it may be possible to explore the fact that weight loss has become a barometer for her self-evaluation. Weight loss has provided a tangible accomplishment for an individual who has for some time experienced a diffuse sense of ineffectiveness. The belief, "if only my weight were a little lower, then I would feel happier," is repeatedly applied. The reading on the scale dictates how the anorexic will feel during the remainder of the day. Although they tell themselves that the "new" goal will be sustaining, most patients are aware that no weight is really low enough, for often it is the loss that becomes rewarding. As the patient's weight declines and further weight loss becomes more difficult, the process that originally provided frequent rewards becomes an unforgiving purveyor of punishment. Fear and guilt become the major determinants of her efforts.

With the bulimic patient, a description of the vicious cycle of bingeing and vomiting that has developed both exposes the paradoxical nature of the behavior (she has become a slave to something which was intended to provide freedom) and demonstrates an awareness of her suffering. Here, vomiting or laxative abuse began as deliberate attempts to control weight. The process often rapidly escalates to the point where vomiting follows every meal. Vomiting, which initially had been the strategy for gaining control, becomes out of control in the sense that the person can no longer *choose* to stop. With this type of explanation most patients are willing to accept the idea that weight gain will be required and that the bulimia-vomiting cycle must be broken. They are more receptive if these are not presented as ends in themselves but rather as the necessary means by which access to significant individual and family issues can be gained. Some patients will maintain that no such psychopathology exists, and this is usually best approached by the therapist's acceptance of this possibility while emphasizing that starvation must be corrected because of its effects upon the thinking, emotions and the entire personality of the patient (Russell, 1981; Strober, 1980).

Specific aspects of psychotherapy are described below. These borrow extensively from the essential features of psychotherapy in general (Bruch, 1974; Frank, 1973; Marmor, 1971, 1976; Rogers, 1967, 1975; Strupp, 1973) but have been adapted to the specific requirements of the anorexic patient. Again, because of the heterogeneity within the disorder, not all elements are equally relevant for all patients. It must be emphasized again that this relationship psychotherapy can proceed and be beneficial to the patient only if the starvation symptoms are ameliorated and she is maintaining a previously agreed upon minimal weight.

## SYMPTOMS AS PLEASURE

The anorexic's rigid dietary control is particularly resistant to treatment because it is simultaneously under the control of a "fear of fatness" and a "drive for thinness." While these appear to be reciprocals of the same motive, they are partially independent forces determining the anorexic's obdurate clinging to her symptoms.

Crisp (1965a, 1978) has described the fear of fatness as a "weight phobia" in which the fear of weight gain reflects avoidance of various demands and expectations of biological maturity. However, the anorexic's behavior is motivated by more than phobic avoidance. There is also an important element of positive reinforcement for her increasing thinness. For the anorexic, weight loss not only holds the solution for avoiding feared circumstances, but is also usually fueled by the gratification obtained from limiting intake and losing weight. Restraint and tangible success in weight loss provide pleasure from the resulting sense of control and accomplishment. It is an exceptional achievement earning the individual distinction for overcoming her biological urges. Selvini Palazzoli (1978) has observed that for the anorexic "every victory over the flesh is a sign of greater control over one's biological impulses" (p. 74). Despite the agony of physical deprivation, the need to attain a sense of virtue through self-restraint and impulse control is the positive force which drives the anorexic. Selvini Palazzoli (1978) has written that the rejection of food is a "magic key to greater power" and a search for "freedom, beauty, intelligence and morality" (Selvini Palazzoli, 1978, pp. 72-73).

Weight gain brings loss of these qualities. This was captured by one young patient who tearfully announced, once she had reluctantly agreed to gain weight, that the therapist had better be prepared to offer compensation for her anticipated loss of mastery. Thus, the anorexic will be resistant to relinguish her sense of power and control. Moreover, the therapist must recognize that unlike other disorders in which avoidance behavior plays a major role, the anorexic does not usually want to be relieved of her anxiety around food and fear of weight gain. For her these aversive experiences are *functional* (Garner and Bemis, 1982) in that the threat they hold assists her in maintaining the higher-order virtue of a low weight. The anxiety aids in the difficult task of oral self-restraint, despite voracious hunger.

The basic pleasure and gratification derived from symptoms distinguish anorexia nervosa from the phobic or depressive disorders. In this sense it is similar to the addictions or sexual fetishes which are maintained by their own potent reinforcement. The positive and negative contingencies controlling the anorexic's behavior must be considered in the approach to treatment. The fundamental premise that thinness is virtuous is an exaggeration and distortion which the patient has applied in a self-destructive manner. This must be discussed gradually and gently with the recognition that this assumption may be the cornerstone of her current belief system.

Treatment must promote the patient's development of alternative sources of pleasure. The patient's understanding of pleasure is often in terms of positive self-evaluations which accrue from self-discipline and superlative performance standards. Mahoney (1974) has described a "cycle of inflationary self-evaluation in which replication of past excellence becomes routinely expected and future endeavors must always set new highs" (pp. 155-156). Patients must learn that positive self-evaluation may be derived from enjoyment of small, personal activities, and not simply from exceptional performances. They may be encouraged to strive for a balance between competence and the liberation of relaxed "standards." As in so many areas in their treatment and lives, learning and accepting "in-betweens" become very important. This involves internalization of new norms from the therapist, a long and difficult process.

## REALITY-ORIENTED FEEDBACK

According to Goldfried (1980), "direct feedback" from the therapist is a clinical strategy common to many different psychotherapies. Depending on the theoretical framework, it is awarded varying degrees of emphasis or acknowledgement for its role in promoting change. Moreover, the substance and the format for the feedback differ in accordance with the particular orientation. Nevertheless, the principle of helping patients become more aware of what they are doing, feeling, and thinking in various situations is fundamental to psychodynamic, behavioral, cognitive, and humanistic approaches.

A major goal of psychotherapy with anorexic patients involves assisting them in the correction of their distorted sense of reality. Faulty thinking and beliefs are applied to the world around them as well as to themselves. While the therapist must help the patient to change these misinterpretations of reality, he must also be cautious not to undermine her confidence that her thoughts and feelings emanate from within. Therefore, the therapist must provide feedback to the patient without negating her own experiences. Faulty thinking, erroneous beliefs, and misperceptions about her body must be identified and labeled as such, while at the same time the patient must be encouraged to trust that her views and perceptions are real for her at this point in time.

The focal point in providing feedback to the anorexic patient is her cognitive distortions. Clinical reports have identified cognitive distortions in the anorexic's thinking (Bliss and Branch, 1960; Bruch, 1973, 1977, 1978; Galdston, 1974; Goodsitt, 1977; Rampling, 1978; Selvini Palazzoli, 1978); these have infrequently been measured objectively (Ben-Tovim, Hunter and Crisp, 1977; Crisp and Fransella, 1972) and only rarely have there been recommendations on how these distortions may be modified in psychotherapy (Beck and Emery, 1979; Hauserman and Lavin, 1977; Hersen and Detre, 1980).

Bruch (1973, 1977, 1978) has repeatedly emphasized that the process of psychotherapy involves the gradual but deliberate relabeling of "misconceptions and errors in the patient's thinking." She concludes that psychotherapy:

> . . . is a process during which erroneous assumptions and attitudes are recognized, defined, and challenged so that they can be abandoned. It is important to proceed slowly and to use concrete small events as episodes for illustrating certain false assumptions or illogical deductions. The whole work needs to be done by reexamining actual aspects of living, by using relatively small events as they come up (1978, pp. 143-144).

She offers specific advice to the therapist who:

> . . . must pay minute attention to the discrepancies in a patient's recall of the past and to the way she perceives or misinterprets current events, to which she will respond inappropriately. The therapist must be honest in confirming or correcting what the patient communicates (1978, p. 136).

Garner and Bemis (1982) have proposed and described in detail an approach to psychotherapy of anorexia nervosa. This is based on cognitive-behavioral principles delineated by Beck and his colleagues for the treatment of depressive and phobic disorders (Beck, 1967, 1976; Beck and Emery, 1979; Beck et al, 1979; Hollon and Beck, 1979). These principles have been adapted specifically to anorexia nervosa so that the patient learns to identify, evaluate, and change faulty thinking patterns and erroneous beliefs. Beck (1976) has identified various types of logical errors in the thinking of depressives and phobics. While anorexics may commit many of these same errors, they also display other distortions (see Chapter 6). The most common reasoning errors observed clinically in anorexic patients are dichotomous thinking, personalization, and superstitious thinking.

## 1) *Dichotomous or All-or-none Reasoning*

The anorexic patient often thinks in absolute terms; splitting is a term commonly used to describe this phenomenon. Rigid attitudes and behaviors are not restricted to weight issues. Careers, studying, and sports are also pursued fanatically. Extreme attitudes which reappear in areas other than weight must be addressed in psychotherapy. The anorexic, for example, often believes that such characteristics as self-control, independence, conflict avoidance, social approval, and self-confidence must be completely and continuously maintained. This leads to idealized and unattainable notions of happiness, self-confidence, and success.

The dichotomous reasoning may also be expressed as an absolute need for certainty, and the perception of any deviation from complete predictability becomes equivalent to chaos. The outcome of potentially unpredictable events is feared and met by attempts to impose rigid control through compulsive "rules" and obsessional or superstitious thinking. Any change is difficult because it is seen in such extreme terms. Many anorexics complain that they are apprehensive at the change associated with the simple passing of time, particularly if it is unstructured. The future cannot be completely predicted or controlled and this is a source of considerable distress.

Psychotherapy must gradually help the patient develop realistic expectations and a sense that there are alternatives to the polarization of experiences in different areas of her life. She must learn to question her own assumption that, if she moves a small distance on a continuum of change, she has assumed the opposite position to that held earlier. The patient must slowly begin to recognize when she is using this style of thinking with its maladaptive consequences, and how to question its validity by examining contradictory evidence from her own experiences. One 22-year-old patient provided an illustration of dichotomous reasoning in the evaluation of her parents. Initially she praised them unconditionally for their loving devotion to their children. During one visit to her parents' home, the patient was overwhelmed by panic and guilt at the realization that her mother was not completely altruistic and wise (splitting). This patient painfully recognized only then that her mother did not accept shortcomings in any of her children but preferred to deny the presence of any faults. She discovered that her panic related to her evaluation of her mother in totally "good" or "bad" terms. Any awareness of fault meant complete rejection and a fear of retaliation. She found it difficult to perceive that both she and her mother possessed a mixture of positive and negative qualities. The revelation was not the end of this patient's tendency to view her mother (or herself) in binary terms but it was an experience that could be referred to again during the course of psychotherapy.

Dichotomous reasoning can also be observed in patients' vacillation between overcompliance and stubbornness with an inability to assume a more moderate position. Accomplishments are approached in extreme terms. A major therapeutic task lies in helping the patient to understand that it is self-defeating to approach every aspect of life in "all-or-nothing" terms.

### 2) Personalization and Self-reference

Anorexic patients often display the egocentric conviction that they are the focus of events which others would describe as impersonal. The patient believes that her behavior is the center of other people's attention. While this may be an understandable outgrowth from an enmeshed family environment, it is often applied to situations which are clearly inappropriate. For example, one patient had become virtually housebound because she believed that when she would walk down the street, complete strangers might notice that she was not "skinny." Another patient expressed a repeated fear in groups that people were thinking critically of her because she had not made significant career advancements. She would interpret their breaking eye contact with her as a sign of rejection. Personalization is often a mechanism by which the patient infers disapproval from others. It becomes another vehicle for self-degradation although, paradoxically, it is based on the somewhat grandiose notion that other people are intensely interested in her. It is a surprise for the individual to discover that people are not concerned with every detail of her existence and a relief that it is not necessary to maintain superlative standards in order to satisfy these others.

Again, the strategy of reality-oriented feedback is the means by which the therapist may assist the patient in overcoming her proclivity for personalization and self-reference. The patient has to learn to identify and evaluate the evidence underlying the assumptions that her behavior or appearance has a significant effect on others. Sometimes, by the technique of "decentering," the therapist can aid the patient's awareness of how infrequently *she* actually attends as closely to the conduct of others as she imagines they do to her own.

Decentering involves applying the same rigorous standards to other people as to one's own behavior. Does the patient spend an inordinate amount of time thinking about the weight or credentials of people whom she meets casually? Does her admiration of friends or acquaintances directly correspond to their weights? Feedback in terms of acknowledgement of change is particularly important. The therapist must try to be aware of small progressions in the patient's thinking and acknowledge her advancement. Commenting on the spontaneous emergence of her own realization and resistance to this type of thinking reinforces the process. This area of difficulty is often deeply ingrained and resists change; however, within a strong therapeutic alliance and after prolonged therapy, patients can use far less personalization.

### 3) *Superstitious Thinking*

The magical belief that there is a cause-effect relationship between unrelated events is common among anorexic patients. They will often assume that every last calisthenic in their exercise regimen must be completed or they will gain weight. One patient developed an elaborate set of exercise rituals in which various situations required her to perform specific rigorous exercise routines. Passing post boxes or street lamps had to be followed by jogging for one block. Initial reduction of her exercise could only be accomplished by mapping "safe" routes that were poorly lit with inadequate postal service. Despite a clear understanding that laxatives will not greatly affect the absorption of calories, another patient continued to ingest laxatives because of her superstition that, "Not using them may promote real weight gains (other than rehydration) through some mysterious process." Laxative abuse served another magical function for this patient who believed that laxatives literally absolved her of guilt from overeating.

As with superstitious behavior in general, the rituals are designed to reduce or delay either specific, or more often obscure but ominous consequences. According to Bandura (1978), avoidance behavior is predominantly under the influence of cognitive control in which "behavior is so powerfully controlled by bizarre internal contingencies that neither the beliefs nor the accompanying actions are much affected even by extremely punishing environmental consequences" (p. 346). Like other avoidance behavior, superstitious rituals are resistant to extinction since the thoughts governing them insulate the patient from information and experience that could change the beliefs. Superstitious thinking, like other types of faulty thinking, is resistant to change but is slowly corrected by the therapist's providing feedback to the patient as well as by reinforcing her own discovery of these distortions.

## 4) *Underlying Assumptions*

Beck et al. (1979) have described maladaptive and underlying or "silent" assumptions which organize and determine much of the depressed patient's disturbed thinking. These differ from faulty beliefs in that the basic assumptions are more general guidelines from which many of the more specific attitudes are derived. They may not be verbalized directly in therapy but may be inferred from the patterns of thinking that reemerge over time. Many of the underlying assumptions identified by Beck and his colleagues with depressed patients are also prominent in the thinking of anorexic patients (for example, "It is crucial to my happiness that I will be liked by everybody" or "My self-worth as a person depends on how other people regard me") (Beck et al., 1979, p. 80).

However, other underlying assumptions have been specifically related to anorexia nervosa. Most important is the idea that "weight, shape, or thinness can serve as the sole or predominant referent for inferring personal value or self-worth" (Garner and Bemis, 1982). Other assumptions common in anorexia nervosa are:

1) Complete self-control and discipline are desirable;
2) fat is intrinsically bad;
3) high calorie foods are intrinsically harmful to health;
4) perfect performance is necessary for self-fulfillment;
5) one *must* live up to the expectations of others; and
6) parents are beyond criticism.

Modifying basic assumptions must be done cautiously with sensitivity to the fact that these principles are often central to the patient's sense of identity. The therapist should not challenge these values prematurely and therapy should never degenerate into arguments over values. Bruch has observed the fundamental nature of these assumptions and the patience required in their modifications:

Patients will adhere to their distorted concepts, the false reality with which they have lived, since it represents their only way of having experiences and communicating; they will let go of this only slowly and reluctantly. Their whole life is based on certain faulty assumptions that need to be exposed and corrected (1978, p. 136).

As these assumptions reappear over the course of therapy, a number of different strategies may be employed to help the patient investigate their validity. These have been described elsewhere (Garner and Bemis, 1982) and may be summarized as follows:

1) The therapist may assist the patient in gathering supporting or refuting evidence for a specific assumption. Its advantages and disadvantages may be weighed and its inconsistency with other important values may be illustrated.
2) The therapist may ask the patient to appy her "rules" to other people. It may be helpful to have her assess others' value strictly in terms of weight and see if this corresponds to her global evaluation of their effectiveness. Has the patient noticed the small fluctuations in the therapist's weight? If she had, would it have had significant implications?
3) Various tests of the patient's assumptions may be devised and given as homework assignments.
4) The mere articulation of the underlying assumptions may reduce their potential impact on the patient's thinking.

This process bears considerable similarity to the feedback recommended by Bruch (1973) but is not dependent on a particular model of pathogenesis. We believe that the deficits observed in anorexia nervosa are multidetermined and that an essential ingredient in successful psychotherapy is the corrective feedback rather than the specific model of causality ascribed to by the psychotherapist. While the aim of this portion of therapy is to provide the patient with feedback, in actual fact the therapist's reactions to the patient and the patient's transference responses interfere with this process. As for distortions in other areas, repeated clarification may be required to deal with transference distortions, particularly as they interfere with therapy (Masterson, 1978).

## AFFECTIVE EXPRESSION

Anorexic patients frequently experience a serious deficit in the area of affective recognition and expression. While it may apply to either group, this is more marked in restricting than bulimic patients. The deficit ranges from "not knowing how they feel" (Bruch, 1973, p. 338) to a lack of trust in and a fear of affective and other internal states. Primary goals in psychotherapy involve facilitating the patient's identification of these internal experiences and helping her overcome the distorted beliefs which inhibit their appropriate expression. This is in accord with Bruch's (1973) recommendations that the therapist confirm genuine expressions of inner feelings, while at the same time be "honest in labeling misconceptions and errors" in the patient's thinking.

Eliciting authentic feeling states must be distinguished from telling the patient what she is *really* thinking or feeling. Interpreting the symbolic meaning or redefining the patient's experience is often accepted without question, for the patient may prefer to rely on the therapist's expertise to answer confusing questions. Classical psychoanalysis has often been criticized for unwittingly validating the idea that the patient really does not know how she feels or what unconscious forces motivate her behavior. Bruch (1974) has argued that it provides a repetition of previous interactions in which others have appeared to know the patient's feelings better than she does herself. The patient's unconditional acceptance of interpretations further confirms the basic mistrust in her own ability to identify feelings or thoughts as emanating from within.

The addition of "parameters" of therapy, as described by Masterson (1978) and others, is necessary to make the psychodynamic approach meaningful to these patients; they stress that the therapist must be fairly active and that the purely passive mirroring therapy is countertherapeutic. On the other hand, some approaches such as Gestalt (Perls, 1969), experiential (Gendlin, 1973), or Encounter (Schultz, 1973) therapies, which confront, interpret, and implore patients to express their feelings, can often be devastating and well beyond the immediate capabilities of the anorexic.

Promoting affective identification or expression must be done gradually and somewhat indirectly. Asking the patient to relate her emotional reactions to a particular situation may be met by a blank stare or a counterquestion such as, "How should I feel?" Often the patient will respond with what she assumes to be the proper or accepted emotional reaction. If she is sufficiently skilled socially, she may be able to discern the therapist's expectations and respond accordingly. However, distortions can often be observed in these contrived expressions. They may lack congruence with other nonverbal behavior, contradict other important aspects of the situation, or simply seem unreal.

When there is denial or absence of seemingly appropriate affect, the circumstances and the patient's thinking should be explored in greater detail. Evidence from the patient's description will begin to emerge which indicates the feeling state is not being recognized. Here it is particularly critical to proceed slowly and to allow the patient to learn to identify the emotions herself. Again, Bruch's (1973) advice is instructive: let the patient discover her inner feelings and "say it first." The continued queries begin to elicit "incipient feelings" which should be acknowledged and confirmed.

This process is illustrated by a 24-year-old bulimic patient who was dieting in competition with her youthful 45-year-old mother. The patient was compelled to eat while her mother adhered to her diet. The patient recognized the hypocrisy, which led to feelings of anger. These were rapidly vitiated because of the contradicting belief that her mother was a flawless, benevolent person who had in mind only the best interests of her starving daughter. The inconsistency was resolved by the patient's concluding that she must not have experienced the anger. Her reasoning was: a) I could only become angry at my mother if she were wrong; b) my mother is not wrong; c) therefore, I must not be angry. Her very experience of the emotion was insufficient for validation because it had to be morally proper. By going over the situation in detail and untangling her logic, she was able to begin to recognize her feelings.

The expression of sadness was completely unacceptable within another patient's family. Her father was always optimistic and her mother masked her own unhappiness with superficiality and conviviality. The patient's attempts to convey her grief were not acknowledged. She remembered the warning in the family maxim: "Laugh and the whole world laughs with you — cry and you cry alone." She idealized her parents and defined her own worth in terms of their acceptance. She suppressed her sadness and denied its legitimacy. Its continual presence made her feel "unreal and alone." She frequently wished that she could return to her prepubescent years when she had felt content. Dieting became an apparent solution to her dilemma. Others commented on how she looked younger as the weight came off and she reported experiencing herself as younger. Further, while her parents were unable to accept her sadness as a legitimate expression, they displayed great concern over the weight loss. This patient reasoned that the emaciation justified her involvement in treatment. Her secret hope was that psychotherapy would indirectly relieve her depression. The initial focus of psychotherapy was the reinforcement, acknowledgment, and acceptance of the patient's rather diffident signs of depression. After she was able to acknowledge its legitimacy, the issues contributing to this persistent mood could be resolved.

In other words, a crucial component of psychotherapy with most patients involves assisting them in identifying accurately their affective states and in promoting a sense of acceptance of these as genuine. Later in therapy the patient may learn to reduce the discomfort created by these emotions.

These goals are gradually achieved through the observations of inconsistencies, incongruities, and inappropriate reactions from the patient to everyday events. These almost invariably come from the patient's trying to respond as she "should," according to the expectations of others. Confirming and reinforcing emotions which seem to be unadulterated expressions of her own experience are essential. A number of specific clinical strategies may also be useful. Through the use of analogies and hypothetical situations, the therapist may be able to help the patient see that her reactions in a specific situation are distorted. She may recognize that in a hypothetical sense anger is acceptable, but only for other people. As therapy progresses, the patient may be encouraged to express "unacceptable" emotions toward the therapist and learn that this does not lead to retaliation or rejection. Finally, the therapist should serve as a model by expressing appropriate affect openly.

### RE-INTERPRETATION OF BODY-IMAGE MISPERCEPTION

Bruch (1973) has written that "patients may gain weight for a variety of reasons but no real or lasting cure is achieved without correction of body image misperception" (p. 90). The assumption appears to be that this aspect of the anorexic's experience is "self-correcting" once more fundamental psychological issues have been resolved. While this is likely true for many patients, specific therapeutic approaches to the patient's self-misperception may accelerate the process.

In a clinical report, Gottheil, Backup and Cornelison (1969) claimed to have successfully treated one anorexic patient's denial of thinness by repeatedly confronting her with motion pictures of her emaciated body. We have found attempts at direct modification of the patient's unrealistic self-perceptions to be unproductive. An alternative to directly altering these misperceptions is to change how patients *interpret* what they claim to experience (Garner and Bemis, 1982; Garner and Garfinkel, 1981). While one of the general goals of therapy is to help the patient develop a sense of trust in her internal perceptions and feelings, the approach that is initially taken with regard to body image is in opposition to this. Early in treatment, the patient's perceptions and beliefs are distorted yet defended tenaciously. By providing the patient with objective evidence for her misperception of size and its fundamental relationship to the disorder, the therapist can encourage the patient to reattribute her refractory self-perception to her illness, rather than to the stimulus properties of her own body. By repeatedly isolating this as a distorted perception/conception, patients begin to question their subjective experiences in this area and ultimately to function despite it.

The patient is encouraged in psychotherapy to generate counterarguments which allow her to override or check the perception of herself as fat and thus not respond by self-defeating dietary restraint. Examples of reattributions are "I know that a cardinal feature of anorexia nervosa is misperception of my own size so I can expect to feel fat" or "When I try to estimate my own dimensions, I am like a color-blind person trying to coordinate his own wardrobe. I will have to rely on objective data or someone I can trust to determine my actual size." Since such statements help patients to *understand* their experiences, rather than deny or diminish them, they are unlikely to provoke confrontations and defiance. Encouraging the patient temporarily to avoid looking in mirrors or to refrain from wearing tight clothing can help reduce intrusive thoughts about shape. An approximate weight goal range of four-to-five pounds of at least 90% of average (using population norms) is established early in therapy. This "thin-normal" weight is associated with objective "health" (Sorlie, Gordon and Kannel, 1980) and can become part of the patient's anchor in a sea of uncertainty about weight and shape. The therapist too becomes an "ambassador to reality" about body size, as well as many other areas of confusion, within the context of a trusting relationship.

## SELF-CONCEPT: SELF-ESTEEM AND PERSONAL TRUST

The concept of "self" has acquired two rather distinct meanings within modern psychological theories (Hall and Lindsay, 1970). In the first instance the self is viewed as an object, and a person's self-concept is reflected by the attitudes, feelings, and perceptions which constitute the individual's evaluation of himself (self-esteem). The second meaning identifies the self as a set of active processes such as perceiving, thinking, and remembering which contribute to personal trust (Hall and Lindsay, 1970). The anorexic patient presents psychological disturbances in both spheres of functioning.

### 1) *Self-esteem*

In many instances, the anorexic patient experiences herself as incompetent in personal and social performance. At some point the anorexic arrives at the idea that weight control will alleviate her self-doubts. This is only one aspect of her more general idea that it is justified to infer her self-worth or essence from her level of performance on specific tasks. However, because of unrealistic performance standards, only exceptional behavior is seen as deserving of a favorable evaluation. Excellence becomes expected and leads to a "cycle of inflationary self evaluation" (Mahoney, 1974) in which performance only "satisfies" when it is superlative.

Weight loss becomes a criterion for inferring self-worth, partly because the evidence for success is objective. Daily acheivement goals may be easily translated into a "number" which must be adjusted downward once its reinforcing power has faded. Psychotherapy must help the patient recognize the limitations of the standards that she has employed to determine her self-worth. To some degree, her self-evaluation must become disconnected from her everyday performance. She must learn that reaching one's potential for excellence is not the requirement for self-acceptance.

Many patients have relied solely on acceptance from others as the criterion for positive self-evaluation, prior to the acquisition of the weight and exercise standard. In these instances psychotherapy is aimed at reinforcing the patient's slow discovery of her own interests and gently challenging performances which seem to be strictly the product of others' expectations. Correcting the perception of worth as a direct product of a quantitative concept of accomplishment is a formidable task because it is contradicted by many messages within our performance-oriented culture.

After dropping university courses that were only taken to please others, one patient began pursuing more leisurely activities for the first time in years. With newfound self-assurance she stated that "some people may think of me as lazy, but I prefer to think of myself as a reformed workaholic." Helping the patient to develop an awareness of unjustified expectations and extreme self-criticism is important. Encouraging self-acceptance despite fallibility is a fundamental role for the psychotherapist working with a patient with poor self-esteem. A self-disclosing therapist makes himself more human and aids the process of self-acceptance in the patient by reducing the idealization of the therapist.

Finally, the patient's sense of helplessness and incompetence can be ameliorated by encouraging her efforts at mastery in areas that she has been frightened of approaching. Occasionally parents have subtly reinforced dependence and conveyed the message that independence-seeking will be inevitably met by failure or even rejection. This may result in the patient's sense of inadequacy and reluctance to pursue goals other than those that are expected by others. These must be countered over a lengthy period of time by support for assertiveness, independence, and reasonable self-expression.

## 2) *Personal Trust*

It has been repeatedly observed that the patient experiences little confidence or trust in the validity of her thinking, feeling, and perception

(Andersen, 1979; Bruch, 1962, 1973, 1978; Frazier, 1965; Goodsitt, 1977; Selvini Palazzoli, 1978; Sours, 1980; Story, 1976). The clinical manifestations of the patient's perceptual and conceptual confusion have been outlined earlier, as have the therapist's strategies for helping the patient develop an awareness of the reliability of her own self-perceptions. The preoccupation with self-control, which is manifest by exaggerated self-discipline and a morbid fear of loss of control, is typical of the confusion surrounding internal functioning. These themes must be met by the therapist by the use of feedback designed to reinforce authentic expressions of internal state (as opposed to feelings that one "should" experience). Fears of loss of control must be met by the temporary imposition of external supports or controls. This may involve hospitalization at one extreme or simply the structuring of the environment and time at the other extreme.

Family therapy sessions are instrumental with many patients in altering the interactional patterns which have come to support the patient's lack of reliance on her own thoughts, emotions, perceptions, and behavior. The family's overinvolvement not only inhibits the development of autonomy but also endorses the patient's sense that her own functioning is inherently deficient. On one level the parents' taking care of every need bears the message of affection, but it may also sabotage the child's self-initiated behavior.

Masterson (1977) has described the parents of many of his anorexic patients as "clinically ill" in their discouragement of their child's self-reliance, while rewarding compliance. He observed that:

> The mother clung to the patient to relieve her own anxiety. She responded to and confirmed the child's clinging behavior. She did not confirm individuative behavior. The father distanced himself from the patient, while at the same time reinforcing the mother's clinging. The patient's regressive behavior played a vital role in maintaining the mother's equilibrium . . . (1977, p. 491).

Although not all patients fit this description, when the family network encourages the child's neglect for her own independent thoughts and feelings, then the structure and interactional patterns of the family system must be modified. The specific strategies for this have been described in detail by others (Liebman et al., 1974a and b; Minuchin et al., 1975, 1978; Rosman et al., 1975, 1978).

In summary, a recurring theme in psychotherapy is the patient's deficiency in self-concept. This is manifested in her negative views of herself and a lack of trust in the validity and reliability of her self-perceptions. Amelioration of the deficient self-concept helps to eliminate the need for weight control as a reference for self-evaluation.

## SEPARATION AND AUTONOMY

Normal adolescence is characterized by a physical, emotional, and cognitive surge in preparation for autonomous psychosocial functioning. While this creates stress for most families, the child eventually separates and emerges to meet the demands of adulthood while the family reintegrates around the strengths of its respective members. The adolescent either meets the challenges of independence or succumbs with maladaptive behavior, but this is usually not reflected in any change in diet or weight. For the potential anorexic, the separation from the family and the new psychosocial demands thus required may precipitate the disorder.

Parents may convey that their daughter's maturity will have destructive consequences for the family or a particular parent. In some cases, the child may feel that her emergent sexuality is a threat to her parents. In one case, the patient's mother began sobbing at her daughter's inquiry about menstruation and she deteriorated into a suicidal depression as a consequence of the daughter's first period. Other sexual events may become the focal point of the adolescent's pubertal crisis. An actual sexual encounter or even an imagined misadventure may be responsible for the desire to retreat from maturity (Crisp 1970, 1980).

Other factors may make adolescence seem overwhelming for the potential anorexic. Social and vocational demands may arouse feelings of inadequacy. For many, performance expectations within the family have been excessive but in the preadolescent years they have been met often with enormous effort. The potential anorexic feels increasingly inadequate to meet the competition in high school or college. This leads to either a conscious or unconscious desire to retreat to the earlier more protected years. All of these focal points for dread have a common motivation which may lie initially just beyond the patient's awareness, namely, the prospect of continued development is unpleasant and must be avoided. To this end, dieting serves as an adaptive mechanism. Success at weight control temporarily compensates for the sense of inadequacy and unhappiness. The resulting physical changes seem to make basic apprehensions and conflicts melt away. Life is simplified when weight and food become the dominant themes.

In addressing the patient's developmental fears, therapy must focus on two issues. First, the patient must understand why it is fundamental that weight gain occurs *prior* to the resolution of psychological conflicts. By her low weight she has avoided the experiences associated with normal weight. Her "fear of gaining weight" ultimately must be understood in terms of the more basic fears associated with separation and autonomous functioning as an adult. These issues cannot be understood or resolved while her experiences are being contaminated by the effects of starvation. She must approach the phobic object — herself at a normal weight.

Secondly, the vicissitudes of adolescence, which form the basis of the anorexic's misgivings, must be addressed. The patient must be reassured that the therapist will not abandon her once the tangible signs of her illness no longer exist. Moreover, she may experience considerable distress and occasionally panic as she approaches her "critical menstrual threshold." The rekindling of her "mature biology" often leaves her with the precarious feeling that she has traversed her entire adolescence in several months. Her adequate preparation for this rapid physical and psychological shift may reduce the discomfort.

Both individual and family therapy may be used to facilitate the process of separation and the development of autonomy when these have become obstacles within the family. While family therapy provides a powerful method for disengaging the enmeshed and overprotective family, individual therapy may achieve similar ends. A major function of individual therapy is to help the anorexic patient visualize herself as a truly separate being without destroying her healthy sense of belonging within the family unit. She comes to therapy with little trust or confidence in the validity of her own perceptions. Her descriptions of her family indicate confusion in interpersonal boundaries and a weak sense of her own identity.

According to Masterson (1977), intense anger, which may be expressed as negativism by the anorexic, results from the demand that independence-seeking be given up in order to obtain approval. Because of its implications for separation, adolescence provokes fear of abandonment and a sense of helplessness in the anorexic. It threatens relationships with family members which have been characterized by a symbiotic clinging. Therapy must provide an opportunity for a relationship in which autonomy is encouraged and separation is met with acceptance.

The patient's fears of abandonment and interpersonal control are continually expressed through the transference relationship and must be repeatedly confronted. She will become increasingly able to accept that the relationship can survive physical separation (i.e., intervals between appointments and vacations) and the development of her own personal autonomy. Similarly, the constancy and dependability of the relationship despite conflict, independence-seeking, or the patient's anger are crucial. She must be reassured that these will not be met with retaliation or abandonment. At the same time, her denial of the seriousness of symptoms must be confronted. Setting limits around issues of weight or eating illustrates the capacity of the relationship to withstand stress. Eventually, she should be able to relinquish the use of food and weight as interpersonal weapons and resort to more conventional expressions of hostility.

Patients often parrot their parents' beliefs while simultaneously feeling the absence of ideas originating within themselves. In therapy, autonomy also may be encouraged by repeated differentiation between parental attitudes and expectations and those of the anorexic patient. The patient may also attempt to introject the therapist's idealized expectations. Previously described clinical strategies of reality-orientated feedback and reinforcement of appropriate affective expression are aimed at helping the patient become aware of her own thoughts and feelings.

Many patients report being unable to identify pleasure in their routine daily experiences. This marked anhedonia may partially result from starvation but may also stem from the rigid value systems which minimize the significance of personal pleasure. Proper conduct and outstanding accomplishment have been more likely to receive approval from others. The development of increasing autonomy requires the differentiation of personal desires and pleasures from the expectation of others. Therapy can provide support for this process.

In summary, separation and the development of greater autonomy may be facilitated by both family and individual therapy. Whereas family therapy enables a direct challenge of dysfunctional communication patterns, individual therapy helps the patient break away from the enmeshed and overprotective environment. Independence-seeking is encouraged and personal needs are differentiated from the expectations of others. Finally, the psychosocial hurdles that have thwarted the anorexic's development are identified and slowly resolved.

## BEHAVIORAL METHODS

The distinction between behavioral, cognitive, and affective approaches is somewhat artificial since they are interdependent. Behavioral principles have been primarily applied in inpatient settings; however, they also may play a part in outpatient therapy. The behavioral approach has been criticized as a coercive and dangerous duplication of the anorexic's intrusive, controlling environment (Bruch, 1974: Cohler, 1977; Goodsitt, 1977; Williams, 1976; see Chapter 9). In defending the method, Wolpe (1975) has blamed the failure of particular behavioral programs on incomplete behavioral assessments of the patient. Behavioral treatment may lend itself to mechanistic misapplication.

While the technology of a particular behavioral approach may be sound, a thorough understanding of the contingencies determining the patients' behavior may be absent. For example, if a behavioral protocol in which privileges are contingent upon daily weight gain is imposed without the patient's collaboration, there may be short-term weight gain. However, it is unlikely that long-term improvement will occur without attention to the reinforcement contingencies determining the patient's "dieting." There have been recent attempts to apply behavioral methods in conjunction with more traditional psychotherapy (Andersen, 1979; Geller, 1975; Hersen and Detre, 1980; Minuchin et al., 1975; Moldofsky and Garfinkel, 1974; Parker et al., 1977). Geller (1975) has advocated an integration of behavior therapy and psychotherapy as "pragmatically suited for the patient with anorexia nervosa" (1975, p. 169). Hersen and Detre (1980) have also argued for this as one component of a "multifaceted approach" in which different strategies may be applied to different aspects of the disorder.

The rigid application of formal operant conditioning procedures may be of limited value, particularly early in outpatient treatment when the patient is most reluctant to part with her symptoms. Furthermore, there are practical limitations in monitoring behavior and obtaining control over the contingencies of outpatients. However, one important behavioral technique that is generally useful is that of having the patient engage in "corrective experiences" or participate in previously avoided activities. This term was originally used by Alexander and French (1946) but Freud had recommended this approach for phobic patients (quoted in Fenichel, 1945). In a report from the Menninger Foundation Psychotherapy Research Project, Horowitz (1974, 1976) concluded that "corrective experiences" are an integral part of psychotherapy. Such diverse approaches as Gestalt, humanistic, psychoanalytic, and behavior therapy have recognized the importance of practicing avoided behavior.

Particular exercises which utilize corrective experiences may be useful for overcoming many activities and experiences avoided by the anorexic patient. The patient may be encouraged to distinguish clearly between "anorexic" and "appropriate" behavioral patterns and to practice the latter even before she feels like spontaneously relinquishing her stereotypic behavior. Even after some patients have begun to make a commitment to improvement, they remain entrenched in their self-defeating behavior patterns. For example, anorexics typically develop peculiar eating habits. They cut food into small pieces, vacillate between menu selection, eat in isolation, and only choose foods which they label as "safe or dietetic." While these are partially starvation-related, some aspects are often maintained in the period immediately after weight restoration. The therapist may enlist the patient's commitment to decide consciously, in advance of a meal, to eat in a "non-anorexic" manner. If the patient is not successful, it may be pointed out that this indicates that she is not yet "in control" of her behavior since that would imply having some "choice." Success in this type of exercise gives the patient practice in "normal" eating and an opportunity to learn that this is not immediately followed by obesity.

Other behavioral exercises can provide the patient with corrective experiences which promote positive change once considerable trust has been achieved. Occasionally the therapist may accompany the patient for meals, not as an invigilator, but as a supporter of normal eating patterns. Here the patient can learn that people may be concerned about her eating without being destructive or intrusive. However, this only applies to some patients and must be appropriately timed. It can be viewed as seductive and needs to be handled with regard to these dangers in the transference. Behavioral homework assignments also may be prescribed to give the patient practice in self-initiated activity, decision-making, and assertive behavior with peers or family. Role-playing may be helpful in practicing these within psychotherapy sessions. The reactions of the patient to these corrective experiences provides meaningful content for other areas of psychotherapy where her thinking, perceptions, and feelings are explored in detail.

Reinforcement has been defined as the "consequences which increase the rate" of a particular behavior (Skinner, 1969). Over the last decade, the operant reinforcement model has been applied extensively to anorexia nervosa in an attempt to promote weight gain (see Chapter 9) but its relevance to psychotherapy has received less attention (Marmor, 1971, 1976). Awareness of the reinforcement contingencies which determine the patient's immediate behavior is valuable in assisting the patient to meet more difficult goals. In anorexia nervosa, the individual's repertoire of reinforcers (positive) rapidly dwindles to the ones associated with the pleasures of weight loss and self-control. The pursuit of these behaviors and those designed to avoid the dreaded consequences of weight gain (negative reinforcement) comprise the major daily activity of most patients.

Sources of negative reinforcement must be eliminated or their influence moderated. In some cases, the patient must gradually learn that the short-term "safety" achieved by avoiding a feared stimulus actually produces greater distress in the future. For example, the bathroom scales may have been relied on for reassurance that a feared weight had been avoided. However, the patient must become aware of how this has developed into an escalating and punitive process in which she has become a slave to the dictates of the scale. While weighing began as a "once-in-the-morning" event, it may now consume a substantial portion of every day. The slightest shift upward leads to a day of panic and depression. Once trust has been established in therapy, the patient may be requested to throw out the scale and agree to weekly weighings by her doctor. This is eventually met with relief and considerably more leisure time.

Finally, the therapist may provide an impetus for the patient to expand the range of activities which provide satisfaction. Encouraging the patient to experiment in purely enjoyable activities can be helpful in promoting a spirit that pleasure is not intrinsically frivolous. This may be met by considerable resistance in the patient for whom "pleasures" have only been tied to superior achievement.

Marmor (1971, 1976) has suggested that an important function of the therapist in any psychotherapy is to provide reinforcement to the patient. The patient's conscious decision to attempt to gain weight may be largely related to the reinforcement properties of the therapist in a global sense. More specifically, through the reinforcement of the patient's self-initiated behavior and accurate self-perceptions, the therapist is able to foster her sense of positive self-awareness. Marmor (1971) has also warned that the unwary therapist may reinforce certain maladaptive perceptions of the patient. Care must be exercised not to duplicate disturbed communication patterns which may have existed within the family. Occasionally a positive therapeutic relationship provides unwitting reinforcement of symptoms. One patient described that in her former psychotherapy "every time I gained weight my appointments were less frequent and when I lost they were more regular. It was necessary for me to maintain my low weight, otherwise my therapist would have abandoned me and then how could I have coped with life?" Awareness of this type of obstacle and discussion within psychotherapy is usually a sufficient remedy.

## DIDACTIC INFORMATION

Anorexic patients are frequently excellent students, yet their performance is too often spawned by over-compliance, perfectionism, approval from others, and a morbid fear of failure. Their goals are "self-improvement" rather than fulfillment of their personal interests and aspirations. While one must be cautious about such patients' reading becoming a purely intellectual endeavour which avoids therapy, "bibliotherapy" can also be a useful clinical strategy for furnishing patients with information about their disorder and providing collateral support on specific therapeutic issues. Excerpts or chapter from the Keys et al. (1950) report on human semi-starvation studies are recommended (particularly Chapter 37 and 38, Vol II) to illustrate that many of the anorexic's distressing symptoms are not due to personal deficiencies but rather to her state of undernutrition. The written material transmits valuable information that may be less compelling if relayed orally. Moreover, sharing the material is seen as evidence of the therapist's openness and desire to let the patient evaluate the "evidence" for herself.

We also recommend that some patients read certain material about anorexia nervosa such as *The Golden Cage* (Bruch, 1978) or *Let Me Be* (Crisp, 1980). This diminishes their feelings of guilt about their disorder and allows them to identify with other patients who have recovered. After reading such material, patients are often more interested in psychotherapy. Later in treatment, particular books may be helpful in providing the patient with additional information on such issues as assertiveness, sexuality, bodily functioning, and healthy eating and weight. These should be offered as an adjunct to discussion of specific issues in psychotherapy and never as a substitute.

## DEALING WITH WEIGHT AND EATING IN PSYCHOTHERAPY

Conducting outpatient psychotherapy with the anorexic often places the therapist in the delicate position of having to encourage the patient to gain or maintain an acceptable weight without allowing this issue to become a battleground as it may have become with her parents, friends, or spouse. Some therapists have approached this by suggesting that weight and eating should largely be ignored in the interest of pursuing the psychological goals (Goodsitt, 1977; Solomon and Morrison, 1972). The assumption is that once the conflicts underlying the behavior have been resolved, the symptoms will cease. As noted previously, because of the self-perpetuating nature of the starvation state, this approach may have dangerous consequences. One method of preventing weight issues from dominating the psychotherapy is to have a physician see the patient regularly for this purpose and a different individual conduct the psychotherapy. Naturally the two must be in close contact. Separating physical from psychological issues in this manner may reinforce the patient's erroneous mind-body distinction. Alternatively, one individual may see the patient for psychotherapy and, as part of this, deal with weight and food concerns.

Helping the patient see the importance of weight while simultaneously attending to psychological concerns illustrates the interdependence of these two aspects of her experience. Also, the process of psychotherapy is dramatically affected by the patient's weight. The profound effects of starvation on cognitive and emotional functioning have been described previously. It is of little value to search for the dynamic roots of experience that is grossly distorted as a direct result of starvation. Because of this, at some level the psychotherapist must be involved with issues about weight.

Before weight and eating can be addressed meaningfully, a therapeutic alliance must exist (Russell, 1981). The patient should be a participant in plans about her weight. The therapist must outline and reiterate several points about the patient's weight status — again, after a positive, trusting relationship has begun to emerge:

1) The patient must be convinced that the therapist's motive is not control but the reduction of her overall suffering.
2) Low weight, seen by the anorexic as a sign of "control," must be reinterpreted as precisely the opposite — a sign that she is *out* of control.
3) It must be understood that outpatient therapy can only proceed if the patient's "weight does not fall below a certain minimum" (Selvini Palazzoli, 1978, p. 126). There are no absolute rules regarding this minimum level of weight since it depends on the patient's overall health, the presence of starvation symptoms and of complicating factors (e.g., hypokalemia, cardiac irregularities, anemia). But once the patient loses 15% of her former weight, her physical status should be regularly monitored by a physician, and generally, when her weight is 25% below average, hospital admission is required.

Some patients' weights will be sufficiently low that "psychotherapy" consists of helping them to understand that hospitalization is absolutely necessary since they are in imminent physical danger. Their protests can be met with an "experiment" in which they attempt to gain 1 kg per week for two weeks to ascertain their degree of "control." For many patients failure will graphically illustrate that they are *not* able to force their weight up, even as a temporary measure to prevent hospitalization. At this point the focus should be to attempt to elicit trust and a sense of collaboration in the hospitalization. Subsequent conflict can be minimized if the patient feels that, at least on some level, she has made the choice for hospitalization. Some patients may need to be told that their behavior, which is assumed to be non-suicidal in intent, cannot be allowed to escalate to fatal proportions. As noted in Chapter 9, on rare occasions patients may require involuntary hospital admission because of their serious weight loss.

We generally recommend to patients that they not weigh themselves but that they be weighed by a nurse, physician, or psychotherapist on a weekly basis. Patients should be informed of their weights. One problem with this is that the scales can never be as accurate as the patients initially demand and there are normally small fluctuations in anybody's weight. For these reasons we establish a goal "range" of 3-4 lbs rather than a specific goal weight. A patient's insistence that she must weigh exactly, say, 105 lbs is impractical, if not impossible. It may be explained that this is analogous to maintaining a heart rate of 60 beats per minute at all times or attempting to steer a car in a straight direction by locking the wheel in a rigid position. Continual adjustments must be made. A stable weight means some fluctuation within an appropriate range.

Some patients will wish to recover but also to remain at either an emaciated weight or one halfway between health and emaciation. This simply cannot be done. If the weight that is chosen requires that the patient be persistently hungry in order to maintain it, she gradually will be drawn again into the full syndrome. Most patients will have an individualized "magic weight" (Selvini Palazzoli, 1978), which is either based on the special meaning that a certain number holds (e.g., 99 versus 100 lbs) or on the biological significance of this weight.

In our experience, patients panic at two points during weight gain. The first is when they initiate their ascent. The second is at the critical weight (body fat) level necessary for the resumption of menses (Frisch and MacArthur, 1974). At this threshold, patients are confronted with the mature shape that they have been dedicated to avoiding (Crisp, 1965b). Pleas for renegotiating a weight below this should be met by firmness on the part of the therapist. The therapist must avoid being seduced or worn down into allowing an unhealthy weight. The patient should be reassured that only if she is able to sustain normal menstrual functioning at a slightly lower weight, will the range be modified. The patient's desire to remain below this level should be interpreted in psychological terms.

There are also a number of general strategies which we have found to be sometimes helpful in promoting weight gain out of hospital. The success of each depends on the particular patient but they are not always useful and some patients can only gain weight in hospital. At some point in therapy, many patients request assistance in controlled weight gain. A dietician may outline a "diet" which will produce a gradual weight gain. This should consist of normal "non-anorexic" foods — the types that were eaten prior to the onset of the disorder. Patients often have come to believe in food myths, such as carbohydrate, sugar, or meat are intrinsically unhealthy. These beliefs should be clearly linked to the disorder. This may be easier if evidence debunking these myths is presented to the patient.

However, these arguments may not change her eating patterns and it may be more productive to recommend that the patient consume the forbidden food in small quantities. This suggestion is typically met with resistance based on the idea that once the anxiety attached to these "bad " foods is removed, the patient will overindulge and become hopelessly overweight. This fear can be answered by a statistic, a promise, and an explanation. First, the statistic: Very few patients actually become obese following treatment (Garfinkel, Moldofsky and Garner, 1977; see Chapter 12). If there has been no premorbid history of obesity, the chances are minimal. Second, if a patient should "lose control" or be unable to level off at a normal weight, she would be hospitalized, and provided with external controls. This form of "loss of control" would be taken as seriously as the patient's emaciation. The reassurance that the goal is not simply to "fatten her up" is of great importance.

Third, the patient needs some explanation that one of the reasons that she feels she will be unable to stop once she begins is because she is operating from the biological orientation of a starving organism. Her voracious hunger will subside gradually after she has reached and maintained an appropriate weight level. There is evidence that weight, like other biological events, is under homeostatic control (Garfinkel and Coscina, 1982). Through strong cognitive control, anorexics have forced their weights well below one that their bodies can defend naturally. With some justification, the anorexic believes that anything that relaxes her cognitive controls will cause a violent counteraction. She may also express a belief that once she "gets into the habit of eating" non-dietetic foods, she will be unable to modify this behavior at a normal weight. But she should know that, with the therapist's or dietitian's assistance, the caloric content of her diet can be adjusted to meet current needs.

External control of intake is necessary until the regulation of eating reassumes natural direction through internal signals. Until that occurs it is most important for the patient not to panic and cut back in response to the first fluctuation of the scale. In some cases keeping records of intake and reviewing these with a dietitian can be beneficial for a patient who is confused about what constitutes an acceptable daily allowance. Of course, this presupposes a strong therapeutic commitment — these methods are premature if the therapist repeatedly hears that the patient has devoured 4500 calories per day and has lost another pound.

Specific assistance with eating may not always be required in therapy. Once some patients understand that the therapist is committed to a relationship which need not be centered around weight, they proceed on their own. Anorexics with a long history of the disorder will be particularly resistant to requesting practical assistance in weight gain. But for many patients, by attending to these areas which are preoccupying her (i.e., loss of control around foods), the therapist demonstrates that her concerns are being taken seriously. Gradually, trust can develop and the patient will reveal her more basic fears. Finally, as weight gain occurs and the starvation state recedes, the more meaningful psychotherapeutic issues become accessible.

## FAMILY THERAPY

Family therapy has been increasingly recognized as an important clinical strategy in anorexia nervosa. It has been recommended as an adjunct to other methods (Andersen, 1979; Bruch, 1973; Crisp, 1970, 1980; Geller, 1975; Hersen and Detre, 1980; Parker et al., 1977) or as the principal mode of treatment (Caille et al., 1977; Conrad, 1977; Minuchin et al., 1978; Selvini Palazzoli, 1978). If the patient is 16 or younger and living at home, it has been our experience that family therapy must be considered as the primary mode of psychotherapy.

Our approach to family therapy relies heavily on the "open systems" model described by Minuchin and his colleagues in Philadelphia and Selvini Palazzoli in Milan. This approach will only be outlined here since it has been presented in detail elsewhere (Liebman et al., 1974a, 1974b; Minuchin et al., 1975, 1978; Rosman et al., 1977; Selvini Palazzoli, 1978). The particular characteristics of these families have been described in Chapter 7. Regardless of whether these characteristics are predispositions or sequelae to the illness, when present they must be addressed in therapy.

Family therapy focuses heavily on challenging the enmeshed styles within the family. Often, these patterns have come into conflict with the developmental pressures for change. An overprotective family life may have discouraged independence-seeking and possibly magnified the apprehensions which normally occur with adolescence. Minuchin et al. (1978) comment on this process further:

> [The anorexic's] overinvolvement with her family handicaps her involvement with the extrafamilial world, causing a developmental lag. . . . With her entrance into adolescence, she finds herself in a crisis. Her wish to participate with a group of peers conflicts with her orientation to the family (p. 60).

The parents' undue need to preserve their child's dependence may be at the core of the overprotective family (Masterson, 1977). The parents and/or the child may be unable to tolerate the prospect of increasing autonomy and both may play a role in thwarting the child's intermittent attempts to assume greater independence. There is a range of fears that the child's adolescence may potentiate in the parents. Her emergent sexual maturity may elicit distress because it provides prominent signs of her growing independence. It also may potentiate disturbed sexual attitudes in the parents. One mother stated that her 14-year-old daughter's vomiting "may be a blessing in disguise" since she was more concerned about food than boys. A daughter's maturation may be seen as a more general threat to the solidarity of the family unit. One 24-year-old patient recalled that her independence-seeking was subtly but effectively discouraged by her mother who continually reminded her that the family had sacrificed everything for a child who was destined to abandon them.

Another 17-year-old patient was blocked from social contacts because of her mother's overwhelming fear that, in the absence of strict controls, the child might fail. Failure had special meaning since from the beginning of marriage the mother had been considered by her powerful mother-in-law as "not good enough." The mother-in-law had openly predicted that "shame would come to the entire family" by the mother's failure in raising her children. Consequently, the mother lived in fear and her daughter was resented for her power to either confirm or disprove the prophecy. This fear motivated the mother's overprotectiveness. Thus, an overvalued child's growing independence can pose a special threat to one or both parents who, in turn, resist their child's attempt to separate.

At times, the parents may require marital psychotherapy to strengthen their relationship. Issues which have led to their emotional estrangement must be openly discussed. The resolution of these conflicts may free the overvalued child from her role of parental support. Firm alliances have often occurred where one parent forms an intense relationship with the anorexic child to the relative exclusion of the spouse. Therapy may focus on realigning these inappropriate coalitions. For example, father and daughter may be encouraged to strengthen their relationship by engaging in activities together. Again, as Selvini Palazzoli (1978) cautions, "great care should be taken that it is not destructive to the mother, who will otherwise feel exclud- ed and may become depressed or hostile" (p. 224). The shifting of alliances may begin to expose serious resentment in the marriage that has endured behind the facade of respectability. The disillusionment may have never been openly acknowledged and the anorexic child's symptoms may have functioned to deflect attention away from the marital conflict.

Therapy sessions may be used to practice less enmeshed patterns of behavior. Extreme care must be taken to avoid blaming particular members for these communicational styles since everyone has contributed to their development. Enmeshment may be gently discouraged by underscoring each individual's separateness. We frequently interview the anorexic patient for a few minutes before or after the family session to emphasize that, while she is part of the family unit, she is also a separate and independent in- dividual. Examples of the anorexic's individual competence are highlighted. Her "differences of opinion" within the family are interpreted not as an in- sult to family unity but as a logical consequence of her different perspective. Moreover, enmeshment is also discouraged by clarifying and supporting the subsystems within the family (Minuchin et al., 1978). The children's inap- propriate intrusion into the parental subsystem is blocked by gently remind- ing the child that some decisions are best made by parents. When ap- propriate, however, the parents are encouraged to let their children, particularly the anorexic child, make decisions themselves and assume greater responsibility for their own behavior. This must be done gently without antagonizing the parents by activating their sensitivity to guilt or by attacking the familial sense of "togetherness."

Selvini Palazzoli (1978) describes the use of "positive connotation" by which she attributes "constructive intentions to the kind of interpersonal behavior that is commonly described as destructive and injurious" (p. 228). This strategy reduces defensiveness and unnecessary resistance. For example, parents' overcontrolling or intrusive behaviors are defined as signs of concern which are inadvertently having a negative effect. The patient's symptoms may be redefined as an understandable attempt to preserve the family unit in the face of developmental stresses.

Therapy sessions provide a relatively protected setting for practicing new interactional styles. Family members are encouraged to express more openly previously avoided emotions such as anger, depression, or affection. Inappropriate attempts to shield family members from criticism are blocked, leading to more direct communication. Implicit rules governing communication are examined in detail and when they are inappropriate they are gently challenged using the "positive connotation" approach. Selvini Palazzoli (1978) has suggested that a common characteristic of families with an anorexic patient is the "disqualification" of communications. This essentially involves a message being sent on one level while being rejected, denied or qualified on a different level. For example, a parent may say that the patient's opinion is vitally important, but interrupt any direct attempt that she makes to speak. One father was particularly insistent on encouraging his 19-year-old daughter to be independent. Yet at one family session he asked her physician to stop her medication, while ignoring his daughter's comments about its efficacy.

Personal preferences may be couched in terms of attempting to meet the needs of others. A change in one person's behavior may be not acknowledged or is even denied. The patient may describe her vomiting in terms that make it sound like an involuntary reaction to stress. These "double messages" can have a negative effect on the members of a family. Minuchin et al. (1978) have suggested that "every human being's sense of identity depends, in large measure, on the validation of self by a reference group" (p. 52). This is where the experience of the family therapist is a distinct asset. Often the contradictory messages within the family are subtle and the meaning of the less complementary interpretation is closely guarded. Family members must be encouraged to speak for themselves and focus attention on taking responsibility for their own viewpoint. They must be taught to disentangle contradictory messages and communicate in a more congruent fashion.

Finally, family therapy may be aimed at increasing parental effectiveness where the child's symptoms reflect the parents' difficulty in maintaining authority and control. Minuchin et al. (1978) have used the therapeutic maneuver of "reframing the symptoms" to redefine the adolescent's refusal to eat as "an act of disobedience, not an illness" (p. 96). In many cases, bulimia, vomiting, and not eating become a means of exerting power and control in a family which is sensitized to illness. By reinterpreting these symptoms, the parents can be mobilized into joining forces against their daughter's rebellion.

This is illustrated by a bright, attractive, upper-middle-class, 16-year-old girl who was brought for consultation by her mother. The mother was terrorized by her daughter's refusal to eat. The mother was pathologically dependent on her daughter (which was in part related to her husband's rejection). A crisis developed as her daughter entered adolescence and began to separate from the family. The mother's overprotection and restriction of her daughter's activities were associated with the development of vomiting. The mother could not discipline or control her daughter effectively and could not enlist support from her husband since his intervention would ensure anger from her daughter ("I will never talk to you again if you tell dad") and from the husband himself for her inability to control the situation. The daughter's dependence on her mother and the inability to express anger openly within the family mitigated against more conventional adolescent rebellion. Her vomiting increased and she began leaving vomitus in conspicuous places around the house. The threat of the father's discovery of the vomitus became the medium for extorting the mother to "relax pressures." Clearly this family required therapy. Once the parents were able to marshall a unified approach to their daughter's behavior, and the mother was able to derive more emotional support from her husband, the vomiting ceased.

## BULIMIA

Little has been written about the psychotherapeutic approach to the bulimic anorexic. Russell (1979) has recently provided a detailed description of a series of 30 bulimic patients. He described the pernicious, self-perpetuating cycle involving an interaction between psychological and pathophysiological mechanisms (Figure 1). Accordingly the patients' psychological disturbances are manifest in a pursuit of thinness which is followed by:

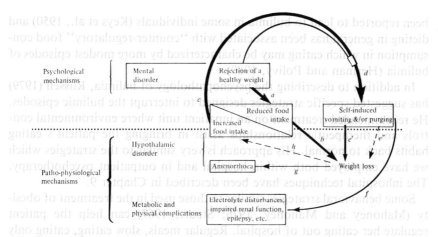

Figure 1, Interactions between the psychological disorder, the loss of weight and the disturbances of eating behavior. The thickness of the lines represents the strength of the evidence favoring each interaction.
Reprinted with permission from Russell, 1979.

. . . reduced food intake (a) and weight loss (b), at least in the common group of patients with an antecedent phase of anorexia nervosa. It is also evident that the patient who rejects her "healthy" weight level is likely to react to the powerful urges to overeat with emotional distress (c): it is this reaction that leads her to rely on devices aimed at counteracting the fattening effects of the food eaten, self-induced vomiting or purging (d). These devices (vomiting (e) more than purging (e")) keep the weight at a reduced level, and give rise to electrolyte and other disorders (f). Weight loss is also an important contributory cause of amenorrhea when this is present (g). . . . bouts of overeating . . . are a response of the hypothalamus to a sub-optimal body weight (h) and this response may also play a part in influencing the patient's attitudes to food as a prelude to or accompaniment of the overeating (pp. 445-446).

These patients struggle to maintain a weight which is below that which occurred prior to the onset of their disorder. In Russell's series, this amounted to an average of greater than 6 kgs below what could be considered a constitutionally determined "healthy weight." It has been hypothesized previously that homeostatic mechanisms act to defend a constitutionally determined "set point" for body weight (Nisbett, 1972; Herman and Polivy, 1980). Deviations from this level are generally countered by biological pressure to return. In accordance with this, semi-starvation has been reported to lead to bulimia in some individuals (Keys et al., 1950) and dieting in general has been associated with "counter-regulatory" food consumption in which eating may be characterized by more modest episodes of bulimia (Herman and Polivy, 1980).

In addition to describing the psychopathology of bulimia, Russell (1979) has suggested specific strategies designed to interrupt the bulimic episodes. He recommended treatment on an inpatient unit where environmental controls and therapeutic relationships assist in bringing the patient's eating habits back to normal. His approach is very similar to the strategies which we have employed both within hospital and in outpatient psychotherapy. The inhospital techniques have been described in Chapter 9.

Some behavioral strategies similar to those used in the treatment of obesity (Mahoney and Mahoney, 1976; Stuart, 1967) can help the patient regulate her eating out of hospital. Regular meals, slow eating, eating only in the presence of others, and keeping detailed records of meals and incidents of vomiting are encouraged. It is also helpful to have patients describe and record their affective states prior to the episode of bulimia/vomiting. Like other anorexics, bulimic patients display confusion in the identification of their affective states. They misinterpret various unpleasant emotions as urges to eat. One patient routinely described herself as feeling "bingy" under certain stressful circumstances. She was not simply being cryptic, she did not have a clear awareness of her emotions except as an antecedent to overeating. By helping the patient piece together various circumstances and listening to details of her descriptions of events, it is possible to provide a differential feedback to reinforce accurate identification of emotions. Then, rather than acting on these emotions by overeating, she may be assisted in exploring more appropriate alternatives.

For the patient who vomits or misuses laxatives to control her weight, it is important to emphasize how these have "reinforced" bulimia in the sense that they have allowed her to overeat and not suffer the caloric consequences. Interrupting the vomiting tends to reduce the frequency of bulimia. When not severe and therefore not requiring hospitalization, there are several strategies that we have found useful in helping patients to break the cycle.

Most bulimic patients oscillate between periods of complete abstinence and overindulgence. They may starve themselves during the day and gorge in the evening or go for several days without food followed by bulimia. These high and low phases must be eliminated. Often a bulimic episode is initiated by a slight deviation from a rigidly prescribed dietary regimen. As observed by Mahoney and Mahoney (1976) with more typical obese dieters, consuming one prohibited food leads to the resigned attitude that the diet has been "blown" and one might as well go all the way. This stems from absolutist thinking in which only flawless behavior is acceptable. Bulimia is also initiated in response to other stresses because it provides temporary solace for the dieter who is feeling deprived. Anger is frequently described as antedating bulimia and the aggression becomes displaced onto food.

Most patients are reluctant to deviate from the bulimic pattern for a number of reasons. One of the strongest forces supporting it is the potent short-term reinforcement that it provides. Sensations of starvation and gastric emptiness become associated in the patient's mind with "virtue, self-control, and the promise of a thinner figure." The patient's starvation provides physical sensations which have specific meaning. She is "being good" and the patient does not want to give up this reliable means of feeling good about herself. While vomiting and laxatives provide relief by removing the food, for many patients they also remove the guilt that has been induced by overeating. Patients may persist with the laxative misuse because they provide a form of penitence whose purpose is to relieve guilt. This cycle may, over time, become disconnected from concerns about weight. One 28-year-old patient took massive dosages of Ex-lax (500-600 tablets, as often as three times per week) and explained: "If I make a fool of myself in a relationship, the only way that I feel that I can go meet someone else is if I have spent two repentant days in bed by suffering for my stupidity." While her behavior was originally tied to a fear of body fat, it expanded to provide atonement for other "sins."

The moralistic interpretation of good = starvation and bad = eating can be extended to interpersonal problems, achievements, and foods. This is identical to the restricting anorexic's interpretation of food in dichotomous terms, except that the bulimic indulges in the prohibited foods during a "binge." In order to make the "forbidden fruit" less attractive, patients are encouraged to consume modest and predetermined amounts of those foods that were previously the object of their binges. These foods should be introduced to the patient as "medication" in the sense that they will be helpful in reducing the psychological cravings and the feelings of deprivation. Patients should eat these foods even if they believe that they can do without. They should be taught to evaluate their thinking in order to identify any vestiges of their dichotomous method of dividing food into moral and immoral categories. They must come to understand that, although their moralistic system does clear up the ambiguity in their personal universe by giving them clear guidelines for conduct, it provides a false sense of security, for it is based on erroneous assumptions, Moreover, patients must realize that their perfectionist, absolutist, and dichotomous thinking is both self-defeating and a distortion of reality. As with modifying other assumptions, the therapist must proceed cautiously and recognize that change occurs in minute gradations.

According to Russell (1979), the bulimic patient must assume a more "healthy" body weight since her "cravings for food are the result of her starved body rebelling and demanding to be fed" (p.447). While bulimia may develop for reasons other than starvation, the patient must understand that many of her difficulties are the result of her reluctance to gain to a level which would be healthier. Such a weight would also be associated with feeling fat. As described earlier, helping the patient modify the fundamental assumptions "I must be thin" and "I must avoid body fat" is one of the most difficult tasks facing the therapist. Patients may have endured years of struggling to lower their weight in the face of serious disabilities. With the bulimic patient a higher weight must be achieved before meaningful therapeutic issues can be explored. Her entire experience is distorted by starvation symptoms and even more by the pernicious effects of her metabolic imbalance. Much of her suffering may be the result and not the cause of "dietary chaos."

As with treatment of other anorexics, a detailed explanation of the effects of starvation (including bulimia) is often helpful. A somewhat simplified version of Russell's (1979) schemata is useful for outlining to the patient the self-perpetuating cycle of bulimia — vomiting — starvation (Figure 2). This graphically illustrates some of the emotions, beliefs and behaviors reported and their physiological effects. It may be elaborated or refined to correspond with the patient's particular experiences. The dangerous consequences of vomiting and laxative abuse are described in detail elsewhere (Chapter

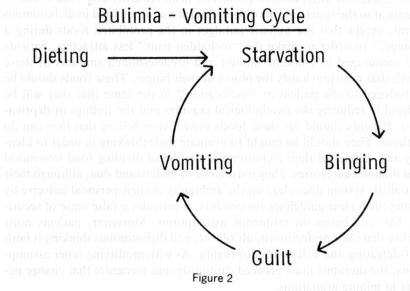

Figure 2

11) and may be placed into the diagram where appropriate . Many engage in the gorging and purging activities for years without connecting the physical and emotional results to their behavior. It may be necessary to underscore this association and the limitation that it imposes on the psychotherapeutic process in other areas.

Until the bulimic's widely fluctuating behavior comes under control and she can accept a higher weight, the therapist is dealing with a personality ravaged by physical complications. The patient has to learn to tolerate a higher weight, rather than like it. In this regard it is often beneficial to explore the patient's dependence on cultural ideals for feminine body shape. Patients may choose to assume a shape based on the fashion models portrayed in the media. However, these standards may be quite unrealistic (Garner, Garfinkel, Schwartz and Thompson, 1980). The patient should be supported in respecting her body without having to alter it drastically to meet the demands and expectation of fashion. We occasionally show patients examples from advertisements in contemporary magazines of women being deprecated by equating female worth with thinness. Other ads recommending ridiculous cosmetic and dietetic practices can sometimes be helpful in assisting the patient to assume a biologically more comfortable weight in healthy defiance of the fashion industry. The patient's giving up an unrealistic body weight is critical in the treatment of bulimia.

## SUMMARY

We have conceptualized anorexia nervosa as a multidetermined disorder — a view that has also been voiced by others (Fries, 1974; Parker et al., 1977; Piazza, Piazza and Rollins, 1980; Rowland, 1970; Russell, 1970; Ryle, 1936; Theander, 1970). Our purpose has been to outline a multifaceted therapy aimed at addressing various aspects of the disorder. Our understanding is derived from our own experience as well as an integration of the writings of Bruch, Crisp, Russell, Selvini Palazzoli, Minuchin, and others.

We have endeavored to present clinical strategies at a level of abstraction that is general enough to cut across diverse therapeutic orientations. On a most basic representational level we have offered a *proximal* model which attributes anorexic behavior to a morbid fear of body weight with a simultaneous desire for thinness. At another representational level, we have linked its expression to various styles of thinking without relying on etiological formulations. On a yet higher level of abstraction, but one that still allows a pragmatic integration with other methods, we have indicated various themes which recur in therapy with particular patients. These overlapping dimensions of disturbed function are: 1) deficiency in self-concept particularly related to effectiveness and personal trust; 2) confused personal identity with an inability to separate and achieve autonomy; and 3) fears of psychosexual and social maturity. Again, it is evident that these are interrelated areas of human functioning; however, their separate discussion allows insight into the issues determining their relationship to a drive for thinness and fear of body fat.

REFERENCES

Alexander, F. and French, T.: *Psychoanalytic Therapy.* New York: Ronald Press, 1946.
Amdur, M.J., Tucker, G.J., Detre, T. and Markhus, K.: Anorexia nervosa: An interactional study. *J. Nerv. Ment. Dis.,* 148:559-566, 1969.
Andersen, A.: Anorexia nervosa: Diagnosis and treatment. *Psychiatry Update Series.* Princeton, N.J.: Biomedia Inc., 1979.
Bandura, A.: The self system in reciprocal determination. *Am. Psychol.,* 33:344-358, 1978.
Beck, A.T.: *Depression: Clinical, Experimental and Theoretical Aspects.* New York: Harper and Row, 1967.
Beck, A.T.: *Cognitive Therapy and the Emotional Disorders.* New York: International Universities Press Inc., 1976.
Beck, A.T. and Emery, G.: *Cognitive Therapy of Anxiety and Phobic Disorders.* Philadelphia: Center for Cognitive Therapy. 1979.
Beck, A.T., Rush, A.J., Shaw, B.F.D. and Emery, G.: *Cognitive Therapy of Depression.* New York: The Guilford Press, 1979.
Bemis, K.M.: Current approaches to the etiology and treatment of anorexia nervosa. *Psychol. Bull.,* 85:593-617, 1978.
Ben-Tovim, D.I., Hunter, M. and Crisp, A.H.: Discrimination and evaluation of shape and size in anorexia nervosa: An exploratory study. *Research Communications in Psychology, Psychiatry and Behavior,* 2:241-257, 1977.
Blinder, B.J., Freeman, D.M.A. and Stunkard, A.J.: Behavioral therapy of anorexia nervosa: Effectiveness of activity as a reinforcer of weight gain. *Am. J. Psychiatry,* 126:1093-1098, 1970.
Blue, R.: Use of punishment in the treatment of anorexia nervosa. *Psychol. Rep.,* 44:743-746, 1979.
Bliss, E.L. and Branch, C.H.H.: *Anorexia Nervosa: Its History, Psychology and Biology.* New York: Paul Hoeber, 1960.
Book, H.E., Sadavoy, J. and Silver, D.: Staff countertransference to borderline patients on an inpatient unit. *Am. J. Psychother.,* 32:521-532, 1978.
Boskind-Lodahl, M.: Cinderella's stepsisters: A feminist perspective on anorexia nervosa and bulimia. *Signs: Journal of Women in Culture and Society,* 2:342-356, 1976.
Bruch, H.: Perceptual and conceptual disturbances in anorexia nervosa. *Psychosom. Med.,* 24:187-194, 1962.
Bruch, H.: *Eating Disorders: Obesity, Anorexia Nervosa and the Person Within.* New York: Basic Books, 1973.
Bruch, H.: *Learning Psychotherapy.* Cambridge, MA: Harvard University Press, 1974.
Bruch, H.: Psychological antecedents of anorexia nervosa. In: R. Vigersky (Ed.), *Anorexia Nervosa.* New York: Raven Press, 1977.
Bruch, H.: *The Golden Cage: The Enigma of Anorexia Nervosa.* Cambridge, MA: Harvard University Press, 1978.
Caille, P., Abrahamsen, P., Girolami, C. and Sorbye, B.: A systems theory approach to a case of anorexia nervosa. *Fam. Process,* 16:455-456, 1977.
Chessick, R.D.: The "crucial dilemma" of the therapist in the psychotherapy of borderline patients. *Am. J. Psychotherapy,* 22:655-666, 1968.

Cohler, B.J.: The significance of the therapist's feelings in the treatment of anorexia nervosa. In: S.C. Feinstein and P. Giovacchini (Eds.), *Adolescent Psychiatry: Volume V Developmental and Clinical Studies.* New York: Jason Aronson, 1977.

Conrad, D.E.: A starving family — an interactional view of anorexia nervosa. *Bull. Menninger Clin.,* 41:487-495, 1977.

Corsini, R.: *Current Psychotherapies.* Itasca, IL: F.F. Peacock Publishers, 1973.

Crisp, A.H.: Clinical and therapeutic aspects of anorexia nervosa: A study of 30 cases. *J. Psychosom. Res.,* 9:67-68, 1965a.

Crisp, A.H.: A treatment regime for anorexia nervosa. *Br. J. Psychiatry,* 112:505-512, 1965b.

Crisp, A.H.: Premorbid factors in adult disorders of weight, with particular reference to primary anorexia nervosa (weight phobia). A literature review. *J. Psychosom. Res.,* 14:1-22, 1970.

Crisp, A.H.: The differential diagnosis of anorexia nervosa. *Proc. Roy. Soc. Med.,* 70:686-690, 1977.

Crisp, A.H.: Some aspects of the relationship between body weight and sexual behaviour with particular reference to massive obesity and anorexia nervosa. *Int. J. Obes.,* 2:17-32, 1978.

Crisp, A.H.: *Anorexia Nervosa: Let Me Be.* New York: Grune and Stratton, 1980.

Crisp, A.H. and Fransella, K.: Conceptual changes during recovery from anorexia nervosa. *Br. J. Med. Psychol.,* 5:395-405, 1972.

Dally, P.J.: *Anorexia Nervosa.* New York: Grune and Stratton, 1969.

Dally, P.J. and Gomez, J.: *Anorexia Nervosa.* London: William Heinemann, 1979.

Ehrensing, R.H. and Weitzman, E.L.: The mother-daughter relationship in anorexia nervosa. *Psychosom, Med.,* 32:201-208, 1970.

Erwin, W.J.: A 16-year follow-up of a case of severe anorexia nervosa. *Journal of Behaviour Therapy and Experimental Psychiatry,* 8:157-160, 1977.

Farquharson, R.F.and Hyland, H.H.: Anorexia nervosa: The course of 15 patients treated from 20-30 years previously. *Can. Med. Assoc. J.,* 94:411-419, 1966.

Fenichel, O.: *The Psychoanalytic Theory of Neurosis.* New York: Norton, 1945, p. 215.

Frank, J.D.: *Persuasion and Healing.* 2nd Ed. Baltimore: John Hopkins University Press, 1973.

Frazier, S.H.: Anorexia nervosa. *Diseases of the Nervous System,* 26:155-159, 1965.

Freud, S.: Recommendations for physicians on the psychoanalytic method for treatment (1912). *Standard Edition,* 12:109-120. London: Hogarth Press, 1957.

Freud, S.: The future prospects of psychoanalytic therapy (1910). *Standard Edition,* 11:139-151. London: Hogarth Press, 1957.

Fries, H.: Secondary amenorrhea, self-induced weight reduction and anorexia nervosa. *Acta Psychiatr. Scan.* [Suppl], 248, 1974.

Frisch, R.E. and McArthur, J.W.: Menstrual cycles: Fatness as a determinant of minimum weight necessary for their maintenance or onset. *Science,* 185:949-951, 1974.

Galdston, R.: Mind over matter — observation on 50 patients with anorexia nervosa. *J. Am. Acad. Child Psychiatry,* 13:246-263, 1974.

Garfinkel, P.E. and Coscina, D.V.: The biology and psychology of hunger and satiety. In: M.R. Zales (Ed.), *Eating, Sleeping, and Sexuality: Treatment for Disorders of Basic Life Functions.* New York: Brunner/Mazel, 1982.

Garfinkel, P.E., Moldofsky, H. and Garner, D.M.: Prognosis in anorexia nervosa as influenced by clinical features, treatment and self-preception. *Can. Med. Assoc. J.,* 117:1041-1045, 1977.

Garner, D.M. and Bemis, K.: A cognitive-behavioral approach to anorexia nervosa. *Cognitive Therapy and Research,* 6:1-27, 1982.

Garner, D.M. and Garfinkel, P.E.: Body image in anorexia nervosa: Measurements, theory and clinical implications. *Int. J. Psychiat. Med.,* 12:263-284, 1981.

Garner, D.M., Garfinkel, P.E., Schwartz, D. and Thompson, M.: Cultural expectations of thinness in women. *Psychol. Rep.,* 47:483-491, 1980.

Geller, J.L.: Treatment of anorexia nervosa by the integration of behavior therapy and psychotherapy. *Psychother. Psychosom.,* 26:167-179, 1975.

Gendlin, E.T.: Experimental psychotherapy. In: R. Corsini (Ed.), *Current Psychotherapies.* Itasca, IL: F.F. Peacock Publishing, 1973.

Goldberg, S.C., Halmi, K.A., Casper, R., Eckert, E. and Davis, J.M.: Pretreatment predictors of weight change in anorexia nervosa. In: R. Vigersky (Ed.), *Anorexia Nervosa.* New York: Raven Press, 1977.

Goldfried, M.R.: Toward the delineation of therapeutic change principles. *Am. Psychol.,* 35: 991-999, 1980.

Goodsitt, A.: Anorexia nervosa. *Br. J. Med. Psychol.,* 42:109-118, 1969.

Goodsitt, A.: Narcissistic disturbances in anorexia nervosa. In: S.C. Feinstein and P. Giovacchini (Eds.), *Adolescent Psychiatry: Volume V Development and Clinical Studies.* New York: Jason Aronson, 1977.

Gottheil, E., Backup, C.E. and Cornelison, F.S.: Denial and self-image confrontation in case of anorexia nervosa. *J. Nerv. Ment. Dis.,* 148:238-250, 1969.

Greben, S.E.: On being therapeutic. *Can. Psychiatric Assoc. J.,* 22:371-380, 1977.

Groen, J.J. and Feldman-Toledano, Z.: Educative treatment of patients and parents in anorexia nervosa. *Br. J. Psychiatry,* 112:671-681, 1966.

Hall, C.S. and Lindsay, G.: *Theories of Personality* (2nd Ed.) New York: Wiley and Sons, 1970.

Hauserman, N. and Lavin, R.: Post-hospitalization continuation treatment of anorexia nervosa. *Journal of Behavior Therapy and Experimental Psychiatry,* 8:309-313, 1977.

Hawkings, J.R., Jones, K.S., Sim, M. and Tibbetts, R.W.: Deliberate disability. *Br. Med. J.,* 2:361-367, 1956.

Herman, C.P. and Polivy, J.: Stress-induced eating and eating-induced stress (reduction): A response to Robbins and Fray. *Appetite,* 1:135-139, 1980.

Hersen, M. and Detre, T.: The behavioral psychotherapy of anorexia nervosa. In: T.B. Karasu and L. Bellak (Eds.), *Specialized Techniques in Individual Psychotherapy.* New York: Brunner/Mazel, 1980.

Hollon, S.D. and Beck, A.T.: Cognitive therapy of depression. In: E.C. Kendall and S.D. Hollon (Eds.), *Cognitive-Behavioral Interventions: Theory, Research and Procedures.* New York: Academic Press, 1979.

Horowitz, L.: *Clinical Prediction in Psychotherapy.* New York: Jason Aronson, 1974.

Horowitz, L.: Internalization as a therapeutic process in psychotherapy and psychoanalysis. Paper presented at the annual meeting of the Society for Psychotherapy Research, San Diego, June 1976.

Hsu, L.K.G., Crisp, A.H. and Harding, B.: Outcome of anorexia nervosa. *Lancet,* 1:61-65, 1979.

Kay, D.W.K. and Schapira, K.: The prognosis in anorexia nervosa. In: J.E. Meyer and H. Feldman (Eds.), *Anorexia Nervosa.* Symposium 24/25 April in 1965 in Gottingen. Stuttgart, Germany: Georg Thieme Verlag, 1965.

Keys, A., Brozek, J., Henschel, A., Mickelsen, O. and Taylor, H.L.: *The Biology of Human Starvation* (2 volumes). Minneapolis: University of Minnesota Press, 1950.

Kiesler, D.J.: Some myths of psychotherapy research and the search for a paradigm. *Psychol. Bull.* 65:110-136, 1966.

King, A.: Primary and secondary anorexia nervosa syndromes. *Br. J. Psychiatry,* 109:470-479, 1963.

Lesser, L.I., Ashenden, B.J., Debuskey, M. and Eisenberg, L.: Anorexia nervosa in children. *Am. J. Orthopsychiatry,* 30:572-580, 1960.

Liebman, R., Minuchin, S. and Baker, L.: An integrated treatment program for anorexia nervosa. *Am. J. Psychiatry,* 131:432-436, 1974a.

Liebman, R., Minuchin, S. and Baker, L.: The role of the family in the treatment of anorexia nervosa. *J. Am. Acad. Child Psychiatry,* 13:264-274, 1974b.

Lorand, S.: Anorexia nervosa: Report on a case. *Psychosom. Med.,* 5:282-292, 1943.

Mahoney, M.J.: *Cognitive and Behavior Modification.* Cambridge, MA: Ballinger Publishing Co., 1974.

Mahoney, M.J. and Mahoney, K.: *Permanent Weight Control. (A Total Solution to the Dieter's Dilemma.)* New York: W.W. Norton, 1976.

Marmor, J.: Dynamic psychotherapy and behavior therapy: Are they irreconcilable? *Arch. Gen. Psychiatry* 24:22-28, 1971.

Marmor, J.: Common operational factors in diverse approaches to behavior change. In: A. Burton (Ed.), *What Makes Behavior Change Possible.* New York: Brunner/Mazel, 1976.

Maslow, A.H.: *The Psychology of Science. A Reconnaissance.* New York: Harper and Row, 1966.

Masterson, J.F.: Primary anorexia nervosa in the borderline adolescent — an object-relations view. In: P. Hartocollis (Ed.), *Borderline Personality Disorders.* New York: International Universities Press, 1977.

Maxmen, J.S., Siberfarb, P.M. and Farrell, R.B.: Anorexia nervosa: Practical management in a general hospital. *JAMA,* 229:801-803, 1974.

Meyer, J.E.: Anorexia nervosa of adolescence: The central syndrome of the anorexia group. *Br. J. Psychiatry,* 118:539-542, 1971.

Minuchin, S., Baker, L., Rosman, B.L., Liebman, R., Milman, L. and Todd, T.C.: A conceptual model of psychosomatic illness in children. *Arch. Gen. Psychiatry,* 32:1031-1038, 1975.

Minuchin, S., Rosman, B.L. and Baker, L.: *Psychosomatic Families: Anorexia Nervosa in Context.* Cambridge: Harvard University Press, 1978.

Moldofsky, H. and Garfinkel, P.E.: Problems of treatment of anorexia nervosa. *Can Psychiatry Assoc. J.* 19:169-175, 1974.

Morgan, H.G. and Russell, G.F.M.: Value of family background and clinical features as predictors of long-term outcome in anorexia nervosa: Four-year follow-up study of 41 patients. *Psychol. Med.,* 5:355-371, 1975.

Nicolle, G.: Prepsychotic anorexia. *Proc. Roy. Soc. Med.,* 32:153-162, 1939.

Nisbett, R.E.: Eating behavior and obesity in men and animals. *Adv. Psychosom. Med.,* 7: 173-193, 1972.

Parker, J.B., Blazer, D. and Wyrick, L.: Anorexia nervosa: A combined therapeutic approach. *South Med. J.,* 70:448-452, 1977.

Parloff, M.B., Waskow, J.E. and Wolfe, B.E.: Research on therapist variables in relation to process and outcome. In: S.L. Garfield and A.E. Bergin (Eds.), *Handbook of Psychotherapy and Behavior Change: An Empirical Analysis.* New York: John Wiley and Sons, 1978.

Perls, F.: *Gestalt Therapy Verbatim.* Lafayette, CA: Real People Press, 1969.

Piazza, E., Piazza, N. and Rollins, N.: Anorexia nervosa: Controversial aspects of therapy. *Compr. Psychiat.,* 21:177-189, 1980.

Quaeritur: Treatment of anorexia nervosa. *Lancet,* 1:980, 1971.

Rampling, D.: Anorexia nervosa. Reflections on theory and practice. *Psychiatry,* 41:296-301, 1978.

Rhoads, J.M. and Feather, B.W.: Transference and resistance observed in behavior therapy. *Br. J. Med. Psychol.,* 45:99-103, 1972.

Rogers, C.R.: Empathic: an appreciated way of being. *Counselling Psychologist,* 5:2-10, 1975.

Rogers, C.R., Gendlin, G.T., Kiesler, D.V. and Truax, C.B.: *The Therapeutic Relationship and Its Impact: A Study of Psychotherapy and Schizophrenics.* Madison: University of Wisconsin Press, 1967.

Rosman, B.L., Minuchin, S. and Liebman, R.: Family lunch session: An introduction to family therapy in anorexia nervosa. *Am. J. Orthopsychiatry,* 45:846-853, 1975.

Rosman, B.L., Minuchin, S., Liebman, R. and Baker, L.: Input and outcome of family therapy in anorexia nervosa. In: S.C. Feinstein and P. Giovacchini (Eds.), *Adolescent Psychiatry: Volume V, Developmental and Clinical Studies.* New York: Jason Aronson, 1977.

Ross, J.L: Anorexia nervosa — an overview. *Bull. Menninger Clin.,* 41:418-436, 1977.

Rowland, C.V.: Anorexia nervosa: Survey of the literature and review of 30 cases. *International Psychiatry Clinics,* 7:37-137, 1970.

Russell, G.F.M.: Anorexia nervosa: Its identity as an illness and its treatment. In: J.H. Price (Ed.), *Modern Trends in Psychological Medicine.* New York: Appleton-Century-Crofts, 1970.

Russell, G.F.M.: The management of anorexia nervosa. In: *Symposium of Anorexia Nervosa and Obesity.* Royal College of Physicians of Edinburgh: 42, 1973.
Russell, G.F.M.: Bulimia nervosa: An ominous variant of anorexia nervosa. *Psychol. Med.,* 9: 429-448, 1979.
Russell, G.F.M.: The current treatment of anorexia nervosa. *Brit. J. Psychiat.,* 138:164-166, 1981.
Ryle, J.A.: Anorexia nervosa. *Lancet,* 2:893, 1936.
Sadavoy, J., Silver, D., and Book, H.: The resident and the borderline in-patient: A supervisor's perspective. *Can. J. Psychiatry,* 26:155-158, 1981.
Schlemmer, J.K. and Barnett, P.A.: Management of manipulative behavior of anorexia nervosa patients. *J. Psychiatr. Nurs.,* 15:35-41, 1977.
Schultz, W.C.: Encounter. In: R. Corsini (Ed.), *Current Psychotherapy.* Itasca, IL: F.F. Peacock Publishing, 1973.
Selvini Palazzoli, M.: *Self-Starvation — From Individual to Family Therapy in the Treatment of Anorexia Nerovsa.* 2nd Ed. New York: Jason Aronson, 1978.
Silverman, J.A.: Anorexia nervosa: Clinical observations in a successful treatment plan. *J. Pediatr.,* 84:68-73, 1974.
Skinner, B.F.: *Contingencies of Reinforcement.* New York: Appleton-Century-Crofts, Inc., 1969.
Solomon, A.P. and Morrison, D.A.R.: Anorexia nervosa: Dual transference therapy. *Am. J. Psychother.,* 26:480-489, 1972.
Sorlie, P., Gordon, T. and Kannel, W.B.: Body build and mortality: The Framingham Study, *JAMA,* 243:1828-1831, 1980.
Sours, J.A.: Anorexia nervosa: Nosology, diagnosis, developmental patterns and power control dynamics. In: G. Caplan and S. Lebovici (Eds.), *Adolescence: Psychological Perspectives.* New York: Basic Books, 1969.
Sours, J.A.: The anorexia nervosa syndrome. *Int. J. Psychoanal.,* 55:567-576, 1974.
Sours, J.A.: *Starving to Death in a Sea of Objects: The Anorexia Nervosa Syndrome.* New York: Jason Aronson, 1980.
Story, I.: Caricature and impersonating the other: Observations from the psychotherapy of anorexia nervosa. *Psychiatry,* 39:176-188, 1976.
Strober, M.: Personality and symptomatological feature in young, nonchronic anorexia nervosa patients. *J. Psychosom. Res.,* 24:353-359, 1980.
Strupp, H.H.: Toward a reformulation of the psychotherapeutic influence. *Inter. J. Psychiat.,* 11:263-327, 1973.
Strupp, H.H.: Psychotherapy research and practice: An overview. In: S.L. Garfield and A.E. Bergin (Eds.), *Handbook of Psychotherapy and Behavior Change: An Empirical Analysis.* New York: John Wiley and Sons, 1978.
Stuart, R.B.: Behavioral control of overeating. *Behav. Res. Ther.,* 5:357-365, 1967.
Szyrynski, V.: Anorexia nervosa and psychotherapy. *Am. J. Psychother.,* 27:492-505, 1973.
Theander, S.: Anorexia nervosa. *Acta Psychiat. Scand.* [Suppl], 214, 1970.
Thoma, H.: *Anorexia Nervosa.* New York: International Universities Press, 1967.
Thoma, H.: Treatment. *Adv. Psychosom. Med.,* 7:300-315, 1972.
Van Buskirk, S.S.: A two-phase perspective on the treatment of anorexia nervosa. *Psychol. Bull.,* 84:529-538, 1977.
Waller, J., Kaufman, M.R. and Deutsch, F.: Anorexia nervosa: Psychosomatic entity. *Psychosom. Med.,* 2:3-16, 1940.
Warren, W.: A study of anorexia nervosa in young girls. *J. Child Psychol. Psychiatry,* 9:27-40, 1968.
Williams, W.: A comprehensive behavior modification programme for the treatment of anorexia nervosa: Results in six cases. *Aust. N.Z. J. Psychiatry,* 10:321-324, 1976.
Wilson, G.T. and Evans, I.M.: The therapist-client relationship in behavior therapy. In: A.S. Gurman and A.M. Razin (Eds.), *Effective Psychotherapy: A Handbook of Research.* New York: Pergamon Press, 1978.
Wolpe, J.: [Letter] Behavior therapy in anorexia nervosa. *JAMA,* 233:317-318, 1975.
Ziegler, R. and Sours, J.A.: A naturalistic study of patients with anorexia nervosa admitted to a university medical center. *Compr. Psychiatry,* 9:644-651, 1968.

# CHAPTER 11

# *Complications*

The complications of anorexia nervosa are due to the starvation process itself, attempts to control weight artifically (by vomiting, laxative or diuretic misuse), complications of weight-restoring treatments, and psychological sequelae. The latter are more fully discussed in Chapter 12. Changes in hypothalamic-pituitary function are described in Chapter 4. Dr. Michael Brotman has reviewed the frequency of a variety of physical complications in our hospitalized anorexic patients (190 admissions of 129 different patients, to June 1980) and the data derived from this are presented in the following discussion. However, it must be emphasized that this sample is biased in the direction of severity of illness, since relatively ill patients are referred to us and then only two-thirds of these are admitted to our hospital unit.

## CARDIOVASCULAR AND RESPIRATORY CHANGES

Bradycardia and hypotension are frequent manifestations of starvation. For example, a resting heart rate of less than 60 was noted in 27% of our patients (Brotman, Darby and Garfinkel, to be published), in 28% of the patients of Seidensticker and Tzagournis (1968), and in 80% of Silverman's (1977) series. An average admission heart rate of 62/minute was recorded by Beck and Brochner-Mortensen (1954) and of 53/minute by Fohlin (1977). In the latter study only four of 31 patients had heart rates of over 60 and rates as low as 28/minute were recorded. Silverman (1977) reported that 52% had resting systolic blood pressures of less than 70, in a relatively young age group. Hypotension (blood pressure of <90/50) was recorded in

86% of Warren and Vande Wiele's (1973) patients. Seidensticker and Tzagournis (1968) reported a systolic blood pressure of less than 100 mm Hg in only 40%. Brotman found that 43% of our inpatients had a diastolic blood pressure of less than 60; in 3% it was less than 40 on admission.

Fohlin (1977) observed that the oxygen uptake at rest was about 20% lower for anorexics than what would be predicted for other individuals of comparable age, sex and body surface area. Keys, Brozek, Henschel, Mickelsen and Taylor (1950) had reported similar changes in their starving subjects in Minnesota. Gottdiener, Gross, Henry, Borer and Ebert (1978) described significant increases in supine and standing heart rates and supine systolic blood pressure after their anorexic patients had regained weight. Fohlin, Freyschuss, Bjarke, Davies and Thoren (1978) have suggested that these changes all reflect an adaptation to the low metabolic rate of starvation.

Fohlin et al. (1978) reported a close correlation between body weight and cardiac volume. But in only five of their patients (out of 26) was the heart volume significantly below the range for healthy children. However, cardiac chamber dimensions and left ventricular mass may be reduced in patients with anorexia nervosa in comparison with controls even after correcting these values for body surface area. Gottdiener et al. (1978) described smaller end-diastolic and end-systolic left ventricular dimensions, reduced left ventricular wall thickness, and smaller left atrial and aortic root dimensions than in normals. They observed these to increase markedly after a mean weight gain of 10 kg in eight of their patients.

In response to maximal exercise both systolic blood pressure and heart rate increased but to a lesser degree than in normals (Fohlin et al., 1978; Gottdiener et al., 1978). Fohlin (1977) also found that the maximal oxygen uptake was reduced, corresponding to findings of the earlier Minnesota studies of starvation. Cardiac output has been studied at rest and in response to exercise. Fohlin et al. (1978) reported this to be within normal limits and to be normally related to oxygen uptake, with a good stroke volume during work. This is indicative of unimpaired myocardial function. Similarly, Gottdiener et al. (1978) reported that left ventricular systolic performance, which was determined at rest by echocardiography, and at rest and during supine exercise by cineangiography, was normal. However, Kalager, Brubakk and Bassoe (1978) found evidence for reduced cardiac contractility based on an altered pre-ejection period and systolic time intervals. These were reversed after weight gain in the single patient restudied.

Electrocardiographic (EKG) changes are common; for example, 69% of Silverman's (1977) patients displayed some "grossly aberrant EKG patterns" and Brotman has found that 60% of our inpatients have electrocardiographic abnormalities. These included sinus bradycardia, extremely low voltage, T-wave inversion, A-V block and several other arrhythmias. These have previously been recorded in experimental semi-starvation (Keys et al., 1950). Thurston and Marks (1974) described nine anorexics; of these seven displayed EKG changes in the absence of electrolyte disturbance. In only one patient was this a sinus bradycardia. Common abnormalities were T-wave inversion and ST segment depression. These changes have been suggested to have little clinical significance (Drossman, Ontjes and Heizer, 1979). Gould, Reddy, Singh and Zen (1980) described a patient with syncope due to a sinus bradycardia and bouts of ventricular tachycardia. Mitchell and Gillum (1980) described a patient with a weight-related arrhythmia characterized by supraventricular premature beats, abnormal P-wave axis and altered PR interval. Palossy and Oo (1977) examined 16 patients when acutely ill and 10 again after recovery. Fourteen displayed initial EKG abnormalities. These included the previously noted T-wave changes and sinus bradycardia; in seven patients U waves were recorded. These became normal in all patients when clinically improved.

Of even greater significance are the occurrence of arrhythmias during exercise. Gottdiener et al. (1978) described one patient (out of 11) who displayed a short run of ventricular tachycardia and three others with occasional ventricular premature beats during exercise. Thurston and Marks (1974) found several of their patients to have a prolonged QT interval; this may be associated with sudden death. This is also seen in starvation from other causes (Simonson, Henschel and Keys, 1948) but did not occur in the patients studied by Gottdiener et al. (1978). These studies have reported EKG abnormalities in the presence of normal electrolytes; however, hypokalemia from repeated vomiting and laxative and diuretic misuse will increase the risk of these, as does the severity of the weight loss (Drossman et al., 1979). Undoubtedly, many deaths due to starvation in anorexia nervosa are related to these cardiac changes.

In addition to these cardiac effects due to starvation, there may be complications secondary to ingestion of emetics. Emetine containing emetics (e.g., Ipecac) are widely available without prescription. Adler, Walinsky, Krall and Cho (1980) have recently described a patient who died of ventricular tachycardia following repeated emetine use for purposes of weight loss. Brotman, Forbath, Garfinkel and Humphrey (1981) have also described a patient with anorexia nervosa and alternating periods of bulimia and starvation. Ipecac syrup was introduced to further control her weight. She consumed approximately 300 ml per week in 85 ml doses during two separate three-month periods. During that time she experienced slowly increasing generalized muscle weakness and lethargy without anxiety. Physical examination revealed marked weakness of a variety of muscles. Laboratory abnormalities included elevated CPK values which persisted for eight weeks after admission to hospital. Electromyographic findings were consistent with a toxic myopathy. EKG readings showed minor nonspecific T-wave changes and a sinus arrhythmia. Two-dimensional echocardiography and nuclear angiography demonstrated a significant asymptomatic abnormality: a left ventricular ejection fraction of 45% at rest and 80% on mild exercise. After nutritional rehabilitation and elimination of the emetic, this patient's cardiomyopathy and peripheral myopathy completely disappeared.

Fohlin (1977) has assessed the peripheral circulation in anorexia nervosa. He found a reduced calf blood flow in the patients when compared to healthy controls. Blood flow in the legs increased significantly after exposure to indirect radiant heat in both the anorexic and control groups, but this was less marked for the anorexics. Anorexics also had reduced blood pressure and skin temperature in the legs. Clinically reported circulatory disturbances include Raynaud's phenomenon or acrocyanosis (Dally, 1969).

There have been few respiratory complications described in the literature. However, four patients with pneumomediastinum and subcutaneous emphysema have been reported (Al-Mufty and Bevan, 1977; Brooks and Martyn, 1977; Donley and Kemple, 1978), perhaps partially related to repeated forceful vomiting.

### RENAL CHANGES

Renal function may be thought to be normal because there is often an absence of protein, glucose, casts, and red blood cells in the urine (Beck and Brochner-Mortensen, 1954). However, there are significant changes in many patients, depending on the nutritional quality of the diet, hydration, weight, and degree of potassium loss. Blood urea nitrogen (BUN) has been observed to be elevated (i.e., >20 mg%) in from 7% to 48% of patients (Seidensticker and Tzagournis, 1968; Silverman, 1974; Warren and Vande Wiele, 1973). Brotman has found that 25% of our patients have an elevated BUN on admission, including several with values in the 70-90 range. Lampert and Lau (1976) reported that seven of their 10 patients had a BUN above 30 mg%, with the highest value being 145 mg%. This differs from what occurs in protein-calorie malnutrition, where there is a normal BUN because of reductions in both protein intake and glomerular filtration rate (GFR) (Klahr and Alleyne, 1973). In anorexia nervosa, protein intake is generally maintained and the elevated BUN may reflect a reduced level of hydration in addition to a reduced GFR.

Fohlin (1977) reported significant reductions in GFR in anorexia nervosa and this has also been described in obese subjects who are fasting (Edgren and Wester, 1971). This is likely related to a reduced plasma flow, but in addition, it has been suggested that there might be a defect in the water permeability of the capillary wall (Aperia, Broberger and Fohlin, 1978; Fohlin, 1977). Several groups have observed a reduced concentrating capacity of the kidneys (Fohlin, 1977; Mecklenburg, Loriaux, Thompson, Andersen and Lipsett, 1974; Russell and Bruce, 1966). It has been suggested that this reversible defect is of renal rather than central origin, since administration of vasopressin does not improve one's ability to concentrate urine (Fohlin, 1977). Reversible changes in concentrating capacity have been reported in protein-calorie malnutrition, but these have been suggested to be vasopressin responsive (Alleyne, 1967; Klahr and Alleyne, 1973).

Other abnormalities may occur less commonly. Berkman (1948) described patients with urinary calculi probably precipitated by fluid restriction. Hirschman, Rao and Chan (1977) reported one patient with non-oliguric ("high output") acute renal failure and acute tubular necrosis secondary to shock after prolonged starvation. Wigley (1960) and Wolff, Vecsei, Kruck, Roscher, Brown, Dusterdieck, Lever and Robertson (1968) have described several anorexic patients with severe, protracted potassium deficiency and secondary renal tubular vacuolation.

## ELECTROLYTES

While Silverman (1974) felt that serum electrolytes were "consistently normal" and Warren and Vande Wiele (1973) observed only one patient with reduced serum electrolyte levels secondary to vomiting, serious depletion of potassium and to a lesser extent of sodium may occur. This will depend on the severity of the dietary restriction and sources of body fluid loss. In this regard the bulimic group of anorexic patients are at serious risk because of their reliance on vomiting, large doses of laxatives and, occasionally, diuretics.

Brotman has found that 6% of our inpatients have serum potassium levels of less than 2.6 mEq/1. Dally (1969) reported that seven of his patients (5%) developed serious hypokalemia (values as low as 1.6 mEq/1); all had chronically misused laxatives. In the restricting group of patients serum potassium levels generally remain normal but there is a depletion of total body potassium. This can be demonstrated in balance studies before and during refeeding (Fohlin, 1977; Russell, 1970). With multiple sources of potassium loss patients may display lowered serum potassium, and to a lesser extent lowered sodium, and an accompanying hypochloremic alkalosis.

Sunderman and Rose (1948) first reported the severe hypochloremia in an anorexia nervosa patient; this was far more marked than in a control individual who underwent a voluntary prolonged fast and was related to the former patient's frequent vomiting. In a careful study of 20 anorexic patients, Elkington and Huth (1959) found hypochloremic alkalosis in one-third of the group; this was closely associated with the severity of weight loss and with vomiting. Warren and Steinberg (1979) described the presence of hypochloremia (<98mEq/1) in three of six patients and a metabolic alkalosis in three of six. Serum chloride levels of less than 90 mEq/1 were found in 8% of our inpatients shortly after admission (Brotman, Darby and Garfinkel, to be published). Vomiting is undoubtedly the major factor in extracellular alkalosis, when it does occur in anorexia nervosa. Given the unusual food habits of some patients, however, ingestion of sodium bicarbonate may be a rare cause of the alkalosis.

Hypokalemia and hyponatremia were also present in one-third of Elkington and Huth's (1959) patients and were found exclusively in those who vomited. Hyponatremia (< 135 mEq/1), however, is relatively uncommon; when it does occur it is generally due to salt restriction or to water intoxication. Warren and Steinberg (1979) reported only one of their patients to have hyponatremia. Brotman has recorded levels of sodium of less than 130 mEq/1 in 3.3% of our inpatients. While rare, hyponatremia may be associated with significant sequelae. Seizures are not uncommon in psychotic patients with delusions that involve water ingestion (Jose, Barton and Perez-Cruet, 1979). We have treated one woman with chronic anorexia nervosa, who, when referred to us, was in her early fifties. She was chronically hyponatremic and on at least one occasion experienced a convulsion.

Hypokalemia is more frequent and potentially serious; its sequelae include muscle weakness or paralysis, tetany, renal tubular vacuolation, cardiac arrhythmias, and death. Of greatest concern is the fact that extreme potassium deficiency can develop gradually in the absence of striking symptoms or signs (Wolff et al., 1968). In addition to Elkington and Huth's (1959) description of hypokalemia in one-third of their patients, Warren and Steinberg (1979) found four of six patients to be hypokalemic and in two there were associated EKG changes. Others have described one or more similar cases (Beck and Brochner-Mortensen, 1954; Luft and Sjogren, 1954; Morgan & Russell, 1975; Rodger and Collyer, 1970,; Siebenmann, 1955; Wigley, 1960).

Wolff et al. (1968) studied nine women with anorexia nervosa who all either chronically vomited or misused laxatives and diuretics. All displayed low total body and serum potassium. Serum sodium was decreased in eight subjects but this was not as marked as potassium loss. Plasma renin concentration was elevated and the aldosterone secretion rate was increased. This is in contrast to the lowered plasma renin and aldosterone that occurs in fasting obese subjects (Tuck, Sowers, Dornfield, Kledzik and Maxwell, 1981). Wolff et al. (1968) suggested that sodium losses through dietary retriction, vomiting, and diuretics stimulated renin and aldosterone production which further contributed to the hypokalemia. They emphasized that multiple routes of electrolyte depletion were the important factor in overwhelming homeostatic mechanisms for potassium conservation. A similar phenomenon was described in a case report by Pasternak (1970).

Anorexia nervosa is generally an illness of several years duration. Because of the serious consequences of these electrolyte abnormalities and because of the renal impairments that occur in starvation, great care must be paid to them in emaciated or vomiting/laxative-misusing patients. Regular monitoring of BUN and electrolytes is indicated and when hypokalemia is evident, serial EKGs are warranted. Patients may require potassium supplements during the active stages and if these are being vomited up, hospitalization becomes necessary. These sequelae also suggest that great care must be used in the rare patient who requires intravenous fluids and that diuretic therapy must be avoided for patients' complaints of bloating.

## EDEMA

Edema is a frequent complication, both in anorexia nervosa (Russell, 1970) and in individuals undergoing experimental semi-starvation (Keys et al., 1950). This is especially seen when a severely emaciated patient is rapidly refed. The frequency of clinically apparent edema in patients ranges from 7-33% (Dally, 1969; Morgan and Russell, 1975; Warren and Vande Wiele, 1973). The mechanisms responsible for it are poorly understood. While often thought to be related to reduced plasma proteins, in anorexia nervosa these are generally normal (Brotman Darby and Garfinkel, to be published; Casper, Chatterton and Davis, 1979; Casper, Kirschner, Sandstead, Jacob and Davis, 1980; Kanis, Brown, Fitzpatrick, Hibbert, Horn, Nairn, Shirling, Strong and Walton, 1974; Lampert and Lau, 1976; Warren and Vande Wiele, 1973) but occasionally are reduced (Berkman, 1948; Berkman, Weir and Kepler, 1947).

Several of our patients have been known to ingest large quantities of salt periodically in order to provoke excessive weight gains and prevent hospitalization. Others drink large quantities of fluids in order to reduce their sense of hunger and this may play a role. In addition, a few patients stand all the time (even when reading or eating) in the belief that this will expend more calories than sitting and there may be a postural component to their edema. The previously noted hyperaldosteronism has also been suggested to play a role (Drossman et al., 1979), as well as alterations in membrane permeability to sodium which occur in kwashiorkor (Patrick, 1979).

## HEMATOLOGICAL CHANGES

There have been many hematological complications described. Anemia, usually of a mild degree, is not infrequent. This is often increased during the initial refeeding period, due to hemodilution. Seidensticker and Tzagournis (1968) and Rieger, Brady and Weisberg (1978) both found that a hemoglobin of less than 12g% occurred in 30% of their sample. Reports of the frequency of moderate anemia (Hb about 10g%) range from 7-17% of anorexics (Berkman, 1948; Morgan and Russell, 1975; Warren and Vande Wiele, 1973) but were much less frequent (3%) in our series. These are often normochromic in nature, but hypochromic anemia has also been described (Berkman, 1948). Severe anemias are probably uncommon, but Crisp (1977) has observed two such cases. In one the individual was found to be removing her own blood.

A detailed hematological study of six patients was conducted by Mant and Faragher (1972). Four experienced mild anemia during some stage of the illness and a fifth had a more severe form. Reticulopenia was common. Anisocytosis and poikilocytosis of the red cells also occurred; spur cells or acanthocytes were present in all six patients and have been described also by others (Amrein, Friedman, Kosinski and Ellman, 1979). Red cell survival was only very slightly altered (Mant and Faragher, 1972). This together with an absence of reticulocytosis suggests that there is no significant hemolysis in these patients. How and Davidson (1977) have described two patients with anorexia nervosa and hemolytic anemia, but the latter may have been secondary to chlorpromazine therapy. Fibrinogen levels have been found to be low and plasminogen activator levels to be elevated. These revert to normal after weight gain (Anyan, 1974; Ogston and Ogston, 1976).

Mant and Faragher (1972) have also assessed hematinic factors; while serum Vitamin B12 was normal in all, one patient displayed a lowered serum folate level (and they stated that two further cases were also low in folate). Extremely wide variations in folic acid levels have also been recorded (Casper et al., 1980). Bone marrow iron stores have generally been absent or reduced (Mant and Faragher, 1972). Both serum iron and total iron-binding capacity have tended to be in the low-normal range but the latter has also been reported to be significantly lower than in controls and responsive to weight restoration (Casper et al., 1980). Mant and Faragher (1972) have recommended more frequent use of iron and folic acid supplements in treating emaciated anorexic patients.

However, these might be of limited value for the normochromic anemia secondary to marrow hypoplasia (Russell, 1970). Bone marrow hypoplasia has been estimated to occur in from 40-50% of anorexics in large studies (Silverman, 1974; Warren and Vande Wiele, 1973). In smaller samples Mant and Faragher (1972) found hypoplasia in five of their six patients, Pearson (1967) in three more, and Lampert and Lau (1976) in all seven patients that they examined. In one instance, it was noted in the same person four years apart (Mant and Faragher, 1972). The marrow in these individuals is characterized by an absence of fat spaces and the presence of an apparently gelatinous material in which marrow cells are embedded. There is often a relative increase in histiocytes and reticulum cells in the marrow. The hypoplasia is readily reversed, after several weeks of refeeding (Mant and Faragher, 1972; Kubanek, Heimpel, Paar and Schoengen, 1977). A mild thrombocytopenia may occur. This was present but slight and considered to be of no clinical significance in three of Mant and Faragher's (1972) six patients, and in four of Lampert and Lau's (1976) ten patients. Silverman (1974), however, has described one patient with marked thrombocytopenia accompanied by generalized petechiae and ecchymoses. Warren and Vande Wiele (1973) noted the presence of petechiae in four of 42 patients. We have measured platelet levels in only 16 of our patients; in two they were significantly reduced (as low as 100,000) and in one instance this was associated with petechiae.

Total peripheral leukocyte counts and absolute neutrophil counts are significantly lower in patients with anorexia nervosa than in control populations (Bowers and Eckert, 1978; Rieger et al., 1978). Twenty-four percent of Silverman's (1974) patients, 38% of Warren and Vande Wiele's (1973) and 50% of Bowers and Eckert's (1978) had leukopenia. Four percent of our inpatients had white blood cell counts of less than 2500. Neutrophils are generally reduced; for example, Bowers and Eckert (1978) found that 37% had low neutrophil counts. Bowers and Eckert (1978) also reported significantly reduced lymphocyte and monocyte counts but this conflicts with other findings of elevated lymphocytes (Brotman, Darby and Garfinkel, to be published; Rieger et al., 1978). Mant and Faragher's (1972) patients all displayed lymphopenia. Of importance, assessment of the marrow granulocyte reserve has been found to be normal in spite of neutropenia (Bowers and Eckert, 1978; Mant and Faragher, 1972) and this may help explain why anorexic patients do not suffer from infections more frequently than they do.

The issue of rate of infection in these patients has not been clearly elucidated. Traditionally, anorexics have been thought to be at high risk for serious infections, especially tuberculosis. Dally (1969) observed that five of his patients developed pulmonary tuberculosis during starvation or shortly after regaining weight. Selvini Palazzoli (1974) described three patients who also developed the illness. Dally (1969) has also suggested that staphylococcal skin infections are common but that viral infections are rare. He observed that many patients complained of losing their immunity to viral illness after their weight had been restored and this has been our experience as well. Berkman (1948) had earlier noted that "these patients are exceptionally free from infections" (p. 239). Bowers and Eckert (1978) found no significant differences in rates of infection between anorexic and control populations during their prehospitalization and hospitalization periods.

Nevertheless, there is some evidence for alterations in the anti-microbial defense system. The peripheral blood granulocytes of three anorexic patients have been found to display a reversibly reduced rate of in vitro bactericidal activity (Gotch, Spry, Mowat, Beeson and MacLennan, 1975). In one patient this was associated with development of an abdominal abscess when emaciated. A further ten patients have been found to have a significant decrease in polymorphonuclear bactericidal capacity in comparison with controls (Palmblad, Fohlin and Lundstrom, 1977). A patient who had low serum complement levels and recurrent staphylococcal skin infections of the feet has also been described (Kim and Michael, 1975). More recently, Palmblad, Fohlin and Norberg (1979) documented reduced plasma levels of complement in ten patients.

Armstrong-Esther, Lacey, Crisp and Bryant (1978) have examined immunological responses in a group of women with anorexia nervosa. Cellular immune responses, as assessed by a tuberculin and macrophage inhibition test, did not differ in anorexic women from a control group. Haemagglutination inhibition titers were also measured against three different viral antigens. While initial responses did not differ between groups, over several months the anorexic woman displayed higher antibody titers. While these alterations in the defense against infectious agents have been noted in small numbers of patients, their overall clinical significance is uncertain.

Other blood constituents may be abnormal. Increased levels of cholesterol are quite common (Blendis and Crisp, 1968; Crisp, Blendis and Pawan, 1968; Kanis et al., 1974; Klinefelter, 1965). Blendis and Crisp (1968) have attributed this to their patients' pattern of alternating bulimia and starvation; however, Halmi and Fry (1974) found no differences between bulimic and restricting patients' cholesterol levels. The basis for the elevation is not certain. It may relate to changes in the thyroid but Crisp et al. (1968) and Mordasini, Klose and Greten (1978) were unable to correlate serum cholesterol with indices of thyroid function. Cholesterol levels tend to normalize after recovery (Blendis and Crisp, 1968; Casper et al., 1980; Mordasini et al., 1978), but not all studies confirm this (Halmi and Fry,

1974). The cholesterol fraction that is elevated is of low-density lipoprotein (Mordasini et al., 1978).

Elevation of serum carotene is common (Casper et al., 1980; Crisp and Stonehill, 1967). Silverman (1974) reported this in 57% of his patients, Warren and Vande Wiele (1973) in 38%, and Dally (1969) in 15%. Robboy, Sato and Schwabe (1974) found elevated levels of $\beta$-carotene, retinol, retinylester, and retinoic acid in eight patients with anorexia nervosa. It is not known if the carotenemia is due to excess ingestion of carotene-containing foods or, more likely, to be an acquired defect in its metabolism (Drossman et al., 1979). Carotenemia may persist for months or years after weight restoration (Dally, 1969; Lucas, 1977) but has also been found to return to normal (Casper et al., 1980). It is unlikely to be of any clinical significance, other than imparting a yellow pigmentation to the skin, especially of the palms and soles.

Vitamin deficiencies are extremely rare; Silverman (1974) reported low plasma levels of vitamin A in some patients. These were not associated with any ophthalmological changes on slit-lamp examination. Casper et al. (1980) did not find abnormal vitamin A levels in their series of 30 patients. Retinol binding was also not altered. There have been rare cases of beri beri (Palmer, 1939; Smitt, 1946), pellagra (Clow, 1932) and vitamin K deficiencies (Aggeler, Lucia and Fishbon, 1942) complicating anorexia nervosa. That these are so rare is not surprising given these patients' food preferences and frequent use of vitamin preparations.

Vitamin preparations may contain little if any minerals. Deficiencies in trace metals may therefore occur. Reduced zinc in particular has been suggested to be a potential factor in some of the symptoms of anorexia nervosa (Bakan, 1979; Horrobin and Cunnane, 1980; Thomsen, 1978). Signs of zinc deficiency include skin lesions, alopecia, nausea, hypoguesia, anorexia and irritability. Lowered zinc may play a role in the elevated carotene levels. Zinc-deficient rats have also been found to display widely varying food intake from day to day. This is unlike their normal eating behavior and is somewhat analogous to bulimia-starvation cycles of humans (Henkin, 1977; Horrobin and Cunnane, 1980).

In a careful study of trace metals and vitamins, Casper et al. (1980) found that plasma and urinary zinc and copper were moderately reduced in anorexic patients. The copper and zinc content of hair was normal. Anorexics also displayed hypoguesia, especially for bitter and sour tastes, but this did not correlate with plasma zinc levels. Taste recognition as well as plasma levels of zinc and copper tended to normalize in the nine patients who were retested. Controlled trials of zinc supplements are warranted to delineate which if any of the anorexic's symptoms can be reponsive to this.

## GASTROINTESTINAL COMPLICATIONS

Constipation is a very common feature of the illness. Many patients resort to laxatives to relieve both this and subjective feelings of bloating. A minority begin to misuse laxatives in attempts to further reduce their weight and chronic diarrhea may occur. The absorptive functions of the jejunum and ileum are not disturbed in these patients (Krejs, Walsh, Morawski and Fordtran, 1977). Radiographs of the upper and lower bowels are generally normal (Beck and Brochner-Mortensen, 1954; Silverman, 1974) but about one-third of patients display a mild non-obstructive jejunal dilatation (Haller, Slovis, Baker, Berdon and Silverman, 1977). Early assessments of gastric motility, using a continuously perfused catheter system with slow rate of infusion, revealed no abnormalities (Silverstone and Russell, 1967).

However, a more recent evaluation using a dye dilution technique found a markedly reduced fractional gastric emptying rate during fasting in 14 of 15 anorexic patients (Dubois, Gross, Ebert and Castell, 1979). Following a standard physiological stimulus, a water load, reduced emptying and increased gastric volume were evident. This partially improved but was still significantly different from normal after weight gain in six patients. Saleh and Lebwohl (1980) recently used a gamma counting technique to assess gastric emptying in seven anorexic patients. Ninety minutes after eating a test meal they found that on average 90% of the meal was retained in the stomach versus only about 40% for a control group. Metoclopromide significantly improved this gastric emptying for the anorexic subjects. Dubois et al. (1979) and Saleh and Lebwohl (1980) have suggested that these data may explain the early satiety and postprandial fullness experienced by many patients.

Selvini Palazzoli (1974) suggested that gastric emptying was delayed in about one-half of her patients based on radiological evidence. Using a barium meal x-ray examination, Scobie (1972) found that gastric emptying was normal but ten of 20 patients had duodenal dilatation. Duodenal ileus has been reported (Ryle, 1939; Scobie, 1973). Phenothiazines may precipitate a paralytic ileus. Duodenal compression by the superior mesenteric artery may be an unusual complication of rapid weight loss from any cause (Burrington and Wayne, 1974). It may be present as an acute or chronic (intermittent) obstructive state but it may be readily overlooked in anorexic patients who regularly vomit. It should be considered when vomiting appears to have become intractable and is associated with severe postprandial abdominal pain. The most helpful finding, diagnostically, is radiologic evidence of a grossly distended stomach and proximal duodenum, with a line of obstruction in its third part. Three recent examples in anorexic patients have been described by Burrington and Wayne (1974) and two further cases by Froese, Szmuilowicz and Bailey (1978) and Sours and Vorhaus (1981).

Markowski (1947) described acute gastric dilatation in prisoners of war who were undernourished and subsequently fed rather rapidly. Similarly, dilatation may occur in patients with anorexia nervosa early in their treatment. Russell (1966) described a 16-year-old girl who developed acute dilatation two days after a high calorie liquid diet was initiated. Evans (1968) reported on a 20-year-old girl with anorexia nervosa who, five days after starting hospital treatment, had an acute dilatation of the stomach which resulted in a perforation. Scobie (1972), Jennings and Klidjian (1974), Browning (1977), Bossingham (1977) and Bruch (1971) have each described two cases of acute gastric dilatation shortly after anorexic patients started a larger diet. One of Browning's (1977) patients died following perforation of a distended stomach and two of Bruch's (1971) male patients died suddenly, with the only autopsy findings being gastric dilatation. Warren and Vande Wiele (1973) have also described a fatal outcome in a patient with an aperistaltic dilated esophagus.

Our only patient who was fed by nasogastric tube developed an acute dilatation shortly after large feedings were initiated; she recovered with conservative treatment. A second developed a gastric perforation following marked bulimic episodes and distention of the stomach. She recovered after surgery. The mortality of uncomplicated gastric dilatation is low, but after perforation is significant (Evans, 1968; Kline, 1979). This emphasizes the need to consider this complication early, whenever anorexic patients are being refed and signs of obstruction develop.

Parotid gland enlargement may occur (Simon, Laudenbach, Lebovici and Mauvais-Jarvis, 1979). This is generally limited to those people who have been inducing vomiting chronically (Dawson and Jones, 1977; Lavender, 1969) with hypokalemic hypochloremic alkalosis, but also has been observed in bulimia without vomiting (Levin, Falko, Dixon, Gallup and Saunders, 1980) and in severe malnutrition or refeeding after starvation (Watt, 1977). Generally the enlarged parotid glands are painless but tenderness may occur. One patient has had a parotid gland biopsy which was normal (Levin et al., 1980).

Several cases of acute pancreatitis complicating anorexia nervosa have been reported (Nordgren and von Scheele, 1977; Schoettle, 1979), and chronic pancreatic disease may result from prolonged starvation (Pitchumoni, 1973). Elevations in serum amylase in the absence of clinical symptoms of pancreatic disease have been reported (Levin et al., 1980; Mordasini et al., 1978). We have measured serum amylase in 28 cases; of these, 13 had elevated values (Brotman, Darby and Garfinkel, to be published). Amylase levels may remain elevated in the immediate period after weight restoration. These individuals display no symptoms suggestive of pancreatic disease. While liver function is generally normal (Casper et al., 1980; Cravario, Cravetto and Autino, 1974), occasional reports of liver enzyme changes (Schoettle, 1979) and hepatic damage exist (Nordgren and von Scheele, 1977; Steele, 1976-1977). Brotman found that while alkaline phosphatase and bilirubin in our patients were elevated in only one instance, clinically significant elevations in SGOT occurred about 6% of the time, due either to hepatic or other tissue wasting in starvation.

## NEUROLOGICAL COMPLICATIONS

Convulsions are not infrequent; 10% of Crisp's (1967) and 9% of Dally's (1969) patients had one or more fits. These are not generally manifestations of idiopathic epilepsy but rather are due to metabolic changes, such as electrolyte disturbances and low blood sugar, or use of drugs such as phenothiazines, insulin and alcohol binges. Electroencephalographic (EEG) changes reflect these varied metabolic states and may be abnormal in non-specific fashion in about 25%-40% (Brotman, Darby, and Garfinkel, to be published; Dally, 1969). Crisp (1967) found only one patient out of 60 who had clinical or EEG evidence of definite brain damage. More ominous EEG changes were recorded in a total of 10 patients by Lundberg and Walinder (1967) and Shimoda and Kitagawa (1973). In a controlled blind evaluation of the EEG in anorexic patients shortly after admission to hospital, Crisp, Fenton and Scotton (1968) found a significant increase in abnormalities in the patients (59%) versus a control group (22%). The abnormalities were most closely related to disturbances in serum electrolytes.

Radiologic examinations of the skull including the sella turcica are normal (Beck and Brochner-Mortensen, 1954; Haller et al., 1977); for example, 55 of our patients have had skull x-rays—all were normal. Air encephalograms have generally been reported to be normal but a few instances of cerebral atrophy have been noted (Geisler, 1953; Heidrich and Schmidt-Matthias, 1961; Lundberg and Walinder, 1967). Cerebral atrophy has been documented by computed tomography (Enzmann and Lane, 1977; Heinz, Martinez and Haenggeli, 1977; Nussbaum, Shenker, Marc and Klein, 1980). While this has been reported to be reversible with weight gain in one patient (Heinz et al., 1977), it was not in two others (Nussbaum et a., 1980). Further investigation is required to clarify the significance of this and its relationship to starvation. Neurological examinations are rarely abnormal except secondarily to other complications. Occasionally a peripheral neuropathy (Nussbaum et al., 1980) or a lateral popliteal palsy are observed (Morgan and Russell, 1975).

## DENTAL CHANGES

Dally (1969) felt that the teeth of his patients were probably not different from those of healthy women of comparable age. Since that time, however, several studies have specifically addressed the issue of dental problems of people with anorexia nervosa. Dental complications may be due to vomiting, the contents of the diet, and reduced saliva either from dehydration or medication with anticholinergic properties. Vomiting appears to produce the most serious sequelae. Erosion of enamel, loss of teeth, increased prevalence of caries, and buccal erosions are all marked in anorexic patients who vomit (Hellstrom, 1974, 1977; Hurst, Lacey and Crisp, 1977).

## SKELETAL MATURATION

Starvation from a variety of causes results in reduced growth, with a reversal of this when nutritional rehabilitation occurs (Prader, Tanner and von Harnack, 1963). Crisp and his colleagues have examined the size and degree of bone maturation of anorexic patients in a series of investigations (Crisp, 1969; Lacey, Crisp, Hart and Kirkwood, 1979; Toms and Crisp, 1972). Crisp (1969) found that anorexic patients did not differ in overall height from a control group but that there was a tendency for patients with an early age of onset to be shorter in stature than the matched controls. The anorexic patients also displayed narrower shoulders and hips; Crisp (1969) related these findings to the reduced estrogenic activity of these emaciated patients. Toms and Crisp (1972) in a single case report of a male documented both stunted growth and delayed puberty which were reversed with high caloric foods.

Lacy et al. (1979) assessed the bone ages of patients and found them to be considerably delayed in relation to chronological age. The delay in bone age was not related to the age of onset of illness but was strongly correlated with the duration of emaciation. These findings suggested that bone maturation ceases when the weight loss has been sufficient to produce amenorrhea but that renourishment reestablishes the mechanism for bone maturation.

### REFERENCES

Adler, A.G., Walinsky, P., Krall, R.A. and Cho, S.Y.: Death resulting from ipecac syrup poisoning. *JAMA,* 243:1927-1928, 1980.
Aggeler, P.M., Lucia, S.P. and Fishbon, H.M.: Purpura due to vitamin K deficiency in anorexia nervosa. *Am. J. Digest Dis.,* 9:227-229, 1942.
Alleyne, G.A.O.: The effect of severe protein calorie malnutrition on the renal function of Jamaican children. *Pediatrics,* 39:400-411, 1967.

Al-Mufty, N.S. and Bevan, D.H.: A case of subcutaneous emphysema, pneumomediastinum and pneumoretropenitoneum associated with functional anorexia. *Br. J. Clin. Pract.,* 31:160-161, 1977.

Amrein, P.C., Friedman, R., Kosinski, K. and Ellman, L.: Hematologic changes in anorexia nervosa. *JAMA,* 241:2190-2191, 1979.

Anyan, W.R., Jr.: Changes in erythrocyte sedimentation rate and fibrinogen during anorexia nervosa. *J. Pediatr.,* 85:525-527, 1974.

Aperia, A., Broberger, O. and Fohlin, L.: Renal function in anorexia nervosa. *Acta Paediatr. Scand.,* 67:219-224, 1978.

Armstrong-Esther, C.A., Lacey, J.H., Crisp, A.H. and Bryant, T.N.: An investigation of the immune response of patients suffering from anorexia nervosa. *Postgrad. Med.,* 54:359-399, 1978.

Bakan, R.: The role of zinc in anorexia nervosa: Etiology and treatment. *Med. Hypotheses,* 5:731-736, 1979.

Beck, J.C. and Brochner-Mortensen, K.: Observations on prognosis in anorexia nervosa. *Acta Med. Scandinav.,* 149:409-430, 1954.

Berkman, J.M.: Anorexia nervosa, anterior-pituitary insufficiency, Simmonds' cachexia and Sheehan's disease; including some observations on disturbances in water metabolism associated with starvation. *Postgrad. Med. J.,* 3:237-246, 1948.

Berkman, J.M., Weir, J.F. and Kepler, E.J.: Clinical observations on starvation edema serum protein and the effect of forced feeding in anorexia nervosa. *Gastroenterology,* 9:357-390, 1947.

Blendis, L.M. and Crisp, A.H.: Serum cholesterol levels in anorexia nervosa. *Postgrad. Med. J.,* 44:327-330, 1968.

Bossingham, D.: Acute gastric dilatation in anorexia nervosa. *Br. Med. J.,* 2:959, 1977.

Bowers, T.K. and Eckert, E.: Leukopenia in anorexia nervosa. Lack of increased risk of infection. *Arch. Intern. Med.,* 138:1520-1523, 1978.

Brooks, A.P. and Martyn, C.: Pneumomediastinum in anorexia nervosa. *Br. Med., J.,* 1:124, 1977.

Brotman, M.C., Forbath, N., Garfinkel, P.E. and Humphrey, J.G.: Ipecac syrup poisoning in anorexia nervosa. *Can. Med. Assoc. J.,* 125:453-454, 1981.

Browning, C.H.: Anorexia nervosa: Complications of somatic therapy. *Compr. Psychiatry,* 18:399-403, 1977.

Bruch, H.: Death in anorexia nervosa. *Psychosom. Med.,* 33:135-144, 1971.

Burrington, J.D. and Wayne, E.R.: Obstruction of the duodenum by the superior mesenteric artery—does it exist in children? *J. Pediatr. Surg.,* 9:733-741, 1974.

Casper, R.C., Chatterton, R.T. and Davis, J.M.: Alterations in serum cortisol and its binding characteristics in anorexia nervosa. *J. Clin. Endocrinol. Metab.,* 49:406-411, 1979.

Casper, R.C., Kirschner, B., Sandstead, H.H., Jacob, R.A. and Davis, J.M.: An evaluation of trace metals, vitamins, and taste function in anorexia nervosa. *Am. J. Clin. Nutr.,* 33:1801-1808, 1980.

Clow, F.E.: Anorexia nervosa. *New England J. Med.,* 207:613-617, 1932.

Cravario, A., Cravetto, C.A. and Autino, R.: Studio della funzionalita epatica nell'anoressia nervosa. *Minerva Med.,* 65:2990-2995, 1974.

Crisp, A.H.: The possible significance of some behavioral correlates of weight and carbohydrate intake. *J. Psychosom. Res.,* 11:117-131, 1967.

Crisp, A.H.: Some skeletal measurements in patients with primary anorexia nervosa. *J. Psychosom. Res.,* 13:125-142, 1969.

Crisp, A.H.: The differential diagnosis of anorexia nervosa. *Proc. Roy. Soc. Med.,* 70:686-690, 1977.

Crisp, A.H., Blendis, L.M. and Pawan, G.L.S: Aspects of fat metabolism in anorexia nervosa. *Metabolism,* 17:1109-1118, 1968.

Crisp, A.H., Fenton, G.W. and Scotton, L.: A controlled study of the EEG in anorexia nervosa. *Br. J. Psychiatry,* 114:1149-1160, 1968.

Crisp, A.H. and Stonehill, E.: Hypercarotenemia as a symptom of weight phobia. *Postgrad. Med. J.*, 42:721-725, 1967.

Dally, P.: *Anorexia Nervosa.* London: William Heinemann, 1969.

Dawson, J. and Jones, C.: Vomiting-induced hypokalemia alkalosis and parotid swelling. *Practitioner*, 218:267-268, 1977.

Donley, A.J. and Kemple, T.J.: Spontaneous pneumomediastinum complicating anorexia nervosa. *Br. Med. J.*, 2:1604-1605, 1978.

Drossman, D.A., Ontjes, D.A. and Heizer, W.D.: Clinical Conference. Anorexia nervosa. *Gastroenterology*, 77:1115-1131, 1979.

Dubois, A., Gross, H.A., Ebert, M.H. and Castell, D.O.: Altered gastric emptying and secretion in primary anorexia nervosa. *Gastroenterology*, 77:319-323, 1979.

Edgren, B. and Wester, P.O.: Impairment of glomerular filtration in fasting for obesity. *Acta Med. Scand.*, 190:389-393, 1971.

Elkington, J.R. and Huth, E.J.: Body fluid abnormalities in anorexia nervosa and undernutrition. *Metabolism*, 8:376-403, 1959.

Enzmann, D.R. and Lane, B.: Cranial computed tomography findings in anorexia nervosa. *J. Comput. Assist. Tomography*, 1:410-414, 1977.

Evans, D.S.: Acute dilatation and spontaneous rupture of the stomach. *Br. J. Surg.*, 55:940-942, 1968.

Fohlin, L.: Body composition, cardiovascular and renal function in adolescent patients with anorexia nervosa. *Acta Paediatr. Scand.* (Suppl.), 268:1-20, 1977.

Fohlin, L., Freyschuss, U., Bjarke, B., Davis, C.T. and Thorén, C.: Function and dimensions of the circulatory system in anorexia nervosa. *Acta Paediatr. Scand.*, 67:11-16, 1978.

Froese, A.P., Szmuilowicz, J. and Bailey, J.D.: The superior-mesenteric-artery syndrome: Cause or complication of anorexia nervosa? *Can. Psychiatr. Assoc. J.*, 23:325-327, 1978.

Geisler, E.: Zur problematik der pubertatsmagersucht. *Psychiat. Neurol. Med. Psychol.*, 5:227-233, 1953.

Gotch, F.M., Spry, C.J.F., Mowat, A.G., Beeson, P.B. and MacLennan, I.C.M.: Reversible granulocyte killing defect in anorexia nervosa. *Clin. Exp. Immunol.*, 21:244-249, 1975.

Gottdiener, J.S., Gross, H.A., Henry, W.L., Borer, J.S. and Ebert, M.H.: Effects of self-induced starvation on cardiac size and function in anorexia nervosa. *Circulation*, 58:425-433, 1978.

Gould, L., Reddy, C.V.R., Singh, B.K., and Zen, B.: Evaluation of cardiac conduction in anorexia nervosa. *PACE*, 3:660-665, 1980.

Haller, J.O., Slovis, T.L., Baker, D.H., Berdon, W.E. and Silverman, J.A.: Anorexia nervosa —the paucity of radiologic findings in more than fifty patients. *Pediatr. Radiol.*, 5:145-147, 1977.

Halmi, K. and Fry, M.: Serum lipids in anorexia nervosa. *Biol. Psychiatry*, 8:159-167, 1975.

Heidrich, R. and Schmidt-Matthias, H.: Encephalogra Phisehe befunde bei anorexia nervosa. *Arch. Psychiat. Nervenkr.*, 202:183-201, 1961.

Heinz, E.R., Martinez, J. and Haenggeli, A.: Reversibility of cerebral atrophy in anorexia nervosa and Cushing's syndrome. *J. Comput. Assist Tomography*, 1:415-418, 1977.

Hellstrom, I.: Anorexia nervosa—odontologiska problem. *Sven. Tandlak Tidskr.*, 67:253-269, 1974.

Hellstrom, I.: Oral complications in anorexia nervosa. *Scand. J. Dent. Res.*, 85:71-86, 1977.

Henkin, R.I.: New aspects in the control of food intake and appetite. *Ann. N.Y. Acad. Sci.*, 300:321-324, 1977.

Hirschman, G.H., Rao, D.D. and Chan, J.C.M.: Anorexia nervosa with acute tubular necrosis treated with parenteral nutrition. *Nutr. Metab.*, 21:341-348, 1977.

Horrobin, D.F. and Cunnane, S.C.: Interactions between zinc, essential fatty acids and prostaglandins: Relevance to acrodermatitis enteropathicia, total parenteral nutrition, the glucagonoma syndrome, diabetes, anorexia nervosa and sickle cell anemia. *Med. Hypotheses*, 6:277-296, 1980.

How, J. and Davidson, R.J.L.: Chlorpromazine-induced haemolytic anaemia in anorexia nervosa. *Postgrad. Med. J.*, 53:278-279, 1977.

Hurst, P.S., Lacey, J.H. and Crisp, A.H.: Teeth, vomiting and diet: A study of the dental characteristics of seventeen anorexia nervosa patients. *Postgrad. Med. J.*, 53:298-305, 1977.

Jennings, K.P. and Klidjian, A.M.: Acute gastric dilatation in anorexia nervosa. *Br. Med. J.*, 2:477-478, 1974.

Jose, C.J., Barton, J.L. and Perez-Cruet, J.: Hyponatremic seizures in psychiatric patients. *Biol. Psychiatry*, 14:839-843, 1979.

Kalager, T., Brubakk, D. and Bassoe, H.H.: Cardiac performance in patients with anorexia nervosa. *Cardiology*, 63:1-4, 1978.

Kanis, J.A., Brown, P., Fitzpatrick, K., Hibbert, D.J., Horn, D.B., Nairn, I.M., Shirling, D., Strong, J.A. and Walton, H.J.: Anorexia nervosa: A clinical, psychiatric and laboratory study. I. Clinical and laboratory investigation. *Q.J. Med.*, 43:321-338, 1974.

Keys, A., Brozek, J., Henschel, A., Mickelsen, O. and Taylor, H.L.: *The Biology of Human Starvation.* Minneapolis: University of Minnesota Press, 1950.

Kim, Y. and Michael, A.F.: Hypocomplementemia in anorexia nervosa. *J. Pediatr.*, 87:582-585, 1975.

Klahr, S. and Alleyne, G.A.O.: Effects of chronic protein-calorie malnutrition on the kidney. *Kidney Int.*, 3:129-141, 1973.

Kline, C.L.: Anorexia nervosa: Death from complications of ruptured gastric ulcer. *Can. J. Psychiatry*, 24:153-156, 1979.

Klinefelter, H.F.: Hypercholesterolemia in anorexia nervosa. *J. Clin. Endocr.*, 25:1520-1521, 1965.

Krejs, G.J., Walsh, J.H., Morawski, S.G. and Fordtran, S.J.: Intractable diarrhea. Intestinal perfusion studies and plasma VIP concentrations in patients with pancreatic cholera syndrome and surreptitious ingestion of laxatives and diuretics. *Am. J. Dig. Dis.*, 22:280-292, 1977.

Kubanek, B., Heimpel, H., Paar, G. and Schoengen, A.: Hamatologishe veranderungen bei anorexia nervosa. *Blut.*, 35:115-124, 1977.

Lacey, J.H., Crisp, A.H., Hart, G. and Kirkwood, B.A.: Weight and skeletal maturation—a study of radiological and chronological age in an anorexia nervosa population. *Postgrad. Med. J.*, 55:381-385, 1979.

Lampert, F. and Lau, B.: Bone marrow hypoplasia in anorexia nervosa. *Eur. J. Pediatr.*, 124:65-71, 1976.

Lavender, A.: Vomiting and parotid enlargement. *Lancet*, 1:426, 1969.

Levin, P.A., Falko, J.M., Dixon, K., Gallup, E.M. and Saunders, W.: Benign parotid enlargement in bulimia. *Ann. Int. Med.*, 93:827-829, 1980.

Lucas, A.R.: On the meaning of laboratory values in anorexia nervosa. *Mayo Clin. Proc.*, 52: 748-750, 1977.

Luft, R. and Sjogren, B.: Disturbed electrolyte metabolism in 2 cases of nervous anorexia. *Acta Endocrinol.*, 17:264-269, 1954.

Lundberg, O. and Walinder, J.: Anorexia nervosa and signs of brain damage. *Int. J. Neuropsychiat.*, 3:165-173, 1967.

Mant, M.J. and Faragher, B.S.: The haematology of anorexia nervosa: *Br. J. Haematol.*, 23:737-749, 1972.

Markowski, B.: Acute dilatation of the stomach. *Brit. Med. J.*, 2:128-130, 1947.

Mecklenburg, R.S., Loriaux, D.L., Thompson, R.H., Andersen, A.E. and Lipsett, M.B.: Hypothalamic dysfunction in patients with anorexia nervosa. *Medicine*, 53:147-159, 1974.

Mitchell, J.E. and Gillum R.: Weight-dependent arrhythmia in a patient with anorexia nervosa. *Am. J. Psychiatry*, 137:337-338, 1980.

Mordasini, R., Klose, G. and Greten, H.: Secondary type II hyperlipoproteinemia in patients with anorexia nervosa. *Metabolism*, 27:71-79, 1978.

Morgan, H.G. and Russell, G.F.M.: Value of family background and clinical features as predictors of long-term outcome in anorexia nervosa: four-year follow-up study of 41 patients. *Psychol. Med.*, 5:355-371, 1975.

Nordgren, L. and von Scheele, C.: Hepatic and pancreatic dysfunction in anorexia nervosa: A report of two cases. *Biol. Psychiatry,* 12:681-686, 1977.

Nussbaum, M., Shenker, I.R., Marc, J. and Klein, M.: Cerebral atrophy in anorexia nervosa. *J. Pediat.,* 96:867-869, 1980.

Ogston, D. and Ogston W.D.: The fibrinolytic enzyme system in anorexia nervosa. *Acta Haematol.,* 55:230-233, 1976.

Palmblad, J., Fohlin, L. and Lundstrom, M.: Anorexia nervosa and polymorphonuclear (PMN) granulocyte reactions. *Scand. J. Haematol.,* 19:334-342, 1977.

Palmblad, J., Fohlin, L. and Norberg, R.: Plasma levels of complement factors 3 and 4, orosomucoid and opsonic functions in anorexia nervosa. *Acta Paediatr. Scand.,* 68:617-618, 1979.

Palmer, H.A.: Beriberi complicating anorxia nervosa. *Lancet,* 1:269, 1939.

Palossy, B., and Oó, M.: ECG alterations in anorexia nervosa. *Adv. Cardiol.,* 19:280-282, 1977.

Pasternak, A.: Anorexia nervosa, secondary aldosteronism and angiopathy. *Acta Med. Scand.,* 187:139-143, 1970.

Patrick, J.: Oedema in protein energy malnutrition: The role of the sodium pump. *Proc. Nutr. Soc.,* 38:61-68, 1979.

Pearson, H.A.: Marrow hypoplasia in anorexia nervosa. *J. Pediat.,* 71:211-215, 1967.

Pitchumoni, C.S.: Pancreas in primary malnutrition disorders. *Am. J. Clin. Nutr.,* 26:374-379, 1973.

Prader, A., Tanner, J.M. and von Harnack, G.A.: Catch-up growth following illness on starvation. *J. Pediat.,* 62:646-659, 1963.

Rieger, W., Brady, J.P. and Weisberg, E.: Hematologic changes in anorexia nervosa. *Am. J. Psychiatry,* 135:984-985, 1978.

Robboy, M.S., Sato, A.S. and Schwabe, A.D.: The hypercarotenemia in anorexia nervosa: A comparison of vitamin A and carotene levels in various forms of menstrual dysfunction and cachexia. *Am. J. Clin. Nutr.,* 27:362-367, 1974.

Rodger, N.W. and Collyer, J.A.: Anorexia nervosa with concealed hyperphagia and self-induced vomiting, hypokalemic alkalosis and normal aldosterone excretion. *Can. Med. Assoc., J.,* 103:169-171, 1970.

Rossier, P.H., Stachelin, D., Buhlmann, A. and Labhart, A.: Alkalose und Hypokaliamie bei anorexia mentalis ("Hunger Alkalose"). *Schweiz Med. Wchnschr.,* 85:465-468, 1955.

Russell, G.F.M.: Acute dilatation of the stomach in a patient with anorexia nervosa. *Br. J. Psychiatry,* 112:203-207, 1966.

Russell, G.F.M.: Anorexia nervosa: Its identity as an illness and its treatment. In: H. Price (Ed.), *Modern Trends in Psychological Medicine.* London: Butterworths, 1970, pp. 131-164.

Russell, G.F.M.: Bulimia nervosa: An ominous variant of anorexia nervosa. *Psychol. Med.,* 9:429-448. 1979.

Russell, G.F.M. and Bruce, J.T.: Impaired water diuresis in patients with anorexia nervosa. *Am. J. Med.,* 40:38-48, 1966.

Ryle, J.A.: Discussion on anorexia nervosa. *Proc. Roy. Soc. Med.,* 32:735-737, 1939.

Saleh, J.W. and Lebwohl, P.: Metoclopramide-induced gastric emptying in patients with anorexia nervosa. *Am. J. Gastroenterol.,* 74:127-132, 1980.

Schoettle, U.C.: Pancreatitis: A complication, a concomitant or a cause of an anorexia nervosa-like syndrome. *J. Am. Acad. Child Psychiatry,* 18:384-390, 1979.

Scobie, B.A.: Acute dilation of the stomach in patients with anorexia nervosa. (Abstr.) *Aust. N.Z. J. Med.,* 2:335, 1972.

Scobie, B.A.: Acute gastric dilatation and duodenal ileus in anorexia nervosa. *Med. J. Aust.,* 2:932-934, 1973.

Seidensticker, J.F. and Tzagournis, M.: Anorexia nervosa—clinical features and long term follow-up. *J. Chronic Dis.,* 21:361-367, 1968.

Selvini Palazzoli, M.: *Self-starvation.* London: Chaucer Publishing, 1974.

Shimoda, Y. and Kitagawa, T.: Clinical and EEG studies on the emaciation (anorexia nervosa) due to disturbed function of the brain stem. *J. Neur. Trans.*, 34:195-204, 1973.

Siebenmann, R.E.: Uber eine todlich verlaufende Anorexia nervosa mit Hypokaliamie. *Schweiz Med. Wchnschr.*, 85:468-471, 1955.

Silverman, J.A.: Anorexia nervosa: Clinical observations in a successful treatment plan. *J. Pediatr.*, 84:68-73, 1974.

Silverman, J.A.: Anorexia nervosa: Clinical and metabolic observations in a successful treatment plan. In: R. Vigersky (Ed.), *Anorexia Nervosa*. New York: Raven Press, 1977, pp. 331-339.

Silverstone, J.T. and Russell, G.F.M.: Gastric "hunger" contractions in anorexia nervosa. *Br. J. Psychiatry*, 113:257-263, 1967.

Simon, D., Laudenbach, P., Lebovici, M. and Mauvais-Jarvis, P.: Parotidomegalie au cours des dysorexies mentales. 10 observations. *Nouv. Presse Med.*, 8:2399-2402, 1979.

Simonson, E., Henschel, A. and Keys, A.: The electrocardiogram of man in semistarvation and in subsequent rehabilitation. *Am. Heart J.*, 35:584-602, 1948.

Smitt, J.W.: Case of anorexia nervosa complicated by beriberi. *Acta Psychiat. et Neurol.*, 21:887-900, 1946.

Sours, J.A. and Vorhaus, L.J.: Superior mesenteric artery syndrome in anorexia nervosa: A case report. *Am. J. Psychiatry*, 138:519-520, 1981.

Steele, R.L.: Anorexia nervosa: A case study. *Psychother. Psychosom.*, 27:47-53, 1976-1977.

Sunderman, F.W. and Rose, E.: Studies in serum electrolytes; changes in serum and body fluids in anorexia nervosa. *J. Clin. Endocrinol.*, 8:209-220, 1948.

Thurston, J. and Marks, P.: Electrocardiographic abnormalities in patients with anorexia nervosa. *Br. Heart J.*, 36:719-723, 1974.

Toms, D.A. and Crisp, A.H.: Weight phobia in an adolescent male with stunted development. *J. Psychosom. Res.*, 16:289-295, 1972.

Thomsen, K.: Zinc, liver cirrhosis and anorexia nervosa. [Letter] *Acta Derm. Venerol.* (Stockh), 58:283, 1978.

Tuck, M.L., Sowers, J., Dornfeld, L. Kledzik, G. and Maxwell, M.: The effects of weight reduction on blood pressure, plasma renin activity, and plasma aldosterone levels in obese patients. *New England J. Med.*, 304:930-933, 1981.

Warren, S.E. and Steinberg, S.M.: Acid-base and electrolyte disturbances in anorexia nervosa. *Am. J. Psychiatry*, 136:415-418, 1979.

Warren, M.P. and Vande Wiele, R.L.: Clinical and metabolic features of anorexia nervosa. *Am. J. Obstet. Gynecol.*, 117:435-449, 1973.

Watt, J.: Benign parotid swellings: A review. *Proc. Roy. Soc. Med.*, 70:483-486, 1977.

Wigley, R.D.: Potassium deficiency in anorexia nervosa, with reference to renal tubular vacuolation. *Br. Med. J.*, 2:110-113, 1960.

Wolff, H.P., Vecsei, P., Kruck, F., Roscher, S., Brown, J.J., Dusterdieck, G.O., Lever, A.F. and Robertson, J.I.S.: Psychiatric disturbance leading to potassium depletion, sodium depletion, raised plasma-renin concentration and secondary hyperaldosteronism. *Lancet* 1:257-261, 1968.

# CHAPTER 12

# *Prognosis*

Opinions have varied about the outcome of anorexia nervosa. Gull (1874) regarded the prognosis as "for the most part favorable," but he did record one death. When Hurst (1939) described his patients he wrote "without exception they have done well." He felt that a "few straightforward conversations are sufficient to reveal and straighten out most mental tangles." On the other hand, others have considered anorexia nervosa to be a serious illness with a high mortality (Kay and Leigh, 1954; Williams, 1958). More recently, most clinicians studying the outcome of anorexia nervosa have recognized how varied it can be (Garfinkel, Moldofsky and Garner, 1977; Hsu, Crisp and Harding, 1979; Morgan and Russell, 1975). Crisp has described this well: "The natural history of anorexia nervosa varies from a mild single illness in adolescence to a life-long recurrent or persistent disorder with a high mortality" (Crisp, 1965).

This diversity of opinion between investigators is related to a number of methodological issues which make comparisons between studies quite difficult (Hsu, 1980; Schwartz and Thompson, 1981). These are outlined below:

1) A major problem with many earlier reports and some recent ones has been the lack of consistent diagnostic criteria for anorexia nervosa. If many patients with schizophrenia or affective disorder are included in the sample, the follow-up results will be seriously affected by these cases. The arguments in favor of a distinct syndrome of anorexia nervosa have been reviewed in Chapter 2. In addition, the diagnostic criteria for the disorder can be made more or less rigorous, thereby influencing the representation of mild cases.

2) The majority of prognostic studies have been retrospective and, as such, are dependent on the deficiencies inherent in medical records. Particularly in the older literature, a review of a hospital's files over 40-50 years may have been contaminated by the individual differences in the details of the physicians' record keeping.

3) Studies have often been unable to locate all patients for the follow-up evaluation.

4) The method of follow-up has been quite variable, from telephone or letter contact to a direct interview. The less direct methods of follow-up are more subject to the individual's distortions or denial and are far more likely to yield inaccurate information. Cremerius (1965) felt that the closer one looked at anorexic patients at follow-up the more one found signs of the illness persisting.

5) Criteria for assessing outcome have varied. Restoration and maintenance of weight are frequently-used indicators of improvement. However, some might argue that weight gain is no more critical than improvement of intrapsychic and interpersonal conflicts (Bruch, 1974; Selvini Palazzoli, 1974). Other criteria of improvement have included menstrual regularity (Dally, 1969; Seidensticker and Tzagournis, 1968), sexual functioning (Crisp, 1965; Dally, 1969), eating habits (Crisp, 1965), and quality of interpersonal relationships (Morgan and Russell, 1975). The most comprehensive assessments have used objective scales based on a variety of these measures to assess an individual's prognosis (Garfinkel et al., 1977; Hsu et al., 1979; Morgan and Russell, 1975).

6) Duration of follow-up has been inconsistent. Outcome studies which assess weight immediately after discharge are of limited value since this is not related to long-term recovery (Browning and Miller, 1968; Dally, 1969; Morgan and Russell, 1975). Similarly, assessing outcome between one and two years after treatment is likely to produce inaccuracies because the assessments do not take into account later relapses and gradual recoveries. Morgan and Russell's (1975) practice of waiting at least four years after inhospital treatment is recommended. Even a four-year follow-up is likely to be brief given the relatively late ages of death (mean age was 27) found by Theander (1970) in his long-term follow-up.

7) A final problem with all the studies that are to be reviewed, based on individuals or groups who specialize in treating anorexia nervosa, relates to the sampling bias. It is likely that such groups generally are referred more chronic cases who have failed elsewhere in treatment. It is difficult to generalize their data to the more mild cases seen in an outpatient department. Similarly, psychiatrists have typically been referred anorexic patients only after they have failed in treatment with other medical personnel (Morgan and Russell, 1975), so that their patients may represent the more intractable cases. Moreover, many patients with the illness never come to medical attention, thus influencing our understanding of its natural history.

These methodological problems make comparisons between different studies difficult, at best. With this in mind, Table 1 provides a review of major prognostic studies reported in English since 1950. We have followed Hsu (1980) in reviewing only those studies with more than 15 patients, in which the definition of anorexia nervosa was such that it was likely that most of the patients were true anorexics. For comparison purposes we have separated those studies dealing almost entirely with a young population (Group A) and those with relatively short follow-up periods (Group B) from the main body of the literature (Group C). This table was compiled using the categories (recovered, improved, unchanged, and dead) developed by the major recent studies (Hsu et al., 1979; Morgan and Russell, 1975) but for some this meant arbitrary placement of a few patients. Also, where the data were provided, the assignment to these categories was based not only on weight and eating habits but rather on global scales which included these data, together with data on menstrual function, social functioning, and educational/vocational performance (Garfinkel et al., 1977). In instances where this was not possible, weight was used — this has been shown to be highly correlated with global outcome scales (Garfinkel et al., 1977; Morgan and Russell, 1975). Finally, while some patients may have recovered from anorexia nervosa, they have later developed other psychiatric illness. This group is not distinguished in this table but is further discussed in this chapter.

Review of these studies shows that:

1) With the exception of some of the studies of younger patients, all investigators have found a marked variability of outcome in their samples;
2) the studies of younger cases show both a higher percentage of recovered patients and a reduced mortality; and
3) the studies of relatively brief follow-up intervals show fewer patients in the recovered but more in the intermediate group and perhaps also a reduced mortality.

Overall, the evaluations which are of long duration and which exclude primarily pediatric samples (Group C) show that over 40% of patients have recovered and 30% are considerably improved at follow-up. However, at least 20% are unimproved or seriously impaired and 9% have died as a result of the illness.

The duration of illness in those who do eventually recover can be quite variable. Both Lasègue (1873) and Janet (1919) believed that patients improved but rarely recovered in less than two years. Weight stabilization, however, can occur relatively soon after weight loss. Dally (1969) found that 97 of his 140 patients recovered in terms of weight. Of these, 83%

## TABLE 1

## Studies Evaluating Prognosis in Anorexia Nervosa

| | Definition of Anorexia Nervosa | N | F:M | Age at onset (years) | Duration ill when seen |
|---|---|---|---|---|---|
| **A) Where patients were predominantly young** | | | | | |
| 1. Lesser et al. (1960) | — | 15 | 15:0 | 13.3 (10-16) | — |
| 2. Blitzer et al. (1961) | + | 15 | 12:3 | 7-14 | 15 months (6-66) |
| 3. Warren (1968) | + | 20 | 20:0 | 12.3 (10.5-15.8) | 18 months |
| 4. Silverman (1974) | — | 29 | 27:2 | 9-15 | 2-30 months |
| 5. Goetz et al. (1977) | — | 33 | 28:2 (3 not followed) | 9.5-16 | — |
| 6. Cantwell et al. (1977) | + | 33 | 32:1 | 13.4 (11-16) | — |
| 7. Minuchin et al. (1978) | + | 53 | 47:6 | 14.4 (9-21) | 6 months (3 >2 years) |
| **TOTALS FOR GROUP A\*** | | | | | |
| **B) Where follow-up was relatively brief** | | | | | |
| 8. Crisp (1965) | + | 21 | 19:2 | — | (10< 2 years) (4 < 5 years) (7 >5 years) |
| 9. Thoma (1967) | + | 30 | 30:0 | 16.5 (13-25) | 2.5 |

+ Appear to meet criteria for anorexia nervosa as described in Chapter 2.
x Recovery from anorexia nervosa but 46% with diagnosis of affective disorder.
\* These percentages are weighted for different Ns.

## TABLE 1
### (continued)

| Method of follow-up | Number not followed | Duration of follow-up from when first seen by investigators (years) | Recovered (%) | Improved (%) | Un-improved % | Dead (%) |
|---|---|---|---|---|---|---|
| Reports from physicians, families and schools | 0 | 5.3 (1-17) | 47 | 47 | 7 | 0 |
| — | 0 | — | 60 | 20 | 13 | 7 |
| 11 interviewed, 4 mothers interviewed, 4 psychiatric | 2 | 2.5 | 61 | 11 | 17 | 11 |
| — | 2 | 2 | 81 | 0 | 19 | 0 |
| 6 patients interviewed; largely telephone conversations with patient or family and letters from patients/ doctors | 3 | 6-14 | 87 | 13 | 0 | 0 |
| 18 patients interviewed; 26 parents interviewed | 7 | 4.9 | 76 × | 20 | 4 | 0 |
| Patient, family and pediatrician | 3 | 1.5-6 (40 > 2) | 86 | 4 | 10 | 0 |
|  |  |  | 76 | 13 | 9 | 2 |
| Personal Interview | 0 | 2.5 | 42 | 19 | 28 | 9 |
| Personal Interview questionnaire or doctors' reports | 11 | 0.5-7 | 21 | 68 | 5 | 9 |

## TABLE 1
### (continued)

| | Definition of Anorexia Nervosa | N | F:M | Age at onset (years) | Duration ill when seen |
|---|---|---|---|---|---|
| 10. Pierloot et al. (1975) | + | 32 | 32:0 | 16.6 ± 3.2 | 3.5 years (3 months- 16 years) |
| 11. Garfinkel et al. (1977) | + | 42 | 40:2 | 17.1 ± 0.4 (11-22) | 3.0 ± 1.1 years |
| 12. Pertschuk (1977) | + | 29 | 27:2 | 12-23 | 31.1 months (6-156 months) |
| TOTALS FOR GROUP B | | | | | |
| C) Where follow-up was relatively long and patients were of variable ages | | | | | |
| 13. Kay (1953) | + | 38 | 34:4 | most frequently 16-20 | ½ > 2 years |
| 14. Beck and Brochner- Mortensen (1954) | + | 28 | 28:0 | 18.2 (11-31) | 3.4 years (0.5-12) |
| 15. Williams (1958) | + | 53 | 53:0 | — | 3 months- 14 years |
| 16. Frazier (1965) | — | 39 | 35:4 | 19 (9-35) | — (4 < 5 years) |
| 17. Farquharson and Hyland (1966) | + | 15 | 12:3 | 12-21 | (7 > 5 years) 5-36 months |
| 18. Seidensticker and Tzagournis (1968) | + | 60 | 59:1 | ½ < 30 | < 1-43 years |
| 19. Browning and Miller (1968) | — | 36 | 36:0 | — | — |
| 20. Dally (1969) | + | 140 | 140:0 | 17.7 (11-33) | — |

+ Appear to meet criteria for anorexia nervosa as described in Chapter 2.

x Recovery from anorexia nervosa but 46% with diagnosis of affective disorder.

* These percentages are weighted for different Ns.

## TABLE 1
### (continued)

| Method of follow-up | Number not followed | Duration of follow-up from when first seen by investigators (years) | Recovered (%) | Improved (%) | Un-Improved % | Dead (%) |
|---|---|---|---|---|---|---|
| — | 0 | 1-6 | 50 | 16 | 34 | 0 |
| Physicians' reports | 0 | 31.7 ± 3.1 months | 17 | 64 | 17 | 2 |
| Telephone interview of patient or family | 2 | 22.4 months (3-45 mos.) | 44 | 33 | 23 | 0 |
| | | | 34 | 41 | 22 | 3 |
| — | 5 | 25 > 5 years | 12 | 48 | 21 | 18 |
| Letters and questionnaire to physicians, some patient interviews | 3 | 11.8 years (1-23) | 80 | — | 16 | 4 |
| Personal interview | 11 | 3-21 years | 55 | 14 | 7 | 24 |
| Patient interview | 0 | — | 28 | 33 | 31 | 8 |
| Patient interviews and physician or relative reports | 0 | 20-30 years | 67 | 20 | 13 | 0 |
| Referring doctors' reports and with patients through Cornell Medical Index | 7 | 16-1-5 years 20-5-10 yrs. 17- >10 yrs. | 38 | 30 | 15 | 16 |
| Questionnaire, personal or telephone interview | 0 | 1-30 years | 50 | 25 | 17 | 8 |
| — | 0 | — | 36 | 24 | 28 | 3 |

## TABLE 1
### (continued)

|  | Definition of Anorexia Nervosa | N | F:M | Age at onset (years) | Duration ill when seen |
|---|---|---|---|---|---|
| 21. Theander (1970) | + | 94 | 94:0 | 17.2 (11-34) | 87% <3 years |
| 22. Rowland (1970) | — | 30 | — | 12 (9-35) | 4 years (<1-12.9) |
| 23. Bruch (1973) | + | 45 | 45:0 | 15.9 (10-26) | 2.8 years (0.5-11) |
| 24. Morgan and Russell (1975) | + | 41 | 38:3 | 15.5 (11-40) | 6 |
| 25. Hsu et al. (1979) | + | 105 | 105:0 | — | 3.5 ± 43 years |

TOTALS FOR GROUP C

+ Appear to meet criteria for anorexia nervosa as described in Chapter 2.
x Recovery from anorexia nervosa but 46% with diagnosis of affective disorder.
* These percentages are weighted for different Ns.

## TABLE 1
### (continued)

| Method of follow-up | Number not followed | Duration of follow-up from when first seen by investigators (years) | Recovered (%) | Improved (%) | Un-Improved % | Dead (%) |
|---|---|---|---|---|---|---|
| Interview with 79 patients | 0 | 16 years (all >8 yrs.) | 58 | 22 | 7 | 13 |
| Interviews with 17 patients | 13 | likely > 10 years | 24 | 24 | 35 | 17 |
| Personal interviews, letters and therapists' reports | 6 | 58% 1-5 yrs. 42% 6-9 yrs. | 33 | 44 | 13 | 10 |
| 34 patient interviews, questionnaires and relative interviews | 0 | 4-10 years | 39 | 27 | 29 | 5 |
| 72 personal interviews 12 questionnaires 13 relative interviews | 3 | 5.9 ± 1.3 yrs. (all >4) | 47 | 30 | 21 | 2 |
|  |  |  | 43 | 28 | 20 | 9 |

regained a stable weight within three years of the onset. Theander (1970) reported reliably knowing the duration of disease in 58 of his patients. In 27 patients (47%) this was less than three years; in 18 (31%) it was three-to-five years and in 13 (22%) more than five years. He felt that if those with mild symptoms were included, the frequency of a course of longer than six years was about 35%.

Some patients have recurrences and these may be differentiated into two types. Some begin to lose weight shortly after discharge from hospital which, according to Dally (1969), may occur in one-third of all patients. Strictly speaking, this does not represent a true recurrence since it is unlikely that the patient has ever achieved a "well" state. In these cases, only weight has improved while underlying predisposing and initiating factors have not been adequately addressed. Others stabilize in weight and eating habits but have a recurrence one or more years later. Theander (1970) reported that this occurred relatively infrequently in 11 of 94 patients. In several of our patients this type of recurrence has occurred after 3-14 years of normal functioning. Usually the recurrence has been associated with a stressful change in the person's life such as a marriage, pregnancy, or move to a new city. Others have also noted pregnancy to be the initiating event in some recurrences (Hsu et al., 1979; Weinfeld, Dubay, Burchell, Millerick and Kennedy, 1977).

Several studies have provided comparable information on various parameters of patients' functioning at the time of follow-up. With regard to weight, Hsu et al. (1979) found that 62% were within 15% of average, while Morgan and Russell (1975) reported 55% and Theander (1970) reported that 51% achieved this standard. In short-term follow-up studies, Pertschuk (1977) found 41% within 15% of average and Garfinkel et al. (1977) reported 58% were within 20% of average weight. Similarly, Dally and Gomez (1979) observed that 38% of their patients weighed more than 90% of average two years after treatment; and after four years this was true of 67% and remained at 70% after ten years. Obesity has been found to be relatively uncommon in most reports, ranging from 2% (Hsu et al., 1979; Theander, 1970) to 7% (Garfinkel, et al., 1977). However, in their study of relatively younger patients, Cantwell, Sturzenberger, Burroughs, Salkin and Green (1977) reported that 12% were obese on follow-up. Halmi, Brodland and Loney (1973) indicated that one-third of their recovered patients were obese at the time of their last follow-up examination, although no definition of degree of obesity was provided. When Hsu (1980) reviewed the prognosis of anorexia nervosa, he found that at least 75% of the reported patients had shown improvement in their weights at the time of follow-up although some patients remained quite symptomatic.

Concerns about weight and fears of fatness remain common; however, these must be considered in light of their frequency in non-anorexic females. For example, 65% of Morgan and Russell's (1975) patients expressed concern about the appearance of their bodies, a figure not out of keeping with the population as a whole (Berscheid, Walster and Hohrnstedt, 1973). Forty-four percent of Hsu et al.'s (1979) patients "worried continuously about their weight and fatness." Thirty percent of Morgan and Russell's (1975) patients felt fat and 40% were fearful of becoming fat. Years after their treatment, Theander (1970) interviewed 79 patients; of these 11 felt their weight was "far too high" but only two were overweight. Fifty percent of Morgan and Russell's (1975) patients and 46% of Hsu et al.'s (1979) continued to display dietary restriction; the latter found only 35% had "normal" eating habits. More indicative of persistent anorexic symptomatology was the presence of anxiety when eating with others (in 51% and 33% respectively).

Bulimia may be fairly common at follow-up, but its relative presence in a sample is highly dependent on referral practices. For example, of the total sample, bulimics represented 50% for Garfinkel et al. (1977), 35% for Pertschuk (1977), 16% for Dally (1969), and 19% for Hsu et al. (1979). Vomiting was present in 14%-28% (Garfinkel et al., 1977; Hsu et al., 1979; Morgan and Russell, 1975; Pertschuk, 1977; Theander, 1970). Laxative misuse on follow-up has been reported in between 10% (Garfinkel et al., 1977; Pertschuk, 1977) and 34% (Hsu et al., 1979; Morgan and Russell, 1975).

Details of the return of menstrual function have been described in Chapter 4; there it was noted that return of menses was related both to weight and to the length of time since weight was restored. Most studies have found that 50-75% of patients are menstruating at follow-up but that menstrual irregularity may be common (Hsu, 1980). However, these investigations have noted that some patients remain amenorrheic, despite achieving a normal weight (Morgan and Russell, 1975; Pertschuk, 1977). For example, Hsu et al. (1979) observed that 28 of their patients remained amenorrheic, although in 11 body weight was normal. Garfinkel et al. (1977) decribed only one patient out of 12 who failed to menstruate after her weight was maintained at greater than 90% of average.

In terms of psychosexual functioning at outcome, the findings seem to parallel those of the course of the anorexia nervosa in general (Theander, 1970). Many patients marry and report close satisfying relationships. Theander (1970) found that 79% of his recovered patients married, approximately the expected rate for women in Sweden; for those who survived but did not recover it was only 30%. Twenty percent of his surviving patients avoided intimate relationships with men. Hsu et al. (1979) found that 15 out of 20 patients who married after recovery from the illness had a satisfactory marital relationship. In contrast, 14 patients were married before or during the course of the illness. Of these, two had died, three divorced and five others reported minimal sexual functioning. Dally (1969) reported similar findings in nine patients who married before or during the illness. Crisp's group found that 17% of their sample had clearly abnormal attitudes toward sexuality. In all but two cases these were in individuals with longstanding low body weight (Hsu et al., 1979). Morgan and Russell (1975) found very similar results, with 60% of patients displaying normal sexual attitudes and 23% an aversion to heterosexual contact, denial of libido, and satisfaction at persistent amenorrhea. The latter were all chronically underweight with the exception of one obese person.

The quality of familial and other relationships can vary. Approximately 40-55% of patients describe persistent familial problems (Hsu, 1980). According to Hsu et al. (1979) the most common finding is heightened dependency, together with hostility toward the family. In addition, anxiety in social situations is not uncommon (25-45%) with subsequent frequent avoidance behavior. This has been reported to occur even after weight recovery (Hsu, 1980). However, patients' work histories tend to be positive despite low body weights (Kay and Schapira, 1965). For example, Theander (1970) reported that 63% of his surviving patients were working to capacity and enjoying their jobs, while a further 23% were working well but were less well-adjusted in their careers.

To summarize, it is noteworthy that of those studies with lengthy follow-up intervals and not restricted to pediatric populations comparable results are generally obtained despite major differences between the investigations. About 40% of all patients are totally recovered, 30% are improved and 30% either die as a result of the illness or are chronically afflicted. Weight and menses tend to become normal in about 50% of the patients and a comparable proportion no longer restrict dietary intake. Psychosexual and interpersonal functioning are generally good in those who maintain a normal weight. Occupational achievement and satisfaction are generally favorable even for those who are chronically underweight.

## MENTAL STATE ON FOLLOW-UP

Few investigators have carefully reviewed and documented the mental status of their returning patients; however, this trend has changed in several recent studies. These are summarized in Table 2. Some appear to have described all their patients, whether weight-recovered or not (Hsu et al.,

TABLE 2

The Mental State in Patients with Anorexia Nervosa on Follow-up

| Investigator | Symptom Free | Depressive Symptoms | Obsessive-Compulsive Symptoms | Phobias (usually social) | Schizophrenia | Antisocial Behavior |
|---|---|---|---|---|---|---|
| Dally (1969)* | — | 23% | 11% | 10% | 1% | 2% |
| Theander (1970)* | 17% | 29% | 13% | 8% | 1% | — |
| Morgan and Russell (1975)* | 40% | 45% | 23% | 45% | — | — |
| Cantwell et al. (1977)* | 21% | 46% | 6% | — | — | 8% |
| Hsu et al. (1979) | 45% | 38% | 21% | 24% | 3% | — |

* indicated review of weight-recovered patients only.

1979; Morgan and Russell, 1975), while the others discuss the psychiatric symptoms only in the weight-recovered group. Cantwell et al. (1977) described patients according to rigorous diagnostic criteria for psychiatric illness. Others have noted subjective symptoms and behavior rather than diagnoses. Theander (1970) reviewed 78 of his patients, excluding those with persistent severe anorexia nervosa and those who died. He found 37% of these improved patients to have significant psychological symptoms and only 17% to be mentally healthy. The proportion of patients who were asymptomatic is considerably higher in the more recent studies from London (Hsu et al., 1979; Morgan and Russell, 1975).

In all these studies the presence of depressive symptoms was noted to be the most frequent complaint. These include both Cantwell et al.'s (1977) description of over 40% of their patients meeting diagnostic criteria for primary affective disorder, and other studies noting the frequency of depressive symptoms, chronic unhappiness, and a lowered sense of self-worth. These findings, together with a higher than expected family history of affective disorder, have been used to support the hypothesis that anorexia nervosa is a variant or predisposition to affective illness (see Chapter 2).

One finding particularly evident from Table 2 is the frequency of social or other phobias on follow-up. Some anorexic patients eventually develop agoraphobia. Anxiety in social situations is not uncommon and may be one factor leading to a gradual withdrawal into isolation. Crisp (1965) has emphasized the phobic quality of the anorexic symptomatology and has suggested that with treatment for the weight "phobia" there may emerge a relatively more healthy social avoidance response.

An increase in phobic thinking in anorexic patients on follow-up has been experimentally demonstrated by Stonehill and Crisp (1977) on the Middlesex Hospital Questionnaire (MHQ) and the Eysenck Personality Inventory (EPI). Shortly after weight gain there were significant reductions in the somatization scale of the MHQ, and both neuroticism and extroversion scales of the EPI. Twenty-nine patients were again studied between four and seven years later, and they displayed a significant increase in their phobic scale scores on the MHQ. These findings have implications for treatment in that specific attention may have to be directed toward treating social anxiety in ongoing psychotherapy.

While depressive, phobic, and obsessional symptoms are common in anorexic patients at the time of follow-up, these symptoms are more frequent in those who are either not weight-recovered, or if so, maintain marked weight and eating preoccupations and related behavioral abnormalities. The presence of such behavior has generally, although not always, been felt to be secondary to the continuing anorexic disorder (Hsu, 1980).

In this sense, the basic psychiatric disturbance in anorexic patients remains constant (Kay and Schapira, 1965). Morgan and Russell (1975) have described that: "In the majority of patients whose illness persisted, the clinical picture continued to be typical of anorexia nervosa. When the eating difficulties receded and were overshadowed by depressive symptoms or maladjustment in social situations, these changes were not entirely new developments but were more in the nature of longstanding problems that became more clearly manifest with the passage of time."

## DEATH IN ANOREXIA NERVOSA

The first anorexic patient described in the medical literature, Mr. Duke's daughter, died of the illness:

Being quickly tired with Medicines, she beg'd that the whole Affair might be committed again to Nature, whereupon, consuming every-day more and more, she was after three Months taken with a Fainting-Fitt, and died (Morton, 1694).

Gull (1874) also recognized the potential fatal course to the illness. Typical of early reports was Ryle's (1939) — of 37 patients referred to him four died, either as a result of starvation or its complications (e.g., tuberculosis, hemorrhaging associated with scurvy). Beck and Brochner-Mortensen (1954) reviewed the outcomes of patients from 12 early studies involving 204 patients. They documented an overall mortality of 8%.

More recently, the frequency of a fatal outcome has varied widely, probably reflecting the methodological problems described earlier in this chapter and consistent medical attention to the starvation state. While mortality figures range from 0-24% (Farquharson and Hyland, 1966; Williams, 1958) of patients who are followed up, the average has been around 9% and is considerably less in the pediatric samples. At least 9 of the studies from Group C in Table 1 have described the causes of death in their patients (Browning and Miller, 1968; Bruch, 1973; Dally, 1969; Hsu, et al., 1979; Kay, 1953; Morgan and Russell, 1975; Rowland, 1970; Theander, 1970; Williams, 1958). These studies document at least 44 anorexia nervosa-related deaths. Of these, 36 were due to starvation and its complications (bronchopneumonia or other infections, renal and cardiac failure), or to electrolyte disturbances secondary to purgatives and vomiting, or to complications of somatic therapies (gastric dilatation, aspiration of tube feedings, and electrolyte imbalances with intravenous fluids). The remaining eight patients were known to have committed suicide. While the metabolic and starvation-related deaths could occur at any time in the illness, suicides tended to occur only after a chronic course (e.g., after five-to-seven years in Theander's sample).

It has been our impression that the bulimic group may be more likely to have a fatal outcome, given their more frequent suicide attempts and reliance on laxatives and vomiting. However, this has not been examined in the literature to date. It is also noteworthy that in the recent large studies from London (Hsu, et al., 1979; Morgan and Russell, 1975) of chronically and seriously ill patients, the overall mortality was less than 3%. This may reflect a reduction due to the consistent safe approach to weight restoration that these groups have employed.

## FACTORS RELATED TO PROGNOSIS

Crisp, Kalucy, Lacey and Harding (1977) and Bemis (1978) have recently examined what is known about specific factors related to outcome of the illness. For the purposes of this review, we have somewhat arbitrarily classified these variables using the following headings: 1) demographic factors; 2) clinical features; 3) psychological factors; 4) factors within the family; and 5) early response to treatment.

### 1) Demographic Factors

#### (a) Age at onset

Probably the most widely agreed-upon finding is that of a better prognosis with an earlier age of onset. This is evident from the overall outcome figures displayed at Table 1. Investigators who have examined and followed patients of varying ages also tend to record similar results. Ryle (1939) first noted that "the younger the patient in my experience the better the result, partly perhaps because the diagnosis is more quickly made, partly because the psychological disturbance is usually of simpler type, and partly maybe, through the natural resistance of childhood" (p. 736). Lesser, Ashenden, Debuskey and Eisenberg (1960) felt that "in children the syndrome is probably commoner, milder and more often spontaneously resolved than in older patients." Theander (1970) found a significant increase of recovered patients in those whose illness began when less than age 17. Similar results have been reported by others (Halmi et al., 1973; Hsu et al., 1979; Morgan and Russell, 1975; Seidensticker and Tzagournis, 1968; Starkey and Lee, 1969). Bruch (1973) also noted more of her young patients to be recovered but stressed that "a higher age of onset and protracted course are not incompatible with recovery" (p. 381).

On the other hand, Dally (1969) suggested a relatively poor outcome in girls less than 14 and Browning and Miller (1968), Pierloot, Wellens and Houben (1975), and Garfinkel et al. (1977) found no relationship between age of onset and prognosis; however, this may reflect the relatively older group of patients seen, at least in the latter study (all but one patient was postpubertal). Age of menarche has not been found to be of prognostic significance (Halmi et al., 1973; Morgan and Russell, 1975; Theander, 1970).

## (b) Sex

Little is known about the long-term outcome of male patients, because few clinicians have had experience with large enough numbers to permit statistical analysis. The St. George group, however, have seen 27 male patients, 8% of their sample (Crisp et al., 1977). They feel that because of the cultural emphasis against slimness in males, they are likely to develop the disorder only when there is serious psychopathology in the individual (often of gender identity) or his family, or when there has been premorbid obesity (Crisp and Toms, 1972). They also feel males are more likely to develop the bulimic form of the disorder (Crisp et al., 1977). Since these features are indicative of a more serious form of the illness, Crisp et al. (1977) suggest that the prognosis for males is worse than for females. Bruch (1973) described the outcome of ten males with the illness, of whom nine were followed for between four months and eight years. Six were considered to be primary anorexics and four "atypical." For the group as a whole, two patients had died, two were confined to state hospitals with a diagnosis of schizophrenia, and one was in residential treatment. Dally (1969) also reported a generally worse prognosis for males. However, all three males in Morgan and Russell's (1975) study were reported to be well on follow-up.

## (c) Marriage

Hsu et al. (1979) reported that being married while ill with anorexia nervosa was associated with a worse prognosis, although this may also be related to the later age of onset in this group. Crisp et al. (1977) had earlier suggested that when someone marries an anorexic or when the anorexia nervosa evolves during a marriage, the marital partners are more resistant to change since the illness is related to "the powerful neurotic needs of both partners." However, they have also reported some success in treating such patients and their husbands, at times even after a chronic illness. In several of our patients, the anorexia nervosa improved only after the marriage ended, while other couples have benefited from marital therapy in addition to individual psychotherapy. Seidensticker and Tzagournis (1968) have also noted that married patients tend to have a relatively poor outcome.

### (c) Social Class

In Chapter 5 it was noted that anorexia nervosa occurs much more commonly in the upper and upper-middle classes, but that it may also becoming more common in adolescents from lower classes. Kalucy, Crisp and Harding (1977) described a far worse outcome for patients in the lower social classes. In their expanded series, Hsu et al. (1979) confirmed these findings. Theander (1970), Pierloot et al. (1975), and Morgan and Russell (1975), however, found no relationship between social class and outcome.

### (e) Chronicity

Patients who have been chronically ill when first seen and who have failed in treatments elsewhere have been noted to do poorly (Hsu et al., 1979; Morgan and Russell, 1975; Pierloot et al., 1975; Seidensticker and Tzagournis, 1968). This is due to the self-perpetuating nature of the illness, the marked social withdrawal, loss of peer relationships, and the development of an "anorexic identity" that may occur with time. However, there are enough examples of chronically ill patients eventually recovering to give credence to Gull's (1874) statement: "As regards prognosis, none of these cases, however exhausted, are really hopeless whilst life exists."

### 2) *Clinical Features*

### (a) Bulimia, Vomiting, and Laxative Misuse

In Chapter 3 we presented the evidence for separating the bulimic form of the disorder from the restricting type. Garfinkel et al. (1977) had previously divided patients into four outcome groups based on their follow-up weight, presence or absence of menses, eating habits, and social and educational/vocational adjustment (Table 3). Bulimia, vomiting, and laxative abuse were quantified using 4-point scales (from 0-absent, to 3-marked, i.e., daily or more frequently). They found that bulimia was associated with a less favorable outcome. Selvini Palazzoli (1974) and Hsu et al. (1979) have also suggested that bulimia carries a more guarded prognosis.

Vomiting was also found to be a sign of poor prognosis by Garfinkel et al. (1977) (Table 3), but this has not been studied separately from bulimia. Hsu et al. (1979) found similar results, although their data were not statistically significant. Theander (1970), Selvini Palazzoli (1974) and Halmi

TABLE 3

Results of Analysis of Food-related Clinical Features
in Patients in the Four Outcome Groups

| Outcome | N | Food fads m ± SEM | Vomiting[a] | Bulimia[a] | Laxative abuse |
|---|---|---|---|---|---|
| Excellent | 7 | 2.3 ± 0.2 | 0.0 | 0.3 ± 0.2 | 0.0 |
| Much improved | 14 | 2.4 ± 0.2 | 0.2 ± 0.2 | 1.0 ± 0.3 | 0.1 ± 0.1 |
| Symptomatic | 13 | 2.9 ± 0.1 | 0.4 ± 0.3 | 1.4 ± 0.3 | 0.7 ± 0.3 |
| Poor | 8 | 2.6 ± 0.2 | 1.6 ± 0.5 | 2.3 ± 0.4 | 0.5 ± 0.4 |

a < 0.01

Reprinted with permission from Garfinkel et al., 1977.

et al. (1973) also reported the association, while Morgan and Russell (1975) and Pierloot et al. (1975) found no relationship between vomiting and outcome.

Laxative abuse was not associated with a poor outcome statistically in the Garfinkel et al. (1977) follow-up (Table 3); however, no patients with "excellent" outcomes had misused laxatives. Halmi et al. (1973) have described an association between laxative misuse and poor outcome but this was not confirmed by Pierloot et al. (1975). This latter group noted that the presence of impulsive behavior (stealing, self-mutilation) was associated with a poor outcome.

(b) Lowest Body Weight

Morgan and Russell (1975) reported that a very low body weight on admission (less than 60% of average) was associated with a less favorable prognosis. This has been observed by several other groups (Hsu et al., 1979; Seidensticker and Tzagournis, 1968; Starkey and Lee, 1969) but not by others (Browning and Miller, 1968; Dally, 1969). Achieving a low body weight may be an important index of denial which may herald a poor outcome if not changed with treatment.

(c) Past History of Obesity

Patients who have been obese premorbidly tend to share certain features which may predispose them to a poor outcome. Often they are the patients with bulimia and vomiting or impulsive behavior. They also tend both to regain weight readily (Stordy, Marks, Kalucy and Crisp, 1977) and to display a greater abhorrence of obesity because of their perceived personal devaluation when they were obese. Crisp et al. (1977) noted that premorbid obesity is associated with bulimia, greater perceptual disturbances, and less favorable outcome, although no data were provided and studies of outcome have not provided much support for this contention. Dally (1969) felt that moderate overweight, premorbidly, was a good sign but severe obesity was a poor prognostic indicator. Morgan and Russell (1975) and Halmi et al. (1973) found no relationship between outcome and previous obesity.

(d) External Precipitants

Halmi, Goldberg, Eckert, Casper and Davis (1977) have suggested that when the illness develops in the absence of external stressors there is a more severe underlying psychopathology and resistance to treatment. This depends in large measure on the definition of an external precipitant, which may vary considerably. However, studies which have attempted to relate these to prognosis have not found an association (Morgan and Russell, 1975; Pierloot et al., 1975; Theander, 1970).

## (e) Premorbid Educational/Vocational Adjustment

Garfinkel et al. (1977) found that patients with good premorbid work and school records had a favorable outcome. Seidensticker and Tzagournis (1968) and Halmi et al. (1973) have both reported favorable outcomes in patients with skilled and professional occupations.

## 3) *Psychological Factors*

Several writers have stressed the importance of premorbid personality for ultimate outcome (Bemis, 1978; Goetz, Succop, Reinhart and Miller, 1977; Lesser et al., 1960). Because of the age of development of the illness, it is generally not possible to describe a premorbid personality that has become fixed prior to the illness. Nevertheless, there is a variety of behavior patterns that are apparent early in childhood and during the illness. Morgan and Russell (1975) and Hsu et al. (1979) described a less favorable outcome in patients who had a variety of earlier childhood behavioral problems, including difficult relationships at school.

There has been little consensus about personality type and its relationship to outcome. Dally (1969) has suggested that obsessional characteristics which are manifest premorbidly and during the illness are associated with a relatively poor prognosis. This has also been reported by others (Bhanji and Thompson, 1974; Halmi et al., 1973), including those studying primarily pediatric age groups (Goetz et al., 1977; Lesser et al., 1960). Pierloot et al. (1975) and Garfinkel (1974) did not find this, although in the latter study behavioral characteristics were assessed quite arbitrarily. Stonehill and Crisp (1977) administered the Middlesex Hospital Questionnaire (MHQ) to a group of patients on presentation and again between four and seven years later. Those who had made a good overall adjustment could not be distinguished from those who were unimproved on initial obsessional scale scores. Hysterical personality traits have been suggested to be associated with a favorable outcome (Goetz et al., 1977; Kay and Schapira, 1965; Lesser et al., 1960), but hysterical scale scores on the MHQ did not distinguish recovered from non-recovered patients in the Stonehill and Crisp (1977) study. Depressive features have been related to a poor outcome by Halmi et al. (1973) but there was a tendency to the opposite in the study by Pierloot et al. (1975).

High levels of somatic distress have been associated with less favorable outcome by Halmi et al. (1973) and high somatic complaint scores on the MHQ were the only ones to be predictive of poor outcome on follow-up by Stonehill and Crisp (1977). More recently, Hsu and Crisp (1980) followed a larger sample of their anorexic patients using the MHQ (now renamed the Crown-Crisp Experiential Inventory). They found only weak correlations between initial MHQ subscale scores and overall outcome four-to-eight years later in 72 patients. High somatic complaint scores on presentation were no longer significantly correlated with outcome. Pierloot et al. (1975) found significant elevations on the MMPI, administered on admission, in their group of unimproved patients at follow-up. The elevations occurred especially in the depression, psychasthenia, and schizophrenia scales.

Garfinkel et al. (1977) found that overestimation of one's body size, as measured by a distorting photograph technique, was an index of poor prognosis several years later (see Chapter 6). These data are presented in Table 4. All patients with poor outcomes had been overestimators of their sizes. When a separate analysis was conducted comparing overestimators versus underestimators, the former displayed little change in their overall clinical condition over time, in comparison with the latter. More recently, Casper, Halmi, Goldberg, Eckert and Davis (1979) found that overestimation of body parts was related to less weight gain during treatment, and greater denial of illness and previous treatment failures, suggestive of an eventual less favorable outcome.

## TABLE 4

### Results of Patients' Self-estimates of Body Size in Four Outcome Groups

| Group | N | $m \pm SEM^a$ (% deviation) | Minimum | Maximum |
|---|---|---|---|---|
| Excellent | 4 | -7.7 ± 1.5 | -10.5 | -4.4 |
| Much Improved | 8 | -1.5 ± 2.0 | -13.1 | + 5.6 |
| Symptomatic | 11 | + 2.0 ± 1.8 | -4.5 | + 12.7 |
| Poor | 5 | + 6.9 ± 1.5 | + 3.6 | + 11.3 |

a < 0.002

Reprinted with permission from Garfinkel et al., 1977.

4) *Familial Factors*

Several groups have documented a relationship between familial psychopathology and outcome. Dally (1969) emphasized the heterogeneous nature of the families of anorexics. He observed an overall rate of psychopathology of 33% in his patients' parents, but in those who eventually recovered from the illness, only 13% had a relative with psychological disturbance. The corresponding figure for his chronically ill group was 59%.

Crisp, Harding and McGuinness (1974) administered the MHQ as an index of psychoneurotic status to parents of their patients on presentation and again after weight restoration. Initially, the parents as a group displayed MHQ profiles that were not greatly different from age-matched suburban parents. After their daughters' weight restoration, the parents of the anorexics displayed elevated anxiety and phobia scales scores, as well as an increased total MHQ score. These investigators also assessed parental psychoneurotic status on presentation and after weight restoration in relation to patients' outcome at six-month follow-up. Those parents who displayed greater initial total MHQ scores and depression scale scores were associated with a poor outcome in their child, six months later. Of interest the worsening of the MHQ scores during the weight-restoration period was not an index of prognosis. Crisp et al. (1977) have used this evidence in suggesting that the increasing psychopathology in parents is often a useful phenomenon which can be addressed within the family psychotherapy.

Morgan and Russell (1975) observed that disturbed familial relationships which antedated the illness were present in 54% of their patients. This was highly correlated with a poor long-term prognosis. Hsu et al. (1979) also reported that the patient's disturbed relationship with her parents prior to the illness and a poor marital relationship were related to less favorable outcome. However, Theander (1970) and Pierloot et al. (1975) did not find an association between outcome and familial relationships. Theander (1970) did note that patients with relatively older mothers tended to display a worse prognosis.

5) *Early Response to Treatment*

Goldberg, Halmi, Casper, Eckert and Davis (1977) have identified a variety of indices which are predictive of short-term inhospital weight gain. Unfortunately, several studies have documented the lack of association between early gains in hospital and ultimate outcome (Browning and Miller, 1968; Dally, 1969; Morgan and Russell, 1975). Crisp et al. (1977) have felt that early motivation for change, as demonstrated on the first interview, may relate to a favorable outcome; however, this is a highly subjective assessment. Of greater significance is the finding of Hsu et al. (1979) that outcome one year after presentation is highly predictive of long-term prognosis.

We agree with Crisp and Russell who feel that it is not known for certain whether treatment has an effect on the long-term course of the illness (Crisp et al., 1977; Russell, 1977). However, as noted earlier in this chapter, it may be that with consistent approaches to weight-restoring treatments, the mortality may be reduced. It is also our belief that long-term therapies, which address the significant predisposing factors, do improve the outlook for many patients. Prospective controlled studies which evaluate this are now required. It is our hope that future reviews will be able to document both a reduced mortality and morbidity due to the illness.

## REFERENCES

Beck, J.C. and Brochner-Mortensen, K.: Observations on the prognosis in anorexia nervosa. *Acta Med. Scand.,* 149:409-430,1954.

Bemis, K.M.: Current approaches to the etiology and treatment of anorexia nervosa. *Psychol. Bull.,* 85:593-617, 1978.

Berscheid, E., Walster, E. and Hohrnstedt, G.: The happy American body: A survey report. *Psychology Today,* November 1973, pp. 119-131.

Bhanji, S. and Thompson, J.: Operant conditioning in the treatment of anorexia nervosa: A review and retrospective treatment study of 11 cases. *Brit. J. Psychiatry,* 124:166-172, 1974.

Blitzer, J.R., Rollins, N. and Blackwell, A.: Children who starve themselves: Anorexia nervosa. *Psychosom. Med.,* 23:369-383, 1961.

Browning, C.H. and Miller, S.I.: Anorexia Nervosa: A study in prognosis and management. *Am. J. Psychiatry,* 124:1128-1132, 1968.

Bruch, H.: *Eating Disorders.* New York: Basic Books, 1973.

Bruch, H.: Perils of behavior modification in the treatment of anorexia nervosa. *JAMA,* 230: 1419-1422, 1974.

Cantwell, D.P., Sturzenburger, S., Burroughs, J., Salkin, B. and Green, J.K.: Anorexia nervosa: An affective disorder. *Arch. Gen. Psychiatry,* 34:1087-1093, 1977.

Casper, R.C., Halmi, K.A., Goldberg, S.C., Eckert, E.D. and Davis, J.M.: Disturbances in body image estimation as related to other characteristics and outcome in anorexia nervosa. *Br. J. Psychiatry,* 134:60-66, 1979.

Cremerius, J.: Zur prognose der anorexia nervosa. *Archiv. Psychiat. fur und Nervenkrank,* 207:378-393, 1965.

Crisp, A.H.: Some aspects of the evolution, presentation and follow-up of anorexia nervosa. *Proc. Roy. Soc. Med.,* 58:814-820, 1965.

Crisp, A.H., Harding, B. and McGuinness, B.: Anorexia nervosa: Psychoneurotic characteristics of parents: Relationship to prognosis. A quantitative study. *J. Psychosom. Res.,* 18: 167-173, 1974.

Crisp, A.H., Kalucy, R.S., Lacey, J.H. and Harding, B.: The long-term prognosis in anorexia nervosa: Some factors predictive of outcome. In: R. Vigersky (Ed.), *Anorexia Nervosa.* New York: Raven Press, 1977, pp. 55-65.

Crisp, A.H. and Toms, D.A.: Primary anorexia nervosa or weight phobia in the male: Report on 13 cases. *Br. Med. J.,* 1:334-338, 1972.

Dally, P.: *Anorexia Nervosa.* New York: Grune and Stratton, 1969.

Dally, P. and Gomez, J.: *Anorexia Nervosa.* London: William Heinemann, 1979.

Farquharson, R.F. and Hyland, H.H.: Anorexia nervosa: The course of 15 patients treated from 20 to 30 years previously. *Can. Med. Assoc. J.,* 94:411-419, 1966.

Frazier, S.H.: Anorexia nervosa. *Dis. Nerv. Syst.,* 26:155-159, 1965.

Garfinkel, P.E.: Perception of hunger and satiety in anorexia nervosa. *Psychol. Med.,* 4:309-315, 1974.

Garfinkel, P.E., Moldofsky, H. and Garner, D.M.: The outcome of anorexia nervosa: Significance of clinical features, body image, and behavior modification. In: R. Vigersky (Ed.), *Anorexia Nervosa.* New York: Raven Press, 1977, pp. 315-329.

Goetz, P.L., Succop, R.A., Reinhart, J.B. and Miller, A.: Anorexia nervosa in children: A follow-up study. *Am. J. Orthopsychiatry,* 47:597-603, 1977.

Goldberg, S.C., Halmi, K.A., Casper, R., Eckert, E. and Davis, J.M.: Pretreatment predictors of weight change in anorexia nervosa. In: R. Vigersky (Ed.), *Anorexia Nervosa.* New York: Raven Press, 1977, pp. 31-42.

Gull, W.W.: Anorexia nervosa. Trans. Clin. Soc. (London), 7:22-28, 1874. Reprinted in: R.M. Kaufman and M. Heiman (Eds.), *Evolution of Psychosomatic Concepts. Anorexia Nervosa: A Paradigm.* New York: International Universities Press, 1964.

Halmi, K., Brodland, G. and Loney, J.: Prognosis in anorexia nervosa. *Ann. Int. Med.* 78: 907-909, 1973.

Halmi, K.A., Goldberg, S.C., Eckert, E., Casper, R. and Davis, J.M.: Pretreatment evaluation in anorexia nervosa. In: R. Vigersky (Ed.), *Anorexia Nervosa.* New York: Raven Press, 1977, pp. 43-44.

Hsu, L.K.G.: Outcome of anorexia nervosa. A review of the literature (1954 to 1978). *Arch. Gen. Psychiatry,* 37:1041-1046, 1980.

Hsu, L.K.G. and Crisp, A.H.: THe Crown-Crisp Experiential Index (CCEI) profile in anorexia nervosa. *Br. J. Psychiatry,* 136:567-573, 1980.

Hsu, L.K.G., Crisp, A.H., and Harding, B.: Outcome of anorexia nervosa. *Lancet,* 1:61-65, 1979.

Hurst, A.: Discussion on anorexia nervosa. *Proc. Roy. Soc. Med.,* 32:744-745, 1939.

Janet, P.: Les obsessions et la psychasthénie. Paris: Felix Alcan, 1919.

Kalucy, R.S., Crisp, A.H. and Harding, B.: A study of 56 families with anorexia nervosa. *Br. J. Med. Psychol.,* 50:381-395, 1977.

Kay, D.W.K.: Anorexia nervosa: A study of prognosis. *Proc. Roy. Soc. Med.,* 46:669-674, 1953.

Kay, D.W.K. and Leigh, D.: Natural history, treatment and prognosis of anorexia nervosa, based on a study of 38 patients. *J. Ment. Sci.,* 100:411-431, 1954.

Kay, D.W.K. and Schapira, K.: The prognosis in anorexia nervosa. In: J.E. Meyer and H. Feldman (Eds.), *Anorexia Nervosa.* Symposium (24/25 April 1965 in Gottingen). Stuttgart, Germany: Georg thieme Verlag, 1965.

Lasègue, C.: De l'anorexie hystérique. *Arch. Gen. de. Med.* (1873) Reprinted in R.M. Kaufman and M. Heiman (Eds.), *Evolution of Psychosomatic Concepts. Anorexia Nervosa: A Paradigm.* New York: International Universities Press, 1964, pp. 141-155.

Lesser, L.I., Ashenden, B.J., Debuskey, M. and Eisenberg, L.: Anorexia nervosa in children. *Am. J. Orthopsychiat.,* 30:572-580, 1960.

Minuchin, S., Rosman, B.L. and Baker, L.: *Psychosomatic Families: Anorexia Nervosa in Context.* Cambridge: Harvard University Press, 1978.

Morgan, H.G. and Russell, G.F.M.: Value of family background and clinical features as predictors of long-term outcome in anorexia nervosa: Four year follow-up study of 41 patients. *Psychol. Med.,* 5:355-371, 1975.

Morton, R.: *Phthisiologica: Or a Treatise of Consumptions.* London: Sam. Smith and Benj. Walford, 1694.

Pertschuk, M.J.: Behavior therapy: Extended follow-up. In: R. Vigersky (Ed.), *Anorexia Nervosa.* New York: Raven Press, 1977, pp. 305-313.

Pierloot, R.A., Wellens, W. and Houben, M.E.: Elements of resistance to a combined medical and psychotherapeutic program in anorexia nervosa. *Psychother. Psychosom.,* 26:101-117, 1975.

Rowland, C.V.: Anorexia nervosa: A survey of the literature and review of 30 cases. *International Psychiatry Clinics,* 7:37-137, 1970.

Russell, G.F.M.: General management of anorexia nervosa and difficulties in assessing the efficacy of treatment. In: R.A. Vigersky (Ed.), *Anorexia Nervosa.* New York: Raven Press, 1977, pp. 277-289.

Ryle, J.A.: Discussion on anorexia nervosa. *Proc. Roy. Soc. Med.,* 32:735-746, 1939.

Schwartz, D.M. and Thompson, M.G.: Do anorectics get well? Current research and future needs. *Am. J. Psychiat.,* 138:319-323, 1981.

Seidensticker, J.F. and Tzagournis, M.: Anorexia nervosa — clinical features and long-term follow-up. *J. Chron. Dis.,* 21:361-367, 1968.

Selvini Palazzoli, M.: *Self-starvation.* London: Chaucer Publishing Co., 1974.

Silverman, J.A.: Anorexia nervosa: Clinical observations in a successful treatment plan. *J. Pediatr.,* 84:68-73, 1974.

Starkey, T.A. and Lee, R.A.: Menstruation and fertility in anorexia nervosa. *Amer. J. Obstet. Gynec.,* 105-374-379, 1969.

Stonehill, E. and Crisp, A.H.: Psychoneurotic characteristics of patients with anorexia nervosa before and after treatment and at follow-up 4-7 years later. *J. Psychosom. Res.,* 21: 189-193, 1977.

Stordy, B.J., Marks, V., Kalucy, R.S. and Crisp, A.H.: Weight gain, thermic effect of glucose and resting metabolic rate during recovery from anorexia nervosa. *Am. J. Clin. Nutr.,* 30: 138-146, 1977.

Theander, S.: Anorexia nervosa: A psychiatric investigation of 44 female cases. *Acta Psychiat. Scand.* [Suppl], 214:1-194, 1970.

Thoma, H.: *Anorexia Nervosa.* New York: International Universities Press, 1967.

Warren, W.: A study of anorexia nervosa in young girls. *J. Child Psychol. Psychiatry,* 9:27-40, 1968.

Weinfeld, R.H., Dubay, M., Burchell, R.C., Millerick, J.D. and Kennedy, A.T.: Pregnancy associated with anorexia and starvation. *Am. J. Obstet. Gynecol.,* 129-698-699, 1977.

Williams, E.: Anorexia nervosa: A somatic disorder. *Br. Med. J.,* 2:190-195, 1958.

# SUBJECT INDEX

Hypophysis, 59
Hypoplasia, 315
Hypotension, 17, 307-308
Hypothalamic-pituitary function, 7, 16, 28,
    29, 58-99, 202-203, 215, 248, 268, 297,
    307
  and fertility, 61-65
  historical perspective on, 58-61
  and hypothalamic function, 65-75
  and menstrual function-fertility, 61-65
  pituitary-thyroid function, 75-89
  and sexuality, 65
  summary on, 89
Hypothyroidism, 16, 60, 79, 81, 249
Hysteria, 12, 16, 20, 24, 25, 40, 50, 54, 59,
    198, 347

Iatrogenic factors and self-control, 209-10
Idealization of feminine beauty, 106-19
Identity, 216, 284
  control of, 33
  gender, 343
  maternal, 205
  and predisposition to anorexia, 193-95
  psychosexual, 50, 144
Ileum, 318
Illness as process, 2
Image-marking method, 132-33, 140
Imipramine, 246
Impulse control, 51, 54
Impulsive behavior, 45-46, 247
Indecisiveness, 22
Insomnia, 13, 21
Insulin, 74, 215, 244, 245, 248
  and appetite, 248
  CSF levels, 84
  resistance to, 82
Internal perceptual (interoception) distor-
    tion, 9, 123, 148-55
  clinical manifestations of, 148-51
  empirical studies of, 151-55
Interviews:
  and prognosis of anorexia, 331, 333, 335
  structure in, 21, 22
Intravenous feeding, 215
Ipecac, 309
IQ, 141
Iron levels, 315
Irritability, 111
Isolation-withdrawal, social, 2, 8, 192, 208,
    227

Jejunum, 318

Karyotyping, 202

Ketosis, 40-41
Ketosteroids, 60
Kwashiorkor, 73

Labeling, affective, 148
Lanugo, 267
Laparoscopy, 202
Laparotomy, 15
Laxatives, 2, 4-6, 15, 16, 27, 61, 150, 246,
    249, 250, 268, 274, 299, 307, 318, 337,
    342
  and anorexia subtypes, 41, 45, 46, 49, 52
  misuse of and prognosis of anorexia,
    344, 346
L-dopa, 74, 86, 215, 247
*Let Me Be* (Crisp), 289
Leucotomy, 215, 247
Leukocytes, 315
Leukopenia, 244, 315
Leighton Obsessional Inventory, 23
Libido. *See also* Sexuality
  denial of, 338
  reduction of, 21
Lipoprotein, 317
Lithium carbonate, 215, 245-47
Locus of control, 138
Loneliness, 2
Lorazepam, 245
Luteinizing hormone (LH), 66-73, 80, 81, 89
  luteinizing hormone releasing hormone
    (LHRH), 68-70, 73
Lymphocyte counts, 315
Lymphopenia, 315

Madame Tussaud's London Wax Museum,
    107
Malnutrition, 25, 73, 79, 311, 319
MANOVA, 138
Marasmus, 73
Marital therapy, 294
Marriage, 21, 181, 192, 338. *See also* Mar-
    ital therapy
  and anorexia of children, 169
  and anorexia subtypes, 44
  and prognosis of anorexia, 343-44
  spouse competition in, 182
Marlowe-Crowne Social Desirability Scale,
    198-99
Masturbation, 13
Maturity, 166, 216
  resistance to, 9
Mayo Clinic, 31, 60
Media, mass, glamorization of anorexia in,
    106
Melatonin, 80-81

# NAME INDEX

364